HISTORICAL COURSE FOR SCHOOLS,

EDITED BY

EDWARD A. FREEMAN, D.C.L.

16mo, cloth.

The object of this series is to put forth clear and correct views of history in simple language, and in the smallest space and cheapest form in which it could be done. It is hoped in time to take in short histories of all the chief countries of Europe and America, giving the results of the latest historical researches in as simple a form as may be. All the volumes are prepared under the supervision of MR. FREEMAN.

I.—GENERAL SKETCH OF HISTORY.

BY EDWARD A. FREEMAN. A new edition in larger type, with an Index and 16 Historical Maps. $1.40

II.—HISTORY OF ENGLAND.

BY EDITH THOMPSON. $1.00

III.—HISTORY OF SCOTLAND.

BY MARGARET MACARTHUR. $1.00

IV.—HISTORY OF ITALY.

BY THE REV. W. HUNT, M.A. $1.00

V.—HISTORY OF GERMANY.

BY JAMES SIME. $1.00

VI.—HISTORY OF THE UNITED STATES.

BY J. A. DOYLE.

With Maps and revisions, by FRANCIS A WALKER. . $1.25

VII.—HISTORY OF FRANCE.

BY C. M. YONGE. $1.00

VIII.—HISTORY OF GREECE.

BY J. ANNAN BRYCE, B.A. . . . . . (*In preparation.*)

FREEMAN'S HISTORICAL COURSE FOR SCHOOLS

GENERAL SKETCH

OF

HISTORY

BY

EDWARD A. FREEMAN, D.C.L.
Late Fellow of Trinity College, Oxford.

ADAPTED FOR AMERICAN STUDENTS

New Edition Revised, with Chronological Table, Maps, and Index

NEW YORK
HENRY HOLT AND COMPANY

TROW'S
PRINTING AND BOOKBINDING CO.,
PRINTERS,
205-213 *East 12th St.*,
NEW YORK.

PREFACE TO THE NEW EDITION.

THE present edition has been thoroughly revised throughout. A Chronological Table, a full Index, and several Maps, illustrating historical Geography at different periods, have been added.

In such a mass of names and dates it is impossible wholly to avoid slips both of the pen and of the press. I have tried to correct all that I found in earlier editions; but I fear that some may have escaped me. I shall be sincerely thankful to any one who will point out to me any that he may come across.

SOMERLEAZE, WELLS,
April 3rd, 1876.

PREFACE TO THE FIRST EDITION.

THE object of the present series is to put forth clear and correct views of history in simple language, and in the smallest space and cheapest form in which it could be done. It is meant in the first place for schools; but it is often found that a book for schools proves useful for other readers as well, and it is hoped that this may be the case with the little books the first instalment of which is now given to the world. The present volume is meant to be introductory to the whole course. It is intended to give, as its name implies, a general sketch of the history of the civilized world, that is, of Europe and of the lands which have drawn their civilization from Europe. Its object is to trace out the general relations of different periods and different countries to one another, without going minutely into the affairs of any particular country, least of all into those of our own. This is an object of the first importance, for, without clear notions of general history, the history of particular countries can never be rightly understood. This General Sketch will be followed by a series of special histories of particular countries, which will take for granted the main principles laid down in the General Sketch. In this series it is hoped in time to take in short histories of all the chief countries of Europe and America, giving the results of the latest historical researches in as simple a form as may be. Those of England and Scotland will shortly follow the present introductory volume, and other authors are at work on other parts of the plan. The several members of the series will all be so far under the supervision of the Editor as to secure general accuracy of statement, and a general harmony of plan and sentiment. But each book will be the original work of its own author, and each author will be responsible for his own treatment of the smaller details. For his own share of the work the Editor has, besides the General Sketch, taken the histories of Rome and Switzerland. The others will be put into the hands of various writers, on whose knowledge and skill he believes that he can rely.

SOMERLEAZE, WELLS,
August 23, 1872.

CONTENTS.

CHAPTER I.

PAGE

ORIGIN OF THE NATIONS 1

CHAPTER II.

GREECE AND THE GREEK COLONIES 18

CHAPTER III.

THE ROMAN COMMONWEALTH. 49

CHAPTER IV.

THE HEATHEN EMPIRE 82

CHAPTER V.

THE EARLY CHRISTIAN EMPIRE 98

CHAPTER VI.

THE ROMAN EMPIRE IN THE EAST 115

CHAPTER VII.

THE FRANKISH EMPIRE 130

CHAPTER VIII.

THE SAXON EMPERORS 146

CHAPTER IX

PAGE
THE FRANCONIAN EMPERORS 154

CHAPTER X.

GENERAL VIEW OF THE MIDDLE AGES 168

CHAPTER XI.

THE SWABIAN EMPERORS 184

CHAPTER XII.

THE DECLINE OF THE EMPIRE 209

CHAPTER XIII.

THE GREATNESS OF SPAIN 244

CHAPTER XIV.

THE GREATNESS OF FRANCE 293

CHAPTER XV.

THE RISE OF RUSSIA 316

CHAPTER XVI.

THE FRENCH REVOLUTION 339

CHAPTER XVII.

THE REUNION OF GERMANY AND ITALY 363

LIST OF MAPS.

THE GREEK COLONIES . . . . *Page* 24

DOMINIONS OF ALEXANDER AND HIS SUCCESSORS " 40

THE MEDITERRANEAN LANDS AT THE BEGINNING OF THE SECOND PUNIC WAR . . . . . " 62

ROMAN EMPIRE AT ITS GREATEST EXTENT . . " 88

EUROPE AT END OF 5TH CENTURY . . . . . " 104

EUROPE UNDER JUSTINIAN . . . . " 114

DOMINIONS OF THE EARLY CALIPHS . . . . " 120

EUROPE UNDER CHARLES THE GREAT . . . . " 128

EUROPE AT THE END OF THE 9TH CENTURY . " 130

EUROPE IN THE 12TH CENTURY . . . . . . " 158

EUROPE TOWARDS THE END OF THE 14TH CENTURY . . . . " 210

EUROPE UNDER CHARLES THE FIFTH . . . . " 242

THE SPANISH AND PORTUGUESE COLONIES . . " 276

EUROPE UNDER LEWIS THE 14TH . . . . . " 284

EUROPE UNDER BUONAPARTE . . . . " 332

EUROPE ACCORDING TO TREATY OF VIENNA . . " 336

CHRONOLOGICAL TABLE.

	B.C.
Messenian Wars	743-668
Solon gives laws to Athens	594
Peisistratos, Tyrant of Athens	560-527
Sardis taken by Cyrus	546
Poems of Theognis of Megara	544
Babylon taken by Cyrus	538
Hippias driven out of Athens	510
The Tarquinii driven out of Rome	510
Battle of Marathôn	490
Battles of Thermopylai and Salamis	480
Battles of Plataia and Mykalê	479
Confederacy under Athens	477
Leadership of Periklês at Athens	444-429
Early Greek Dramatic Poets	472-388
Beginning of the Peloponnesian War	431
Thucydidês, fl.	c. 431-411
Xenophôn, fl..	c. 410-362
Athenian expedition against Syracuse	415
Defeat of the Athenians	413
Dionysios I., Tyrant of Syracuse	406-367
Battle of Aigos-potamos	405
Government of the Thirty at Athens	404
Deliverance of Athens by Thrasyboulos	403
Veii taken by Camillus	396

	B.C.
Battle of the Allia ; Rome taken by the Gauls . . .	**390**
Spartan Campaigns in Asia Minor	**399-394**
Corinthian War	**394**
Peace of Antalkidas	**387**
Kadmeia of Thebes taken by the Spartans	**382**
The Spartans driven out of Thebes ; leadership of Pelopidas and Epameinôndas	**379**
Olynthian Confederacy suppressed by Sparta. . . .	**379**
Battle of Leuktra	**371**
Dionysios II., Tyrant of Syracuse	**367-356**
The Arkadian League ; foundation of Megalopolis .	**369**
Restoration of Messênê	**369**
Lucius Sextius first Plebeian Consul	**366**
Battle of Mantineia ; death of Epameinôndas . . .	**362**
Philip, King of Macedonia	**359**
Dêmosthenês, fl.	c. **356-322**
Olynthos taken by Philip	**347**
First Samnite War	**343**
Latin War	**340**
Battle of Chairôneia	**338**
Alexander the Great, King of Macedonia.	**336**
Thebes destroyed by Alexander	**335**
Battle of the Granikos	**334**
Battle of Issos	**333**
Foundation of Alexandria	**332**
Battle of Arbêla	**331**
Second Samnite War	**326**
Death of Alexander	**323**
The Lamian War	**323**
Submission of Athens to Antipatros	**322**
Beginning of Kingdom of Pergamos	**280**
Agathokles, Tyrant of Syracuse	c. **310-286**
Battle of Ipsos	**301**
Third Samnite War.	**298-290**
Pyrrhos, King of Epeiros	**295**
Dêmêtrios Poliorkêtês, King of Macedonia	**294**
War between Pyrrhos and the Romans	**281**
Gaulish Invasion of Greece and Macedonia	**280**

	B.C.
Revival of the Achaian League	**280**
Gaulish Settlement in Asia	**279**
Battle of Beneventum	**275**
Death of Pyrrhos at Argos	**272**
Hierôn II., King of Syracuse	**270-216**
First Punic War	**264-241**
Sikyôn joins the Achaian League	**251**
Rise of the Parthian Dynasty	**250**
Aratos, General of the Achaian League	**247**
Hamilcar Barcas, General of the Carthaginians	**245**
Kleomenês, King of Sparta	**236**
War between Rome and Illyria	**229**
War between Sparta and the Achaian League	**227**
Corinth given up to Antigonos Dôsôn	**223**
Battle of Sellasia	**221**
Death of Kleomenês	**221**
Hannibal, General of the Carthaginians	**221**
The Confederate War	**220-217**
Second Punic War	**218**
The Scipios in Spain	**218-206**
Battle of Lake Trasimene	**217**
Battle of Cannæ	**216**
First Macedonian War	**213-205**
Publius Cornelius Scipio in Africa	**206-201**
Philopoimên, General of the Achaian League	**208**
Battle of Zama	**202**
Second Macedonian War	**200**
Battle of Kynoskephalê	**197**
Defeat of Antiochos the Great at Thermopylai	**191**
Roman Conquest of Cisalpine Gaul	**191**
Defeat of Antiochos at Magnêsia	**191**
Roman Conquest of Ætolia	**189**
Polybios, fl.	c. **182-146**
Third Macedonian War	**171**
The Lykian League	**168**
Battle of Pydna	**168**
Third Punic War	**149**
Fourth Macedonian War	**149**
Macedonia becomes a Roman Province	**148**

	B.C.
Carthage taken by the Romans	146
War between Rome and Achaia; destruction of Corinth	146
Attalos bequeaths Pergamos to the Romans	133
Roman Conquest of Numantia	133
Tribunate of Tiberius Gracchus	133
First Roman Province in Transalpine Gaul	125
Tribunate of Caius Gracchus	123
Jugurthine War	111-106
Invasion of Gaul by Cimbri and Teutonês	109
Caius Marius, Consul	107
Defeat of the Teutones at Aquæ Sextiæ	102
Defeat of the Cimbri at Vercellæ	101
The Social War	90
Civil War between Marius and Sulla	88-82
First Mithridatic War	88
Battles of Chairôneia and Orchomenos	87
Dictatorship of Sulla	82
Second Mithridatic War	74-64
Roman Conquest of Syria	64
Jerusalem taken by Pompeius	63
Conquests of Cæsar in Gaul	58-51
Cæsar's Invasions of Britain	55-54
Parthian Expedition and Death of Crassus	54-53
Civil War of Pompeius and Cæsar	49
Defeat of Pompeius at Pharsalos	48
Perpetual Dictatorship of Cæsar	45
Death of Cæsar	44
Second Civil War	43
Battle of Philippi	42
War between Cæsar and Antonius	32
Battle of Aktion	31
Title of Augustus taken by Cæsar	27
Beginning of the Roman Empire	27
Campaigns of Drusus and Tiberius in Germany	11-9
	A.D.
Defeat of Varus by Arminius	9
Tiberius, Emperor	14
Campaigns of Germanicus	15-16

	A.D.
Caligula, Emperor	37
Claudius, Emperor	41
Claudius in Britain	43
Nero, Emperor	54
Galba, Otho, Vitellius, Emperors	68-69
Revolt of Civilis	69-70
Destruction of Jerusalem	70
Vespasian, Emperor	70
Domitian	79
Titus	81
Final Conquest of Britain by Agricola	84
Dacian War	86
Nerva	96
Trajan	98
Hadrian	117
Antoninus Pius	138
Marcus Aurelius	161
Commodus	180
Septimius Severus	193
Antoninus Caracalla	211
Alexander Severus	222
Sassanid Dynasty in Persia	226
Valerian	253
Gallienus	260
Kingdom of Palmyra	261
Claudius II.	263
Defeats of the Goths by Claudius	269, 270
Aurelian, Emperor	270
Overthrow of the Kingdom of Palmyra	273
Diocletian, Emperor	284
Maximian, joint Emperor with Diocletian	286
Abdications of Diocletian and Maximian	305
Constantine the Great (sole Emperor)	323
Foundation of Constantinople	324
Council of Nikaia	325
Constantius (sole Emperor)	350
Campaigns of Julian in Gaul	356-360
Julian, Emperor	360-363

	A.D.
The Goths cross the Danube	376
Battle of Hadrianople	378
Theodosius the Great (sole Emperor)	393
Arcadius and Honorius	395
Alaric in Italy	402
Stilicho defeats Alaric	403
Rome taken by Alaric	410
The Roman Legions leave Britain	410
Beginning of the Gothic Kingdom in Spain and Gaul	414
Settlement of the Vandals in Africa	429
English Conquest of Britain	449-547
Defeat of Attila at Châlons	451
Majorian, Emperor in the West	457-461
Reunion of the Empires under Zeno	476
Odoacer governs Italy as Patrician	476
Reign of Theodoric in Italy	493-526
Justinian, Emperor	527-565
Chosroes or Nushirvan, King of Persia	531
Campaigns of Belisarius in Africa	534
Italy recovered by Belisarius and Narsês	536-554
Lombard Settlements in Italy	568
Birth of Mahomet	569
Maurice, Emperor	582
Chosroes Parviz, King of Persia	590
Conversion of the English	597-681
Phokas, Emperor	602
Beginning of Mahomet's Mission	609
Heraclius, Emperor	610
Campaigns of Chosroes	611-615
Heraclius overthrows the Persian power	623-628
Death of Mahomet; Abu-Bekr Caliph	632
Saracen Conquest of Syria	632-639
Saracen Conquest of Persia	632-651
Saracen Conquest of Egypt	638
Saracen Conquest of Africa	647-709
First Siege of Constantinople	673
Carthage taken by the Saracens	698
Saracen Conquest of Spain	710-713

	A.D.
Second Siege of Constantinople	**716**
Leo the Isaurian, Emperor	**717**
Iconoclast Controversy in Italy	**728**
Battle of Tours; defeat of the Saracens by Charles Martel	**732**
Constantine Koprônymos, Emperor	**741-775**
Pippin, King of the Franks	**753**
End of the Ommiad Dynasty at Damascus	**750**
Abd-al-rahman founds the Ommiad Dynasty in Spain	**755**
The Saracens driven out of Gaul	**755**
Charles the Great overthrows the Lombard Kingdom	**774**
Deposition of Constantine VI.	**797**
Charles the Great, Emperor of the West	**800**
Ecgberht, King of the West-Saxons	**802-837**
Lewis the Pious, Emperor	**814**
Saracen Conquest of Crete	**823**
Saracen Conquest of Sicily	**827-878**
Treaty of Verdun	**843**
Alfred, King of the West-Saxons	**871**
The Macedonian Emperors in the East	**867-1028**
Paris besieged by the Northmen	**885**
Division of the Karolingian Empire	**887**
Settlement of Rolf in Gaul	**913**
Edward the Elder, Lord of all Britain	**924**
Otto the Great crowned Emperor	**962**
Otto the Second, Emperor	**972**
Otto the Third, Emperor	**983**
Mahometan Invasion of India	**1001-1026**
Danish Conquest of England	**1013-1016**
Cnut, King of all England	**1017-1035**
Edward the Confessor	**1042**
Conrad II. — King **1024**,* Emperor	**1027**
End of the Ommiad Dynasty in Spain	**1031**
Union of Burgundy with the Empire	**1032**

* In the case of the Western Emperors the first date is that of election and coronation as King or, in the case of a King crowned in his father's lifetime, his accession as sole King; the second date is that of his coronation as Emperor.

	A.D.
Henry III. . . . . King **1039**, Emperor	**1046**
Rise of the Seljuk Turks	**1035**
Togrel Beg helps the Caliph Al Kayem against the Dilemites	**1055**
Henry IV. . . . . King **1056**, Emperor	**1084**
Norman Conquest of Sicily	**1060-1090**
Battle of Senlac	**1066**
Battle of Manzikert	**1071**
Revolt of the Saxons against Henry IV.	**1073**
Henry IV. at Canosa	**1077**
Alfonso of Leon takes Toledo	**1084**
Dynasty of the Almoravides in Spain	**1087**
Division of the Seljuk Empire	**1092**
Council of Clermont	**1095**
The First Crusade	**1096**
Jerusalem taken by the Crusaders	**1099**
Henry I., King of England	**1100-1135**
Henry V. . . . . King **1106**, Emperor	**1111**
Alfonso of Aragon takes Zaragoza	**1118**
John Komnênos, Eastern Emperor	**1118-1143**
The Concordat of Worms	**1122**
Norman Kingdom of Sicily	**1130**
Lothar of Saxony . . . . King **1125**, Emperor	**1133**
Conrad III., King	**1138**
Manuel Komnênos, Eastern Emperor	**1143**
The Almohade Dynasty in Spain	**1146**
The Second Crusade	**1147**
Henry II. of England	**1154**
Frederic Barbarossa . . . King **1152**, Emperor	**1155**
The Lombard League	**1167**
Conquest of Ireland	**1171**
Saladin overthrows the Fatimite Dynasty	**1171**
Manuel, Eastern Emperor, defeated by the Turks . .	**1176**
Philip Augustus, King of France	**1180**
Peace of Constanz	**1183**
Saladin takes Jerusalem	**1187**
Henry VI. . . . . King **1190**, Emperor	**1191**
Conquest of Sicily by Henry VI.	**1194**

	A.D.
Battle of Alarcos	**1195**
John, King of England	**1199**
Alliance between the Crusaders and Venetians	**1201**
First Latin Siege and taking of Constantinople	**1203**
Second Latin Conquest of Constantinople	**1204**
Theodore Laskarês, Emperor of Nikaia	**1204**
Invasion of the Moguls under Jenghiz Khan	**1206**
Crusade against the Albigenses	**1208**
Battle of Tolosa	**1212**
James the Conqueror, King of Aragon	**1213–1276**
Battle of Bouvines	**1214**
The Great Charter granted by John	**1215**
Henry III., King of England	**1216–1272**
Ferdinand III., King of Castile	**1217–1252**
Frederick II.	King **1215**, Emperor **1220**
John Vatatzês, Emperor of Nikaia	**1222**
Mogul Invasion of Persia	**1222**
Saint Lewis of France	**1226**
Frederick II. crowned King of Jerusalem	**1228**
The County of Toulouse joined to France	**1229**
Ferdinand III. unites Castile and Leon	**1230**
The Teutonic Order conquers Prussia	**1230–1260**
Kingdom of Granada	**1237**
Rise of the Ottoman Turks	**1240**
Battle of Lignitz	**1241**
Jerusalem taken by the Chorasmians	**1244**
First Crusade of St. Lewis of France	**1248**
Death of Frederick II. Conrad IV., King	**1250**
End of the Swabian Dynasty	**1254**
The Interregnum	**1254–1273**
Manfred, King of Sicily	**1258**
End of the Bagdad Caliphate	**1258**
Michael Palaiologos, Eastern Emperor	**1259**
Recovery of Constantinople	**1261**
Battle of Evesham	**1265**
Dante born	**1265**
Conquest of Sicily by Charles of Anjou	**1266**
Gregory X., Pope	**1271**

	A.D.
Edward I., King of England	**1272**
Rudolf of Habsburg, King	**1273–1292**
The Sicilian Vespers	**1282**
Wales united to England	**1282**
Albert, Duke of Austria	**1282**
Genoese Defeat of the Pisans off Meloria	**1284**
Acre taken by the Mahometans	**1291**
Beginning of the Swiss League	**1291**
Adolf, King	**1292**
Albert I., King	**1299**
Battle of Courtray	**1302**
Boniface VIII., Pope	**1294–1303**
Clement V., Pope	**1305**
Edward II., King of England	**1307**
Popes at Avignon	**1309**
Robert, King of Naples	**1309**
Henry VII.	King **1308**, Emperor **1312**
Lewis of Bavaria	King **1314**, Emperor **1328**
Philip the Fair annexes Lyons to France	**1314**
Battle of Mortgarten	**1315**
Edward III., King of England	**1327**
Independence of Scotland	**1328**
First Passage of the Turks into Europe	**1341–1347**
Lewis, King of Hungary	**1342**
Jane I., Queen of Naples	**1343**
Battle of Crecy	**1343**
Rienzi at Rome	**1347**
Dauphiny of Vienne becomes an appanage of France	**1349**
Charles IV.	King **1346**, Emperor **1355**
The Golden Bull	**1356**
Battle of Poitiers	**1356**
Peace of Bretigny	**1360**
Philip of Valois, Duke of Burgundy	**1361**
Hadrianople taken by the Turks	**1361**
Battle of Najara	**1366**
Rise of Timour	**1370**
Return of the Popes to Rome	**1376**
Beginning of the Great Schism	**1378**

	A. D.
Beginning of the War of Chioggia	1378
Timour conquers Persia	1380-1393
John the Great, King of Portugal	1385
Battle of Sempach	1386
Union of Poland and Lithuania	1386
Bajazet, Sultan of the Ottomans	1389
Gian Galeazzo Visconti, Duke of Milan	1395
Victory of Bajazet at Nikopolis	1396
The Union of Calmar	1397
Bajazet defeated by Timour at Angora	1402
John the Fearless, Duke of Burgundy	1404
Death of Timour	1405
Pisa becomes subject to Florence	1406
Sicily united to Aragon	1409
Council of Pisa	1409
Sigismund . . . . King, **1410**, Emperor	1433
Henry V., King of England	1413
Battle of Agincourt	1415
Council of Constanz	1415
John Huss burned	1415
Alfonso V., King of Aragon	1416
Jane II., Queen of Naples	1419
Philip the Good, Duke of Burgundy	1419
Henry V. takes Rouen	1419
Treaty of Troyes	1420
Amurath II., Sultan	1421
Siege of Constantinople	1422
Council of Basel	1431
Treaty of Arras	1435
Council of Florence	1439
Frederick III. . . . . . . King **1440** Emperor	1452
Battle of St. Jacob near Basel	1444
Battle of Varna	1444
Death of Filippo Maria Visconti, Duke of Milan . .	1447
Christian I., King of Denmark	1448
Constantine Palaiologos, Eastern Emperor	1448
Francesco Sforza Duke of Milan	1450
Mahomet II., Sultan	1451

	A.D.
End of the Hundred Years' War	1453
The Turks take Constantinople	1453
Wars of York and Lancaster	1455–1485
John Huniades drives back the Turks from Belgrade	1456
Matthias Corvinus, King of Hungary	1458
Mahomet II. conquers the Empire of Trebizond	1461
Casimir IV., King of Poland, wins West Prussia from the Teutonic Knights	1466
Union of Castile and Aragon	1471
Ivan Vasilovich frees Russia from the Moguls	1477
Discovery of the Cape of Good Hope	1486
Conquest of Granada	1492
Christopher Columbus discovers America	1492
Charles VIII. of France enters Italy	1494
Florence gets rid of the Medici	1494
Pisa regains her liberty	1494
Lewis XII. of France conquers the Duchy of Milan.	1500
Shah Ismael, first Sophi of Persia	1501
Ferdinand of Spain and Sicily conquers Naples	1504
League of Cambray	1508
Maximilian I. takes the title of Emperor-elect	1508
Henry VIII., King of England	1509
Pope Julius II. forms the Holy League	1511
Ferdinand conquers Navarre	1512
Battle of Ravenna	1512
The Medici return to Florence	1512
Selim the Inflexible, Sultan	1512
Germany divided into Circles	1512
Christian II., King of Denmark and Norway	1513
Francis I., King of France	1515
Battle of Marignano	1515
Charles V., (I.) King of Spain	1516
Beginning of the Reformation	1517
Charles V. elected Emperor	1519
Ulrich Zwingli preaches at Zürich	1519
Christian II. of Denmark becomes King of Norway	1520
Mexico conquered by Hernando Cortez	1519–21
Suleiman the Lawgiver, Sultan	1520

	A.D.
Suleiman takes Belgrade	**1521**
War between Charles V. and Francis I.	**1521**
Luther before the Diet of Worms	**1521**
Knights of St. John driven out of Rhodes	**1522**
Gustavus Vasa, King of Sweden	**1523**
Frederick I., King of Denmark and Norway	**1523**
Battle of Pavia	**1525**
Foundation of the Duchy of Prussia	**1525**
Lewis II. of Hungary killed at the Battle of Mohacs	**1526**
Baber, Emperor of Hindostan	**1326**
Sack of Rome by the Imperialists	**1527**
The Medici driven out of Florence	**1527**
Peace of Cambray	**1529**
Diet of Speyer	**1529**
Sultan Suleiman besieges Vienna	**1529**
Charles V. crowned Emperor	**1530**
Fall of Florence	**1530**
Confession of Augsburg	**1530**
The Portuguese colonize Brazil	**1531**
The Smalcaldic League	**1531**
Death of Zwingli	**1531**
Peru conquered by Francisco Pizarro	**1532–1536**
Ivan IV. (the Terrible), Czar of Russia	**1533**
Duke Charles of Savoy besieges Geneva	**1534**
The Society of Jesus founded by Ignatius Loyola	**1540**
Mary, Queen of Scots	**1542**
Nizza besieged by the Turks	**1543**
Council of Trent	**1545**
Death of Luther	**1546**
Henry II. of France	**1547**
Edward VI. of England	**1547**
Henry II. of France seizes the Three Bishopricks.	**1552**
Mary, Queen of England	**1553**
The Fall of Sienna	**1555**
Abdication of Charles V.	**1555**
Peace of Augsburg	**1555**
Philip II. of Spain	**1556**
Akbar, Emperor of Hindostan	**1556**

	A.D.
Cosmo de' Medici, Duke of Florence, gets possession of Sienna	1557
Battles of St. Quentin and Gravelines	1557
The French take Calais	18
Elizabeth, Queen of England	18
Peace of Câteau-Cambresis	1559
Francis II. of France	1559
Frederick II. of Denmark and Norway	1559
Charles IX. of France	1560
Death of Gustavus Vasa	1560
Religious Wars in France begin	1562
First French Settlement of Carolina	1562
Cyprus taken by the Turks	1571
Battle of Lepanto	1571
Massacre of Saint Bartholomew	1572
The Polish Crown becomes purely elective	1573
Henry III. of France	1574
Philip II. annexes Portugal to Spain	1580
Charles Emmanuel, Duke of Savoy	1580
Union of the Seven Provinces	1581
Death of William the Silent	1584
Sir Walter Raleigh founds the Colony of Virginia	1585
Mary of Scotland beheaded	1587
Philip II. sends the Armada against England	1588
Christian IV. of Denmark and Norway	1588
Henry IV. of France	1589
End of the Dynasty of Ruric in Russia	1589
Philip III. of Spain	1598
Treaty of Lyons	1601
James I. of England	1603
Jehangir, Emperor of Hindostan	1605
Lewis XIII. of France	1610
Expulsion of the Moriscos from Spain	1610
Union of Prussia and Brandenburg	1611
Gustavus Adolphus, King of Sweden	1611
Beginning of the Romanoff Dynasty in Russia	1613
Beginning of the Thirty Years' War	1618
Philip IV. of Spain	1621

	A.D.
Massacre of Amboyna	**1623**
Christian IV. of Denmark Head of the Protestant League	**1625**
Charles I. of England	**1625**
Shah Jehan, Emperor of Hindostan	**1627**
Gustavus Adolphus, Head of the Protestant League	**1630**
Battle of Lützen	**1632**
Christina, Queen of Sweden	**1632**
Ferdinand III., Emperor	**1637**
Beginning of the Dynasty of Braganza in Portugal	**1639**
English Settlement at Madras	**1640**
Lewis XIV. of France	**1643**
War of Candia	**1645**
Peace of Westphalia	**1648**
Charles I. of England beheaded	**1649**
Oliver Cromwell, Protector of England	**1653**
Prussia independent of Poland	**1657**
Death of Oliver Cromwell	**1658**
Leopold I. Emperor	**1658**
Aurungzebe, Emperor of Hindostan	**1658**
Peace of the Pyrenees	**1659**
Restoration of Charles II. of England	**1660**
Treaties of Oliva and Copenhagen	**1660**
Denmark becomes an absolute Monarchy	**1660**
Charles II. sells Dunkirk to Lewis XIV.	**1663**
War between England and the United Provinces	**1664–1667**
The Plague of London	**1665**
The Great Fire of London	**1666**
Lewis XIV. conquers Franche Comté and part of Flanders	**1667**
The Triple Alliance against Lewis XIV.	**1668**
The Turks take Candia	**1669**
William III., Stadholder	**1672**
John Sobieski, King of Poland	**1674**
Peace of Nimwegen	**1678–1679**
Lewis XIV. seizes Strassburg	**1681**
Sweden becomes an absolute Monarchy	**1682**
The Turks besiege Vienna	**1683**

	A.D.
Lewis XIV. revokes the Edict of Nantes	1685
James II. of England	1685
The Hungarian Crown becomes hereditary	1687
Lewis XIV. seizes Avignon	1688
William and Mary, King and Queen of England	1689
Peter the Great, sole Emperor of Russia	1689
Russian Conquest of Azof	1696
Peace of Ryswick	1697
Charles XII., King of Sweden	1697
Augustus the Strong, King of Poland	1697
English Settlement at Calcutta	1698
Peace of Carlowitz	1699
Battle of Narva	1700
War of the Spanish Succession	1700
Frederick I., first King of Prussia	1701
Anne, Queen of England	1702
Stanislaus, King of Poland	1704
Gibraltar taken by the English	1704
Joseph I., Emperor	1705
Union of England and Scotland	1707
Beginning of the East India Company	1708
Charles VI., Emperor	1711
Treaty of Utrecht	1713
Victor Amadeus II. of Savoy, King of Sicily	1713
Frederick William I., King of Prussia	1714
George I. of England	1714
Lewis XV. of France	1715
War between Austria and Turkey	1715
The Turks win back Peloponnêsos from Venice	1715
Jacobite Rebellion in England	1715
Peace of Passarowitz	1718
Death of Charles XII.	1718
Quadruple Alliance against Spain	1718
Victor Amadeus II., King of Sardinia	1720
The Pragmatic Sanction	1720
Mahmoud I., Sultan	1730
War of the Polish Election	1733
Peace of Belgrade	1739

	A.D.
Maria Theresa, Queen of Hungary	**1740**
Frederick II. (the Great) of Prussia	**1740**
Frederick conquers Silesia	**1740**
War of the Austrian Succession	**1741–1748**
Charles VII., Emperor	**1742**
Francis I., Emperor	**1745**
Second Jacobite Rebellion	**1745**
Battle of Culloden	**1746**
William IV. Hereditary Stadholder	**1747**
The Seven Years' War	**1756**
Suraj-ad-dowla takes Calcutta	**1756**
Battle of Plassey	**1757**
English Conquest of Canada	**1759**
George III. of England	**1760**
The Family Compact	**1761**
Catharine II., Empress of Russia	**1762**
Russian conquest of Crim Tartary	**1762**
Peace of Paris	**1763**
Joseph II., Emperor	**1765**
Annexation of Lorraine to France	**1766**
Annexation of Corsica to France	**1768**
First Partition of Poland	**1772**
Abolition of the Society of Jesus	**1773**
Peace of Kainardji	**1774**
Lewis XVI. of France	**1774**
Revolt of the American Colonies	**1775**
Declaration of Independence	**1776**
Independence of Ireland	**1782**
Convocation of States-General in France	**1789**
Constitution of the United States	**1789**
Selim III., Sultan	**1789**
Leopold II., Emperor	**1790**
Francis II., Emperor	**1792**
National Convention in France	**1792**
Treaty of Jassy	**1792**
Wars of the French Revolution	**1793–1815**
Second Partition of Poland	**1793**
Execution of Lewis XVI.	**1793**

	A.D.
Third Partition of Poland	1795
Batavian Republic	1795
Paul, Emperor of Russia	1796
Helvetic Republic	1798
Battle of the Nile	1798
Union of Great Britain and Ireland	1800
Alexander, Emperor of Russia	1801
Peace of Luneville	1801
Peace of Amiens	1802
Napoleon Buonaparte, Emperor of the French	1804
Buonaparte, King of Italy	1805
Battle of Austerlitz	1805
Peace of Pressburg	1805
Battle of Trafalgar	1805
Francis II. resigns the Imperial Crown	1806
Battle of Jena	1806
Peace of Tilsit	1807
Mahmoud II. Sultan	1807
The Peninsular War begins	1808
Battle of Wagram	1809
Revolt of the Spanish Colonies in America	1810
French Invasion of Russia	1812
War between England and the United States	1813-1815
Battle of Leipzig	1813
First Peace of Paris	1814
Abdication of Napoleon Buonaparte	1814
Congress of Vienna	1815
Return of Buonaparte. Battle of Waterloo	1815
Second Peace of Paris	1815
The German Confederation	1815
Greek War of Independence	1821
Separation of Brazil from Portugal	1822
Charles X. of France	1824
Nicholas, Emperor of Russia	1825
Battle of Navarino	1827
War between Russia and Turkey	1828
French Revolution of July	1830
Separation of Belgium from the Netherlands	1830

	A.D.
Insurrection in Central Italy	1831
Polish Revolution	1831
Civil War in Spain	1833
Independence of Egypt	1841
Pius IX., Pope	1846
War of the Sonderbund in Switzerland	1847
Frederick VII. of Denmark	1848
Second French Republic	1848
Louis Napoleon Buonaparte, President	1848
First War of Independence in Italy	1848
War of Sleswick and Holstein	1848
Swiss Federal Constitution	1848
Battle of Novara	1849
Victor Emmanuel II., King of Sardinia	1849
Fall of Rome and Venice	1849
French Republic destroyed by Louis Napoleon Buonaparte	1851
Buonaparte calls himself Emperor	1852
The Crimean War	1854-1856
Alexander II., Emperor of Russia	1855
Indian Mutiny	1857
Freedom of Lombardy	1859
Garibaldi frees Sicily and Naples	1860
Victor Emmanuel, King of Italy	1861
Secession War in America	1861
Polish Revolt	1863
Battle of Königsgrätz	1866
Sleswick and Holstein joined to Prussia	1866
France declares war against Prussia	1870
Battle of Sedan	1870
Rome the Capital of Italy	1870
William I. of Prussia, German Emperor	1871
Surrender of Paris	1871
Peace of Frankfurt	1871

GENERAL SKETCH

OF

HISTORY.

CHAPTER I.

ORIGIN OF THE NATIONS.

Different nations of the world (1)—*difference between East and West* (2)—*the Aryan nations* (3)—*connexion among their languages* (3)—*amount of progress made by them before their dispersion* (4)—*their advances in religion and government* (5)—*the Semitic nations* (6)—*their religious influence on the world* (6)—*the Turanian and other Non-Aryan nations* (7)—*their extent in Asia* (7)—*traces of them in Europe* (7)—*movements of the Aryans in Europe and Asia* (8)—*geographical shape of Europe* (9)—*the three great peninsulas* (10)—*advance of the successive Aryan swarms* (11)—*the Greeks and Italians* (11, 12)—*the Celts* (12)—*the Teutons* (13)—*the Slaves and Lithuanians* (14)—*later Turanian settlements in Europe; Hungarians and Turks* (14)—*different degrees of importance among the Aryans of Europe* (15)—*Rome the central point of all European History* (1)—*Division of periods before and after the Roman Dominion* (16).

1. **Different Aspects of History.**—The history of the various nations of mankind may be looked at in many and very different ways; and the importance

of different parts of history varies widely according to the way in which they are looked at. One who wishes to trace out the history of religion, or of language, or of manners and customs, will often find as much that is useful for his purpose among savage nations, who have played no important part in the world, as among the most famous and civilized people. But researches of this sort cannot be put together into a continuous tale; they are not *history* strictly so called. By *history* in the highest sense we understand the history of those nations which have really influenced one another, so that their whole story, from the beginning to our own time, forms one tale, of which, if we wholly leave out any part, we cannot rightly understand what follows it. Such a history as this is found only in the history of the chief nations of Europe, and of those nations of Asia and Africa which have had most to do with them.

2. **Difference between East and West.**—Between the history of the East, as we may vaguely call it, that is chiefly the history of *Asia* and *Africa*, and the history of the Western world in *Europe* and *America*, the gap is in many ways wide. To take one point of difference among many, the history of the *East* does not give the same political teaching as that of the *West*. It is in a much greater degree the history of a mere succession of empires and dynasties, and in a much less degree the history of the people. We shall therefore do right if we deal with the history of the West as our main subject, and treat of the history of the East only so far as it bears on the history of the West. For history in the highest sense, for the history of man in his highest political character, for the highest developements of art, literature, and political freedom, we must look to that family of mankind to which we ourselves belong, and to that division of the world in which we ourselves dwell. The branch of history which is history in the highest

and truest sense is the history of the *Aryan* nations of Europe, and of those who have in later times gone forth from among them to carry the arts and languages of Europe into other continents. The history of these nations forms *Western* or *European* history, the history of *Europe and of European Colonies.* But here too we shall find some periods and countries of higher interest and importance than others. Still the whole from the earliest times to which we can trace it back, forms one connected story. No part is altogether void of interest in itself, none is altogether cut off from connexion with the general thread of continuous history. And with regard to particular times and places, this part of history reaches the highest degree of interest and importance that history can reach. It takes in the history of those times and places which most directly concern ourselves, and it takes in the history of those times and places which have had the deepest and most lasting influence on the world in general. It is then to the history of Europe, and of the Aryan nations in Europe and in European colonies elsewhere, that the present sketch, and the more detailed histories which are to follow it, will mainly be devoted. The history of other parts of the world, and of other families of the human race, will be dealt with only so far as those other nations and countries are brought into connexion with the long unbroken tale of European history.

3. **The Aryan Nations.**—Some readers may perhaps by this time have asked what is to be understood by a word which has been already used more than once, namely, the *Aryan* nations. That is the name which is now generally used to express that division of the human race to which we ourselves belong, that which takes in nearly all the present nations of Europe and several of the chief nations of Asia. The evidence of language shows that there was a time, a time of course long before the beginning of

recorded history, when the forefathers of all these nations were one people, speaking one language. *Sanscrit,* that is the ancient language of India, *Persian, Greek, Latin, English,* and other tongues, many of which we shall soon have occasion to speak of, are really only dialects of one common speech. They show their common origin both by their grammatical forms, such as the endings of nouns and verbs and the like, and also in a way which is more easily understood by people in general, by their still having many of the commonest and most necessary words, those words without which no language can get on, essentially the same. Now many of the nations which now speak these languages have for ages been so far parted from one another that it is quite impossible that they can have borrowed these words, and still less these grammatical forms, from one another. We can thus see that all these nations are really kinsfolk, that they once were only one nation, the different branches of which parted off from one another at a time long before written history begins.

4. **Early State of the Aryan Nations.**—But what we know of the languages of the various Aryan nations tells us something more than this. By the nature of the words which are common to all or most of the kindred tongues, we can see what steps the forefathers of these various nations had already taken in the way of social life and regular government in the days before they parted asunder. And we can see that those steps were no small steps. Before there were such nations as Hindoos and Greeks and Germans, while the common forefathers of all were still only one people, they had risen far indeed above the state of mere savages. They had already learned to build houses, to plough the ground, and to grind their corn in a mill. This is shown by the words for ploughing, building, and grinding being still nearly the same in all the kindred languages. It is easy for any-

one to see that the word *mill* is the same as the Latin *mola*, and that the old word to *ear*—that is, to *plough*—the ground, which is sometimes used in the Old Testament, is the same as the Latin *arare*, which has the same meaning. But no one ought to fancy that the English word is derived from the Latin, or that we learned the use of the thing from any people who spoke Latin, because the same words are found also in many other of the kindred languages, even those which are spoken in countries which are furthest removed from one another. We see then that words of this kind—and I have chosen only two out of many—are really fragments remaining from the old common language which was spoken by our common forefathers before they branched off and became different nations. It is therefore quite plain that the things themselves, the names of which have thus been kept in so many different languages for thousands of years, were already known to the Aryan people before they parted into different nations. And I need not say that people who build houses, plough the ground, and grind their corn, though they may still have very much to learn, are in a much higher state than the people in some parts of the world are in even now.

5. **Early Aryan Religion and Government.**—But language again tells something more of the early Aryan people besides the progress which they had made in the merely mechanical arts. We find that the names for various family relations, for the different degrees of kindred and affinity, *father*, *mother*, *brother*, *sister*, and the like, are the same in all or most of the kindred tongues. We see then that, before the separation, the family life, the groundwork of all society and government, was already well understood and fully established. And we see too that regular government itself had already begun; for words meaning *king* or *ruler* are the same in languages so far distant from one another as Sanscrit, Latin, and

English. The Latin words *rex*, *regere*, *regnum*, are the same as the Old-English *rica*, *rixian*, *rice*, words which have dropped out of the language, but which still remain in the ending of such words as *bishoprick*, where the last syllable means *government* or *possession*. And we can also see that the Aryans before their dispersion had already something of a religion. For there is a common stock of words and tales common to most of the Aryan nations, many of which they cannot have borrowed from one another, and which point to an early reverence for the great powers of the natural world. Thus the same name for the sky, or for the great God of the sky, appears in many of the kindred languages, as *Dyaus* in Sanscrit, *Zeus* in Greek, and the Old-English God *Tiw*, from whom we still call the third day of the week *Tiwesdæg* or *Tuesday*. And there are a number of stories about various Gods and heroes found among different Aryan nations, all of which seem to come from one common source. And we may go on and see that the first glimpses which we can get of the forms of government in the early days of the kindred nations show them to have been wonderfully like one another. Alike among the old Greeks, the old Italians, and the old Germans, there was a *King* or chief with limited power, there was a smaller *Council* of nobles or of old men, and a general *Assembly* of the whole people. Such was the old constitution of England, out of which the present constitution has grown step by step. But there is no reason to think that this was at all peculiar to England, or even peculiar to those nations who are most nearly akin to the English. There is every reason to believe that this form of government, in which every man had a place, though some had a greater place than others, was really one of the possessions which we have in common with the whole Aryan family. We see then that the common Aryan forefathers, in the times when they were still one people, times so long ago that we cannot hope to give them any certain date, had already made advances in civilization which placed them far above mere savages. They already had the family life; they already had the beginnings of religion and government; and they already knew most of those simple arts which are most needed for the comfort of human life.

6. **The Semitic Nations.**—Such then were the original Aryans—that one among the great families of mankind to which we ourselves belong, and that which has played the greatest part in the history of the world. Still the Aryan nations are only a small part among the nations of the earth. It is not needful for our purpose to speak at any length of the nations which are not Aryan; but a few words must be given to the two great families which have always pretty well divided Europe and Asia with the Aryans, and with whom the history of the Aryans is constantly coming in contact. Next in importance to the Aryans we must place those that are called the *Semitic* nations, among which we have most to do with the *Hebrews*, the *Phœnicians*, and the *Arabs*. And in one point we must set them even above the Aryans; for the three religions which have taught men that there is but one God—the *Jewish*, the *Christian*, and the *Mahometan*—have all come from among them. But those among the Semitic nations to whom this great truth was not known seem often to have fallen into lower forms of idolatry than the Aryans. Now the Semitic nations have, so to speak, kept much closer together than the Aryans have. They have always occupied a much smaller portion of the world than the Aryans, and they have kept much more in the same part of the world. Their chief seats have always been in south-western Asia; and, though they have spread themselves thence into distant parts of the world, in Asia, Africa, and even Europe, yet this has mainly been by settlements in comparatively late times, about whose history we

know something. Their languages also have parted off much less from one another than the Aryan languages have; the Semitic nations have thus always kept up more of the character of one family than the Aryans.

7. **The Turanian Nations.**—The rest of Asia, which is not occupied either by Aryan or by Semitic people, is occupied by various nations whose tongues differ far more widely from one another than the Aryan tongues do. Still there is reason to believe that many of them at least were originally one people, and at all events it is convenient for our purposes to class together all those nations of Europe and Asia which are neither Aryan nor Semitic. The people of the greater part of Asia are commonly known as the *Turanian* nations. In the old Persian stories *Turan*, the land of darkness, is opposed to *Iran* or *Aria*, the land of light; and it is from this *Iran*, the old name of Persia, that it has been thought convenient to give the whole family the name of *Aryans*. And besides that large part of Asia which is still occupied by the Turanians, it is plain that in earlier times they occupied a large part of Europe also. But the Aryans have driven them out of nearly all Europe, except a few remnants in out-of-the-way corners, such as the *Fins* and *Laps* in the north. The *Basques* also on the borders of Spain and Gaul, whether akin to the Turanians or not, are at least neither Aryan nor Semitic, so that for our purpose they may all go together. Except these few remnants of the old races, all Europe has been Aryan since the beginning of written history, except when Semitic or Turanian invaders have come in later times. But in Asia the nations which are neither Aryan nor Semitic, the *Chinese*, *Mongols*, *Turks*, and others, still far outnumber the Aryan and Semitic nations put together.

8. **The Aryan Dispersion.**—We have seen that there was a time, long before the beginning of recorded

history, when the forefathers of the various Aryans dwelled together as one people, speaking one language. And the advances which they had made towards civilization show that they must have dwelled together for a long time, but a time whose length we cannot undertake to measure. Nor can we undertake to fix a date for the time of the great separation, when the families which had hitherto dwelled together parted off in different directions and became different nations, speaking tongues which are easily seen to be near akin to each other, but which gradually parted from one another so that different nations could no longer understand each other's speech. All that we can say is that these are things which happened long before the beginnings of written history, but which are none the less certain because we learn them from another kind of proof. The various wandering bands must have parted off at long intervals, one by one, and it often happened that a band split off into two or more bands in the course of its wanderings. And in most cases they did not enter upon uninhabited lands, but upon lands in which men of other races were already dwelling. Among these they came as conquerors, and, for the most part, they drove them out of the best parts of the land into out-of-the-way corners. First of all, there are the two great divisions of the *Eastern* and the *Western*, the *Asiatic* and the *European*, Aryans, divisions which became altogether cut off from one another in geographical position and in habits and feelings. From the old mother-land one great troop pressed to the south-east and became the forefathers of the *Persians* and *Hindoos*, driving the older inhabitants of India down to the south, into the land which is properly distinguished from *Hindostan* by the name of the *Deccan*. The other great troop pressed westward, and, sending off one swarm after another, formed the various Aryan nations of Europe. The order in which they came can be known only by their geographical position. The first waves of the migration must be those whom we find furthest to the *West* and furthest to the *South*. But, in order fully to take in the force of the evidence furnished by the geographical position of the various Aryan nations in Europe, it is needful to say a few words as to the geographical aspect of the continent of Europe itself.

9. **Geographical Shape of Europe.**—A glance at the map will show that, of the three continents which form the Old World, *Europe*, *Asia*, and *Africa*, the first two are far more closely joined to one another than either of them is to the third. Africa is a vast peninsula—in our own day indeed it may be said to have become an island—united to the other two by a very narrow isthmus. But Europe and Asia form one unbroken mass, and in some parts the boundary between the two is purely artificial. Some maps, for instance, make the *Don* the boundary; others make it the *Volga*. The most northern and the most central parts of Europe and Asia form unbroken geographical wholes; it is only the southern parts of the two continents which are quite cut off from one another. And it is in these southern parts of each that the earliest recorded history, at all events the earliest recorded history of the Aryan nations, begins. Central Europe and central Asia form one great solid mass of nearly unbroken land. The southern parts of each continent, the lands below these central masses, consist of a series of peninsulas, running, in the case of Europe, into the great inland sea called the *Mediterranean*—the sea which brings all three continents into connexion—in the case of Asia into the *Ocean* itself. Europe thus consists of a great central plain, cut off by a nearly unbroken mountain range from a system of islands and peninsulas to the south, which is again balanced to the north by a sort of secondary system of islands and peninsulas, the *Baltic* being a

kind of northern Mediterranean. We might almost say the same of Asia, as the mouths of the great rivers which run to the north form several peninsulas and inland seas. But then this part of the world has always been, so to speak, frozen up, and it never has played, nor ever can play, any part in history.

10. **The three great European Peninsulas.**—We thus see that the southern part of Europe consists mainly of three great peninsulas, those of *Spain, Italy,* and what we may roughly call *Greece.* Of these, the two eastern peninsulas are purely Mediterranean, while Spain, from its position at one end of the Old World, could not help having one side to the Ocean. So Northern Europe may be said to consist of the two *Scandinavian peninsulas* and of the *British Islands*, which in a certain way balance Spain, and which, in a general glance, seem peninsular rather than insular. Now of the three southern peninsulas, it will be seen at once that the eastern one has a character of its own. Though the nearest to Asia, it is in its geographical character the most thoroughly European. As Europe is, more than either of the other continents, a land of islands and peninsulas, so Greece and the countries near to it are, more than any other part of Europe, a land of islands and peninsulas. It is therefore hardly more than we should expect when we find that the recorded history of Europe begins in this eastern peninsula, that is to say, in Greece; that for several ages the history of Europe is little more than a history of this and the neighbouring peninsula, that is to say, of *Greece* and *Italy;* that the third peninsula, that of *Spain*, first appears in European history as a kind of appendage to the other two; and that the historical importance of central and northern Europe belongs to a later time still.

11. **The Aryan Settlement of Europe. The Greeks and Italians.**—This does not however

necessarily prove that the two peninsulas of Greece and Italy were positively the first parts of Europe which received Aryan inhabitants. There can be no doubt, from the close likeness of the *Greek* and *Latin* languages, that the Aryan inhabitants of those two peninsulas branched off from the original stock as one swarm. They afterwards parted and became two nations, or rather two groups of many nations; but the fact that the Greek and Latin languages agree so closely together shows that there was a time when the forefathers of the *Greeks* and the forefathers of the *Italians* had already parted off from the forefathers of the Hindoos and Germans, but had not yet parted off from one another. Now the time when they occupied these two peninsulas must have been long before the beginnings of recorded history, so that it is impossible to give any details of the way in which the land was conquered. Still it is not in the least likely that they found the land uninhabited. They may have found earlier inhabitants who were not Aryans, as the Aryans certainly did in many other parts of Europe, or they may even have found Aryan settlers earlier than themselves. The exact relations between the Greeks and the other ancient nations of south-eastern Europe are in some respects very hard to make out, and the little that can be said about it in such a sketch as this will be better said when we come to speak of Greece somewhat more particularly. But of the people whom the Italians found in the middle peninsula of the three, we must say something more.

12. **The Italians and Celts.**—In the case of the Italians, we know a little more of the nations, both Aryan and otherwise, whom they seem to have found in their peninsula. In some parts they most likely found a non-Aryan people, and it can hardly be doubted that, if they entered their peninsula by land from the head of the Hadriatic Gulf, they

already found a *Celtic* people in the northern part of it. The *Celts* were the first wave of the Aryan migration in central Europe, and we therefore find them further to the west than any other Aryan people. In historical times we find them in *Gaul*, in the *British Islands*, in parts of *Spain* and *Italy*, and in the border lands of *Italy* and *Germany* south of the Danube. Now it is not likely that they found any part of these lands quite uninhabited ; it is far more likely that they found an earlier people dwelling in them, whom they slew or drove out. In Spain indeed and in Southern Gaul we know that they found an earlier people dwelling, because, as has been already said, there is a small district on each side of the Pyrenees where a non-Aryan tongue is still spoken. The people who speak it, the *Basques*, are, we cannot doubt, remnants of the earlier people who inhabited Spain and Southern Gaul, and most likely other parts of Western Europe, before either the Celts or Italians came. And we can hardly doubt that the Italians found people of this race, perhaps in their peninsula itself, and at any rate on its borders. But the Italians never settled far to the west of their own peninsula ; the first Aryans who pushed their way into Western Europe as far as the Ocean were the Celts. But we must now mark that, as the Aryans pressed upon and slew or drove out the earlier people whom they found in the lands into which they came, so presently other Aryan swarms came pressing upon the first Aryans, and dispossessed or drove them out in like manner. Thus, in Western Europe, while the earlier inhabitants have been driven up by the Celts into very small corners indeed, the Celts themselves were in the end also driven up into corners, though not into quite such small corners. Thus, out of all the lands where the Celts once dwelled, their languages, of which the *British* or *Welsh*, the *Breton*, and the *Irish* tongues still survive, are now spoken only in certain parts of Gaul,

Britain, and Ireland. This change is partly because, as we shall see as we go on, a large part of the Celts were conquered by the *Romans*, and learned to speak their language. But it is also partly because another wave of Aryan settlement presently came into Western Europe, which pressed upon the Celts from the east, and drove them out of a great part of the land, just as they had driven the earlier people. And so in later times, other branches of the Aryan family have pressed backwards and forwards, and have conquered and displaced other Aryan nations, just as much as those that were not Aryan. But there can be no doubt that the Celts were the first Aryans who made their way into the western lands of Spain, Gaul, and Britain.

13. **The Teutons or Dutch.**—The second Aryan swarm in Western Europe, that which came after the Celts, is the one with whose history we are more concerned than with that of any other; for it is the branch of the Aryan family to which we ourselves belong. These are the *Teutons*, the forefathers of the *Germans* and the *English*, and of the *Danes*, *Swedes*, and *Norwegians* in Northern Europe. The Teutons do not appear in history till a much later time than the Celts, and then we find them lying immediately to the east of the Celts, chiefly in the land which is now called *Germany*. From this they spread themselves into many of the countries of Europe; but in most cases they got lost among the earlier inhabitants, and learned, like them, to speak the language of the Romans. The chief parts of Europe where *Teutonic* languages are now spoken are *Germany*, *England*, and *Scandinavia*. In Scandinavia we cannot doubt that the present Teutonic inhabitants were the first Aryan settlers; for they found a Turanian people there, some of whom still remain, by the name of *Laps* and *Fins*, in the extreme north of Sweden and Norway and on the eastern coast of the Baltic. But in most places

the Teutons, as the second wave, came into lands where other Aryan settlers had been before them. Sometimes they may have simply come in the wake of the Celts as they were pressing westward; but, sometimes they found the Celts in the land and drove them out, as was specially the case in Britain. Of the first coming of the Teutons into Europe we can say nothing from written history, any more than of the first coming of the Celts. But many of their chief settlements, and among them the settlement in Britain, happened so late that we know a good deal about them. The true name of the Teutons is *Theodisc* or *Dutch*, from *Theod, people*, as one might say, "the people," as opposed to foreigners. The Germans still call themselves *Deutschen* in their own language, and not so long ago the word *Dutch* was still used in English in a sense at least as wide as this, and did not mean only the people to whom alone we now commonly give the name.

14. **The Slaves and Lithuanians.**—The third wave of Aryan settlement in the central parts of Europe consisted of the *Slaves* and *Lithuanians*, whom for our purpose we may put together, It must not be thought that the word *Slave*, as the name of a people, comes from *slave* in its common sense of *bondman*. It is just the other way, for the word *slave* got the sense of *bondman* because of the great number of bondmen of *Slavonic* birth who were at one time spread over Europe. This third swarm forms the Aryan inhabitants of the central part of Eastern Europe, of *Old Prussia* and *Lithuania*, of *Russia*, *Poland*, *Bohemia*, of parts of *Hungary*, and of a large part of the countries which are subject to the *Turks*. They thus lie to the east of the Teutons, who in after-times turned about and greatly enlarged their borders at their cost. And it is also among these Slavonic people that we find the only instances in Europe of a Turanian people turning about and establishing themselves at the cost of Aryan

nations. One of these is the *Hungarians* or *Magyars*, a people allied to the Fins, who pressed in as conquerors, and founded a kingdom which still lasts, and where the old Turanian tongue is still spoken. The other case is that of the *Ottoman Turks*, who still bear rule over many of the Greeks, Slaves, and other Aryan and Christian people in south-eastern Europe. And as we go on, we shall find other cases in eastern Europe of Turanian nations invading or ruling over Aryans; but it is only the Hungarians and the Ottoman Turks who founded kingdoms which have lasted to our own time. The last Aryan people to be mentioned in this survey of Europe are the *Lithuanians*, whose language and history are closely connected with those of the Slaves. They are the smallest, as the Slaves are the largest, of the great divisions of the Aryan settlers in Europe. But they are of great importance, because their language is in some sort the very oldest in Europe; that is, it is the one which has undergone the least change from the common Aryan tongue from which all set out. But it is only in a very small part of Europe, on the south-east corner of the Baltic, that the Lithuanian tongue is still spoken.

15. **Rome the Centre of European History.**—Such is a very short sketch of the settlement of the chief Aryan nations in Europe. The history of these nations forms European history. But, even among these Aryan nations in Europe, some have played a much more important part than others. Thus the Lithuanians and Slaves have always lagged behind the other nations. Nor have the Celts played any great part in history, except when they have come under either Roman or Teutonic influences. The nations which have stood out foremost among all have been the *Greeks*, the *Romans*, and the *Teutons*. And among these it is the *Romans* who form the centre of the whole story. Rome alone founded a universal

Empire in which all earlier history loses itself, and out of which all later history grew. That Empire, at the time of its greatest extent, took in the whole of what was then the civilized world, that is to say, the countries round about the *Mediterranean Sea*, alike in Europe, Asia, and Africa. The *Roman Empire* was formed by gradually bringing under its dominion all the countries within those bounds which had already begun to have any history, those which we may call the states of the *Old World*. And it was out of the breaking up of the great dominion of Rome that what we may call the states of the *New World*, the kingdoms and nations of modern Europe, gradually took their rise. Thus through the whole of our sketch we must be ever thinking of Rome, ever looking to Rome, sometimes looking forward to it, sometimes looking back to it, but always having Rome in our mind as the centre of the whole story. In the former part of our sketch we have to deal with kingdoms and nations which are one day to come under the power of Rome. In the latter part of our sketch we have to deal with kingdoms and nations, many of which actually formed part of the Roman dominion, and all of which have been brought, more or less fully, under Roman influences. In this way Rome will never pass out of our sight.

16. **Division of Periods.**—We may thus say that the history of the civilized part of the world falls into three parts. There is the history of the states which were in being before the Roman dominion began, and out of whose union the Roman dominion was formed. Then there is the history of the Roman dominion itself. Lastly, there is the history of the states which arose out of the breaking up of the Roman dominion. But we shall have much more to say about the states which grew up out of the breaking up of the Roman dominion than about the states which were brought together to form it. There are

two reasons for this. History which we can fully trust, history which was written down at or soon after the time when things happened, begins only a few hundred years before the Roman power came to its full growth. But a far longer time has passed since the days when the Roman dominion began to break in pieces. Thus the portion of trustworthy history which comes after the days of the Roman dominion is much longer than the portion which comes before it. And in these later times we have to deal with many great and famous states, among which are those which have grown into the chief powers of Europe in our own day. But in the earlier time, the time before the Roman dominion, we know very little of most of the European nations: the history of most of them may be said to begin at the time when the Romans began to conquer them. Of most of them therefore the little that we have to say will be best said when we come to speak of the Roman conquests. But there is one European country which has a history of its own before its conquest by the Romans, and a history longer and nobler than that of the Romans themselves. This country is *Greece.* Of Greece then, and of Greece alone, we must give a separate sketch in the next chapter, before we begin to trace the steps by which Rome won her universal dominion.

CHAPTER II.

GREECE AND THE GREEK COLONIES.

Connexion between the Greeks and Italians (1)—*their relation to other neighbouring nations* (1)—*their early advances over their kindred* (1)—*meaning of the name* Hellas (2)—*geographical character of the country* (2)—*number of islands and peninsulas* (2)—*consequent number of small states* (2)—*early political superiority of Greece* (3)—*relations between the Greeks and Phœnicians* (4)—*extent of the Phœnician Colonies* (4)—*extent of the Greek Colonies* (5)—*distinction between Greeks and Barbarians* (6)—*relations of the Greeks to the kindred nations* (6)—*relations among the cities of Greece* (7)—*relations of the colonies to the mother cities* (7)—*early constitutions of the Greek cities; likeness of those to other Aryan nations* (8)—*Kingship, Aristocracy, Democracy* (8)—*Tyranny* (9)—*Greek religion and mythology* (10)—*the Homeric poems* (11)—*the Dorian migration* (11)—*the Messenian wars* (11)—*reforms of Solôn at Athens* (11)—*growth of the Persians* (12)—*their conquests of Lydia and the Greek cities of Asia* (12)—*first Persian invasion of Greece; Battle of Marathôn* (13)—*second Persian invasion of Greece; Battles of Salamis, Plataia, and Mykalê* (13)—*greatness of Athens* (14)—*beginning of the Peloponnesian War* (15)—*Athenian expedition to Sicily* (15)—*Athens overcome by Sparta* (15)—*the dominion of Sparta* (16)—*the Peace of Antalkidas* (16)—*rise of Thebes* (17)—*rise of Macedonia under Philip; his supremacy in Greece* (18)—*conquests of Alexander the Great* (19)—*effects of his conquests; spread of Greek civilization in Asia* (20)—*the Successors of Alexander in Asia and Egypt* (21)—*the later Kings of Macedonia and Epeiros* (22)—*character of the later history of Greece* (23)—*prevalence of Federal Governments in later Greece; Leagues of Achaia, Ætolia, and elsewhere* (24)—*greatness of Sparta under Kleomenês* (25)—*interference of Rome in Greek affairs* (25)—*Summary* (26).

1. **The Greek People.**—Whether the Greeks were the first Aryan people to settle in Europe or in Eastern Europe we cannot tell for certain. But we do know for certain that they were the first Aryan nation whose deeds were recorded in written history; and there never was any nation whose deeds were more worthy to be recorded. For no nation ever did such great things, none ever made such great advances in every way so wholly by its own power and with so little help from any other people. Yet we must not look on the Greeks as a nation quite apart by themselves. We have already seen that the Greek people

were part of a great Aryan settlement which occupied both the two eastern peninsulas, and that the forefathers of the Greeks and the forefathers of the Italians must have kept together for a good while after they had parted company from the other branches of the Aryan family. And there is some reason to think that some of the other nations bordering near upon Greece, both in the eastern peninsula and in the western coast of Asia, in *Illyria*, *Thrace*, *Phrygia*, and *Lydia*, were not only Aryan, but were actually part of the same swarm as the Greeks and Italians. However this may be, it seems quite certain that most of the nations lying near Greece, as those in *Epeiros* and *Macedonia*, which lie to the north, those in *Sicily* and *Southern Italy*, and in some parts of the opposite coasts of Asia, were very closely akin to the Greeks, and spoke languages which came much nearer to Greek even than the languages of the rest of Italy. The people of all these countries seem to have had a power beyond all other people of adopting the Greek language and manners, and, so to speak, of making themselves Greeks. The Greeks seem, in fact, to have been one among several kindred nations which shot in advance of its kinsfolk, and which was therefore able in the end to become a teacher to the others. And one thing which helped the Greeks in thus putting themselves in advance of all their kinsfolk and neighbours was the nature of the land in which they settled.

2. **Geographical Character of Greece.**—Any-one who turns to the map will see that the country which we call *Greece*, but which its own people have always called *Hellas*, is the southern part of the great eastern peninsula of Europe. But we must remember that, in the way of speaking of the Greeks themselves, the name *Hellas* did not mean merely the country which we now call Greece, but any country where *Hellênes* or Greeks lived. Thus there might be patches, so to speak, of Hellas anywhere; and there were such

patches of Hellas round a great part of the Mediterranean Sea, wherever Greek settlers had planted colonies. But the first and truest Hellas, the mother-land of all Hellênes, was the land which we call Greece, with the islands round about it. There alone the whole land was Greek, and none but Hellênes lived in it. It is, above all the rest of Europe, a land of islands and peninsulas; and that was, no doubt, one main reason why it was the first part of Europe to stand forth as great and free in the eyes of the whole world. For in early times the sea-coast is always the part of a land which is first civilized, because it is the part which can most easily have trade and other dealings with other parts of the world. Thus, as Greece was the first part of Europe to become civilized, so the coasts and islands of Greece were both sooner and more highly civilized than the inland parts. Those inland parts are almost everywhere full of mountains and valleys, so that the different parts of the land, both on the sea-coast and in the inland parts, were very much cut off from one another. Each valley or island or little peninsula had its own town, with its own little territory, forming, whenever it could, a separate government independent of all others, and with the right of making war and peace, just as if it had been a great kingdom.

3. **Character of Grecian History.**—The geographical nature of the land in this way settled the history of the Greek people. It is only in much later times that a great kingdom or commonwealth can come to have the same political and intellectual life as a small state consisting of one city. In an early state of things the single city is always in advance of the great kingdom, not always in wealth or in mere bodily comforts, but always in political freedom and in real sharpness of wit. Thus the Greeks, with their many small states, were the first people from whom we can learn any lessons in the art of politics, the

art of ruling and persuading men according to law. The little commonwealths of Greece were the first states at once free and civilized which the world ever saw. They were the first states which gave birth to great statesmen, orators, and generals who did great deeds, and to great historians who set down those great deeds in writing. It was in the Greek commonwealths, in short, that the political and intellectual life of the world began. But, for the very reason that their freedom came so early, they were not able to keep it so long as states in later times which have been equally free and of greater extent.

4. **The Greeks and the Phœnicians.**—Whether the Greeks found any earlier inhabitants in the land which they made their own is a point on which we cannot be quite certain, but it is more likely that they did than that they did not. But it is certain that, when they began to spread themselves from the mainland into the islands, they found in the islands powerful rivals already settled. These were the *Phœnicians*, as the Greeks called them, who were a Semitic people, and who played a great part in both Grecian and Roman history. Their real name among themselves was *Canaanites*, and they dwelled on the coast of *Palestine*, at the east end of the Mediterranean Sea, especially in the great cities of *Sidon*, *Tyre*, and *Arados* or *Arvad.* They were a more really civilized people, and made a nearer approach to free government, than any other people who were not Aryans. They were especially given to trade and to everything which had to do with a seafaring life. They had thus begun to spread their trade, and to found colonies, over a large part of the Mediterranean coast, before the Greeks became of any note in the world. They had even made their way beyond what the Greeks called the *Pillars of Hêraklês*, that is, beyond the *Strait of Gibraltar*, and had sailed from the Mediterranean Sea into the Ocean. They had there founded

the city of *Gades*, which still keeps its name as *Cadiz*, and they founded other colonies, both in Spain and on the north-west coast of Africa, of which the most famous was *Carthage*. They had also settlements in the islands of the Ægæan Sea, as well as in the greater islands of *Cyprus* and *Sicily;* and it was in these islands that they met the Greeks as enemies. But, even before the Greeks had begun to send out colonies, they had a good deal of trade with the Phœnicians. And, as the Phœnicians were the more early civilized of the two nations, the Greeks seem to have learned several things of them, and above all, the *alphabet*. The Greeks learned the letters which the Phœnicians used to write their own language, which was much the same as the *Hebrew*, and they adapted them, as well as they could, to the Greek language. And from the Greeks the alphabet gradually made its way to the Italians, and from them to the other nations of Europe, with such changes as each nation found needful for its own tongue. The Phœnicians did much in this way towards helping on the civilization of the Greeks: but there is no reason to believe that the Phœnicians, or any other people of Asia or Africa, founded any settlements in Greece itself after the Hellênes had once made the land their own.

5. **Foundation of the Greek Colonies.**—From the mainland of Greece the Greek people gradually spread themselves over most of the neighbouring islands, and over a large part of the Mediterranean coast, especially on the shores nearest to their own land. In fact, we may say that the Phœnicians and the Greeks between them planted colonies round the whole coast of the Mediterranean, save in two parts only. One of these was *Egypt* on the south; the other was Central and Northern *Italy*, where the native inhabitants were far too strong and brave to allow strangers to settle among them. The Greeks thus spread themselves over all the islands of the Ægæan Sea, over the coasts of

Macedonia and *Thrace* to the north and of Asia Minor to the east, as well as in the islands to the west of Greece, *Korkyra* and the others which are known now as the *Ionian Islands.* A great part of this region became fully as Greek as Greece itself, only even here, on some parts of the coast, the Greek possessions were not quite unbroken, but were simply a city here and there. And nowhere, except in Greece itself, did the Greek colonists get very far from the sea. Other colonies were gradually planted in *Cyprus*, in *Sicily* and *Southern Italy*, and on the coast of *Illyria* on the eastern side of the Hadriatic. And there was one part of the Mediterranean coast which was occupied by Greek colonies where we should rather have looked for Phœnicians; that is, in the lands west of Egypt, where several Greek cities arose, the chief of which was *Kyrênê.* These were the only Greek settlements on the south coast of the Mediterranean. But some Greek colonies were planted as far east as the shores of the *Euxine*, and others as far west as the shores of *Gaul* and *Northern Spain.* One Greek colony in these parts which should be specially remembered was *Massalia*, now *Marseille.* This was the only great Greek city in the western part of the Mediterranean, and it was the head of several smaller settlements on the coasts of Gaul and Spain. In the southern part of Spain, and in the greater part of northern Africa, the Greeks could not settle, because there the Phœnicians had settled before them. And no Greek sailors were ever bold enough to pass the Pillars of Hêraklês and to plant colonies on the shores of the Ocean.

6. **Greeks and Barbarians.**—We have thus seen the extent of country over which the Greek people spread themselves. There was their own old country and the islands nearest to it, where they alone occupied the whole land; and there were also the more distant colonies, where Greek cities were planted here and there, on the coasts of lands which were occupied by

men of other nations, or, as the Greeks called them, *Barbarians*. This word *Barbarians*, in its first use among the Greeks, simply meant that the people so called were people whose language the Greeks did not understand. They called them Barbarians, even though their blood and speech were nearly akin to their own, if only the difference was so great that their speech was not understood. It followed that in most parts of the world it was easy to tell who were Greeks and who were Barbarians, but that along the northern frontier of Greece the line was less strongly drawn than elsewhere. Along that border the ruder tribes of the Greek nation, the *Ætolians*, *Akarnanians*, and others, lived alongside of other tribes who were not Greek, but who seem to have been closely allied to the Greeks. If you turn to the map, you will see along this northern border the lands of *Macedonia*, *Epeiros*, *Thessaly*. *Macedonia* was ruled by Greek Kings, but it was never reckoned to be part of Greece till quite late times. *Thessaly*, on the other hand, was always reckoned as part of Greece, though the people who gave it its name seem not to have been of purely Greek origin. In *Epeiros* again the same tribes are by some writers called Greeks and by others Barbarians, and it was only in quite late times that Epeiros, like Macedonia, was allowed to be a Greek land. So, among the colonies, though all were planted among people whom the Greeks looked on as Barbarians, yet it made a great practical difference whether the people among whom they were planted were originally akin to the Greeks or not. Thus, in many countries, as in the lands round the Ægæan and also in Italy and Sicily, the Greeks settled among people who were really very near to them in blood and speech, and who gradually adopted the Greek language and manners. In this way both Sicily and Southern Italy became quite Greek countries, though in Sicily the Greeks had to keep up a long struggle against the

Phœnicians of Carthage, who also planted several colonies in that island. In Cyprus also the same struggle went on, and the island became partly Greek and partly Phœnician. But in those of the Ægæan islands where the Phœnicians had settled, the Greeks drove them out altogether. For there was no chance of the Phœnicians taking to Greek ways as the Italians and Sicilians did.

7. **The Greek Commonwealths.**—Greece itself, the land to the south of the doubtful lands like Macedonia and Epeiros, was the only land which was wholly and purely Greek, where there was no doubt as to the whole people being Greek, and where we find the oldest and most famous cities of the Greek name. Such, in the great peninsula called *Peloponnêsos*, were *Sparta* and *Argos*, and, in early times, *Mykênê*; *Corinth* too on the *Isthmus*, and beyond the Isthmus, *Megara*, *Athens*, *Thebes*, and, in very early times, *Orchomenos*. Each Greek city, whenever it was strong enough, formed an independent state with its own little territory; but it often happened that a stronger city brought a weaker one more or less under its power. And in some parts of Greece several towns joined together in *Leagues*, each town managing its own affairs for itself, but the whole making war and peace as a single state. Thus in Peloponnêsos, first *Mykênê*, then *Argos*, and lastly *Sparta*, held the first place, each in turn contriving to get more or less power over a greater or smaller number of other cities. And it would seem that in very early times the Kings of Mykênê had a certain power over all Peloponnêsos and many of the islands. Still, even when a Greek city came more or less under the power of a stronger city, it did not wholly lose the character of a separate commonwealth. And when the cities of Old Greece began to send out colonies, those colonies became separate commonwealths also. Each colony came forth from some city in the mother country, and it often hap-

pened that a colony sent forth colonies of its own in turn. Each colony became an independent state, owing a certain respect to the mother city, but not being subject to it. And as the colonies were commonly planted where there was a rich country or a position good for trade, many of them became very flourishing and powerful. In the seventh and sixth centuries before Christ, many of the colonial cities, as *Milêtos* in Asia, *Sybaris* in Italy, and *Syracuse* in Sicily, were among the most flourishing of all Greek cities, greater than most of the cities in Greece itself. But the colonies were for the most part not so well able to keep their freedom as the cities in Greece were.

8. **Forms of Government.**—In the earliest days of Greece we find much the same form of government in the small Greek states which we find among all the Aryan nations of whose early condition we have any account. But both the Greeks and the Italians were unlike the Teutons and some of the other Aryan nations in one thing. That is because they were gathered together in cities from the very beginning, while some of the other nations were collections, not so much of *cities* as of *tribes*. Still the early form of government was much the same in both cases. Each tribe or city had its own *King* or chief, whose office was mostly confined to one family, for the Kings were commonly held to be of the blood of the Gods. The King was the chief leader both in peace and war; but he could not do everything according to his own pleasure. For there was always a *Council* of elders or chief men, and also an *Assembly* of the whole people, or at least of all those who had the full rights of citizens. This kind of kingship lasted in Greece through the whole of the earliest times, through what are called the *Heroic Ages*, and in the neighbouring lands of Epeiros and Macedonia a kingship of much the same kind lasted on through nearly the whole of their history. But in Greece itself the kingly

power was gradually abolished in most of the cities, and they became commonwealths. At first these commonwealths were *aristocracies;* that is to say, only men of certain families were allowed to fill public offices and to take part in the assemblies by which the city was governed. These privileged families were in most cases the descendants of the oldest inhabitants of the city, who did not choose to admit new-comers to the same full rights as themselves. Some of the Greek cities remained aristocracies till very late times; but others soon became *democracies;* that is to say, all citizens were allowed to hold offices and to attend the assemblies. But it must be remembered that everyone who lived in a Greek city was not therefore a citizen. For in most parts of Greece there were many *slaves;* and, if a man from one city went to live in another, even though the city in which he went to live was a democracy, neither he nor his children were made citizens as a matter of course. In a few cities the name *King*, in Greek *Basileus*, remained in use as the title of a magistrate, though one who no longer held the chief power. And in Sparta they always went on having Kings of the old royal house, two Kings at a time, who kept much power both in military and in religious matters, though they were no longer the chief rulers of the state.

9. **The Tyrants.**—All the three chief forms of government, *Monarchy*, *Aristocracy*, and *Democracy*, were held by the Greeks to be lawful; but there was another kind of power which was always deemed unlawful. This was *Tyranny*. It sometimes happened, especially in cities where the nobles and the people were quarrelling as to whether the commonwealth should be aristocratic or democratic, that some man would snatch away the power from both and make himself *Tyrant*. That is to say, he would, perhaps with the good will of part of the people, seize the power, and much more than the power, of the old

Kings. The word *Tyrant* meant at first no more than that a man had got the power of a King in a city where there was no King by law. It did not necessarily mean that he used his power badly or cruelly; though, as most of the Tyrants did so, the word came to have a worse meaning than it had at first. The time when most of the Tyrants reigned in Greece was in the seventh and sixth centuries before Christ; and the most famous of them were *Peisistratos* and his sons, who ruled at Athens in the sixth century. In the colonies, and especially in Sicily, Tyrants went on rising and falling during almost the whole time of Grecian history. But in old Greece we do not hear much of them after the sons of Peisistratos were driven out, about the end of the sixth century, till quite the later times of Grecian history, when Tyrants again were common, but Tyrants of quite another kind.

10. **The Greek Religion.**—The religion of the Greeks was one of those forms of mythology which have been already spoken of as growing up among most of the Aryan nations. All the powers of nature and all the acts of man's life were believed to be under the care of different deities, of different degrees of power. The head of all was *Zeus*, the God of the sky, and he is described as reigning on *Mount Olympos* in Thessaly, where the Gods were believed to dwell, with his Council and his general Assembly, much like an early Greek King on earth. The art and literature of the Greeks, and indeed their government and their whole life, were closely bound up with their religion. The poets had from the beginning many beautiful stories to tell about the Gods and about the *Heroes*, who were mostly said to be the children of the Gods. And, when the Greeks began to practise the arts, it was in honour of the Gods and Heroes that the noblest buildings and the most beautiful statues and pictures were made.

11. **The Early History of Greece.**—Of the

earliest times of Grecian history we have no accounts written at the time; we have to make out what we can from the traditions preserved by later writers, and from the notices of the poets. For composition in verse always goes before composition in prose, and the earliest Greek works that we have are those of the poets. The poems which go by the name of *Homer*, the *Iliad* and *Odyssey*, give us a picture of the state of things in the earliest days of Greece, and allusions and expressions in them also help us to some particular facts. But scholars no longer believe that the story of the war of *Troy* is a true history, though the tale most likely arose out of the settlements of the Greeks on the north-west coast of Asia. These settlements were among the earliest of the Greek colonies, the very earliest probably being the settlements in the southern islands of the Ægæan, which Homer himself speaks of. These were made so early that it is vain to try to give them any exact date. Presently we get glimmerings, which seem to have been preserved partly by poets and partly by tradition, of a great movement by which the *Dorians*, a people of Northern Greece, came and conquered the *Achaians* in Peloponnêsos and dwelled in their chief cities, Argos, Sparta, Corinth, and others. The other chief division of the Greek nations was the *Ionians*, whose chief city was Athens, and who are said to have planted many colonies in Asia about the same time when the Dorians came into Peloponnêsos. And when we get down to times to which we can give something more like exact dates, we have remains of several poets which sometimes help us to particular facts. Thus there was a war in which Sparta conquered her neighbours of *Messênê*, of which we learnt something from the poems of the minstrel *Tyrtaios*, who made songs to encourage the Spartan warriors. This was in the seventh century before Christ; and in the next century, *Solôn*, the famous lawgiver of Athens, made laws for his own city, and first gave the mass of the people a share in the government, which was the beginning of the famous democracy. Solôn was also a poet, and we have some remains of his verses, which throw light on his political doings. So again, the poems of *Theognis* of Megara throw some light on the disputes between the nobles and the people in that city. But from fragments like these we can get no connected history, so that most of what we know of these days comes from later writers, who did not live near the time, and whose accounts therefore cannot be trusted in every detail. It is only when we come to the *Persian Wars*, in the beginning of the fifth century before Christ, that we begin to have really trustworthy accounts. For those times we have the history of *Hêrodotos*, who, though he did not himself live at the time, had seen and spoken with those who did. By this time the chief cities of Greece had settled down under their several forms of government, aristocratic or democratic. And most of the colonies had been founded, especially those in Italy and Sicily, which were at this time very flourishing, though many of them were under Tyrants. Greece had now pretty well put on the shape which she was to wear during the greatest times of her history, and she had now to bear the trial of a great foreign invasion and to come out all the stronger for it.

12. **The Persians.**—The people of *Persia*, though they lived far away from the shores of the Mediterranean, in the further part of Asia beyond the great rivers *Euphrates* and *Tigris*, were much more nearly allied to the Greeks in blood and speech than most of the nations which lay between them. For they belonged to the Eastern branch of the Aryan family, who had remained so long separate from their kinsfolk in Europe, and who now met them as enemies. The Persians first began to be of importance in the sixth century before Christ, when, under their King *Cyrus*,

they became a conquering people. He took *Babylon*, which at that time was the great power of Asia, and also conquered the kingdom of *Lydia* in Asia Minor. This conquest first brought the Persians across the Greeks, first in Asia and then in Europe. For the Greeks who were settled along the coast of Asia had been just before conquered by *Crœsus*, King of Lydia, the first foreign prince who ever bore rule over any Greeks; and now, as being part of the dominions of Crœsus, they were conquered again by Cyrus. The Greek cities of Asia, which had, up to this time, been among the greatest cities of the Greek name, now lost their freedom and much of their greatness. And from this time various disputes arose between the Persian Kings and the Greeks in Europe. The Athenians had now driven out their Tyrants and had made their government more democratic. They were therefore full of life and energy, and they gave help to the Asiatic Greeks in an attempt to throw off the Persian yoke. Then the Persian King *Darius* wished to make the Athenians to take back *Hippias*, the son of Peisistratos, who had been their Tyrant. At last Darius made up his mind to punish the Athenians and to bring the other Greeks under his power; and thus the wars between Greece and Persia began.

13. **The Persian Wars.**—The first Persian expedition against Greece was sent by Darius in the year 490 B.C. A Persian fleet crossed the Ægæan, and landed an army in Attica. But, far smaller as their numbers were, the Athenians, under their general *Miltiadês*, utterly defeated the invaders in the famous battle of *Marathôn*. In this battle the Athenians had no help except a small force from their neighbours of *Plataia*, a small town on the Bœotian border, which was in close alliance with them. This was the first of all the victories of the *West* over the *East*, the first battle which showed how skill and discipline can prevail over mere numbers. As such, it is

the most memorable battle in the history of the world. Ten years later, in 480 B.C., a much greater Persian expedition came under King *Xerxês* himself, the son of Darius. He came by land, and all the native kingdoms and Greek colonies on the north coast of the Ægæan, and even a large part of Greece itself, submitted to him. Some Greek cities indeed, especially Thebes, fought for the Barbarians against their countrymen. But Athens, Sparta, and several other Greek cities withstood the power of Xerxês, and in the end drove his vast fleet and army back again in utter defeat. In this year 480, were fought the battle of *Thermopylai*, where the Spartan King *Leônidas* was killed, and the seafight of *Salamis*, won chiefly by the Athenian fleet under *Themistoklês*. After this Xerxês went back ; but in the next year his general *Mardonios* was defeated by the Spartans and other Greeks in the battle of *Plataia*, and the same day the Persians were also defeated both by land and sea at *Mykalê*, on the coast of Asia. These three battles, Salamis, Plataia, and Mykalê, decided the war, and the Persians never again dared to invade Greece itself. But the war went on for several years longer before the Persians were driven out of various posts which they held north of the Ægæan. Still, they were at last wholly driven out of Europe, and they were even obliged to withdraw for a time from the Greek cities of Asia.

14. **The Growth of Athens.**—At the beginning of the Persian Wars, Sparta was generally looked up to as the chief state of Greece; but, as Athens was much the stronger at sea, it was soon found that she was better able than Sparta to carry on the war against the Persians, and to recover and protect the islands and cities on the coasts. Most of these cities therefore joined in a League, of which Athens was the head, and which was set in order by the Athenian *Aristeidês*, surnamed the *Just*. But, after a time, Athens, instead of being merely the head, gradually became the

mistress of the smaller states, and most of them became her subjects, paying tribute to her. Athens thus rose to a wonderful degree of power and splendour, beyond that of any of the other cities of Greece. The chief man at Athens at this time was *Periklês*, the greatest statesman of Greece, perhaps of the world, under whose influence the Athenian government became a still more perfect democracy. In his time Athens was adorned with the temples and other public buildings which the world has admired ever since. This was also the time of the great dramatic poets, *Æschylus*, *Sophoklês*, *Euripidês*, and *Aristophanês*. Æschylus had fought in all the great battles with the Persians. Euripidês and Aristophanês were younger men who lived on through the next period. Oratory, which was so needful in a democratic state, began to be studied as an art, and so were the different forms of philosophy; in fact, there never was a time when the human mind was brought so near to its highest pitch as in these few years of the greatest power and splendour of Athens.

15. **The Peloponnesian War.**—But the great power of Athens raised the jealousy of many of the other Greek cities, and at last a war broke out between Athens and her allies on the one side, and Sparta and her allies on the other. This war, which began in the year 431 B.C. and lasted for twenty-nine years almost without stopping, was known as the *Peloponnesian War*, because it was waged by the Athenians against Sparta and her allies, among whom were the greater part of the cities of *Peloponnêsos*, besides Thebes and some other cities in other parts of Greece. Of this war we know all the events in great detail, because we have the history of it from writers who lived at the time. The history of the greater part of the war was written by *Thucydidês*, who was not only living at the time, but himself held a high command in the Athenian army. And the history of the latter years of

the war was written by *Xenophôn*, another Athenian writer, who also lived at the time. This war might be looked on as a war between Ionians and Dorians, between democracy and oligarchy. For Athens was the chief of the Ionian and democratic states, and Sparta the chief of the Dorian and aristocratic states. But the two parties were never exactly divided either according to descent or according to forms of government. It is perhaps more important to remark that Sparta had many free and willing allies, while Athens had but few such, so that she had to fight mainly with her own forces and those of allies who were really her subjects. During the first ten years of the war, down to the year 421, the two parties strove with nearly equal success, the Athenians being much the stronger by sea, and the Spartans and their allies by land. A peace was then made, but it was not very well kept ; so that Thucydidês says that the years of peace ought to be reckoned as a part of the war. Then, in 415, the Athenians sent a fleet to attack the city of *Syracuse* in Sicily. The Syracusans got help from Sparta, and so the war began again ; but, after two years of fighting and siege, the Athenians were altogether defeated before Syracuse. The allies of Athens now began to revolt, and the war during the later years was carried on almost wholly on the coasts of Asia. The Persians now began to take a share in it, because they were eager to drive away the Athenians from those coasts, and to get back the Greek cities in Asia. But they did more in the way of giving, and sometimes only promising, money to the Spartans than by actually fighting. Several battles, chiefly by sea, were fought in these wars with varying success ; and it is wonderful to see how Athens regained her strength after her loss before Syracuse. At last, in the year 405, the Athenians were defeated by the Spartan admiral *Lysandros* at *Aigospotamos* in the Hellespont. Athens was now besieged, and in the next year she had to surrender. She now lost all her dominion and her great naval power, and was obliged to become a member of the Spartan alliance. Her democratic government was also taken away, and an oligarchy of thirty men was set up under the protection of Sparta. But in the next year, 403, the oligarchy was put down, and Athens, though she did not get back her power, at least got back her freedom.

16. **The Dominion of Sparta.**—At this time, at the end of the fifth century before Christ, *Sparta* was more than ever the greatest power of Greece. From this time Athens has no longer any claim to be looked on as holding the first place. But she still remained one of the greatest among the Grecian cities, and, as her political power grew less, she became more and more the acknowledged chief in all kinds of literature and philosophy. Her loss of power, which left Sparta for a while without a rival, presently led to great changes. New powers began to come to the front. We shall, first of all, see the foremost place in Greece held for a while by *Thebes*, the chief city of Bœotia, which had always been reckoned one of the greater cities of Greece, but which in the Peloponnesian war had played only a secondary part as one of the allies of Sparta. We shall next see the power over all Greece fall into the hands of a state which had hitherto not been reckoned to be Greek at all, through the victories of the great *Macedonian* Kings, *Philip* and *Alexander*. But for a while the Spartans had it all their own way. No state in Greece could stand up against them; the government of most of the cities passed into the hands of men who were ready to do whatever the Spartans told them, and in many cities there even were Spartan governors and garrisons. A few years after the end of the Peloponnesian war, the Spartans made war upon Persia, and their King *Agêsilaos* waged several successful campaigns in Asia Minor. But by this time several of the

Greek cities had got jealous and weary of the Spartan power, and the Persian King *Artaxerxês*, against whom the Spartans were fighting, was naturally glad to help them with both money and ships. So in the year 394 Agêsilaos had to come back to withstand a confederacy formed against Sparta by Athens, Argos, Corinth, and Thebes. Several battles were fought; and, though the Spartans commonly had the victory, yet it was shown that the Theban soldiers were able to do great things. In the former part of this war the Persian King sent his great Phœnician fleet to help the Athenians; but afterwards he was persuaded to change sides, and in 387 a peace was made, called the *Peace of Antalkidas*, by which the Greek cities of Asia were given up to Persia, and those of Europe were declared to be every one independent. But in truth the power of Sparta now became greater than ever, and the Spartans domineered and interfered with the other cities even more than before. Among other things, they treacherously seized the *Kadmeia* or citadel of Thebes, and put a Spartan garrison in it. They also put down a confederacy which the city of *Olynthos* was making among the Greek cities on the coasts of Macedonia and Thrace, and thus took away what might have been a great check to the growing power of the Macedonian Kings.

17. **The Rise of Thebes.**—It was when the power of Sparta was at its very highest that it was overthrown. The Thebans, who had shown in the former war that they were nearly as good soldiers as the Spartans themselves, now rose against them. In 379 the Spartans were driven out of Thebes; a democratic government was set up, and Thebes under two great citizens, *Pelopidas* and *Epameinôndas*, became for a while the chief power of Greece. The Spartans were defeated in 371, the first time they had ever been defeated in a pitched battle, at *Leuktra* in Bœotia. After this Epameinôndas invaded Peloponnêsos

several times. He greatly weakened the power of Sparta by restoring the independence of *Messênê*, which the Spartans had long ago conquered, and by persuading the *Arkadians* to join in a League and to found *Megalopolis* or the *Great City*, near the Spartan frontier. During the first part of this war the Athenians took part with Thebes, and in the latter part with Sparta, and in the course of it they won back a great deal of their power by sea, and again got many of the islands and maritime cities to become their allies. At last, in 362, Epameinôndas was killed at *Mantineia* in a battle against the Spartans and Athenians, and after his death, as there was no one left in Thebes fit to take his place, the power of the city gradually died out.

18. **The Rise of Macedonia.**—We have already seen that, though the Macedonians seem to have been closely allied to the Greeks, and though the Macedonian Kings were acknowledged to be of Greek descent, yet *Macedonia* had hitherto not been reckoned as a Greek state. Its Kings had not taken much share in Greek affairs, but several of them had done much to strengthen their kingdom against the neighbouring Barbarians, and also to bring in Greek arts and civilization among their own people. Just at this time there arose in Macedonia a King called *Philip*, the son of Amyntas, who did much greater things than any of the Kings who had gone before him. His great object was, not exactly to conquer Greece or make it part of his own kingdom, but rather to get Macedonia acknowledged as a Greek state, and, as such, to win for it the same kind of supremacy over the other Greek states which had been held at different times by Mykênê, Argos, Sparta, Athens, and Thebes. He artfully contrived to mix himself up with Grecian affairs, and to persuade many of the Grecian states to look upon him as their deliverer, and as the champion of the god *Apollôn*. The temple of *Delphi* had been plundered by the

Phôkians, and Philip put himself forward as the avenger of this crime, and got himself admitted as a member of the *Amphiktionic Council*, the great religious assembly of Greece, which looked after the affairs of the Delphian Temple. This was much the same as formally acknowledging Macedonia to be a Greek state. Philip also conquered the Greek city of Olynthos in the neighbourhood of his own kingdom, and made the peninsula called *Chalkidikê*, which runs out as it were with three fingers into the Ægæan, part of Macedonia. This he would hardly have been able to do if the Spartans had not already destroyed the great Greek alliance which the Olynthians had begun to make in those parts. Philip was several times at war with Athens, and it was during these wars that the great orator *Dêmosthenês* made himself famous by the speeches which he made to stir up his countrymen to act vigorously. Philip's last war was against Athens and Thebes together, and in 338 he gained a victory over them at *Chairôneia* in Bœotia, from which the overthrow of Grecian freedom may be dated. After this, all the Greeks, except the Spartans, were partly persuaded, partly compelled, to hold a synod at Corinth, where Philip was elected captain-general of all Greece, to make war on Persia and avenge the old invasions of Greece by Darius and Xerxês. But, while he was making ready for a great expedition into Asia, he was murdered in the year 336 by one of his own subjects.

19. **Alexander the Great.**—Philip was succeeded by his son *Alexander*, known as *Alexander the Great*. He was presently acknowledged as the leader of Greece against the Persians, as his father had been. Thebes however, where Philip had put a Macedonian garrison, now revolted, but it was taken and destroyed by Alexander. In the next year, 334, Alexander set out on his great expedition, and he never came back to Europe. In the course of six years he altogether

subdued the Persian Empire, fighting three famous battles, at the river *Granikos* in Asia Minor in 334, at *Issos*, near the borders of Cilicia and Syria, in 333, and at *Arbêla* or *Gaugamêla* in Assyria in 331. In these last two battles the Persian King *Darius* was present, and was utterly defeated. Between the last two battles Alexander beseiged and took *Tyre*, and received the submission of *Egypt*, where he founded the famous city which has ever since borne his name, *Alexandria*. Soon after the battle of Gaugamêla Darius was murdered by some of his own officers, and Alexander now looked upon himself as King of Persia. He afterwards set out, half exploring, half conquering, as far as the river *Hyphasis* in northern *India*, beyond which his soldiers refused to follow him. At last he died at *Babylon* in 323, having made greater conquests than were ever made by any European prince before him or after him. And there was no conqueror whose conquests were more important, and in a certain sense more lasting; for, though his great empire broke in pieces almost at once, yet the effects of his career have remained to all time.

20. **Effects of the Conquests of Alexander.**—The conquests of Alexander, though they were won so quickly, and though a large part of them were soon lost again, made a great and lasting change throughout a large part of the world. Both he and those who came after him were great builders of cities in Asia Minor, Syria, Egypt, and as far as their conquests reached. In each of these cities was placed a Greek or Macedonian colony, and in the western part of Asia most of these cities lived and flourished, and some of them, like Alexandria in Egypt and *Antioch* in Syria, soon took their place among the greatest cities in the world. The Greek language became the tongue of all government and literature throughout many countries where the people were not Greek by birth. It was thus at the very moment that Greece began to lose

her political freedom that she made, as it were, an intellectual conquest of a large part of the world. And though, in the cities and lands which in this way became partially *Hellenized*, there was neither the political freedom nor the original genius of the great statesmen and writers of old Greece, yet mere learning and science flourished as they had never flourished before. The Greek tongue became the common speech of the civilized world, the speech which men of different nations used in speaking to one another, much as they use French now. The Greek colonies had done much to spread the Greek language and manners over a large part of the world. The Macedonian conquests now did still more; but they did not, as the old colonies had done, carry also Greek freedom with them.

21. **The Successors of Alexander.**—The great empire of Alexander did not hold together even in name for more than a few years after his death. He left no one in the Macedonian royal family who was at all fit to take his place, and his dominions were gradually divided among his generals, who after a little while took the title of Kings. Thus arose the kingdom of the *Ptolemies* in *Egypt*, and that of the descendants of *Seleukos* in the East, which gradually shrank up into the kingdom of *Syria*. In the countries beyond the Tigris the Macedonian power gradually died out; but various states arose in Asia Minor, which were not strictly Greek, but which had a greater or less tinge of Greek cultivation. Such were the kingdom of *Pergamos* and the League of the cities of *Lykia*. These arose in countries which had been fully subdued by Alexander, and which won their independence only because the descendants of Seleukos could not keep their great dominions together. But Alexander's conquests had been made so fast that some parts even of Western Asia were not fully subdued. Thus out of the fragments of the

Persian Empire several kingdoms arose, like those of *Pontos* and *Bithynia*, which were ruled by native Kings, but which also affected something of Greek civilization. And some real Greek states still contrived to keep their independence on or near the coast of Asia, as the city of *Byzantion*, the island of *Rhodes*, and the city of *Hêrakleia*, which last was sometimes a commonwealth and sometimes under Tyrants. Of many of these states we shall hear again as they came one by one under the power of Rome. But we are now more concerned with what happened in Macedonia and in Greece itself.

22. **The later Macedonian Kings.**—The death of Alexander was followed by a time of great confusion in Macedonia and Greece. Even while Alexander was away in Asia, the Spartans, under their king *Algis*, had tried to throw off the Macedonian yoke, but in vain. After Alexander's death another attempt was made by several of the Greek states, especially the Athenians, who were again stirred up by Dêmosthenês, and the *Ætolians*. These last were a people of western Greece, the least civilized of all the Greek states, but which now began to rise to great importance. This was called the *Lamian War*. In the end the Athenians had to yield, and they were obliged by the Macedonian general *Antipatros* to change their constitution, making it much less democratic than before, and depriving many of the citizens of their votes. For many years there was the greatest confusion in Macedonia and Greece and all the neighbouring countries. And things were made worse by an attack from an enemy with whom the Greeks had never before had anything to do. Greece and Macedonia were invaded by the *Gauls*. By these we need not understand people from Gaul itself, but some of those Celtic tribes which were still in the east of Europe. After doing much mischief in those parts, the Gauls crossed over into Asia, and there

founded a state of their own which was called *Galatia*, and, as they too began to learn something of Greek civilization, *Gallo-græcia.* Meanwhile Kings were being constantly set up and overthrown in Macedonia, and each of them tried to get as much power and influence as he could in Greece itself. At this time too *Epeiros*, a country which had hitherto been of very little importance, became a powerful state under its King *Pyrrhos*, who at one time obtained possession of Macedonia. He also waged wars in Italy and Sicily, which will be spoken of in the next chapter, and he had a great deal to do with the affairs of Peloponnêsos, where he was at last killed in besieging *Argos*, in 272. From this time things became rather more settled; a second time of freedom, if not of greatness, began in Greece, and a regular dynasty of Kings fixed itself in Macedonia. The old royal family was quite extinct, and the second set of Macedonian Kings were the descendants of *Antigonos*, one of the most famous of Alexander's generals. His son *Dêmêtrios*, surnamed *Poliorkêtês* or the *Besieger*, got possession of the crown of Macedonia in 294. Both he and his son *Antigonos Gonatas* were driven out more than once, but in the end Antigonos contrived to keep the Macedonian crown, and to hand it on to his descendants, who held it till Macedonia was conquered by Rome.

23. **The later History of Greece.**—The last days of Grecian history, before the country came altogether under the power of the Romans, are in several ways very unlike times which went before them. The states which are most important in these times are not the same as those which were most important in the old days of the Persian and Peloponnesian Wars. First of all we must remember that Macedonia and Epeiros must now be reckoned as Greek states, and that a large part of Greece, especially in the north, was now subject to the Mace-

donian Kings, or at least altogether under their influence. And, among the states of Greece itself, the division of power was very different from what it had been in earlier times. In the days which we have now come to neither Athens nor Thebes was of any great account, and, though Sparta was of great importance during part of the time, yet its greatness was only, as we may say, by fits and starts. We may say that the chief powers of Greece now were *Macedonia*, *Achaia*, *Ætolia*, and *Sparta*. Achaia and Ætolia are states of which but little is heard in Grecian history since the heroic times, and the strength which they had now chiefly came from a cause which must be explained a little more at length.

24. **The Achaian and Ætolian Leagues.**—What chiefly distinguishes this part of Grecian history from earlier times is that we have now but little to do with single cities, but with cities and tribes bound together so as to make states of much greater size. With the exception of Sparta, the Greek states which play the greatest part at this time were joined together in *Leagues*, so as to form what is called a *Federal* Government, such as there is now in Switzerland and in the United States of America. That is to say, several cities agreed together to give up a part of the power which naturally belonged to each city separately to an Assembly or Council or body of magistrates in which all had a share. In a government of this kind the central power commonly deals with all matters which concern the League as a whole, while each city still acts much as it pleases in its own internal affairs. There had been several Leagues of this kind in Greece from the beginning, but they were chiefly among the smaller and less famous parts of the Greek nation, and they did not play any great part in Grecian affairs. The only one which was of much note in earlier times was the League of Bœotia, and that could hardly be with any truth called a League, for Thebes was so

much stronger than the other Bœotian cities as to be practically mistress of all of them. But now the Federal states of Greece come to be of special importance, because it was found that, as long as the cities stood one by one, they had no hope of keeping their freedom against the Macedonian Kings, and that their only chance of doing so was by several cities acting together in matters of peace and war as if they were one city. The greatest of these Leagues was that of Achaia, which began with the ten small Achaian cities on the south side of the Corinthian Gulf. These cities had been joined together in a League in early times, but in the times of the Macedonian power they had gradually fallen asunder, and in the days of Antigonos Gonatas several of them were in the hands of Tyrants, who reigned under Macedonian protection. This was the case with many other cities of Greece also, and it was the great object of the League, as it grew and strengthened, to set free these cities and to join them on to its own body. It was about the year 280 that the old Achaian towns began to draw together again, the chief leader in this work being *Markos* of *Keryneia*. About thirty years after, in 251, the League began to extend itself by admitting the city of *Sikyôn* as a member of its body. Sikyôn had just been set free by *Aratos*, who now became the leading man in the League, and, under his administration and that of *Philopoimên*, who followed him, the League took in one city after another, *Corinth*, *Megalopolis*, *Argos*, and others, at first only with their own good will, but afterwards sometimes by force. At last all the cities of Peloponnêsos and some cities beyond the Isthmus became members of the League. The Ætolian League on the other side of the Corinthian Gulf did not bear so good a character as the Achaian, though its form of government was much the same. For the Ætolians, though a brave people and always stout in defending their own freedom, were ruder and fiercer than most of the Greeks, and were much given to plunder both by sea and land. The Ætolian League thus greatly extended itself, and became more powerful than that of Achaia, but its policy was not so just and honourable as that of Achaia commonly was. There were also smaller Leagues in *Phôkis* and *Akarnania*, besides the League of *Epeiros*, which was now counted as a Greek land, and which had got rid of its Kings and had changed itself into a Federal commonwealth. Thus, except Sparta at one end and Macedonia at the other, by far the greater part of Greece was parted out among the different Leagues.

25. **The last Days of Independent Greece.**—For a long time the great object of the Achaians was to set free the cities which were more or less under the Macedonian power. But at last they became jealous of Sparta, which was again becoming a great power, and in 227 a war broke out between Sparta and the League. Sparta had now a great King called *Kleomenês*, who had upset the old oligarchy and had greatly increased the power both of the Kings and of the people. By so doing he put quite a new life into his country, and he pressed the Achaians so hard that at last, in 223, they asked help of *Antigonos Dôsôn*, King of Macedonia, which they only got by giving up to him the citadel of *Corinth*. The Macedonians and Achaians together defeated Kleomenês, and Sparta's second time of greatness died with him. The next King of Macedonia, *Philip*, kept on the alliance with Achaia, and the Achaians and Macedonians fought together in a war with Ætolia ; but, though the League gained in extent, it lost in real power and freedom by joining with a prince who was strong enough to be its master. Peace was made over all Greece in 216, but by this time the Romans had begun to meddle in Greek affairs, and from hence the history of Greece and Macedonia chiefly consists of the steps by which

they were swallowed up in the Roman dominion. This last stage of their history will therefore best be told in our sketch of the history of Rome.

26. **Summary.**—The history of Greece which we have thus run through, though it is the history only of a small part of the world for a few hundred years, is worth fully as much study as any later and wider part of history. It is, as it were, the history of the world in a small space. There is no lesson to be taught by history in general which is not taught by the history of Greece. The Greeks too, we should never forget, were the first people to show the world what real freedom and real civilization were. And they brought, not only politics, but art and science and literature of every kind, to a higher pitch than any other people ever did without borrowing of others. In all these ways Greece has influenced the world for ever. Still the influence of Greece upon later history has been to a great degree indirect. Greece influenced Rome, and Rome influenced the world. But with the history of Rome an unbroken chain of events begins which is going on still. We will now try and trace it from the beginning.

CHAPTER III.

THE ROMAN COMMONWEALTH.

Ancient extent of Italy (1)—*Gauls, Venetians, and Ligurians within its modern boundary* (1)—*effect of the geography of the country on its history* (1)—*inhabitants of Italy; the Etruscans and the Greek colonists* (2)—*two chief branches of the Italian race, Oscans and Latins* (2, 3)—*language, religion, and government; tendency to the formation of Leagues* (4)—*origin of Rome; characteristics of its history* (5)—*the Roman Kings* (6)—*dynasty and expulsion of the Tarquinii* (6)—*the powers of the Kings transferred to the Consuls* (7)—

disputes between Patricians and Plebeians (7)—*wars of Rome with her neighbours; taking of Veii* (8)—*taking of Rome by the Gauls* (8)—*wars with the Samnites and Latins; gradual conquest of Italy* (9)—*state of Italy under the Romans; distinction of Romans, Latins, and Italians* (10)—*war with Pyrrhos* (11)—*origin and history of Carthage* (12)—*First Punic War* (13)—*cession of Sicily; nature of the Roman Provinces* (14)—*Second Punic War; campaigns of Hannibal and Scipio* (15)—*Third Punic War; destruction of Carthage* (16)—*first dealings of the Romans with Greece* (17)—*First Macedonian War* (17)—*Second Macedonian War; alliance of Rome with Ætolia and Achaia* (18)—*campaign of Antiochos in Greece; Roman conquest of Ætolia* (19)—*Third Macedonian War; dismemberment of the Macedonian Kingdom* (20)—*Fourth Macedonian War; Macedonia becomes a Province* (21)—*war with Achaia; destruction of Corinth* (21)—*the Macedonian states in Asia; revolt of the Parthians* (22)—*war with Antiochos; and extension of Roman influence in Asia* (22)—*formation of the Province of Asia* (22)—*conquest of Cisalpine Gaul* (23)—*conquest of Spain* (24)—*inhabitants of Transalpine Gaul* (25)—*affairs of Massalia; formation of the Roman Province in Gaul* (25)—*invasion of the Cimbri and Teutones; their defeat by Marius* (26)—*Rome dominant round the Mediterranean; her relations with Egypt* (27)—*internal disputes at Rome; her relations to her allies; murder of the Gracchi* (27)—*the Social War; final conquest of the Samnites* (28)—*Civil War of Marius and Sulla; Dictatorship of Sulla* (28)—*war with Mithridates; campaigns of Sulla and Pompeius* (29)—*Roman conquest of Syria; dealings with Parthia* (30)—*disputes at Rome; rise of Cæsar* (31)—*Cæsar's conquests in Gaul; his campaigns in Germany and Britain* (32)—*Civil War of Pompeius and Cæsar; Dictatorship and death of Cæsar* (33)—*Second Civil War; Battles of Philippi and Aktion; Egypt becomes a province* (34)—*the younger Cæsar becomes Augustus; beginning of the Roman Empire* (35).

1. **The Geography of Italy.**—We now come to the history of the second of the three great peninsulas, that of *Italy*. But we must remember that in early

times the name of Italy did not take in all the land that we now understand by that name, and that a great part of its inhabitants did not belong to the race of whom we shall have to speak of as *Italians*. The greater part of Northern Italy, all north of the *Po* and a good deal to the south of it, was counted as part of Gaul, and was inhabited by Celtic people akin to those on the other side of the Alps. Thus there was *Cisalpine Gaul*, Gaul *on this side*—that is the Italian side—of the Alps, as well as *Transalpine Gaul*, or Gaul *beyond* the Alps. *Milan*, *Verona*, *Bologna*, and other famous Italian cities thus stand in what in early times was part of Gaul. And the country in the extreme north-east was held by the *Venetians*, a people whose origin is not very clear. They gave their name to the province of *Venetia*; but it must be remembered that they had nothing to do with the city of *Venice*, which did not begin till many ages later. And the land between the Gulf of Genoa and the Po was held by the *Ligurians*, a people who were most likely not Aryans at all, but a remnant of the older inhabitants, like the Basques. And people akin to the Ligurians seem also to have held the islands of *Sardinia* and *Corsica*, and part of *Sicily*. None of these lands were counted as part of Italy in the earliest times, so that the name of Italy belonged much more strictly to the peninsula than it does now. The name seems to have been first given to quite the southern part only, and to have gradually spread itself northwards. The map will at once show that the peninsula of Italy, though it is so long and narrow and has so great an extent of sea-coast, is not so broken up by bays and arms of the sea, nor has it so many islands round about it, as the peninsula of Greece. And though many parts of Italy are mountainous, and though the great chain of the *Apennines* runs from one end of the peninsula to the other, yet the whole land is not cut up into little valleys in the way the greater part of Greece is. Two things came of this difference between Greece and Italy. First, the Italians never became a seafaring people in the same degree that the Greeks did, nor did they in the same way send out colonies to all parts of the world that they knew. Secondly, there never were so many great cities in Italy as there were in Greece, and the small Italian towns were less jealous of their separate independence, and more ready than the Greek cities to join together in leagues.

2. **The Inhabitants of Italy.**—Setting aside those countries which were not then reckoned as part of Italy, we find at the beginning of history three chief nations dwelling in the peninsula. The part of Italy between the Arno and the Tiber was called *Etruria*, the land of the *Rasena* as they called themselves, otherwise called *Tyrrhenians*, *Tuscans*, and *Etruscans*. The origin of the Etruscans is a great puzzle, but most likely they were an Aryan people, though their tongue was very unlike those of the other nations of Italy. In early times they seem to have spread over a much larger country both northwards and southwards, but in trustworthy history they appear only in the lands already spoken of on the western coast, where they formed a confederation of twelve cities. They were great builders and skilful in many of the arts, and they were held to be specially wise in divination and all other matters belonging to the worship of the Gods. The Etruscans, like the Gauls and Ligurians, were settled in what we now call Italy before authentic history begins. At the other end, quite in the south, the Greeks planted many colonies, but these belong to a later time, when trustworthy history was beginning among the Greeks, though it had not yet begun among the Italians. The map will show that this part of Italy is much more like Greece, much more broken up by bays and peninsulas, than the rest of Italy. The Greeks were

therefore, as we have already seen, able to found many colonies here, some of which flourished so greatly in early times that the country was known as *Great Greece.* But at the time when history begins, all Italy in the older sense (that is, not reckoning Liguria and Cisalpine Gaul), except Etruria, was inhabited by people whom we may specially call *Italians.* These, as we have already said, belonged to the same Aryan swarm as the Greeks, and the common forefathers of both must have stayed together after they had parted off from the forefathers of the Celts, Teutons, and others. The greater part of Italy was occupied by tribes sprung from this one swarm, some of whom however were more closely allied to the Greeks than others. But all may be looked on as coming nearer to the Greeks than to any other branch of the Aryan family. But long before history begins, the Greeks and the Italians had parted off into distinct nations, and the Italians had also parted off into distinct nations among themselves.

3. **The Latin and Oscan Races.**—We thus see that, setting aside the Etruscans and the Greeks who settled in later times, all the other nations of ancient Italy were allied to one another, and all were more remotely allied to the Greeks. But they had parted far more widely among themselves than the different tribes of the Greek nation ever did. The Italian nations fall naturally into two great groups, which we may call roughly the *Oscans*, lying to the north-east, and the *Latins*, lying to the south-west. Of these the Latins were those who were more nearly allied to the Greeks. The *Siculi* or *Sikels* especially, in southern Italy and in Sicily, to which island they gave their name, and some other of the tribes in the south, seem to have been as near to the Greeks, and to have been as easily Hellenized, as their neighbours in Epeiros and on the coast of Asia. The Oscan tribes, *Sabines, Umbrians,* and others, were much less nearly akin to the Greeks,

and presently the Oscan races began to press southward at the expense both of the Latins and Greek colonies. It was these Oscans of the south, the *Samnites*, *Lucanians*, and others, whose incursions gradually destroyed the greatness and freedom of the Greek colonies in Italy.

4. **Language, Religion, and Government.**—Our knowledge of all the ancient nations of Italy, except the Romans, is very scanty, but it would seem that the differences between the Latin and Oscan races answered rather to the differences between the Greeks and their most nearly allied neighbours than to the differences of Dorians and Ionians among the Greeks themselves. Still they always had much in common in language, religion, and government. The old languages of Italy all gradually gave way to the Latin, and we have only a few fragments remaining of any of them. And of their religion, even of that of the Latins, we know very little, because, when the Greeks and Romans came to have dealings with one another, they began to call each other's Gods by the names of those among their own Gods which seemed most like them. Thus the Greek *Zeus* and the Latin *Jupiter* got confounded, and the other Gods in the like sort. But one thing we can see, that none of the Italian nations had so many stories to tell about their Gods as the Greeks had. As for their government, we can see the same elements as among the Greeks and other Aryans,—the King or other chief, the nobles, and the ordinary freemen. In fact, owing, as we have already said, to the nature of the country, the common form of government in ancient Italy was much the same as that common in the ruder parts of Greece, several kindred districts or small towns joining together in a League. Of these Leagues the most famous in history was that of the *Samnites*, an inland people of the Oscan stock, and that of the thirty cities of the *Latins* on the west coast south of the Tiber.

5. The Origin of Rome.—But there was one Latin city which was destined to be mighty and famous above all, and to become the mistress of Latium, of Italy, and of the world. This was the town of *Rome* on the Tiber. There were all manner of traditions in ancient times, and all manner of conjectures have been made by ingenious men in later days, as to the origin of this greatest of all cities. Into these we cannot go now. The story most generally believed by the Romans themselves was that Rome was founded by *Romulus*, a son or descendant of *Æneas* (in Greek *Aineias*), one of the Trojan heroes who was said to have escaped after the taking of Troy, and to have taken refuge in Italy. But *Romulus* or *Romus* is merely one of those names which were made up because people fancied that every city and nation must have taken its name from some man. The tales about the foundation of Rome, and about its early Kings, are mere legends which cannot be trusted. There can be little doubt that Rome began as a border town of the Latins, on the *march* or frontier, both of the Etruscans beyond the Tiber, and of the Sabines in the mountains. The first Rome was a settlement on the hill by the Tiber called the *Palatine,* held by the Latin tribe of the *Ramnes* or Romans. This settlement on the Palatine and other settlements on the neighbouring hills gradually joined into one city. Of these the first and chief was the Sabine settlement of the *Titienses* on the *Capitoline* hill. The beginning of the growth of Rome was when the Latin Ramnes and the Sabine Titienses made a league together, so that their people gradually became two tribes in one city, instead of two distinct cities. This was the beginning of the way in which Rome became the greatest of all cities, namely by constantly granting its citizenship both to its allies and to its conquered enemies. Step by step, the people of Latium, of Italy, and of the whole civilized world, all became *Romans.* This is what really distinguishes the Roman history from all other history, and it is what made the power of Rome so great and lasting.

6. **The Roman Kings.**—There can be no doubt that Rome, like the Greek cities, was at first governed by Kings, who ruled by the help of a Senate and an Assembly of the People. But the Roman Kings, unlike those in Greece, were not hereditary, nor were they even chosen from any particular family. It is said, and it is not at all unlikely, that the old rule was to choose the King in turn from the two tribes of the Ramnes and Titienses. The legend gives us the names of seven Kings, and it is most likely that the two or three last names on the list are those of real persons. These are the dynasty of the *Tarquinii*, about whom there have been many opinions, but who most likely were Etruscans, and who seem to have adorned Rome with buildings and works of Etruscan art. At all events they greatly extended the power of Rome, so that she became the greatest of all Latin cities. The last King, *Lucius Tarquinius*, called *Superbus* or the *Proud*, is said to have acted as a cruel tyrant, and to have had no regard for the laws of the Kings who had gone before him. He was therefore driven out with his family, and the Romans now said they would have no more Kings, and they ever after hated the very name of King. This is said to have happened B.C. 510, about the same time when the Tyrant Hippias, son of Peisistratos, was driven out of Athens. There can be no doubt that the driving out of the Kings of Rome is a real event, but, as we have no accounts of it written at the time, or for ages after, we cannot be certain as to the details of the story, or as to the exact time when it happened.

7. **The Roman Commonwealth.**—The Roman history is, for want of contemporary accounts, very uncertain for a long time after the driving out of the

Kings. Much of what commonly passes for Roman history is really made up of legends, which are often most beautiful as legends, but which still are not history. Much of it also comes from what is much worse than legends, namely, mere inventions in honour of Rome or of some particular Roman family. It is not till two hundred years and more after the Kings that we come to history of which we can fully trust the details. Still we can make out something, both as to the internal constitution of Rome and as to the steps by which she made her way to the headship of Italy. The chief thing to be remembered is that Rome was a city bearing rule over other cities. The government of the Roman commonwealth was the government of a city; and so it always remained, even after Rome had come to be the head of Italy, and even of the world. When the Kings were driven out, the powers which had belonged to the Kings were entrusted to two magistrates, who were at first called *Prætors* and afterwards *Consuls*, and who were chosen for one year only. The Senate and the Assembly of the People went on much as they had done under the Kings, but, soon after the Kings were driven out, there began to be great dissensions within the Roman Commonwealth. For there was a very old division of the Roman people into *Patricians* and *Plebeians* or *Commons*, of whom the Patricians for a long time kept all the chief powers of the state in their own hands. Most likely the Patricians were the descendants of the first citizens, and the Plebeians were the descendants of allies or subjects who had been afterwards admitted to the franchise. This division must have begun in the time of the Kings, as it began to be of great importance very soon after they were driven out. At first the Consuls and other magistrates were chosen from among the Patricians or old citizens only, though the Plebeians voted in choosing them. There were long disputes between the two orders, as the privileges of the Patricians were felt to be very oppressive, and gradually the Plebeians obtained the right to be chosen to the consulship and other high dignities. The first plebeian Consul was *Lucius Sextius* in B.C. 366, about the time when Epameinôndas was warring in Peloponnêsus. After this the two orders were gradually reconciled, and many of the greatest men in the later history of Rome were Plebeians.

8. **Wars of Rome with her Neighbours.**—At the time when the kingly government of Rome came to an end, she was strong enough to make a treaty with *Carthage*, in which she contracts, not only on her own behalf, but also on that of all the Latin cities of the coast as her subjects or dependent allies. But she seems to have lost a good deal of her power after the Kings were driven out. Her chief enemies were the Etruscans on the one side of her, and the various Oscan nations, especially those called the *Æquians* and *Volscians*, on the other. With the Latin cities she was for a long time in close alliance, Rome, as a single city, being one party to the treaty, and the other Latin cities, as a League, being the other party. About B.C. 396 Rome greatly extended her power by the conquest of *Veii*, the nearest of the great Etruscan cities. This was taken by *Marcus Furius Camillus*, who was then *Dictator;* that is, he received, for six months only, greater powers than the Consuls themselves, as was often done in times of special danger and difficulty. But soon after this the Roman power received a great check, for in B.C. 390 the Romans were defeated at the river Allia by the *Gauls*, who, it will be remembered, held most of the northern part of what is now called Italy. They were now pressing southward, and invaded Etruria. The city of Rome itself was taken, but the Gauls were soon either driven out or paid to go away, and it is wonderful how soon Rome got over this great blow. And from this time the Roman history becomes somewhat more trust-

worthy, for we at all events have the lists of the Consuls and other magistrates, though there is still much falsehood and exaggeration in our accounts of their actions. The Romans had still to withstand several invasions of the Gauls, and they had many wars with their neighbours, in which, on the whole, they went on increasing their territory, and ever and anon admitting those whom they conquered to their own citizenship.

9. **The Roman Conquest of Italy.**—At last, about B.C. 343, there began a series of greater wars in Italy, in which the Romans may truly be said to have been fighting for the dominion of the whole land. And in the space of about sixty years they gradually won it. The *Samnites*, a nation of the race which we have roughly called Oscan, were now the chief people in the South of Italy: they were a brave and stout people, quite able to contend with the Romans on equal terms. The first war with the Samnites did not last long, and it was followed in 340 by a war between Rome and her old allies the *Latins*. The Latins wished for a more complete union with Rome, and for one of the Consuls to be always a Latin; but to this the Romans would not agree. The end of the war was that the Latin League was broken up and the cities were merged in the Roman state one by one. Then, in 326, came a second Samnite War, which lasted eighteen years, and a third lasted from 298 to 290. In these two latter wars the Samnites were helped by the Etruscans and Gauls, but all were gradually subdued, and by the year 282 Rome was pretty well mistress of all Italy, except some of the Greek cities in the South.

10. **The Italian States under Rome.**—The condition of the Italian states under the Roman dominion was very various, but we may say that the free people of Italy now formed three main classes, *Romans*, *Latins*, and *Italians*. Many of the allied and con-

quered states were altogether merged in Rome at a very early time; their people became Romans, and formed tribes in the Roman Assembly. Rome, in the end, gradually admitted all the people of Italy to her own citizenship. But, till an Italian city which was subject to Rome received the Roman citizenship, its people had no voice at all in the general government, in choosing the magistrates, or in matters of peace and war. And, after such a city received the Roman citizenship, the only way in which its citizens could influence such matters was by themselves going to Rome and giving their votes in the Roman Assembly. This should be carefully borne in mind throughout, as it was the natural consequence of the Roman government always being the government of a city. Among the states whose people did not at once become Romans, some had the *Latin* franchise, as it was called, the franchise which was at first given to the cities of Latium and afterwards to others in different parts. This did not give full Roman citizenship, but it made it much easier to obtain it. Lastly, the *Italians* or *Allies* kept their independent constitutions in all internal matters, but they had to follow the lead of Rome in all matters of peace and war. Thus it was that the Roman dominion in Italy was a dominion of a city over cities.

11. **The War with Pyrrhos.**—We now come to the beginning of the wars of the Romans with the nations out of Italy, beginning with one in which they had to fight for their newly-won dominion in Italy itself. Soon after the Roman power had reached into Southern Italy, the people of the Greek city of *Taras* or *Tarentum* contrived to offend the Romans, and they then asked *Pyrrhos*, King of Epeiros, to come and help them as the champion of a Greek city threatened by Barbarians. Pyrrhos came over in 281, and the Romans had now to try their strength against a way of fighting quite different from their own, and that under

the most famous warrior of the age. Pyrrhos was joined by some of the lately conquered nations in Southern Italy, who were glad of a chance of throwing off the Roman yoke. He defeated the Romans in two battles, but with so much loss on his own side that he was glad to make a truce and to go over into *Sicily*, where some of the Greek cities had asked him to help them against the *Carthaginians*. In 276 he came back to Italy, but in the next year he was defeated at *Beneventum* and left Italy altogether. In the next few years the small part of Italy which still held out against Rome was subdued.

12. **Carthage.**—Rome was now mistress of Italy, and she soon began to be entangled in wars beyond its boundaries. The greatest power besides Rome in the western Mediterranean lands was the city of *Carthage* on the north coast of Africa. This, as we have already said, was a *Phœnician* city, one of the colonies of the older Phœnician cities of Tyre and Sidon. Carthage, like Rome, was a city bearing rule over other cities; for she had gained a certain headship over the other Phœnician cities in Africa, much as Rome had over the Latin and other cities in Italy. And besides the kindred Phœnician cities, Carthage bore rule also over many of the native tribes whom the Phœnician settlers found in Africa. And, unlike Rome up to this time, she had, as trading cities and countries always strive to have, large dominions beyond the sea. Carthage at this time bore rule over the islands of Sardinia and Corsica, and she had also large possessions in Sicily. But in Sicily a constant warfare was kept up between the Phœnician and the Greek settlements, in which the Tyrants who at different times reigned in Syracuse specially distinguished themselves. Such were *Gelôn*, who reigned at the time of the Persian War, *Dionysios*, who reigned at the time of the war between Sparta and Thebes, and *Agathoklês*, who lived in the time of Pyrrhos. As

Tyrants in their own city, these men did many evil things; still they deserve some honour as champions of the Greek nation against the Phœnicians. Sicily thus became the great battle-field between the Aryan and Semitic races, and it became so still more after the Romans stepped in. The wars between Rome and Carthage also bring out one great point of difference between the two cities. For, while the Romans waged their wars by the hands of their own citizens and allies, the wars of Carthage were mainly carried on by barbarian mercenaries, that is, soldiers serving simply for pay, whom they hired both in Africa and in Gaul and Spain. A state which does this can never hold up for good against one which uses native armies; and it is a sign of the great wealth and power of Carthage, helped still more by a few very great men who appeared among her citizens, that Carthage could hold up so long as she did. Carthage had indeed one other great advantage, namely that, as a trading city, she was very strong by sea, while the Romans had as yet had hardly anything to do with naval affairs. Thus Carthage and Rome were the two great states of the West, and it could hardly fail but that war should spring up between them about something. And it was the more likely, as the island of Sicily lay between them, where the Greek cities which were threatened by Carthage were closely connected with the Greek subjects of Rome in Southern Italy.

13. **The First Punic War.**—A cause of quarrel was soon found in the disputes among the different towns in Sicily. Rome, as the head of Italy, undertook to protect the *Mamertines*, a body of Campanian mercenaries who had seized the town of *Messênê* on the strait. Their enemies were *Hierôn* King of Syracuse—for those who were formerly called *Tyrants* now called themselves *Kings*—and Carthage. Thus arose the first *Punic* War, so called from the Latin

form of the name *Phœnician.* This war went on between Carthage and Rome for twenty-four years, beginning in B.C. 264, and Hierôn had soon to change the Carthaginian alliance for the Roman. During so long a time the two great cities contended with very varied success, the war being chiefly carried on in and about Sicily, though at one time the Roman Consul *Marcus Atilius Regulus*, who is one of the most famous heroes of Roman legend, carried the war into Africa. For a long time the Carthaginians had greatly the advantage at sea; but gradually the Romans came to be their match at their own weapons, and at last a great naval victory was won by the Consul *Caius Lutatius Catulus*, which made the Carthaginians ask for peace. The First Punic War ended in B.C. 241.

14. **Beginning of the Roman Provinces.**—This victory over the Carthaginians was the beginning of a new state of things, and gave Rome quite a new class of subjects. For, when peace was made, Carthage had to give up her possessions in Sicily, and the island, except the part which belonged to Hierôn, became a Roman *province.* This was the beginning of the Roman *Provinces*, that is the dominions of Rome out of Italy. Their condition was much worse than that of the Italian allies, for the provinces were ruled by Roman governors, and had to pay tribute to Rome. The *Provincials* in fact were mere subjects, while the Italians, though dependent allies, were still allies. Though they were bound to serve in the Roman armies and to follow Rome in all matters of war and peace, they still kept their own constitutions and no Roman governors were sent to rule them.

15. **The Second Punic or Hannibalian War.**—Twenty-three years passed between the end of the first Punic War and the beginning of the second. But in the meanwhile the Romans got possession, rather

unfairly, of the islands of *Sardinia* and *Corsica*, which Carthage had kept by the peace. On the other hand a Carthaginian dominion was growing up in *Spain* under *Hamilcar Barkas*, one of the greatest men that Carthage ever reared, his son-in-law *Hasdrubal*, and his son *Hannibal*, the greatest man of all, and one of the greatest generals that the world ever saw. Another quarrel arose between Carthage and Rome, when Hannibal took the Spanish town of *Saguntum*, which the Romans claimed as an ally. War began in 218, and Hannibal carried it on by invading Italy by land. This was one of the most famous enterprises in all history. Never was Rome so near destruction as in the war with Hannibal. He crossed the Alps and defeated the Romans in four battles, the greatest of which was that of *Cannæ* in B.C. 216. Many of the Italian allies revolted against Rome, and the war went on in Italy till B.C. 203. By that time the Romans had taken *Syracuse*, which, after Hierôn's death, had forsaken their alliance, so that all Sicily was now a Roman province. They had also, while Hannibal was in Italy, conquered the Carthaginian possessions in Spain. Lastly, the Roman general who had been so successful in Spain, *Publius Cornelius Scipio*, crossed over into Africa, so that Hannibal had to leave Italy and go back to defend Carthage itself. He was defeated by Scipio in the battle of *Zama* in B.C. 202. Peace was now made, by which Carthage gave up all her possessions out of Africa, and bound herself not to make war without the consent of the Romans. That is to say, Carthage now became a dependent ally of Rome. The Semitic races could no longer dispute the dominion of the Mediterranean lands with the Aryans.

16. **The Third Punic War.**—The last war with Carthage began about fifty years after the second. The Carthaginians were always at variance with their neighbour *Massinissa* King of *Numidia*, who had

been a useful ally of Rome in the former war. The Romans always favoured Massinissa, and in B.C. 149 war broke out again between Rome and Carthage. Three years later Carthage was taken by the younger Scipio, *Publius Cornelius Scipio Æmilianus;* the city was destroyed; part of its territory was given to Massinissa, and part became the Roman province of *Africa*. This is an example of the way in which Rome advanced step by step. By the *First* Punic war Carthage lost territory, but it remained quite independent. The *Second* made it a dependent ally of Rome, but left it free in its internal government. The *Third* destroyed the city and made the country a province. It is perhaps hardly needful to say that *Africa*, as the name of a Roman province, does not mean the whole continent, but only the immediate territory of Carthage.

17. **The First Macedonian War.**—We see the same way of advancing step by step in the next great conquest made by Rome, which was going on at the same time as the Punic Wars. This was the conquest of *Macedonia* and *Greece*. Many things were beginning to bring the Romans and the Greeks together, and, when any people began to have anything to do with Rome, however friendly their dealings might be at first, it always ended in the other nation being sooner or later swallowed up in the Roman dominion. The Romans already had Greek subjects in Italy and Sicily. They were now beginning to know something of the language and literature of Greece, and to imitate them in writings of their own. For it is about this time that the Roman literature which we now have begins. The Romans now began to have dealings with the Greeks in Greece itself; but their first dealings were quite friendly. A war broke out with *Illyria* in B.C. 229, which ended in the island of *Korkyra* and the cities of *Apollônia* and *Epidamnos* submitting to Rome. These were

Greek cities on the Illyrian coast, and they welcomed the Romans as deliverers. But Rome had now got possessions on the Greek side of the Ægæan, and the conquest of those lands had really begun. In 215 Philip King of Macedonia made a league with Hannibal, and in 213 the *First Macedonian War* began, while the second Punic War was still going on. In this war Philip was helped by the leagues of *Achaia*, *Akarnania*, and *Epeiros*, while Rome found allies in the League of *Ætolia*, in *Attalos* King of *Pergamos* in Asia, and *Nabis* Tyrant of *Sparta*. Since the fall of Kleomenês, Sparta had been in a state of great confusion, and she had had several wars with the Achaians, in which *Philopoimên*, the last great general of Greece, greatly distinguished himself. Peace was at last made in 205, and some changes of frontier were made; but the chief result of the war was that Rome had now begun steadily to interfere in Greek and Macedonian affairs.

18. **The Second Macedonian War.**—The first war with Macedonia, like the first war with Carthage, did not affect the position of that kingdom, or of any other of the Greek states, as independent powers. The *Second Macedonian War*, which began in B.C. 200, marks another stage in the progress of conquest. The Romans now stepped in to help the Athenians, who were their allies, and who had been attacked by Philip. The Ætolians took the Roman side from the beginning, and the Achaians joined them in 198. In 197 the war was ended by the defeat of Philip at *Kynoskephalê* in Thessaly, and the next year, 196, the Roman Consul *Titus Quinctius Flamininus* proclaimed the liberty of all those parts of Greece which had been under his power. Philip thus lost a large part of his territory, and had to become a dependent ally of Rome. And from this time we may count the Greeks allies of Rome, though nominally free, as practically dependent.

19. **The Conquest of Ætolia.**—The Ætolians now invited the Seleukid King *Antiochos the Great* to cross over from Asia and attack the Romans in Greece. He crossed over in 192, and several Greek states joined him, but the Achaians held steadily to Rome. In 191 Antiochos was defeated at *Thermopylai* by the Consul *Manius Acilius Glabrio*, and his allies the Ætolians were presently, in 189, obliged to become a Roman dependency, being the first within the borders of Greece itself. Rome also took the islands of *Zakynthos* and *Kephallênia*, and the Achaian League was extended over all Peloponnêsos. Rome was now really mistress of Greece, and Grecian history from this time consists mainly of her dealings with the states which had practically become her subjects.

20. **The Third Macedonian War.**—The *Third Macedonian War*, waged with *Perseus* the son of Philip, began in 171. Most of the Greek states were now on the Macedonian side, for it had become plain that Rome was much more dangerous than Macedonia. But the Achaians remained allies of Rome, though they were from this time treated with great insolence. The war ended with the victory of *Lucius Æmilius Paullus* at *Pydna* in 168. The Macedonian kingdom was now cut up into four commonwealths, all dependencies of Rome. *Epeiros* was subdued and most of its cities destroyed.

21. **Final Conquest of Macedonia and Greece.**—The *Fourth Macedonian War* happened at exactly the same time as the Third Punic War, in 149. The Macedonians rose under one *Andriskos*, who called himself Philip, and gave himself out as the son of Perseus. He was successful for a time, but he was overthrown in 148, and Macedonia, after so many stages, at last became a Roman province. There were also many disputes between Rome and Achaia, which now grew into a war, and in 146 the Achaians were defeated by *Lucius Mummius*, and *Corinth* was

destroyed in the same year as Carthage. The League was dissolved for a while, and the Achaian cities became formally dependent on Rome. But *Athens* and several other Greek cities and islands still remained nominally independent. The history of these times was written by *Polybios*, a leading man in the Achaian League, but who, being a prisoner at Rome, formed a close friendship with the younger Scipio and other chief Romans. He was thus able to look with his own eyes at two different stages of the world's history in a way that perhaps no one else ever could.

22. **The Romans in Asia.**—Macedonia and Greece formed easy stepping-stones for the Romans to meddle in the affairs of Asia. By far the greatest of the Macedonian kingdoms in Asia was that of the descendants of *Seleukos*, which for a while took in all Alexander's conquests in Asia. But this great dominion was cut short in the East about B.C. 256 by the revolt of the *Parthians* in Northern Persia. They established a kingdom under the descendants of their first leader *Ashk* or *Arsakês*, which in after times was the chief rival of Rome. The eastern provinces of the Seleukid Kings thus fell away one by one, but at the time of the Second Punic War their dominion reached to the Ægæan at one end and stretched far beyond the Tigris at the other. But it must be remembered that there were several states in Western Asia, both native and Macedonian, like the kingdoms of *Pergamos* and *Bithynia*, which did not form part of their dominion. All these states were more or less tinged with Greek culture. We have already seen how Antiochos, called the Great, had crossed over into Greece and had been there defeated by the Romans. The Romans then crossed into Asia, and Antiochos was defeated by *Lucius Scipio* at *Magnêsia* in 189. Antiochos had now to give up all his dominions west of Mount Tauros, and the great dominion of the Seleukid Kings shrank up into a

mere kingdom of *Syria.* But their capital *Antioch* on the Orontês still remained one of the chief seats of Greek culture, and one of the greatest cities of the world. The Romans now became really masters of all Western Asia, though after their manner, they did not as yet formally take any part of the land to themselves. What Antiochos gave up they divided among their allies, giving the largest share to *Eumenês* King of *Pergamos.* The kingdom of Eumenês thus became the greatest state in Western Asia, and his capital, like Antioch, became a great seat of Greek culture and learning. And a little later the cities of *Lykia* joined together in a free and most wisely managed Confederation, much after the pattern of the Achaian League. But from this time Pergamos, Lykia, and all these Macedonian or Hellenized states looked up to Rome, just as the Greeks in Greece itself had already learned to do. At last in 133 *Attalos*, the last king of Pergamos, left his dominions to the Roman people, and the greater part of them were made into a Roman province, by the name of the *Province of Asia*, the first province that Rome held beyond the Ægæan.

23. **The Romans in Western Europe. Conquest of Cisalpine Gaul.**—In all these wars with Carthage, Macedonia, and Syria, Rome had to struggle with enemies on something like equal terms. All were civilized states, and the Macedonian Kings, both in Macedonia and in Asia, had kept up the military discipline of Philip and Alexander. We must now see how Rome dealt with the people of the *West*, the forefathers of the chief nations of modern Europe, but who then were only brave barbarians. Her first conquest among these was naturally that of those lands within the Alps which are now reckoned part of Italy, but which were then known as *Cisalpine Gaul.* The Gauls, it will be remembered, had once taken Rome itself, and they had shown themselves dangerous enemies to Rome by helping

the Samnites and Etruscans against her. It was no wonder then that the conquest of Cisalpine Gaul began almost as soon as the conquest of Italy was over. The lands south of the *Po* were won before the first Punic War, and in the time between the first and the second Punic Wars the conquest went on, and several colonies were planted beyond the Po. The Gauls greatly helped Hannibal in his invasion of Italy, but they presently paid dearly for so doing. For, as soon as the second Punic War was over, the conquest of Cisalpine Gaul went on, and was ended by about 191. The land was now full of Roman and Latin colonies, and it soon became a Roman land and began to be reckoned part of Italy. *Liguria* and *Venetia* were conquered soon afterwards, so that the Roman power took in all within the Alps, all that we now call Italy.

24. **The Conquest of Spain.**—Meanwhile the third and most western of the three great peninsulas, that of *Spain*, was being added, like Greece and the neighbouring countries, to the Roman dominion. Spain was the only one of the great countries of Europe where the mass of the people were not of the Aryan stock. The greater part of the land was still held by the *Iberians*, as a small part is even now by their descendants the Basques. But in the central part of the peninsula *Celtic* tribes had pressed in, and we have seen that there were some *Phœnician* colonies in the south, and some *Greek* colonies on the east coast. In the time between the First and Second Punic Wars, Hamilcar, Hasdrubal, and Hannibal had won all Spain as far as the Ebro for *Carthage*. But during the second Punic War, between the years 211 and 206, the Carthaginian territories in Spain were all won for Rome by the Scipios. Rome thus became the chief power in Spain, even before the second Punic War was over, and before she had conquered all Cisalpine Gaul. But Spain has always been a hard

country to conquer, and the Romans had constant wars with the native tribes. Still we may look on the Roman dominion in Spain as finally established in B.C. 133, when the younger *Scipio* took *Numantia.* This, it will be remembered, was in the same year as the bequest of Attalos which gave Rome her first Asiatic possession, and Numantia was taken by the same general who had taken Carthage. From this time all Spain was a Roman province, except some of the mountainous parts in the north, where native tribes still remained free.

25. **Beginning of the Conquest of Transalpine Gaul.**—The conquests of Rome in *Transalpine Gaul,* Gaul beyond the Alps, began a little later. Gaul in the geographical sense, the land between the Rhine, the Alps, the Pyrenees, and the Ocean, was then, as now, peopled by different races, speaking different languages. In the south the old non-Aryan inhabitants still held their ground. The districts near the Alps were chiefly held by *Ligurians,* while *Aquitaine,* a name which then meant the land between the Pyrenees and the Garonne, was *Iberian.* In the centre the Aryan *Celts* had settled, but the next wave, the *Teutons,* were most likely already pressing upon them, though when our kinsfolk first crossed the Rhine it would be hard to say. The Mediterranean coast of Gaul was fringed by that group of Greek cities of which *Massalia* was the head. Massalia was a great trading city, and it became an ally, at first a really equal and independent ally, of Rome. This was in 218, at the beginning of the second Punic War. The Romans had once or twice to cross the Alps to defend their Greek allies, and at last, in 125, a Roman *province* was formed in Transalpine Gaul, in the land which has ever since kept the name of *Provence.* At the same time the colony of *Aquæ Sextiæ,* now *Aix,* was founded. As usual, the Roman dominions advanced, and twenty years later

the Roman province reached as far as *Geneva* to the north and *Tolosa* or *Toulouse* to the west.

26. **The Cimbri and Teutones.**—It is not unlikely that the Romans would now have gone on and conquered the whole of Gaul, if an event had not happened which put a stop for some time to their further progress in those parts. For about this time Gaul was invaded by a vast host of barbarians called *Cimbri* and *Teutones*, who came from the North, but about whom there has been much doubt whether they really were of Celtic or of what we call Teutonic race. They defeated several Roman commanders in Gaul, but in 102 the *Teutones* were utterly defeated by the Consul *Caius Marius* near *Aquæ Sextiæ*, and in the next year the war was finished by the two Consuls Marius and *Quintus Lutatius Catulus* overthrowing the Cimbri also at *Vercellæ* in Cisalpine Gaul. This was the same kind of danger from which Rome had been saved long before by Camillus, the danger of being overthrown, not by the chief of a civilized people like Pyrrhos or Hannibal, but by a people who were still altogether barbarous. If any of our ancestors had a hand in this invasion, it gives it a special interest for us; but, at all events, as saving Rome from this great danger, the defeat of the invaders was one of the greatest events in Roman history, and Caius Marius is one of Rome's most famous men. But, fully to understand the condition of Rome, and especially to understand the position of Marius, we must look back a little at the state of things in Italy while these great conquests were going on abroad. It will however be better to keep the details of the internal affairs of Rome, as far as may be, for the special History of Rome, and to speak chiefly of those things which concern the relations of Rome to her allies and subjects.

27. **Rome and her Allies.**—We have thus seen that, in the space of about two hundred years, from the beginning of the Samnite Wars to the conquest of

Numantia and the inheritance of the province of Asia, Rome had come to be the mistress of all the lands round the Mediterranean Sea. The whole was not as yet fully annexed and made into provinces, but no power was left which had the least chance of holding against Rome. The only great power with which Rome had had no war was the kingdom of *Egypt.* There the descendants of the first *Ptolemy*, all of whom bore his name, still reigned, and Egypt was the richest and most flourishing of the Macedonian kingdoms, and its capital *Alexandria* was the greatest seat of Greek learning and science. But when the Romans began to be powerful in Asia, even the Ptolemies, who often had wars with the Seleukids, began to look to Rome as a protector. It was this vast dominion, while it made Rome so great in the face of other nations, which led to the corruption of her constitution within, and at last to the utter loss of her freedom. The form of government which had done so well for a single city with a small territory did not at all do for the government of so large a portion of the world. Throughout the Roman dominions the Roman People was sovereign; the Assembly of the People made laws and chose magistrates for Rome itself, and sent out generals and governors to conquer and rule in the subject lands. The *provincials*, and even the *allies*, had no voice in settling the affairs of the vast dominion of which they had become a part, and they were often greatly oppressed by the Roman officers. Meanwhile in Rome itself the great offices had been gradually thrown open to the *Plebeians* as well as the *Patricians*, and hardly any legal distinction was left between the two orders. The constitution was therefore really *democratic;* for the sovereign power lay in the Assembly of the whole People, which made the laws and chose the magistrates. And, in choosing the magistrates, they also indirectly chose the Senate, as the Senate was mainly made up of men who had held the different magistracies. Still the constitution had a great tendency to become practically *aristocratic*. For the men who had held great offices, whether patricians or plebeians, began to form a class by themselves, and their descendants, who were now called *nobles*, began to think that they only had a right to hold the offices which their forefathers had held. Then again the old citizens of Rome were largely cut off in the endless wars, and many *freedmen*—that is, men who had been slaves—and strangers got the citizenship, so that the character of the Roman People was greatly lowered. And, as every citizen who wished to vote had to come to Rome in his own person, the Roman Assembly had become far too large, and gradually turned into a mere mob. Then again many citizens were wretchedly poor, while rich men had made themselves great estates out of the land which rightly belonged to the commonwealth. Thus, instead of the old political strife between *patricians* and *plebeians*, there had come, what was a great deal worse, a social strife between the *rich* and the *poor*. While Rome had still powerful enemies to strive against, these evils did not make themselves so much felt; but, when Rome had nothing more to fear, they began to be very glaring, and men had to seek for remedies for them. And, along with this, the Italian allies, who had not been raised to Roman citizenship but who had borne a great part in the wars of Rome, now demanded to be made Romans. The cause of the poor against the rich was taken up by *Tiberius Sempronius Gracchus*, in the year 133; and the cause both of the poor and of the allies was taken up by his brother *Caius* in 123. But both of them were murdered by the oligarchs, who wished to keep all power and wealth in their own hands.

28. **The Social War.**—After the death of the Gracchi the ill will between the nobles and the people, and the further ill will between the Romans and the Italians, still went on. The next great leader of the popular party was *Caius Marius*, of whom we have

already heard as the conqueror of the Teutones. He was not of any high family, but was born at Arpinum, an old town of the Volscians, whose people did not obtain the full Roman citizenship till 188. His sympathies therefore lay with the people against the oligarchs, and still more with the Italians against either the nobles or the mob of Rome. He was an excellent soldier, and first began to distinguish himself in the war with *Jugurtha*, who had usurped the kingdom of *Numidia*, whose King Massinissa had been so useful to Rome in the Punic War. This war began in 111, and in 106 Marius brought the war to an end and led Jugurtha in triumph. Very soon after came the invasion of the Cimbri and Teutones and Marius' great success against them. He was now the chief man in Rome and the leader of the popular party. But the complaints of the Italians still went on, and in the year 90 most of them rose in arms. This was called the *Social War*, that is the war with the *Socii* or *Allies* of Rome. It was ended in the course of the next year by all the allies, except the *Samnites* and *Lucanians* in the south of Italy, submitting and being made Roman citizens. The Samnites, whom it had cost Rome so much trouble to conquer two hundred years before, still held out. Marius held a command in this war, and so did *Lucius Cornelius Sulla*, who had been his lieutenant in the war with Jugurtha; but Marius did little or nothing, and went far to lose his old credit, while Sulla showed himself the rising man of Rome. Presently a *Civil War*, the first in Roman History, broke out between *Marius* and *Sulla*, in which the war with the Samnites, which had never quite come to an end, merged itself. At one stage of this war *Sertorius*, a Roman general on the Marian side, held *Spain* almost as a separate power, having a Senate of his own, which he said was the real Roman Senate. In 83 Sulla came back from his wars in the East, of which we shall speak directly, and the Samnites joined with the Marian party, and began openly to declare that Rome must be destroyed. Rome had never been in such danger since quite the old times, and there can be no doubt that Sulla, who now saved Rome and crushed the Samnites and the Marian party, fixed the future history of the world far more than Cæsar or anyone else who came after him. Sulla now took to himself the supreme power at Rome, with the title of *Perpetual Dictator.* But, when he had quite rooted out the Marian party, and had passed a series of laws to confirm the dominion of the aristocracy, he gave up his power, and lived as a private man till he died soon after. Rome had now passed through her last trial within her own peninsula. The Samnites, who had withstood to the last, had been utterly cut off, and the other Italians had become Romans.

29. **The Mithridatic War.**—While Rome went through this great trial at home, she had to undergo another almost as great abroad. She had to wage a war greater than any that she had waged since the conquest of Carthage and Macedonia. One of those states in Asia Minor which had arisen, as was before mentioned, out of the ruins of the old Persian Empire, was *Pontos*, the Kingdom of the *Euxine Sea*—*Pontos* in Greek meaning the *Sea*, and specially the Euxine Sea. Its Kings were of native blood, but, like all their neighbours, they made a certain pretence to Greek culture, and the acquisition of the province of Asia by the Romans made them neighbours of Rome. Pontos was now ruled by *Mithridatês* the Sixth or the *Great.* A war with him broke out while the Social War was going on in Italy, and Mithridatês succeeded in winning all Asia. He then ordered all the Romans and Italians who were settled in Asia to be massacred in one day, which the people everywhere did very willingly—they had made themselves so hateful. Then his generals, like Antiochos, crossed over into Greece, where many of the Greeks took his side. Sulla then,

in 87, came into Greece, stormed Athens, won two great battles at *Chairôneia* and *Orchomenos* in Bœotia, and then, being called home by the news of the successes of Marius, patched up a peace by which Mithridatês gave up all his conquests. Such a peace was not likely to last, and, as soon as he had a good opportunity, Mithridatês began the war again. This was in 74, and the second war between him and the Romans, first under *Lucius Licinius Lucullus* and then under *Cnæus Pompeius*, called *Magnus* or the Great, lasted ten years. It ended in the overthrow of the Pontic kingdom, which was split up in the usual way, and in the complete re-establishment of the Roman power in Asia.

30. **The Conquest of Syria.**—In the history of Rome one conquest always led to another, and, after the overthrow of Mithridatês, the Roman arms were carried by Pompeius much further towards the East than they had ever gone before. *Tigranês*, King of *Armenia*, who had helped Mithridatês, was utterly humbled; *Syria*, the remains of the great Seleukid kingdom, was partly made a Roman province, partly divided among dependent princes. Pompeius also took *Jerusalem* in the year 63, and *Palestine* was henceforth under the Roman power, though it was often held by vassal Kings, such as the *Herods* in the New Testament. The Roman power now reached from the Ocean to the Euphrates, and the Roman Commonwealth may be looked on as having taken the place of Alexander and his successors in Asia, as the champion of the West against the East. But each increase of dominion laid it open to fresh enemies. The *Parthian* Kings became formidable enemies, and indeed rivals, of Rome. We shall hear a great deal of the wars and other dealings between Rome and Parthia. But the first attempt of the Romans against Parthia, which was made by *Marcus Lucinius Crassus* in the year 54, was utterly unsuccessful. Crassus was

defeated and killed, and the more part of his army were made prisoners.

31. **State of Things at Rome.**—Meanwhile it became more and more plain how unfit the government of the single city of Rome was to rule all Italy and the world. New discontents arose out of the admission of the Italians to the Roman citizenship, and the commonwealth was torn in pieces by the disputes of the leading men. We now come to the famous men of the last days of the Commonwealth,—*Pompeius* and *Crassus*, of whom we have already heard, *Marcus Tullius Cicero* the great orator, *Marcus Porcius Cato*, and the most famous of all, *Caius Julius Cæsar*. We shall say more of their doings at home in the special History of Rome. It may here be enough to say that, as far as natural gifts went, Cæsar was perhaps the greatest man that ever lived, being great in all ways, equally as soldier, statesman, and scholar. He was of an old patrician house, but he was connected with the family of Marius, and he took up the cause of the people not honestly, like the Gracchi, but to serve his own ends. The whole Commonwealth was now utterly corrupt; still Pompeius and Cicero, though there were plenty of faults on their side, did strive to defend the law and constitution, such as it was, while the Roman people had sunk into a mere mob, which men like Cæsar could use as they chose.

32. **Cæsar's Conquests in Gaul.**—In the year 59 Cæsar was Consul, and in the next year he went into *Gaul*, which had been given him as his province, and where he spent about seven years in conquering the whole of the country. Instead of a small part of southern Gaul, the Roman dominion now reached to the Rhine and the British Channel. In this war the Romans first had to deal both with people of our own race and with the land now called Britain. Our own ancestors, the *English*, were still in their

old land by the *Elbe*, and Cæsar never came near them. But there were several Teutonic tribes in north-eastern Gaul, and in the year 55 Cæsar crossed into *Germany* itself, but he did not conquer any part of the land. In the same year 55, and again in 54, he crossed over into *Britain*, but he made no lasting conquest, and left no Roman troops behind him. Britain was then inhabited by a Celtic people, the *Britons*, who gave their name to the island, and whom our fore-fathers, when they came into Britain long after, called the *Welsh* or *strangers*. Both the German and the British expeditions were made rather to show the power of Rome than to make conquests which it would have been hard to keep. The *Rhine* thus became the boundary of the Roman province of Gaul; that is to say, the Germans on the left bank of the Rhine became subjects of Rome, along with the Iberian and Celtic inhabitants of Gaul, while the Germans on the right bank remained free. This conquest of Gaul by Cæsar is one of the most important events in the history of the world. It is in some sort the beginning of modern history, as it brought the old world of southern Europe, of which Rome was the head, into contact with the lands and nations which were to play the greatest part in later times, with Gaul, Germany, and Britain.

33. **The Civil War of Pompeius and Cæsar.**—Cæsar had been all this time winning fame and power in Gaul, in order to make himself master of his country. Things got into great confusion while he was away, which was just what he wanted. At last, in the year 49, Cæsar openly rebelled, and another Civil War now began, in which Pompeius commanded the armies which were faithful to the Commonwealth. But now that the Roman dominion took in so large a part of the world, a civil war between Romans was not necessarily fought in Italy. The power of Pompeius lay chiefly in the lands east

of the Hadriatic; so, while he was gathering his forces there, Cæsar marched to Rome and got the People to make him, first Dictator, and then Consul for the year 48. Then he crossed over to Epeiros, and presently defeated the army of Pompeius and the Senate at *Pharsalos* in Thessaly. Pompeius was soon after murdered in Egypt, and in about three years' time Cæsar was able to overcome all who withstood him in Africa, Spain and elsewhere. The battle of Pharsalos is one of the most important battles in history, as it really ended the Roman Commonwealth, and began the *Roman Empire*, which we may almost say has gone on ever since. The forms of the Commonwealth lasted long after, but from this time the Roman world always had a master. Cæsar was now master of the Roman dominions, and was made Dictator for life. He was also called *Imperator* (the word which is cut short into *Emperor*), a title which in some sort belonged to every Roman general, but which Cæsar was allowed to use in a special way. But he was not satisfied with being Dictator and Imperator; he wished to be *King* and to wear a diadem. This was more than men could bear; so many of the senators, among whom the chief were *Caius Cassius* and *Marcus Junius Brutus*, conspired and slew him in the senate-house (March 15th, B.C. 44). Cæsar was a *Tyrant;* he had overthrown the freedom of his country and had seized a power beyond the laws. But it should not be forgotten that for the provinces it was a distinct gain to get one master instead of many. The real lesson to be learned from the overthrow of the Roman Commonwealth is that states which boast themselves of their own freedom should not hold other states in bondage.

34. **The Second Civil War.**—After the death of Cæsar followed a time of great confusion, lasting for thirteen years. Brutus and Cassius, who had killed Cæsar, stood up for the Commonwealth, and there was

a war between them and the partizans of Cæsar undeı *Marcus Antonius*, one of Cæsar's officers, and Cæsar's great-nephew, *Caius Octavius.* Cæsar had adopted Octavius as his son; so his name became *Caius Julius Cæsar Octavianus.* These two, along with *Marcus Æmilius Lepidus*, formed what was called a *Triumvirate* for settling the affairs of the Commonwealth. Meanwhile Brutus and Cassius, like Pompeius, had gone to the East, and in 42 the battle of *Philippi* in Macedonia was fought between them and the Triumvirs, and the hopes of the party of the Commonwealth were crushed. Presently Antonius professed to make war upon the Parthians, but he did nothing great, for he was utterly bewitched by *Kleopatra*, Queen of Egypt, the last of the dynasty of the Ptolemies. War presently followed between Cæsar and Antonius, and Antonius and Kleopatra were altogether defeated in a sea-fight at *Aktion*, near Ambrakia, on the west coast of Greece (31). Antonius and Kleopatra presently killed themselves, and *Egypt* became a Roman province. All the lands round the Mediterranean had now come under the Roman dominion, though here and there there were principalities and commonwealths which had not been formally made into provinces.

35. **The Beginning of the Empire.**—There was now no one left to withstand Cæsar, and the Senate and People gradually voted him one honour and office after another, which made him practically master of the state, though the outward forms of the Commonwealth went on as before. But he was never called King, or even Dictator, like his uncle, for that title had become almost as hateful as that of King. But the new title of *Augustus* was voted to him, and all who succeeded him in his power called themselves *Cæsar* and *Augustus.* But he is specially known as *Augustus Cæsar.* This is the beginning of the Roman Empire, for, of the various titles borne by Augustus and his successors, that of *Emperor* (*Impe-*

rator) or chief of the army was the one which prevailed in the end. The rest of the history of Europe is the history of the Roman Empire in one shape or another, and we shall see that the title of Roman Emperor went on almost to our own times. The first Emperor then was Caius Julius Cæsar Octavianus, and we may count the Empire as beginning in B.C. 27, when he received the title of Augustus. The last Emperor was *Francis, King of Germany*, who gave up the Empire in A.D. 1806. The differences between the early and the later Emperors we shall see as we go on, but there was a continuous succession between them without any break.

CHAPTER IV.

THE HEATHEN EMPIRE.

Extent of the Roman Empire; distinction of the Latin, Greek, and Oriental Provinces (1)—*nature of the Roman dominions; all the inhabitants of the Empire gradually become Romans* (2)—*reign of Augustus; stealthy introduction of Monarchy* (3)—*wars with the Germans; victory of Arminius* (3)—*Roman Literature and Art* (4)—*the Claudian Emperors; conquest of Britain; the Empire passes from the Cæsarian family* (5)—*the Flavian Emperors; wars with the Jews, Batavians, and Dacians* (6)—*the Good Emperors; origin of the Roman Law* (7)—*Emperors chosen by the army; distinction of Romans and Barbarians; the Illyrian Emperors* (8)—*the Tyrants* (9)—*restoration of the Kingdom of Persia; wars between Persia and Rome* (10)—*wars with the Teutonic nations; first appearance of the Goths* (10)—*origin of Christianity; its advance and persecutions* (11)—*reign of Diocletian; his division of the Empire* (12)—*last persecution of the Christians; Constantine embraces Christianity* (12)—*Summary* (13).

1. **Extent of the Roman Empire.**—At the time when the government of Rome practically

changed from a commonwealth to a monarchy, the Roman power had spread over all the lands which could be looked on as forming the civilized world. These lands fall naturally under three heads, the distinction between which will be found to be of great importance as we go on. In the Western provinces, as Gaul and Spain, to which we may add Africa, where Carthage had been restored by Cæsar as a Roman colony, the Romans appeared, not only as a conquering, but as a civilizing people. Roman customs and the use of the Latin language took firm root; the whole civilization of these lands became Roman, and the native tongues and customs lived on only in out-of-the-way corners, such as the mountain land of the Basques in Spain and southern Gaul. But in Greece, and in those lands whither the Greek speech and customs had been carried by Greek colonists or by Macedonian conquerors, the Greek civilization, the older and the higher of the two, still held its ground. These lands became politically Roman, but they remained socially and intellectually Greek, and Greek still went on as the language of literature and polite life. But in the further East, in the lands beyond Mount Tauros, in Syria and Egypt, though those lands had been ruled by Macedonian Kings, and though great Greek cities had arisen as their capitals, the native languages and religions and general habit of thought never died out, nor were they driven, as in the West, into out-of-the-way corners. It is only in a very superficial sense that these lands can be said to have ever become either Greek or Roman. This distinction between what we may call the *Latin*, the *Greek*, and the *Oriental* provinces must be carefully borne in mind throughout. It was not a distinction made by law, but it was one which had most important practical results. Speaking roughly, the Roman dominion was bounded by the Rhine, the Danube, the Euphrates, and the great deserts of

Africa. It did not reach quite so far as this at the very beginning of the Empire, but the few outlying lands which were needed to bring it to those boundaries were added during the reigns of Augustus and the other earlier Emperors. And, within those boundaries, we may look on the *Latin* provinces as reaching from the Ocean to the Hadriatic, the *Greek* as reaching from the Hadriatic to Mount Tauros, and the *Oriental* as taking in the lands beyond.

2. **Nature of the Roman Dominion.**—It must always be remembered that the establishment of the Roman Empire was not a formal revolution. The old republican forms went on in Rome, and the relations between the ruling city and the allied and subject states were in no way changed. But as the Empire, as the power of one man, became step by step more firmly established, the tendency was to break down the old distinctions. Particular families, and sometimes whole cities and regions, were admitted to the Roman franchise, till at last all the free inhabitants of the Empire were declared to be Roman citizens. From this time all the subjects of the Empire were legally equal, and all who spoke either Latin or Greek began to look on themselves as *Romans*. The Empire, which had once been a collection of cities and provinces in different degrees of subjection to one ruling city, gradually changed into a vast dominion, all the inhabitants of which were alike fellow-subjects of the Emperor. Rome, instead of being the ruling city, thus became merely the capital or seat of government. And we shall see that, as time went on, Rome ceased even to be the seat of government, and other cities took its place.

3. **The Reign of Augustus.**—Counting the reign of Augustus to begin when he received that new and special title, it lasted forty-one years, from B.C. 27 to A.D. 14. During all that time he was practically master of Rome and of the whole Empire. He be-

came so by the means of uniting various great offices in his own person, and by having special grants of authority made to him by the Senate for periods of ten years. Men thus became gradually used to the rule of one man, and, though all the old magistracies and the old forms went on, they gradually sank into mere forms. The legions were kept up as a standing army, and the government gradually became a military monarchy. Augustus however never took on himself anything of the pomp of royalty, but behaved simply as the first magistrate of the commonwealth. He did not seek to make any great conquests; still several wars, both successful and unsuccessful, were carried on during his reign. The small part of Spain which remained independent was subdued, and the lands between the Alps and the Danube were added to the Empire. There were also wars at this time which more concern us, for the two *Claudii*, the stepsons of Augustus, first *Drusus* and then *Tiberius*, waged long wars with the Germans beyond the Rhine, and it was hoped that Germany would be subdued as well as Gaul. Had this happened, the future history of the world must have been utterly changed. And everyone who speaks English or any other Teutonic tongue ought to honour the name of the German hero *Arminius*, who in A.D. 9 cut off three Roman legions under *Publius Quinctilius Varus*, and stopped all fear of Germany becoming a Roman province. Drusus had in some of his wars reached the Elbe, so that it is quite likely that he may have come across some of our own forefathers.

4. **Roman Literature and Art.**—The reign of Augustus is also famous as the time when many of the best-known Latin writers lived. There is nothing in the Latin language which at all answers to the native literature of Greece. Before the Punic wars we have only a few scraps. From that time the existing Latin literature begins. But the Latin writers, especially

the poets, were too much given to imitation of Greek models to produce anything at all equal to them. But there were many great Latin writers in the time of the Civil Wars, as Cicero and Cæsar, who were so famous in other ways, and the poets *Lucretius* and *Catullus*. But the *Augustan Age*, as it is called, became specially famous for the number of poets, such as the well-known names of *Virgil*, *Horace*, and *Ovid*, who lived at that time, and sang the praises of Augustus, and of their great patron, his minister *Caius Cilnius Mæcenas*. *Livy* also (*Titus Livius*), the historian of Rome, lived at this time. But both he and the greatest of the Augustan poets had grown up under the Commonwealth. Horace, for instance, (*Quintus Horatius Flaccus*), had fought against Augustus at Philippi, having been an officer in the army of Brutus and Cassius. The most truly original Latin writers, the satirist *Juvenal* and the historian *Tacitus*, to whom we may add the great Roman lawyers, belong to a later time. Of all branches of knowledge and literature, law is the only one in which the Romans were thoroughly original, and it is that by means of which they did most to influence other lands and times. The art of Rome is very like her literature. The Romans of the Augustan age imitated the Greeks in their buildings and in their works of art generally, and it was only gradually that a really genuine and national form of Roman architecture was worked out.

5. **The Claudian Emperors.**—As Rome was not legally a monarchy, it is plain that the supreme power could not pass at the will of the last Emperor. But the stepson of Augustus, *Tiberius Claudius Nero*, whom he had adopted, and who therefore became his son according to Roman law, succeeded without any difficulty, and the Senate voted him all the honours which Augustus had held. The Empire thus passed into a new family, that of the *Claudii*. But, according to the

law of adoption, they counted as *Cæsars*, and the Cæsars became a kind of artificial family, for no Emperor at this time was ever succeeded by his own son. Four Emperors reigned by this kind of succession, *Tiberius*, *Caius*, *Claudius*, and *Nero*. All of these were Cæsars by adoption, though not by blood, and Caius, Claudius, and Nero were really descended from Augustus in the female line. The first of these four, Tiberius, reigned from A.D. 14 to A.D. 37. The Empire was on the whole prosperous in his time; but he did many jealous and cruel things, causing the death of all of whom he was in any way afraid, especially of his nephew *Germanicus*, the son of Drusus, and Germanicus' wife, *Agrippina*. Germanicus took his name from his wars in Germany, where he advanced as far as the Weser, but he was happily called back by the jealousy of Tiberius. Caius, commonly called *Caligula*, the son of Germanicus, succeeded Tiberius, and reigned four years, from 37 to 41. He seems to have been quite mad, and did the wildest and wickedest things in every way, and at last he was killed by some of his officers. The soldiers then chose Claudius, the brother of Germanicus and uncle of Caius, and the Senate had to confirm their choice. This was the first time that an Emperor was chosen by the army. Claudius was a well-meaning man, but he was constantly led astray by his wives and favourites. It was in his time that the Roman conquest of Britain began, and Claudius himself went for a short time into Britain in the year 43. He reigned till 54, when he was poisoned by his last wife *Agrippina*, who was the daughter of Germanicus and his own niece. She had made him adopt her son *Nero*, who then succeeded, and reigned well for a while, but gradually became the worst of the whole family for every form of vice and cruelty. At last the soldiers in the distant provinces began to rebel, and Nero was deposed by a vote of the Senate, and died by his own hand in the year 68. The Empire now passed quite away from the Cæsarean family; those who followed no longer pretended to belong to that family, even by adoption; yet all who succeeded to the Empire still went on calling themselves *Cæsar* and *Augustus* to the very end.

6. **The Flavian Emperors.**—A time of confusion followed on the death of Nero. The armies in various parts of the Empire chose their own generals to be Emperors, and several of them obtained possession of Rome, and were acknowledged by the Senate and People for a little while. Thus *Galba*, *Otho*, *Vitellius*, succeeded one another very quickly, each reigning a little time and then being killed. At last, in the year 70, a more permanent power was established by *Titus Flavius Vespasianus*, who kept the Empire till his own death in 79, and was succeeded by his sons *Titus* and *Domitian* in succession, the first time that an Emperor had been succeeded by his own son. Vespasian made a much better ruler than any of the Emperors who had gone before him, and a long time of comparative peace and good government now began. In Vespasian's time the *Jews*, who had rebelled in the time of Nero, were subdued by his son Titus, and *Jerusalem* was destroyed. And during the times of confusion, the *Batavians*, a people near the mouth of the Rhine, very nearly akin to ourselves, had revolted and tried to set up an empire of their own in Gaul. This movement too was put down about the same time as that of the Jews, The power of Vespasian and his family was now firmly established, but it is to be noticed that the *Flavian* Emperors did not, like the Julian and Claudian, spring from any of the great and ancient families of Rome. This is a sign of the way in which old distinctions were breaking down. Titus reigned but two years after the death of his father; he was called the *Delight of Mankind*, but his brother Domitian, who succeeded

him, and who professed to be a careful and severe assertor of the laws, gradually became as great a tyrant as any of the Claudii. In his time the conquest of Britain was completed by *Agricola*, and Rome found a new enemy to strive against in the *Dacians* beyond the Danube. Domitian was killed in 96, and the Flavian dynasty ended with him.

7. **The Good Emperors.**—We now come to a time which in some sort continues the Flavian dynasty. The Roman world had now got thoroughly used to the rule of a single man, and there can be no doubt that the provinces were better off under the rule of the Emperors than they had been under the Commonwealth. And, from the accession of Vespasian onwards, there was a great feeling in favour of legal and regular government, of strict observance of the law and of respect for the authority of the Senate. It was about this time that Law began to be a matter of special study, and that the great Roman lawyers began to put together that system of Roman Law known as the *Civil Law*, which has been the groundwork of the law of most parts of Western Europe except England. Several famous writers, both in Greek and Latin, flourished at this time, especially the great historian *Tacitus*. The Emperors of this time, who are often called specially *the Good Emperors*, formed a kind of artificial family, like that of the first Cæsars, each man being succeeded, not by his real son, but by one whom he had adopted. Five thus reigned in order, *Nerva* from 96 to 98, *Trajan* from 98 to 117, *Hadrian* from 117 to 138, *Antoninus Pius* from 138 to 181, and *Marcus Aurelius* from 161 to 180. Of these Trajan was the first Emperor who was born out of Italy, being a native of Spain. It was in his time that the Empire reached its greatest extent. He had wars with the Parthians, from whom he won several provinces in the East, so that for a moment the Empire reached the Caspian Sea. But this was only for a moment, for these

Eastern conquests were at once given up by Trajan's successor Hadrian. And in Europe also Trajan won the province of *Dacia* beyond the Danube. But this too, though it was kept longer than the conquests in the East, was not a really lasting possession. From this time the Romans made no more great conquests, for they commonly found that they had enough to do to defend their own frontiers. Thus Marcus had to wage wars with the Germans along the Danube. He was a philosopher, who left some excellent moral writings behind him. With him the time of the Good Emperors ended. For he was succeeded by *Commodus*, who was his own son, and not merely a son by adoption. He was the first Emperor who was born during the reign of his father. But he proved very unlike his father, being, for vice and cruelty, one of the worst princes that ever reigned, and was at last murdered in 192.

8. **Emperors chosen by the Army.**—A time now followed, lasting for nearly a hundred years, from 192 to 285, during which there is no need to go through all the Emperors by name. Many of them reigned only a very short time. The soldiers set up and slew Emperors as they chose, and the Senate was obliged to make the usual votes in favour of those who were thus set up. It was quite a rare thing for the Empire to pass from father to son, or by fair election by the Senate, or in any other peaceful and lawful way. For a little while there was an attempt to keep up a dynasty or succession of Emperors in the same family, or at least in the same name; for *Septimius Severus*, who reigned from 193 to 211, and his sons called themselves *Antoninus*, though it does not seem that they were descended from, or even adopted by, any of the Emperors of that name. Under Severus the government became still more military than it had been before. He was succeeded by his wicked son *Antoninus*, who was commonly called *Caracalla*.

And, after he was murdered in 217, two Syrian youths, *Elagabalus* and *Alexander Severus*, who were said to be Caracalla's sons, were set up in succession, who both took the names of Aurelius and Antoninus. Of these Elagabalus was one of the worst, and Alexander one of the best, of the Emperors. In the time of Caracalla the old distinctions of *Romans*, *Latins*, *Italians*, and *Provincials* were quite wiped out. Roman citizenship was now given to all the free inhabitants of the Empire, so that a man in Britain or Greece or anywhere else called himself a *Roman*, as in the East men have done ever since. It therefore happened that many of the best and bravest Emperors, especially towards the end of this time, were what would before have been called *Barbarians*. That word now meant those who were altogether outside the Empire. Many of the best of these later Emperors came from *Illyria*. *Decius*, *Claudius*, *Aurelian*, and others, brave and wise men who rose by their merits, followed one another in swift succession, and had much fighting with the different enemies of Rome. At last one of the greatest of their number made a complete change in the constitution of the Empire, which we must presently speak of.

9. **The Tyrants.**—While Emperors were thus set up and put down by the soldiers, it often happened that there were several Emperors or claimants of the Empire at once; that is to say, the armies in different parts of the Empire had each set up its own general to be Emperor. And towards the end of this period it often happened that one of these pretenders contrived to keep some part of the Empire for several years, so that there were Emperors reigning in Gaul or Britain or some other province or provinces only. But these local Emperors must not be mistaken for national rulers of the provinces where they reigned; they claimed to be Roman Emperors, and they of course aimed at getting the whole Empire, if they

could. Sometimes the reigning Emperor found it convenient to acknowledge them as colleagues; if they were unsuccessful, they were called *Tyrants*. As in old Greece a Tyrant had meant a man who unlawfully seized on kingly power in a commonwealth, so now it meant a man who called himself Emperor, but who was held not to have a lawful right to the title. In the time of *Gallienus*, who reigned from 260 to 268, the whole Empire was split to pieces among various pretenders of this kind. One of these should be specially noticed, because it is the only case among all these divisions of anything like a real national state being founded. This was at *Palmyra* in Syria, where one *Odenathus* was acknowledged as Emperor, and after him his wife *Zênobia*, one of the most wonderful women in history, reigned as *Queen of the East.* But this new kingdom was put down by *Aurelian*, one of the ablest of the Illyrian Emperors, in 271.

10. **Wars with the Persians and Germans.**—We have seen that a new state of things begins after the reign of Trajan, for from that time the Romans had to fight, not as in former times to make new conquests, but to keep what they had got already. The wars went on along the Eastern frontier, with the Parthians as long as their power lasted, and after that with a new enemy who stepped into their place. These were the real old *Persians*, who had been kept in bondage ever since the time of Alexander, but who rose up about the year 226 and founded a new Persian kingdom. Their first king was *Ardeshir* or *Artaxerxes*, whose descendants, called the *Sassanidæ*, ruled over Persia more than four hundred years. Many of the Emperors had to wage war with the Persians, and among them *Alexander Severus* and *Valerian*, the father of Gallienus, who reigned from 253 to 260. He was taken prisoner by the Persians, and died in captivity. At a later time the Romans gained territory from the Persians and then lost it again, and so things went on for some

ages; Rome and Persia were always fighting and making small conquests from one another, but, till a much later time, neither dealt any real blow at the main strength of the other. But the wars which the Romans had to wage in the West were of quite another kind. They have a more special interest for us, because they were wars with our own kinsfolk, and they also mark one of the greatest stages in the history of the world. For it was now that the race came to the front which was to take the place which had been held, first by the Greeks and then by the Romans, as the leading race of the world. From the time of Marcus Aurelius onwards the Teutonic nations began really to threaten the Empire. The chief business of the Roman armies now was to drive the Germans back; and, if they made any conquests, it was now merely winning back lands which had been lost. We now first hear of the famous nation of the *Goths*, a people whose speech was very nearly akin to our own, and also of the *Franks*, whose name has in later history been more famous still. The great Illyrian Emperors had much to do in fighting both with the Persians and with the Goths and other Teutonic people. And *Claudius*, who reigned before Aurelian from 268 to 270, won a great victory over the Goths, who for some time afterwards kept more quiet. But Aurelian thought it wise to give up Trajan's province of Dacia, so that the Danube again became the boundary. We now come to a time of great changes in the internal state of the Empire.

11. **The Growth of Christianity.**—All this while, almost from the very beginning of the Empire, a new religion had been growing up in the world. Our Lord Jesus Christ was born in the reign of Augustus and was crucified in the reign of Tiberius. Ever since that time Christianity had been gradually preached in most parts of the Empire, and the Christians were now a large and important body. The Christians were often cruelly persecuted, but it should be carefully

noticed that, as a rule, it was not the worst Emperors who most persecuted them. The truth is that the heathen religion of ancient Rome was looked on as part of the constitution of the state. Other Gods might be worshipped, if only the old Gods did not lose their worship; but a religion which taught that the Gods of Rome and of all other nations were alike false, and which strove to win over all mankind to that belief, was looked on as dangerous to the Empire. Those Emperors therefore who were most zealous to keep up the old laws and customs of Rome were commonly the most anxious to put down the new faith, and we therefore find that the Christians really suffered most under good and reforming princes like Trajan and Marcus Aurelius. Still the Church constantly advanced and made converts, for men had now but little real faith in the old Gods, and their worship was mainly kept up as a matter of state policy. And Christianity also had no small influence even on those who did not accept it as a religion. A higher standard of morals and higher notions of the divine nature became common even among the heathens, and many a philosopher who professed to hate and despise Christianity was a better man for Christianity having been preached. At last it became plain that a deadly struggle must come between the old faith and the new. Those who held that the greatness and glory of Rome were bound up with the worship of the old Gods of Rome saw that the time was come when a stand must be made. The Christians were now grown so powerful that several of the later Emperors, especially *Decius* and *Valerian*, looked on them as dangerous to the state, and severe persecutions went on during their reigns. After that time, there was a lull; the Christians were not molested for a long time, and their doctrine spread among all classes of people everywhere. At last, at the time which we have now reached, among many important changes, came the last and greatest persecution.

12. Diocletian and his Successors.—During this time the notion of the Roman Commonwealth, the forms of which had been so carefully kept up under the earlier Emperors, had almost wholly died out. The Empire had become a military monarchy, in which the power of the prince rested mainly on the support of his soldiers. And another change gradually happened. All the inhabitants of the Empire were now equally Romans, and the Emperors had to move about wherever the needs of constant warfare called them. Italy therefore ceased to be any longer distinguished from the rest of the Empire, and even the importance of Rome itself, as the centre of the Empire, was greatly lessened. These great changes, which had already taken place in fact, were now formally acknowledged. In the year 284 the Empire fell to *Diocletian*, another of the able Illyrians of whom so many had risen to the throne. He began quite a new order of things. There were to be two Emperors, with the title of *Augustus*, reigning as colleagues, with two *Cæsars* under them. Speaking roughly, this fourfold division answered to *Italy* itself and the neighbouring countries, the *Western provinces* (Gaul, Spain, and Britain), the *Greek*, and the *Oriental* provinces. Many of the forms of royalty which had been unheard of before were now brought into use, though even now no Roman prince dared to take the title of *King*, and the Senate and Consuls still went on in name. But Rome was now quite forsaken as a dwelling-place of the Emperors, who found it better to live near the frontiers, whence they could keep watch against the Persians, Germans, and other enemies of the Empire. Thus Diocletian and his colleague *Maximian* lived respectively at *Nikomêdeia* in Asia and at *Milan*, while one of the *Cæsars* was commonly placed in Gaul or Britain, at *Trier* or at *York*. In 303 Diocletian abdicated, and made his colleague Maximian abdicate also. But towards the end of their reign they put forth a series of cruel edicts against the Christians, and the heaviest of all the persecutions now took place. But the Church lived through all attempts to destroy it, and its greatest worldly success followed soon after this great persecution. The system of Augusti with Cæsars under them was not regularly kept up for any long time. A series of civil wars followed, till at last the whole Empire was joined together again in the hands of *Constantine* called *the Great.* He began to reign at York in 306 ; after that he reigned at Trier, till he obtained the whole Empire in 323 and kept it till his death in 337. He was the first Emperor who acknowledged himself a Christian, and other important changes were made in his time, which will be spoken of in the next chapter.

13. **Summary.**—We have thus gone through the history of heathen Rome both under the Commonwealth and under the Empire. It began as a single city ; it gradually gained the dominion, first over Italy, and then over all the lands round the Mediterranean Sea, and it gradually admitted its subjects and allies to its own citizenship. When the government of a single city became quite unable to act as the government of the whole civilized world, all power gradually came into the hands of one man, and the practical holding of all power by one man gradually changed the state into an avowed monarchy. Then, when all the inhabitants of the Empire were alike Romans, the city of Rome became, as it were, lost in the Roman Empire, and other cities began to be seats of government. At the same time new enemies, namely our own kinsfolk, were beginning to threaten the Empire, and a new religion, that which we ourselves believe, was beginning to supplant the old religion of Rome. We have thus come to a time of very great and speedy change, and to the first beginnings of the state of things which still goes on in modern Europe. There is in some things a greater change between the first Emperors and the Emperors after Constantine than there was between the old Kings of Rome and the first Emperors.

CHAPTER V.

THE EARLY CHRISTIAN EMPIRE.

History of Constantine; his changes in the government of the Empire (1)—*he fixes his capital at Constantinople or New Rome* (1)—*reigns of Constantius and Julian* (1)—*establishment of Christianity; disputes and Councils in the Church* (2)—*forms assumed by Christianity in different parts of the Empire* (2)—*revival of paganism under Julian; its final extinction* (2)—*Teutonic settlements within the Empire* (3)—*movements of the Goths; defeat and death of Valens* (4)—*reigns of Theodosius and his sons* (4)—*Rome taken by Alaric* (4)—*foundation of the Gothic kingdom in Spain* (4)—*invasion of Attila* (5)—*later Emperors in the West; the two Empires nominally reunited; rule of Odoacer in Italy* (5)—*settlements of the Burgundians and Franks in Gaul; reign and conquests of Chlodwig* (6)—*settlement of the Vandals in Africa* (7)—*reign of Theodoric in Italy* (7)—*intermixture of Romans and Teutons; origin of the Romance nations* (8)—*growth of the Romance languages* (9)—*distinctions of High and Low Dutch* (10)—*the English conquest of Britain; its differences from the other Teutonic settlements* (11).

1. **Constantine and his Family.**—The changes which were wrought by Constantine made him one of the most famous of all the Emperors. He was the son of *Constantius*, who had reigned under Diocletian and Maximian in Britain, Spain, and Gaul, and who, though not a Christian himself, had, out of justice and humanity, done what he could to protect the Christians. Constantine himself for a long time did the same. He protected the Christians, but he did not profess their religion till the last civil war in 323, which gave him possession of the whole Empire. He presently made a change which had a great effect upon the later history of the Empire. Rome, as we have seen, had

ceased to be the usual dwelling-place of the Emperors. Constantine now fixed the capital of the Empire in the old Greek city of *Byzantion* on the Bosporos, which he greatly enlarged and called *New Rome*, but which has ever since been better known as *Constantinople* or the *City of Constantine.* From this time, whatever changes and divisions there were, Constantinople remained the capital of the whole Empire when it was united, and of the Eastern part when it was divided. The chief power was thus placed in a city which was Christian from what we may call its new birth, and which had none of the heathen associations of the Old Rome. And, as Constantinople was in its origin a Greek city, it soon again became, though it was the capital of the Roman Empire, a city more Greek than Roman, and it gradually took the place of Antioch and Alexandria as the chief seat of Greek culture and learning. Constantine too in his new capital was able to set more fully in order the despotic system of government which had been brought in by Diocletian. From this time, though the Senate and the Consuls still went on, we may look on the Empire as being an absolute monarchy in form as well as in fact. And moreover Constantine not only reigned longer than any Emperor since Augustus, but he established his power so firmly that the Empire lasted in his family as long as any of his family were left. But they were mostly cut off by their own kinsfolk. Constantine divided his dominions among his three sons, but at last, in 353, the Empire was again united in his son *Constantius*, who reigned at Constantinople till 361. There were several revolts and rival Emperors in his time, as well as many disputes in the Church, and unsuccessful wars with the Germans and Persians. But his cousin *Julian*, who was *Cæsar* under him in the West, drove the Germans out of Gaul, and thus made himself a great name. At last his soldiers proclaimed him *Augustus*, and, as Constantius died soon after

Julian got possession of the whole Empire without much trouble. But his reign did not last long, as in 363 he died in war against the Persians, and the family of Constantine ended with him.

2. **The Establishment of Christianity.**—When Constantine embraced Christianity, the long struggle between the Church and the power of heathen Rome came to an end. The Church conquered the Empire. Not only did the Empire become Christian, but Christianity became in a special way the religion of the Empire. Christianity has hardly anywhere taken firm and lasting root, except in those countries which either formed part of the Roman Empire or learned their religion and civilization from it, and from this time the history of the Church and of the Empire go together. Constantine, as was often done at that time, put off his baptism till just before his death. Yet he acted throughout as the chief ruler of the Church; and when *Arius*, a priest of Alexandria, put forth new doctrines as to the more mysterious points of Christian belief, it was by the Emperor's authority that a Council of Bishops was gathered together at *Nikaia* in Bithynia in 325. This is commonly called the *Council of Nice*, and here the *Nicene Creed* was drawn up. This was the first of what are called the *General Councils* of the Church, several of which were held in this and the next century. For men were at this time constantly disputing about the deepest doctrines of the Christian religion, and each *heresy*, that is, each new and strange kind of teaching, commonly called for a Council to settle the dispute. The truth is that the despotic system of the Empire had so thoroughly crushed men's minds in all political matters that it was only on points of religion that there was any free play of thought at all. Moreover, while Christianity is essentially the religion of the Roman Empire, different forms of Christianity took their firmest root in different parts of the Empire, accord-

ing to the character and turn of mind of the people. Thus in the West, where Latin was spoken, men thought less about subtle points of doctrine; but we shall see that, before long, Rome again became the ruling and Imperial city in ecclesiastical matters, as she had once been in temporal dominion. Meanwhile, in the Greek-speaking provinces men's minds were more given to hard questions of doctrine. As the Greeks had in old times produced so many subtle philosophers, so they now produced equally subtle divines. And in the further East, in Syria and Egypt, in the lands which had never thoroughly become either Greek or Roman, men fell off into doctrines which both Greeks and Latins thought heretical. This was the only way that was left to them of asserting their national independence. Thus the whole Empire gradually embraced Christianity; but Christianity took different shapes in different parts, and there were long disputings on various points of doctrine, and of course men did not become Christians of any kind all at once. Many still clave to the old heathen worship, especially what we may call the two ends of mankind, that is to say, the philosophers who trusted in their own wisdom, and the rude peasantry in the country-places. For Christianity was everywhere preached first in the towns; hence it came that the word *paganus*, which at first simply meant a *countryman*, came to mean a *pagan* or heathen or worshipper of false Gods. Still, from the time that Constantine professed himself a Christian, Christianity grew and paganism went back, though it cannot be doubted that the spread of Christianity was greatly hindered by the endless disputes in the Church. Constantius favoured the Arians, and, after his death, paganism got a new start for a moment. For Julian, though he had been brought up as Christian, and though in his own life he was one of the best of all the Emperors, fell back again to the worship of the old Gods. But all the Emperors after him were Christians, and by the end of the fourth century after Christ, the Christians were, to say the least, the great majority in most parts of the Empire. Under the Emperors *Gratian* and *Theodosius*, who reigned between them from 367 to 395, the public profession of paganism was quite put an end to.

3. **The Teutonic Invasions.**—We have now come to the time when the nations of our own race began to make their way into the Empire. We have seen that the different *German* tribes had been most dangerous enemies of Rome ever since the time of Augustus, and that many of the most valiant Emperors had much ado to defend the Empire against them. So it was still; Constantine and Julian had to fight hard against the Germans, and so had *Valentinian*, the next Emperor but one after Julian. But in all these wars, though the Germans were constantly driven back, yet they grew stronger and stronger, while the Romans grew weaker and weaker. Some of the Germans made their way into the Empire in arms: others took service in the Roman armies, and often received grants of land as their reward. In both ways they learned something of Roman civilization and Roman military discipline, without losing anything of their own strength and courage. Presently it became not uncommon for a Gothic or other Teutonic chief to be at once King of his own people and to bear some title as a Roman general or magistrate. In such cases he and his people served the Emperors or fought against them, pretty much as they thought good, or according as they were well or ill treated. And at the same time they learned something of the religion of Rome, so that most of the Teutonic nations became Christians, before they settled in the Empire or very soon after. But it was for the most part in its Arian form that they embraced Christianity. Thus we find *Barbarians*, who for the most part however were

Christians, settled within the Empire; and before long they began to occupy whole provinces. We have now come to the time when the Teutonic settlements and conquests become the most important facts in history. It often happens that the migrations and victories of one nation are caused by some other nation pressing upon it. And so it happened now. The movements of the Teutonic nations into the Roman Empire which had already begun was greatly hastened and strengthened by the pressure of Turanian tribes who were pushing their way from the East. The chief of these were the *Huns*, who had been themselves driven out of *China* in the extreme east of Asia, and who were now making their way into Europe. Though the Huns did not themselves enter the Empire till long afterwards, and though they never actually settled within it at any time, yet this migration of theirs had a most important effect on the state of the Empire, by the stir which it caused among the Teutonic nations.

4. **The Goths.**—The first Teutonic people whom the Huns met were the Goths, who had lately formed a great kingdom in the land north of the Danube, which had been Trajan's province of Dacia, but from which the Romans had withdrawn under Aurelian. They were beginning to become Christians of the Arian sect, under the teaching of a Bishop named *Wulfila* or *Ulfilas*, whose translation of the Scriptures into the Gothic tongue is the oldest Teutonic writing that we have. The Huns now came upon them like a storm; some of the Goths submitted to the new invaders, while others were allowed to cross the Danube and settle within the Empire. This was in 376. The first Valentinian was now dead: the reigning Emperors were his brother *Valens* in the East and his sons *Gratian* and *Valentinian* in the West. The Goths were so ill-treated by the officers of Valens that they took to arms; a battle was fought near *Hadrianople*

in 378, in which Valens was killed. After this the Goths were never driven out of the Empire, though many of them took service in the Roman armies. But strangely enough, when the Goths came to found a lasting kingdom, it was not in the eastern part of the Empire into which they had first passed, but quite away in the West. This was a most wretched time for the Empire; for, besides the movements of the Barbarians, various Emperors or Tyrants rose and fell in different provinces, especially in Gaul and Britain. Things went on a little better during the reign of *Theodosius*, who is called *the Great*, and who reigned, first as a colleague of the sons of Valentinian, and afterwards alone, from 379 to 395. Theodosius is famous for the penance to which he submitted at the hands of Saint *Ambrose*, the Archbishop of Milan, who refused him admittance to the church till he had repented of a massacre which he had ordered among the turbulent people of *Thessalonica*. Theodosius was the last Emperor who reigned over the whole Empire before it was divided and dismembered; as soon as he died it began to fall in pieces. He left two sons, of whom *Honorius* reigned in the West, and *Arcadius* in the East. The *West-Goths*, under their famous king *Alaric*, presently revolted, and, though they were kept in check for a while by the Roman general *Stilicho*, at last, in 410, they took and sacked Rome, which had never been taken by a foreign enemy since the time of Brennus the Gaul. Alaric died soon after, and the next Gothic King *Athaulf* made a treaty with the Empire and passed into Gaul and Spain. German tribes of all kinds were now pressing into Gaul, and from Gaul into Spain, and rival Emperors were rising and falling. Athaulf went in name as a Roman officer to restore the province of Spain to the Empire. In reality this was the beginning of an independent Gothic kingdom in Spain and southern Gaul, and the way in which this kingdom began is a good example of the way in which the Roman Empire, its laws and titles, still exercised a powerful influence on the minds of those who were really its conquerors.

5. **End of the Emperors in Italy.**—Meanwhile the Western Empire was being cut short in all quarters by the settlements of the *Franks*, *Burgundians*, *Vandals*, and other Teutonic tribes in the different provinces, settlements which we shall speak of again presently. No Teutonic kingdoms were founded in the East; but, while the Western provinces were falling off one by one, the East had much ado to hold up against the attacks of the Persians. Presently the Romans of both Empires, and the Goths and other Teutons who had settled within the Empire, were all threatened by the Turanian hordes under the famous *Attila*, King of the Huns. He went on for a while ravaging and conquering far and wide, till at last he was defeated in the great battle of *Châlons* in 451 by the united powers of Romans, Goths, and Franks. This was one of the most important battles in the history of the world; it was a struggle for life and death between the Aryan and Turanian races, and Christianity and civilization, and all that distinguishes Europe from Asia and Africa, were at stake. The names therefore of *Aetius*, the Roman general, and of the West-Gothic King *Theodoric* who died in the battle, are names which should always be held in honour. It is needless to go through the names of all the Emperors of this time: the only one in the West who is worth remembering on his own account is *Majorian*, a wise and brave man, who reigned from 457 to 461. At last, in 476, the succession of the Western Emperors came to an end, and the way in which it came to an end marks the way in which the names and titles of Rome were kept on, while all power was passing into the hands of the Barbarians. The Roman Senate voted that one Emperor was enough,

and that the Eastern Emperor *Zeno* should reign over the whole Empire. But at the same time Zeno was made to intrust the government of Italy, with the title of *Patrician*, to *Odoacer*, the chief of the German mercenaries in the service of the Western Empire. Thus the Roman Empire went on at Constantinople or New Rome, while Italy and the Old Rome itself passed into the power of the Barbarians. Still the Roman laws and names went on, and we may be sure that any man in Italy would have been much surprised if he had been told that the Roman Empire had come to an end. We shall presently see what important events came of this long keeping on of the old Roman names and feelings.

6. **Settlements of the Burgundians and Franks.**—It was through these settlements of the Teutonic tribes within the Roman Empire that several of the chief nations of modern Europe arose. We may perhaps call the Spanish kingdom of the West-Goths, of which we have already spoken, and which began about 414, the first of the kingdoms of modern Europe, the first which arose out of the breaking up of the Roman Empire. For some while it was not merely a Spanish kingdom, for it took in all *Aquitaine* or Gaul south of the Loire, and the capital of the West-Gothic kings was at *Toulouse*. Meanwhile the *Burgundians* and *Franks*, whose names are so famous in later history, began to settle, at first under a nominal subjection to the Empire, in other parts of Gaul. The Burgundians settled in the south-eastern part of Gaul, where their name has lived on in several kingdoms and duchies. And, towards the end of the fifth century, the kingdom of the Franks took firm root in Gaul under their King *Chlodwig* or *Clovis*—the same name which was afterwards written *Ludwig*, *Louis*, and *Lewis*—who reigned from 481 to 511. He became a Christian, and not only a Christian but a Catholic, which greatly favoured his con-

quests, as all the other Teutonic Kings were Arians. The dominions of the Franks now took in part of their old country in Germany and also their conquests in Gaul. And they have given their name to parts of both countries; for part of Germany is still called *Franken* or *Franconia*, and part of Gaul is still called *France*. In Latin both names are the same, *Francia*. But the Franks gradually spread their conquests over a much larger part both of Gaul and of Germany, bringing the different nations of both lands into more or less of subjection to them. Thus in Gaul they conquered the kingdom of the Burgundians and won Aquitaine from the West-Goths, leaving to them only a small part of Gaul on the coast of the Mediterranean. But it was only in Northern Gaul that the Franks really settled. It was out of these settlements of the West-Goths, Franks, and Burgundians that all the modern states of Germany, Gaul, and Spain have arisen.

7. **The Vandals and the East-Goths.**—But there were other Teutonic settlements in the Empire which did not in this way give birth to modern states and nations, because the Emperors were, as we shall presently see, able to join them again to the Empire. Among these were what we may call the worst and the best of the Teutonic settlements, those namely of the *Vandals* in Africa and of the *East-Goths* in Italy. The Vandals were for some time settled in Spain, but in 429 they crossed over into Africa and founded a kingdom of which *Carthage* was the capital. The Vandals were Arians, and they cruelly persecuted the Catholic Romans whom they found in the country, and this seems to have been one reason among others why their kingdom did not last. The kingdom of the East-Goths in Italy was very different. Their King *Theodoric* entered Italy in 489 by a commission from the Emperor Zeno, overthrew Odoacer, and reigned himself from 493 to 526. But, though he

reigned in Italy, he was never called King of Italy, but only King of his own Goths. Though he was an Arian, he in no way persecuted the Catholics, and he let the Romans keep their own laws and all that they were used to. Every year he named one of the Consuls, while the other was named by the Emperor at Constantinople. Italy under Theodoric was the most peaceful and flourishing country in the world, more peaceful and flourishing than it had been for a long time before or than it has ever been since till quite lately. The dominions of Theodoric stretched far beyond Italy to the north, east, and west, and he ruled the West-Gothic kingdom in Gaul and Spain as guardian for his grandson. But this great dominion of the East-Goths did not last any more than that of the Vandals in Africa, and none of the modern states or nations of Europe can be said to spring from either of them.

8. **Origin of the Romance Nations.**—We thus see that new states arose out of the settlements of the Teutonic nations in the western provinces of the Empire. And we may say that not only new states arose, but also new nations. For, out of the mixture of the Roman inhabitants and the Teutonic settlers, there arose a new state of things, which was neither Roman nor Teutonic, but a mixture of the two. The Goths and the other Teutons who settled in Italy, Spain, and Gaul were by no means mere destroyers who swept everything before them. They let the Romans keep their own laws and language and part of their lands. And in Spain and Gaul those nations, like the Goths and Burgundians, which had been converted by Arian Bishops gradually came over to the Catholic faith. Moreover, as the Romans had all the learning and civilization on their side, the clergy were for a long time almost always Romans, and they kept the property and influence which they had before, and indeed added to it. Thus the two nations were

gradually mixed together; and the conquerors, as being the smaller in number, gradually came to adopt a great deal of the laws and manners, and especially the language, of the conquered. Thus there arose the modern *Spanish* and *Italian* nations, and the two nations of Gaul, the people of *Provence and Aquitaine* south of the Loire and the *French* to the north. But of the languages which were thus formed we must speak a little more fully.

9. **Origin of the Romance Languages.**—By the time the Teutonic settlements in Western Europe took place, *Latin* had become the common speech of Gaul and Spain no less than of Italy. The old languages which were spoken before the Romans came lived on only in a few out-of-the-way corners, like the country of the Basques. The language therefore which the Teutonic settlers found prevailing, and which they had to learn in order to get on with the people of the provinces, was Latin. That is to say, it was such Latin as was spoken at the time, which of course was not quite the same as the Latin of the great Roman writers of earlier times, and the language no doubt differed more or less in different provinces. And, as the Germans learned to speak Latin, the language naturally became still more corrupted, and a good many German words crept into it. Thus the common language of Italy, Gaul, and Spain became a kind of corrupt Latin, which men used in common speech; in writing they used fairly good Latin for ages after. No one thought of writing in the common speech, which began to be called *Roman*, in distinction from the *Latin* which men wrote. Thus, out of the various dialects of this *Roman* language, several of the chief languages of modern Europe very gradually arose. These are those which are called the Romance languages, those namely which have their origin in Latin. The chief of these are *Italian* and *Spanish* in their different dialects, *Provençal* in

Southern, and *French* in Northern, Gaul. These languages had their beginning at the time of which we are now speaking, but it was not until long afterwards that men began to understand that quite new languages had really grown up. And, besides these four great Romance languages, a fifth, distinct from any of them, which is still specially called *Romansch*, is spoken in the eastern parts of Switzerland, in what was anciently the Roman province of *Rœtia*. And, stranger still, in the lands which formed the province of Dacia, which the Romans held only from the time of Trajan to that of Aurelian, a Romance language is still spoken, and the people still call themselves *Roumans*. Of the fourth great Latin-speaking country, Africa, we have nothing to say in this way, for, as we go on, we shall see how in Africa everything Roman and everything Teutonic was utterly swept away.

10. **High and Low Dutch.**—Such was the way in which the Teutonic nations established themselves in the western provinces of the Continent. Meanwhile other Teutonic settlements of quite another kind, and made by another branch of the Teutonic race, were going on elsewhere. This is a good place to stop and explain that there are two great divisions of the *Teutonic* or *Dutch* people, the *High* and the *Low*. It must always be remembered that, though we now commonly use the word *Dutch* to mean only the people of Holland, yet the word is always used in German, and was formerly used in English, to mean the whole of the German people. And, as the Germans called their own speech *Thiotisc*, *Deutsch*, or *Dutch*, meaning the language which could be understood, those people whose language could not be understood were called *Welsh* or strangers. The *High-Dutch* are those who live inland, in the south of Germany away from the sea, while the *Low* are those who live near the sea, by the mouths of the great rivers Rhine, Weser, and Elbe. Into the greater part of their country the Romans had

never come since the days of Drusus and Germanicus, and for a long time they knew very little of the Romans, and the Romans knew very little of them. They had not served in the Roman armies, and they knew nothing about the Christian religion. They were therefore in quite a different state from the other tribes who had made their way into the continental provinces; for these last knew something of the civilization and religion of Rome, even before they entered the Roman dominions. Of the earlier Teutonic settlers the greater part belonged to the High-Dutch division, though the language of the Goths had much more in common with the Low. But, though the Low-Dutch and Gothic languages are thus closely connected, yet the settlements of the Goths have historically nothing to do with the settlements of the Low-Dutch. Those Low-Dutch settlements which have had most effect on the history of the world, and in which we have the deepest interest, were made in quite another part of the Empire, and in quite another way. The settlements of the Goths and Franks were mainly made by land, while the great settlement of the Low-Dutch tribes was made by sea.

11. **The English Conquest of Britain.**—We have seen that in the island of *Britain*, of which the greater part became a Roman province in the time of Agricola, the Romans found a Celtic people, the *Britons*. But in the north of the island, and in the other great island of *Ireland*, there was another Celtic people, the *Scots* or *Irish*. The Romans never even tried to conquer Ireland, and they never conquered the whole of Britain. The northern part of what is now called *Scotland* always remained free. In the rest of the island the Britons were conquered, and the land became a Roman province. But in the fourth century, when the power of Rome began to get weaker, the free Celts in the northern part of the island, the *Picts* and *Scots*, began to pour into the Roman pro-

vince, and other enemies began to invade the land from the east by sea. These last were no other than the forefathers of the *English* of to-day. For the *English* people belong to the Low-Dutch stock, and entered Britain from the old Low-Dutch lands by the Elbe and the Weser. It was in the latter part of the fourth century that these Low-Dutch tribes, and, first among them, the *Saxons*, began to make attacks on Britain by sea. The Saxons are also heard of as pressing into Gaul by land, and they even made one or two small settlements there; but their attacks on Britain by sea were those which led to the greatest results. The first great Saxon invasion was in the time of Valentinian, but it was driven back by *Theodosius*, father of the Emperor of that name. But when the Roman power began altogether to give way in the reign of Honorius, the Roman troops were withdrawn from Britain, about the year 410, and the island was left to shift for itself. The Teutonic invasions now naturally began again, and now it was that the invaders began to settle in the land. No doubt men of many different Low-Dutch tribes joined in these expeditions; but there were three tribes which stood out above the others. These were the *Angles*, the *Saxons*, and the *Jutes*. The Celts, the Britons and Scots, have always called Englishmen *Saxons*, most likely because it was the Saxons who made the first attack in Valentinian's time. But, as soon as the different Teutonic tribes in Britain began to join together into one people, the name by which they called themselves was *Angles* or *English*, and the land was called *Anglia* or *England*. Thus it was that the English people went from their old homes on the mainland, and won for themselves new homes in the isle of Britain. They knew nothing and cared nothing for the laws or language or arts of Rome. They did not, like the Goths and Franks, adopt the language and religion of the Romans; they swept everything before them, and the Britons were either killed, or made slaves, or took refuge in the western parts of the island. The Germans everywhere called the people of the Roman provinces, whose tongue they did not understand, *Welsh*, and that word in German is still applied to the French and Italians. But in Britain of course the name meant the Britons; they were called, and are still called the *Welsh*, and the part of the island which they still keep is called *Wales*. The first English kingdom founded in Britain was that of *Kent*, a kingdom of the Jutes, founded in 449, two years before Aetius and Theodoric overthrew Attila at Châlons. Presently other kingdoms, Anglian and Saxon, were founded, and, in a little more than a hundred years, the greater part of that land which had been the Roman and Christian province of *Britain* had become the heathen land of the *Angles* and *Saxons*. Thus it was that the *English* people settled in the land which thus became *England*, settling in quite another way from that in which the other Teutonic nations had settled in the other parts of the Empire. Our forefathers kept their own language and their own religion. The other Teutons did not become Christians till about a hundred and fifty years after the English Conquest began, and then they were not converted by those whom they had conquered. But the tongue which we still speak, though, like other tongues, it has gone through many changes, is still in its main substance the old Teutonic speech of our fathers.

12. **Summary.**—Thus, in the course of the fourth and fifth centuries, the Roman Empire gradually became Christian. The capital was moved to *Constantinople*, and, when the Empire was divided, Constantinople always remained the capital of the Eastern part. Meanwhile the *Goths*, *Franks*, and other Teutonic nations pressed into the Empire, and out of their settlements the *Romance* nations of modern Europe arose. The invasion of the *Huns* was driven back by

the united powers of Romans and Teutons. The series of Emperors in the West came to an end, and the Empire was nominally reunited, *Theodoric* the Goth reigning in *Italy*. Meanwhile the *Low-Dutch* tribes, the *Angles* and *Saxons*, were settling in *Britain*, and making the beginning of the *English* nation.

CHAPTER VI.

THE ROMAN EMPIRE IN THE EAST.

Continuation of the Roman Empire at Constantinople (1)—*condition of the Eastern Church* (1)—*reign of Justinian, his legislation and buildings* (2)—*exploits of Belisarius and Narsês; recovery of Africa and Italy* (2)—*Lombard conquest of Italy; relations of Rome and Venice to the Empire* (2)—*wars with the Turks and Avars* (3)—*greatness of Persia under the two Chosroes; Persian victories of Heraclius* (3)—*rise of the Saracens; preaching of Mahomet; spread of his religion* (4)—*the first Caliphs; their wars with the Empire; conquests of Syria and Egypt; sieges of Constantinople* (5)—*Saracen conquests in Africa, Spain, and Southern Gaul* (5)—*Saracen conquest of Persia; breaking up of the Saracenic dominion; position of the later Caliphs* (6)—*the Isaurian Emperors; dispute about images; decline of the Imperial power in Italy* (7)—*advance of the Lombards in Italy* (8)—*the Merwings in Gaul; they are succeeded by the Karlings* (8)—*Pippin invited into Italy; he becomes Patrician of Rome* (8)—*Charles the Great conquers the Lombards; his election as Emperor* (8, 9)—*Summary* (10).

1. **The Roman Emperors at Constantinople.**—The succession of Roman Emperors thus came to an end in the West, but the Empire still went on at Constantinople. The Emperors who reigned there still claimed to be sovereigns of the whole Empire, though they had no real power west of the Hadriatic.

The parts of the Empire which were really under their dominion were chiefly those which either were originally Greek, or where the Greek language and civilization had been spread by the conquests of Alexander. That is, they ruled over the lands which I have before spoken of as the Greek and the Oriental provinces. Still it must be borne in mind that these Emperors were strictly *Roman* Emperors. The Imperial succession went on without any break; the laws and titles of Rome were kept up, and, though Greek was the language which was most spoken, yet Latin remained for a long time the official language, that which was used in drawing up laws and public documents of all kinds. There is no need to say much about the Emperors who reigned at Constantinople between the death of Theodosius the Great and the nominal reunion of the Empire in 476. Their time was mainly taken up with wars with the Persians, in which the Romans generally got the worst, with the invasion of Attila and his Huns, and with ecclesiastical disputes within the Empire. The people of the Oriental provinces especially, who had never thoroughly become either Greek or Roman, were constantly putting forth or adopting doctrines which the Catholic Church, both of the Old and of the New Rome, looked on as heretical. Several Councils of the Church were held during this time, and this was the time of some of the most famous of the Greek *Fathers*, especially the great preacher Saint *John Chrysostom*, that is, the *Goldenmouth*, who was Patriarch of Constantinople. The *Patriarchs* of Constantinople or New Rome were the chief Bishops in the East, but, as the Emperors were always at hand, they never won anything like the same power which the Bishops of the Old Rome won in the West. Thus, though the history of the Eastern Empire is largely a history of ecclesiastical disputes, yet we never find there the same kind of disputes between Church and State, between the ecclesiastical and the temporal powers, which make up so great a part of Western history.

2. **The Recovery of Italy and Africa.**—As the claims of the Emperors who reigned at Constantinople to rule over all the dominions of their predecessors were never forgotten, so they were put forward whenever there was any chance of making them good. And soon after the Emperors came to an end in the West, the Emperors at Constantinople had several opportunities of meddling in Western affairs. The Franks were too powerful and too far off for the Emperors to have any chance of winning back Gaul; so they were commonly held to be friends of the Empire, and in 510 Chlodwig himself was made Roman Consul for the year. With Italy the Emperors had much more to do. We have seen that both Odoacer and Theodoric entered Italy with a nominal commission from the Emperor Zeno, which at least kept up the memory of the claims of the Emperors to rule in Italy. As long as Theodoric lived, there was no hope of anything more than this; but after his death the power of the Goths in Italy declined. So did also that of the Vandals in Africa, and the reigning Emperor now began to think that it would be possible to make both countries again really, as well as nominally, parts of the Empire. This Emperor was *Justinian*, who reigned from 527 to 565, and was one of the most famous of all the Emperors. He was famous for his buildings, especially for the great church of *Saint Sophia* at Constantinople, and still more for putting the laws of Rome into the shape of a regular code. Thus was formed that complete system of Roman law, called the *Civil Law*, which has formed the groundwork of the law of the greater part of Europe. Justinian was also famous for the great conquests made in his reign, though he had not much to do with making them himself. His general *Belisarius* was perhaps the greatest commander that

ever lived, as he did the greatest things with the smallest means. He did something to check the Persians, who were now very powerful under a great King called *Chosroes* or *Nushirvan*. In 534 Belisarius put an end to the *Vandal* kingdom in *Africa*, and the next year, being then Consul, he landed in Sicily, and a long war between the Romans and Goths went on under Belisarius and his successor *Narsês*, till, in 553, the whole of Italy was recovered to the Empire. Meanwhile the southern part of *Spain* was also recovered from the West-Goths, so that Justinian reigned both in the Old and in the New Rome, and the Roman dominion again stretched from the Ocean to the Euphrates. It would have been far wiser if Justinian had left the West alone, and had given his whole mind to defending his Eastern dominions against the Persians and against the various enemies who were always attacking the Empire from the north. While his great generals were conquering Italy, the Slavonic tribes ravaged the Illyrian and Thracian provinces at pleasure. In fact these great conquests were really a source of weakness rather than of strength. Still it is not wonderful that Justinian, as Roman Emperor, could not withstand the temptation, and he most likely thought it his duty, to recover as many of the old provinces of the Empire as he could. But, after all, it was only for a very few years that the Emperors were able to keep the whole of Italy. Three years after Justinian's death, in 568, a Teutonic people called the *Lombards* began to pour into Italy, and they presently conquered the whole North and some parts of the South. Still a large part of Italy, including Rome and Ravenna, most part of the South, and the islands of Sicily, Sardinia, and Corsica, remained to the Empire. *Venice* also, a state which began to spring up in the fifth century, when men fled for fear of the Huns and sought shelter in the small islands of the Hadriatic, also kept up its connexion with the

Empire, but its connexion gradually became one rather of alliance than of subjection.

3. **Wars with the Persians.**—We thus see that, at the end of the sixth century, the Empire, though so large a part of it had fallen away, still took in the greater part of the countries round the Mediterranean Sea, and still kept all the greatest cities of Europe, Asia, and Africa. But it was threatened on all sides, not only by the Lombards in the West but by the Slavonic and Turanian nations who were pressing in from the North in the countries by the Danube, and still more by the Persians in the East. It was in the reign of Justinian that we first began to hear of the *Turks*. That name does not mean those particular Turks who made their way into the Empire long afterwards, and who hold Constantinople still. The Turks with whom we have now to do belonged to other branches of the great Turkish race, a race which is perhaps the most widely spread of all the Turanian races of Asia, and of the different branches of which we shall often hear again. Another Turanian people, the *Avars*, also appear on the borders of the Empire at this time, and several Emperors, especially *Maurice*, who reigned from 582 to 602, had much ado to defend their northern frontier against them. Meanwhile the Persians were at the height of their power; and, under another *Chosroes*, a grandson of Chosroes called Nushirvan, they bade fair to subdue all the Eastern provinces of the Empire. Between the years 611 and 615 the Persian armies overran the whole of Syria, Egypt, and Asia, reaching to the Hellespont, and encamping at Chalkêdôn within sight of Constantinople. The Empire was then ruled by *Heraclius*, one of the greatest names in the whole list of Roman Emperors. He had been *Exarch* or Governor of Africa, and had risen to the throne by destroying *Phocas*, who had rebelled and murdered the Emperor Maurice. For a while he seemed to do

nothing to stop the Persian invasions; but at last he arose; he restored the old discipline of the Roman armies, and in a series of great campaigns, from 620 to 628, he altogether broke the Persian power, and won back all that Chosroes had conquered. But, while the Romans and Persians were thus disputing for the dominion of Asia, the Empire was again cut short in the West, for the Gothic Kings now won back the Roman province in Spain; and it was presently cut short in the East in a far more terrible way. For a power was now arising which was to overthrow the Persians and Goths altogether, and to strike a deadly blow at the power of Rome.

4. **Rise of the Saracens.**—We now come to the rise of a great Semitic power, the only Semitic power which has played any great part in history since the time of the great dominion of Carthage. For it must not be forgotten that the Persians, though so widely cut off from their Western brethren, were just as much Aryans as the Italians, Greeks, or Teutons. We also come to the rise of a new religion, the last of the three great religions which have come out from among the Semitic nations, and all of which taught men that there is but one God, and bade them to keep from the worship of idols. First came *Judaism*, then *Christianity*, and now the religion of *Mahomet.* Mahomet was an Arab of *Mecca*, the holy city of Arabia, where he was born in 569. He gave himself out for a prophet, and taught that, though both the Jewish and the Christian religion were sent from God, yet he had himself received a revelation more perfect than either. In his own country there can be no doubt that Mahomet was a great reformer. He swept away the idolatry of the Arabs; he greatly reformed their laws and manners, and gathered their scattered tribes into one nation. In his early days he had to bear much persecution; but, as he grew powerful, he began to teach that his new religion was to be forced

upon all men by the sword. So the Arabs, or *Saracens* as they are also called, as soon as they had embraced the faith of Mahomet, held it to be their duty to spread their faith everywhere, which in fact meant to conquer the whole world. They everywhere gave men the choice of three things, *Koran*, *tribute*, or *sword;* that is, they called on all men either to believe in Mahomet and to accept the *Koran*, a book which contained his revelations, to submit to the Saracens and pay tribute, or else to fight against them if they could. By these means the religion of Mahomet was spread over a large part of Asia and Africa, and we shall see that it made its way into Europe also. As Christianity became the religion of the Empire and of the nations which learned their civilization from either the Old or the New Rome, so Mahometanism became the religion of the Arabs, and of those nations who were conquered by them or learned their civilization from them. We may call it the religion of the *East*, as far as we have to do with the East, just as Christianity is the religion of the *West*. It has spread at different times as far as from Spain to India. The people of all the countries which were conquered by the Saracens and other Mahometan powers had either to embrace the Mahometan religion or else to buy the right to practise their own, whether Christian or heathen, by the payment of tribute.

5. Wars between the Saracens and Romans.—As soon as all Arabia had been joined together under the authority of Mahomet, he and his followers began to spread their power over the neighbouring countries; that is, of course, mainly over the dominions of Rome and Persia. Mahomet himself died in 632, before any serious attack was made upon either, and he was succeeded in his power by rulers called his *Caliphs* or *Successors*, the first of whom was his father-in-law *Abu-Bekr*. The Caliphs were at once spiritual and temporal rulers, much the same as if in

Christendom the same man had been Pope and Emperor at once. Under the first two Caliphs *Abu-Bekr* and *Omar*, the Roman provinces of *Syria* and *Egypt* were conquered between the years 632 and 639. Now it should be remembered that these two were the provinces in which Greek and Roman civilization had never thoroughly taken root, where the mass of the people still kept their old languages, and where men were always falling away into forms of belief which were counted heretical according to the faith both of the Old and New Rome. In these provinces therefore men may well have deemed that they had little to lose by a change of rulers. It followed then that, though the Saracens had to fight several hard battles against the Roman armies in Syria, yet they met with no general resistance from the whole people, and in Egypt they met with no resistance at all. The great cities of *Antioch* and *Alexandria*, as well as *Jerusalem*, were thus lost to the Empire. But in the lands on this side of Mount Tauros, where the influence of Greek culture and Roman law was more deep and abiding, the Saracens never gained any lasting footing. They often invaded the country, and twice, in 673 and 716, they besieged Constantinople itself, but they made no abiding conquests. In *Africa* too, which had been far more thoroughly Romanized than Syria and Egypt, they met with a long resistance. Their invasions began in 647, but Carthage was not taken till 698, and the whole country was not fully subdued till 709. From no part of the Empire have all traces either of the Roman dominion or of the Teutonic settlement of the Vandals been so utterly swept away as from Africa. From Africa in 710 the Saracens crossed into *Spain*, and in about three years they subdued the whole land, except where the Christians still held out in the mountain fastnesses of the North. They conquered also a small part of Gaul, namely the province of *Narbonne* or *Septimania*. But this was the end of their conquests in Western Europe. In 732 they were defeated in the great battle of *Tours* by the Frank *Charles Martel*, of whom we shall presently hear again. In 755 they were altogether driven out of Gaul, but it took more than seven hundred years more to drive them out of the whole of Spain.

6. **The Saracen Conquests in the East.**—The Saracens thus lopped off the Eastern and Southern provinces of the Empire, so that the Romans no longer held anything in Africa, nor anything in Asia beyond Mount Tauros. Meanwhile they were pressing on with equal vigour against the other great empire of *Persia.* In about nineteen years, from 632 to 651, the whole kingdom of Persia was conquered, and the native dynasty of the *Sassanides*, which had reigned in Persia since the time of Artaxerxes, came to an end. Persia now gradually became a Mahometan country. The Saracens thence pressed northwards and eastwards into *Sind*, the most western part of India, and into the *Turkish* lands beyond the Oxus. For a short time the whole of this vast dominion held together, and a single Caliph was obeyed in Spain and in Sind. But, before long, disputes and civil wars arose among the Saracens themselves, as to the right succession of the Caliphate, and in 755 their empire was divided, and was never joined together again. Spain was lost, and in the East the Turkish tribes were pressing into the Saracenic empire, very much in the same way in which the Teutonic tribes had pressed into the Empire of Rome. The governors of the different provinces gradually made themselves independent, and various dynasties, chiefly Turkish, arose, whose obedience to the Caliph became quite nominal. Various sects also arose among the Mahometans, just as they arose among the Christians, and each sect looked on the others as heretics. There were opposition Caliphs in Spain and in Egypt; but those who gave themselves out as the orthodox fol-

lowers of Mahomet always looked up to the Caliph who reigned at Bagdad. So the Caliphs may be looked on as keeping something like the power of a Pope after they had lost the power of an Emperor.

7. **The Loss of Italy.**—The descendants of Heraclius went on reigning till about the end of the seventh century. Then came a time of confusion, till at last, in 718, the Empire fell to a valiant man named *Leo,* a native of *Isauria,* whose descendants reigned after him till the beginning of the ninth century. The second siege of Constantinople by the Saracens was then going on, and it was mainly owing to his valour and wisdom that the invaders were beaten back. This defeat of the Saracens by Leo is really one of the greatest events in the world's history; for, if Constantinople had been taken by the Mahometans before the nations of Western Europe had at all grown up, it would seem as if the Christian religion and European civilization must have been swept away from the earth. But, if Leo thus secured the Empire towards the East, his dealing in religious matters did much to weaken its power in the West. Though Spain and Africa had been lost, the Emperors still kept Rome and all that part of Italy which was not conquered by the *Lombards*, as well as all the great islands of *Sicily*, *Sardinia*, and *Corsica.* The Italian possessions of the Empire were ruled by an *Exarch* or governor, who lived, not at Rome but at *Ravenna.* Thus, as neither the Emperor nor his deputy lived at Rome, the power of the Popes or Bishops of Rome grew greater and greater. At last, during the reign of Leo, another religious dispute broke out, about the worship or reverence paid to images and pictures in churches. This worship Leo held to be idolatrous, and so did his son *Constantine,* called *Koprônymos,* who succeeded him and reigned from 741 to 775, and who also was a valiant warrior against the Saracens. The party who thought with them were called *Iconoclasts* or breakers

of images, and there were constant disputes about this matter in the Eastern Church all through the eighth and part of the ninth century. But in Italy, when the Emperors tried to put away the worship and even the use of images, men everywhere withstood them, the Popes *Gregory the Second* and *Gregory the Third* taking the lead against them. The result was that the Emperors lost all real power in Rome. But they kept *Southern Italy* for a long time afterwards, and even at Rome their authority was acknowledged in name down to the end of the eighth century. We must now see how even its formal acknowledgment came to an end.

8. **The Franks in Italy.**—Meanwhile the *Lombards* were extending their dominion in Italy. Under their Kings *Liudprand* and *Astolf*, they took Ravenna and more than once threatened Rome. There was no hope of any help coming from the Emperors at Constantinople; so the Popes and the Roman people sought for help in quite a new quarter, namely at the hands of *Pippin* the King of the Franks. The Franks had now long been the ruling people of Germany and Gaul. The descendants of Chlodwig, the German King and Roman Consul, went on reigning, though their dominions were often divided into several small kingdoms, and in the south of Gaul, especially in Aquitaine, they had but little real power. These descendants of Chlodwig, the *Merwings* or *Morowingians* as they were called, were one of the worst dynasties that ever reigned; few parts of history are more full of crimes, public and private, than the accounts of the early Frankish Kings. Latterly they became weak as well as wicked, and all real power passed into the hands of the *Karlings*, who governed by the title of *Mayors of the Palace.* They came from the Eastern, the most German, part of the Frankish dominions, and their rise to power was almost like another German conquest of Gaul. One of these

Mayors was *Karl* or *Charles*, called *Martel* or the *Hammer*, who won the great victory over the Saracens at Tours in 732. He was succeeded by his son *Pippin*, who in 753 was chosen King of the Franks, the Merowingian King *Chilperic* being deposed, for it was thought foolish that the title of King should belong to one man and the kingly power to another. Thus began the dynasty of the Karlings, the *sons of Charles*, the second Frankish dynasty in Germany and Gaul. Of their doings in Germany and Gaul we shall speak presently; we have now to do with them in Italy. King Pippin came at the prayer of Pope *Stephen the Third*, and saved Rome from the Lombards and won back from them the *Exarchate*, that is the country about Ravenna, which they had conquered. He became the virtual sovereign of Rome, but, as it was still not thought right wholly to throw away the authority of the Emperors, he was called, not King or Emperor, but *Patrician*. That word had quite changed its meaning since it had meant the highest class of the Roman people; it was now used rather vaguely, and it sometimes meant the governor of a province; this last must have been the sense in which they used it now. Pippin's son, *Karl* or *Charles* the *Great*, altogether conquered the Lombard kingdom in 774. He then called himself *King of the Franks and Lombards and Patrician of the Romans*. As such, he was ruler of all Italy, except the part in the south which the Emperors still kept. The Franks were thus the head people in all Western Christendom.

9. **Charles elected Emperor.**—But a greater honour still was in store for the Franks and their King. In 797, the Emperor *Constantine the Sixth*, the grandson of Constantine Koprônymos, was deposed by his mother *Eirênê*, who put out his eyes and reigned in his stead. This gave the Pope and the people of Rome a good excuse for throwing off the authority of the Emperors at Constantinople altogether.

They now said that a woman could not be Cæsar and Augustus, and that the Old Rome had as good a right to choose the Emperor as the New. So in the year 800 the Romans of the Old Rome chose their Patrician Charles to be Emperor, and he was crowned by Pope *Leo* as *Charles Augustus, Emperor of the Romans.* The Empire was now finally divided, and for many ages there was one Emperor reigning in the East and another in the West, each claiming to be the true Roman Emperor. The Eastern Emperors never got back Rome again, nor any part of Northern Italy, but they kept, and sometimes enlarged, their dominions in Southern Italy, where the Greek tongue was still not wholly forgotten, for more than two hundred years longer.

10. **Summary.**—Thus, through the sixth, seventh, and eighth centuries, there was only one Emperor, who reigned at *Constantinople.* Under *Justinian* a very large part of the Empire was won back again from the Goths and Vandals. But, in the course of the sixth and seventh centuries, a great part of the recovered provinces, together with *Syria* and *Egypt*, were lost again. The *Lombards* established themselves in *Italy*, and the *Saracens* overthrew the kingdom of *Persia*, conquered the *Eastern* and *African* provinces of Rome, and established themselves in *Spain.* In the eighth century the dispute about images led to the gradual separation of *Rome* and what was left to the Empire in Northern Italy, and in its last year Rome parted off altogether from the Eastern Empire, and chose the Frank *Charles* as separate *Emperor of the West.*

CHAPTER VII.

THE FRANKISH EMPIRE.

Divison of the Empire; the Western Empire held by the Frankish kings (1)—*the Ommiad Caliphs; accession of the Abbassides* (2)—*division of the Caliphate; relations between the two Caliphates and the two Empires* (2)—*conquests and losses of the Saracens* (2)—*reign of Charles the Great; extent of his Empire* (3)—*division of the Frankish Kingdoms; Kingdoms of Germany, Lotharingia, Karolingia, Burgundy, and Italy; different meanings of the word* Francia (4)—*final division of the Empire; end of the Karlings in Germany* (5) —*Odo King of the West-Franks; shifting of the Kingdom between Laon and Paris* (6)—*Duchies of France, Burgundy, and Aquitaine; distinction between Northern and Southern Gaul* (6)—*Hugh Capet elected King; beginning of the modern kingdom of France* (6)—*settlements of the English in Britain; their conversion to Christianity* (7)—*the Northmen; their invasions of Gaul and Britain* (8)—*supremacy of Wessex in Britain; invasion and settlements of the Danes; formation of the Kingdom of England* (9)—*settlements of the Northmen in Gaul; settlement of Rolf at Rouen; growth of the Duchy of Normandy* (10)—*Summary* (11).

1. **The Division of the Empire.**—The Roman Empire was now finally divided, and it might seem to have altogether passed away from the true Romans. The Emperors of the West from this time were Germans; they did not live much at Rome itself, and their native language was German, though Latin remained the language of law, government, and religion. In the Eastern Empire the tongue commonly spoken was Greek; Latin had gone out of use even as an official language; and, from the time of the loss of Rome and Ravenna, the Roman Empire of the

East answered pretty well to those parts of Europe and Asia which had thoroughly accepted the Greek language and Greek civilization. Still each Empire gave itself out as the continuation of the old Empire, and the old Imperial titles went on. Only, while in the East the Emperor was a Roman Emperor and nothing else, in the West the Emperor was *King of the Franks* as well as *Emperor of the Romans*. In truth, the choice of a German King to be Roman Emperor was the greatest of all changes, and it was really the beginning of quite a new state of things. But men at the time talked as if things had gone regularly on, and they spoke of Charles the Great as the lawful successor of Constantine the Sixth. And in this way, through the union of the Roman and German crowns, a large territory was now held to belong to the Roman Empire which had never belonged to the Empire in old times. And, though the new line of German Emperors lived but little in their old capital of Rome, yet, for seven hundred years after the election of Charles, it was held that no king had a right to be called *Emperor* or *Cæsar* till he had been crowned at Rome by the Pope. The Eastern Emperors meanwhile kept Constantinople, or the New Rome, as their capital, and they were crowned by Patriarchs of Constantinople in the church of Saint Sophia.

2. **Division of the Caliphate.**—We mentioned in the last chapter that, about fifty years before the final division of the Empire, the Mahometan power was divided in much the same way. The first four Caliphs, *Abu-Bekr*, *Omar*, *Othman*, and *Ali*, were all among the immediate friends or kinsmen of Mahomet. Then came the dynasty of the *Ommiads*, who reigned at *Damascus*. But in 750 they were overthrown by the descendants of *Abbas*, the uncle of Mahomet, who founded the dynasty of the *Abbassides*, by whom the seat of their dominion was after a while moved to *Bagdad* on the Tigris. But a prince of the Ommiad family,

Abd-al-rahman by name, escaped to *Spain*, and was the founder of the dynasty of the Ommiads of *Cordova*. These princes at first called themselves only *Emir* or prince, but afterwards they took the title of Caliph, and from the beginning they were the enemies of the Abbassides. Thus there were two rival Empires among the Christians and two rival Caliphates among the Mahometans; and, as was to be expected, each of the Christian powers was at enmity with the Mahometan power which was its own neighbour and on good terms with the Mahometan power at a distance. The Caliphs of Cordova were the natural enemies of the Western Empire, and the Caliphs of Bagdad were the natural enemies of the Eastern Empire. But there was commonly peace and friendship between the Western Empire and the Eastern Caliphate and between the Eastern Empire and the Western Caliphate. And, just as the two Empires not only parted asunder from one another, but each split up into various kingdoms, so the two Caliphates gradually split up also. Many Mahometan powers arose, which professed at most a nominal allegiance to the Caliph either at Bagdad or Cordova. And some of these powers went on conquering at the expense of the Christians. In the course of the ninth century independent Saracen powers arose in the great Mediterranean islands of *Sicily* and *Crete*, which had up to that time belonged to the Eastern Empire. In Spain itself the Saracens never conquered quite the whole of the country, as the Christians always maintained their independence in the mountains of the North, whence they gradually won the whole peninsula back again. In the ninth century then the four great powers of the civilized world were the two Christian Empires and the two Mahometan Caliphates. The *British Islands* were independent of all, standing alone in being both Christian and independent. The other parts of Europe which acknowledged neither Emperor nor Caliph were still heathen and barbarous.

3. **Charles the Great.**—The first Frankish King who became Roman Emperor, the first man of Teutonic blood who was called Cæsar and Augustus, was, as we have said, Charles the son of Pippin, called *Karolus Magnus* or *Charles the Great.* In after times he became a great subject of French romance, in which he is called by the French name of *Charlemagne.* Under him the power of the Franks rose to its highest pitch. *Francia,* the *land of the Franks,* took in all Central Germany and Northern Gaul. Besides this, Charles more thoroughly established the Frankish dominion over Southern Gaul and Southern Germany, that is over *Aquitaine* and *Bavaria,* and also over *Armorica,* the north-western corner of Gaul. Here a great number of the Welsh from the Isle of Britain had settled when their country was conquered by the English. Thus the land was known as the *Lesser Britain* or *Britanny,* and the Celtic language, which had perhaps never quite died out, was kept up by their coming. Charles also subdued the German people to the north of his own *Francia,* that is our own kinsmen, the *Saxons* who had stayed behind in Germany and had not gone into Britain. They were still heathens, but he forced them to embrace Christianity. He thus became master of all Germany and Gaul. And, as we have seen, as Emperor and King of the Lombards he held the greatest part of Italy, and he had also Spain as far as the Ebro. He had also much fighting with the nations to the east and north of Germany. To the north lay the *Scandinavian* nations, called the *Northmen,* of whom we shall have presently to speak more at large. Of these Charles had a good deal of fighting with the *Danes,* and he brought them into some degree of submission to the Empire. To the north-east of Germany beyond the Elbe lay the *Slavonic* nations who were spoken of in the first chapter, who grew up into the different nations of the *Wends,* the *Poles,* and the *Czechs* or *Bohemians,* all of whom had at different times

to make submission to the Emperors, and a large part of whose country has long formed part of Germany. To the south-east were other Slavonic nations who had been allowed to settle on the frontiers of the Eastern Empire. Between these two branches of the Slaves, in a great part of modern Hungary, the Turanian people of the *Avars* had fixed themselves. With all these border nations the Emperor Charles had much fighting, and most of them were brought into more or less of submission. Under him then the Western Empire was at a greater height of power than it had ever been since the division after the death of Theodosius, and in all his vast dominions Charles did what he could to encourage learning and religion by promoting learned men, founding bishopricks and monasteries, and making laws for the government of his Empire. He first united Germany under one head, and he won the rank of Roman Emperor for the German King. Like Constantine and Theodosius, he thought of dividing the Empire among his sons, but, as all his sons, except *Lewis*, surnamed the *Pious*, died before him, the whole Empire passed at his death in 814 to that one son Lewis.

4. **The Frankish Kingdoms.**—So great a dominion as had been brought together under Charles the Great needed a man like Charles himself to keep it together. The second Frankish Emperor Lewis was a good but weak man, and his sons were always rebelling against their father and quarrelling with one another. Several divisions of the Empire were made during his lifetime, and after his death his dominions were, after much fighting, divided in 843 among his sons *Lothar*, *Lewis*, and *Charles*. Lothar was Emperor, and, as such, he reigned in Italy, and he was meant to have at least a nominal supremacy over his brothers. For his own kingdom he took Italy and a long narrow strip of territory reaching from the Mediterranean to the Northern Ocean, and taking in

what is now *Provence* at one end and *Holland* at the other. Part of his kingdom spoke German and part Romance. To the east of him his brother Lewis, who is called *the German*, reigned over a purely German kingdom, the lands between the Rhine and the Elbe. Charles reigned in Gaul to the West of Lothar. On Lothar's death Italy passed to his son the Emperor *Lewis the Second*, while a second *Lothar* reigned in the borderland of Germany and Gaul. From having been the kingdom of two Lothars, this land was called *Lotharingia*, and part of it still keeps the name in the form of *Lothringen* or *Lorraine*. Just in the same way Charles's kingdom was at first called *Karolingia*, only the one name has gone out of use, while the other has lived on. But the different kingdoms which were now formed had no regular names. All the different Kings were *Kings of the Franks*, much as in earlier times there had been several Emperors at once. There now came a time of great confusion, during which the different kingdoms were split up and joined together again in various ways. But there was still always one King who was Emperor, though he soon lost all real power over the others. And all the Kings were of the house of the Karlings, save only in the *Burgundian* land between the Rhone, the Saône, and the Alps, where Kings of other houses reigned, and which was called the *Kingdom of Burgundy* or *Arles*. At last, in 884, all the Frankish kingdoms except Burgundy were joined together under the Emperor *Charles the Fat*. But in 887 all his kingdoms agreed to depose him, and each kingdom chose a King of its own. And the kingdoms which were now formed began to answer more nearly to real divisions of nations and language than had hitherto been the case. Thus from this time the Eastern and Western Franks were never again united, and the word *Francia* henceforth has two meanings. Eastern or Teutonic *Francia* was the old Frankish land in Germany, forming part of the *Eastern* Kingdom. Western or Latin *Francia* was the land between the Loire and the Seine, where men spoke Romance and not German, and which formed part of the *Western* Kingdom. Between them lay *Lotharingia*, the border land, taking in modern *Belgium*. This had no longer a King of its own, but it was often disputed between the Eastern and Western Kings, the Kings of Germany and *Karolingia*. In South-eastern Gaul the *Burgundian* Kingdom went on, sometimes forming one kingdom, sometimes two. And in Italy, during the first half of the tenth century, there were several rival Kings, some of whom got to be crowned Emperors. But they had no power out of Italy, and not much in it. And it must be remembered that all this time Southern Italy still belonged to the Eastern Emperors, and that Sicily had been conquered by the Saracens.

5. **The End of the Karlings in Germany.**—After the division in 887 the *Eastern* or *German* Kingdom still stayed for a while in the family of Charles the Great. For the East-Franks chose as their King *Arnulf*, who was a Karling, though not by lawful descent. But the Western Franks in Karolingia chose *Odo*, Count of *Paris*, who had been very valiant in defending his city against an attack of the Northmen, of whom we shall hear presently. But King Arnulf was the head King, and King Odo of Paris did *homage* to him for his crown ; that is, he became his *man*, and promised to be faithful to him. Arnulf afterwards went to Rome and was crowned Emperor. But the German crown did not stay long among the Karlings. The line of Arnulf died out in his son *Lewis*, called the *Child*, and then the Eastern Kingdom fell to men of other families, connected with the Karlings only in the female line or not at all. From this time the Kingdom of Germany went on as a separate kingdom, but we shall soon see that it had a great deal to do with the other kingdoms which arose

out of the breaking up of the Frankish Empire. And it had much to do in other ways with the Slavonic and Turanian people to the East, and in the end it greatly extended itself at the cost of its Slavonic neighbours.

6. **Beginning of the Kingdom of France.**—After the election of Odo of Paris to the Western Kingdom, there followed a hundred years of shifting to and fro between his new family and the old family of the Karlings. Sometimes there was a King of one house and sometimes of the other. The Karlings still spoke German, and, when they held the kingdom, their capital was *Laon*, in its north-eastern corner. The family of Odo were called *Dukes of the French*, and they spoke *French*, as we may now call the Romance speech of Northern Gaul, and their capital was Paris. Their Duchy, the *Duchy of France*—that is, *Western* or *Latin Francia*—was, even when its Dukes were not Kings, the most powerful state north of the Loire. But whichever family held the crown, the Kings had very little power south of the Loire. For, in these times of confusion, the *Dukes* and *Counts*, who at first were only governors of the different provinces, both in the Eastern and Western Kingdoms, had grown up into hereditary princes, paying a merely nominal homage to the King, whether he reigned at Laon or Paris. The princes north of the Loire, the *Counts of Flanders*, the *Dukes of the Normans* (of whom we shall say more presently), the native princes of *Britanny*, and the *Dukes of Burgundy*, were often at war with the Kings, and with one another. These Dukes of Burgundy held the northern part of Burgundy, that of which *Dijon* is the capital; this did not form part of the Kingdom of Burgundy, but of the Western Kingdom or Karolingia. South of the Loire, where men spoke, not French but Provençal, the *Dukes of Aquitaine* and *Gascony*, and the Counts of *Toulouse* and *Barcelona*

had hardly anything to do with the Kings at all. The most famous among the Karolingian Kings at Laon was *Lewis the Fourth*, called *From-beyond-sea*, because he had been brought up by his uncle King *Æthelstan* in England. He had much striving with *Hugh the Great*, Duke of the French, the nephew of King Odo, who refused the crown more than once, but who never had any scruple about rebelling against the King. But on the death of the last Karolingian King at Laon, *Lewis the Fifth*, *Hugh Capet*, the son of Hugh the Great, was chosen King in 987. This was the real beginning of the modern Kingdom of *France*. The *Duke of the French* was now *King of the French*. Paris became the capital of the Kingdom, and, as the Kings of the French got hold of the lands of their vassals and neighbours bit by bit, the name of *France* was gradually spread, as it is now, over the greater part of Gaul.

7. **The English in Britain.**—We have thus seen how the kingdoms and nations of Germany, Italy, Burgundy, and France were formed by the breaking up of the great Frankish Empire. Meanwhile the English nation was growing up in the Isle of Britain, which formed no part of the Empire, and which men spoke often of as a world of itself. We have already seen how the three *Low-Dutch* tribes, the *Angles*, *Saxons*, and *Jutes*, settled in Britain, how they drove the *Britons* or *Welsh* into the western part of the Island, and how, as they gradually became one people, the whole nation was called *Angles* or *English*. They formed a great number of principalities in Britain, among the chief of which were the Kingdom of the Jutes in *Kent*, the oldest of all, the Kingdom of the *West-Saxons*, which began in what is now Hampshire and gradually spread over all South-western Britain, the Kingdom of the *Mercians* in the middle of England, and the Kingdom of the *North-umbrians*, which, sometimes under one King, some-

times under two, stretched from the Humber to the Firth of Forth. The Kingdoms of the *South-Saxons*, *East-Saxons*, and *East-Angles* should also be noticed, but they were less powerful than the other four. All these kingdoms had much fighting with one another, as well as with the Britons or Welsh to the west of them and with the other Celtic tribes of the *Picts* and *Scots* to the north beyond the Forth. Sometimes one of their Kings gained a certain authority over the other kingdoms; he was then called a *Bretwalda* or *Wielder of Britain*. As we have already said, the English remained heathens for about one hundred and fifty years after their first settlement in Britain. Then, in 597, Pope *Gregory the Great* sent over *Augustine*, who converted the Kentish King *Æthelberht*, who was then Bretwalda; so *Kent* was the first Christian kingdom among the English. Gradually all the English kingdoms were converted, some by missionaries from Kent or straight from Rome, some by the Scots, who were already Christians, but none, it would seem, by the Welsh. And presently the English began themselves to send missionaries to convert those of their kinsfolk in their old land who were still heathens. One of them, *Winfrith* or *Boniface*, in the time of Pippin, was called the *Apostle of Germany*. This was quite another way of being converted from that of the Goths and Franks who embraced Christianity while they were pressing into the Empire. But, even after they became Christians, the English still went on making conquests from the Welsh, and also carrying on wars among themselves. During the seventh and eighth centuries the three great kingdoms of the West-Saxons, Mercians, and Northumbrians were ever striving for the mastery. Sometimes one had the upper hand and sometimes the other; but at the beginning of the ninth century the different English kingdoms began to be more closely united together, and they had also a common enemy from without to withstand.

8. **The Northmen.**—We have already spoken of the Aryan people in Northern Europe, called the *Northmen* or *Scandinavians*. These were a Teutonic people, whose speech is more nearly akin to the Low-Dutch than to the High. They had settled in the great peninsula to the north-east of the Baltic, where they were gradually making their way against the Turanian inhabitants, the *Fins* and *Laps*, and they had also occupied the peninsula called the *Cimbric Chersonêsos* or *Jütland*, which is divided from Saxony by the river *Eider*. In these peninsulas and the neighbouring islands they gradually formed three kingdoms, those of *Norway*, *Sweden*, and *Denmark*. The Danes in the southern peninsula had often to yield more or less of submission to Charles the Great and his successors. But the Northmen of the northern peninsula never submitted to the Empire, and indeed the Swedes had for a long time to come but little to do with the general affairs of Europe. They had enough to do in striving with their own Turanian neighbours, and in conquests toward the East, where they came to bear rule over the Slavonic land of *Russia*. But the Western Scandinavians, the Danes and the Norwegians who were more specially called *Northmen*, began, towards the end of the eighth century, to be fearful scourges both to Britain and to all the coasts of the Empire. Even while Charles the Great lived, they had begun to sail about and plunder in various parts; and after he was dead, and when the Empire began to break in pieces, they were able to ravage almost wherever they pleased. After a while they began, not only to plunder, but to make settlements, both in Gaul and in Britain. They also settled in *Iceland*, in the *Orkneys* and in the other islands near Scotland, in the northern part of Scotland itself, and in the towns on the east coast of Ireland. But we have most to do with their settlements in England and in Northern Gaul. For through their settlement in

Gaul a new power in Europe arose, and, what we should hardly have looked for, their settlements in England had a great deal to do with the making of the different English kingdoms in Britain into one.

9. **Formation of the Kingdom of England.**—We have seen that, up to the end of the eighth century, the chief power among the English in Britain was always passing from one of the English kingdoms to another. But at the beginning of the ninth century it came permanently into the hands of *Wessex*. This was under *Ecgberht*, who was King of the West-Saxons from 802 to 837. He was a friend of Charles the Great, with whom he had taken shelter when he was banished from his own country. It was no doubt the friendship and example of Charles which set him upon doing in Britain much the same as Charles had done in Germany. Ecgberht gradually brought all the other English kingdoms and the Welsh both of *Cornwall* and of what we call *Wales*, into more or less of subjection to his own kingdom of the West-Saxons. Other Kings went on reigning, but they were his men and he was their lord, like the Emperor among the Kings and princes on the mainland. Thus a great step was taken towards joining all the English in Britain into one kingdom. But the Scots beyond the Forth and the Northern Welsh in *Cumberland* and thereabouts remained independent, so that Ecgberht was still far from being master of the whole island, and presently the Danish invasion seemed likely to shatter the newly founded West-Saxon power altogether. King *Ælfred* or *Alfred*, the grandson of Ecgberht and the most famous of all our ancient Kings, who began to reign in 871, had much fighting with the Danes. The northern part of England was conquered by them, and Danish Kings and Earls reigned at York. Presently they invaded Wessex, whence they were driven out by Alfred in 878. But he found it needful to make a treaty with the Danish

King *Guthrum*, by which Guthrum was allowed to hold all the eastern part of England, on condition of becoming King Alfred's man and also becoming a Christian. For the Danes were still heathens, as the English were when they first entered Britain, and they seem to have taken special delight in destroying the churches and monasteries. The Kings who came after Alfred, his son *Edward* and his grandsons *Æthelstan* and *Edmund*, had much fighting with the Danes in Britain. But at last they were able to bring all the Teutonic people in Britain, both English and Danish, into one kingdom; so they were called *Kings of the English* and not merely *Kings of the West-Saxons.* And all the princes of the Welsh and of the Scots also became their men, so that they were *Lords of all Britain.* Sometimes, as being lords of the other world where the Roman Emperors had no power, they were called *Emperors of Britain*, or in Greek *Basileus*, in imitation of the Emperors of the East. It was King Edward who first received the homage of all Britain in 924. But it was not till a long time after that the Danes in the North of England were thoroughly subdued. But these settlements of the Danes, by breaking up the other English kingdoms and by making Englishmen everywhere ready to join against the invaders, really did much to help the West-Saxon Kings in winning the lordship of the whole island.

10. **Foundation of the Duchy of Normandy.**—The Danes and other Northmen also made many invasions of Gaul through the whole latter half of the ninth century. They more than once sailed up the Seine and besieged Paris. There was one specially famous siege of Paris in 885, when Count Odo did great things in withstanding the Northmen, in reward of which he was before long, as we have seen, elected King. Soon after this the Northmen began to make settlements in Gaul as they did in Britain, and one of their settlements rose to great importance. This

was the settlement made at *Rouen* by a chief named *Rolf*, or in Latin *Rollo.* This was in 913, when *Charles the Simple*, who was King of the West-Franks —he was of the House of the Karlings and reigned at Laon—and *Robert,* Duke of the French, who was brother of King Odo and was afterwards King himself, granted the land at the mouth of the Seine to Rolf. For this he became King Charles's man, and he served his lord much more faithfully than ever the Dukes of the French did. Rolf was baptized, as Guthrum had been, and the Northmen who settled in Gaul gradually became Christians and learned to speak French. Their name was softened into *Normans*, and their land was called *Normandy,* and their prince the *Duke of the Normans.* The Dukes of the Normans of the House of Rolf became the most powerful princes in Northern Gaul, and we shall presently hear of them in England.

11. **Summary.**—Thus, in the course of the ninth and tenth centuries the great *Frankish Empire* broke in pieces; the *Kingdom of France* arose in Gaul; the *Kingdom of England* grew up in Britain; the *Danes* and *Northmen* settled both in Britain and in Gaul, and their settlement in Gaul grew into the *Duchy of Normandy*. During this time the *Romance* languages had hardly begun to be written, but men were finding out that they were distinct languages from Latin. Books on the Continent were still wholly written in Latin. Thus *Eginhard*, the Secretary of Charles the Great, wrote the Life of his master, and there were other good writers of history in all the Frankish kingdoms. But the *English Chronicle* began to be put together in England in these times, so that we have, what no other people in Western Christendom has, our ancestral history written in our own tongue from the beginning.

CHAPTER VIII.

THE SAXON EMPERORS.

The Kingdom of Germany; dealings with the Magyars and Slaves (1)—*the Saxon Kings; victories of Henry the Fowler and Otto the Great over the Magyars* (2)—*Otto the great crowned Emperor; relations between the Empire and the German Kingdom* (2, 3)—*the later Saxon Emperors* (3)—*disputes between the Eastern and Western Churches* (4)—*the Macedonian Emperors in the East; their victories over the Saracens* (4)—*Slavonic settlements in the Eastern Empire; wars with the Russians and Bulgarians* (5)—*greatness of England under Edgar* (6)—*Danish invasions of England; reign of Cnut in England* (6)—*greatness of the Scandinavian nations; great dominion of Cnut; effects of the Scandinavian settlements in Gaul and Russia* (6, 7)—*conversion of the Scandinavians and Russians to Christianity* (7)—*Summary* (8).

1. **The German Kingdom.**—The division of 887 separated for ever the Kingdoms of the East and West Franks, those which answer to Germany and France. But the Kingdoms of Italy and Burgundy were, after a while, once more united with Germany. But this was not just yet. The Kings of the East-Franks, the *Eastern Kings* as they were called, were the head Kings, but as yet they only held their own land, the *Teutonic Kingdom* or Germany. They had much ado to defend themselves against the inroads of the Danes, to defend and extend their border against the Slaves to the north-east, and to drive back some new and fearful enemies who had begun to show themselves to the south-east. These were the *Magyars* or *Hungarians*, of whom we have already spoken, who were pressing into Central Europe, and who, wherever they came, did as much mischief by land as the Northmen

did by sea. They were still heathens, but in the end, before the tenth century was out, they became Christians, and settled down into a regular and powerful Christian kingdom. They have held their place among the kingdoms of Europe ever since, and their land is still called the *Kingdom of Hungary*. But, before the Hungarians had thus settled down among Christian nations, the German Kings had to fight many battles against them to keep them out of their own dominions. As a safeguard against the Hungarian invasions they founded a *Mark* or border-state under a chief called a *Markgraf* or *Marquess;* this was called the *Eastern Mark*, *Ostmark* or *Oesterreich*. This grew into the Duchy of *Austria*, the Dukes of which have, oddly enough, for a long time past been also Kings of Hungary. To the north of Hungary several Slavonic states grew up during this time into Christian dukedoms and kingdoms, especially those of *Poland* and *Bohemia;* but the *Wends* on the south of the Baltic remained heathens for a long time, and the *Prussians* to the east of them for a longer time still. Thus the Kingdom of Germany was the central state of Europe, and it had to do with all parts of Europe, East, West, North, and South. And it was soon to rise to greater things still.

2. **The Saxon Kings.**—The dynasty which had most to do with raising the German Kingdom to greatness was that of the *Saxons*, whose Duke, *Henry*, was elected King in 918. He did much to make his kingdom flourishing and powerful, and he had to wage many wars against the Magyars, especially by the foundation of towns. He was succeeded in 936 by his son *Otto*, called the *Great*. He finally defeated the Magyars in a great battle in 954. He had also much to do with the affairs of the Western Kingdom, and he often stepped in to help the Karolingian King *Lewis*, who was his brother-in-law, against his enemies in France and Normandy. But he is most famous

for again uniting the *Roman Empire* to the *German Kingdom*. Since Arnulf no Emperor had been generally acknowledged, though some of the Kings of Italy had been crowned Emperors at Rome. In truth, Italy, during the whole half of the tenth century, was altogether torn in pieces by the struggles of rival Kings and wicked Popes. In 951 Otto was invited into Italy, and he made the King *Berengar* become his man. In 962 he was again called on by the Pope and the Italians to deliver them from Berengar altogether. So he entered Italy a second time, and was crowned Emperor at Rome, by the Pope *John the Twelfth*, one of the worst of all the Popes.

3. **The Restoration of the Empire.**—The coronation of Otto the Great as Emperor put the Western Empire on quite a new footing. Hitherto the Empire had had no special connexion with any one of the several kingdoms which had arisen out of the break-up of the dominion of Charles the Great. The Imperial crown had been sometimes held by one King, and sometimes by another, and very often there had been no Emperor at all. But now Germany had, under the Saxon Kings, become so much the greatest of all the Frankish kingdoms that it was able to join the Empire to itself. The change was in truth a restoration of the Empire in a more regular shape after a time of confusion. From this time the Empire was always held by a German king. As long as the Empire lasted, the rule was that whoever was chosen King in Germany had a right to be crowned *King of Italy* at Milan, and to be crowned *Emperor* at Rome. There was not always an Emperor, because some of the German Kings never got to Rome to be crowned Emperors; but there always was either an Emperor or a King who alone had the right to be crowned Emperor. Thus the Kingdom of Italy was again united with the Kingdom of Germany. But both Burgundy and Karolingia or the Western Kingdom

still remained cut off from the Empire, Burgundy for a while and Karolingia for ever. Still the Emperors kept a good deal of influence in Burgundy, and in the Western Kingdom too as long as any of the Karlings reigned at Laon. But when the *Kingdom of France* was finally established, when the long line of Kings of the French of the blood of Hugh Capet began to reign at Paris, France left off having anything to do with the Empire at all. Otto the Great died in 972, and after him reigned his son *Otto the Second* till 983. He had wars with the Danes, whose King *Harold*, called *Blaatand* or *Bluetooth*, he forced to become a Christian, and also with the Eastern Emperors in Southern Italy. Then came *Otto the Third* from 983 to 1002. He was called the *Wonder of the World.* His great wish was to make Rome again the head of the world and to reign there again, like one of the old Emperors. But he died young, and his plans were all cut short. Then came *Henry the Second*, a descendant of Henry the First, but not of Otto the Great, who was the last Saxon Emperor. He died in 1024.

4. **The Eastern Empire.**—It is now time to say something of what had happened in the East since the election of Charles the Great in the West. The Eastern Empire, as I before said, was now chiefly confined to the Greek-speaking parts of Europe and Asia. And, after the Eastern and Western Empires were separated, disputes gradually arose between the Eastern and Western Churches. They differed on some points both of doctrine and ceremony, but the real ground of quarrel was chiefly because the Eastern Church would never admit the claims of the Bishops of Rome. The Iconoclast controversy went on during a great part of the ninth century, but in the end the worshippers of images gained the day. After Eirênê there were several Emperors of different families, some of whom were weak men, while others ruled well and fought manfully against the Saracens. At last, in the

latter part of the ninth century, a dynasty arose under which the Eastern Empire won back a great deal of its former power. This was the *Basilian* or *Macedonian* dynasty, the first Emperor of which, *Basil the First* or the *Macedonian*, began to reign in 867. He was a law-giver, and under him the Byzantine dominions in Italy were greatly increased. But the time when the Eastern Empire reached its greatest amount of power after the final division was from 963 to 1025. Three Emperors, one after the other, *Nikêphoros Phôkas*, *John Tzimiskês*, and *Basil the Second*, won back many of the provinces which had been lost. The Saracens, as we have already seen, were now cut up into many small states, and, though the Caliphs went on, they could no longer meet the Emperors on equal terms. Nikêphoros won back Crete, and both he and John Tzimiskês, who murdered him and reigned in his stead, waged wars in the East, won back Antioch and other cities which had been taken by the Saracens in their first conquests, and again carried the Roman frontier to the Euphrates.

5. **The Slavonic Invasions.**—We said at the beginning that the *Slavonic* nations were the last of the great Aryan swarms which had pressed into Europe, and that which had played the least part in the general affairs of the world. As yet we have not heard much of them, except so far as the German Kings had greatly extended their dominion to the West at their expense. But we have now reached a very important period in their history, chiefly with regard to their dealings with the Eastern Empire. For a long time past various nations had been pressing into the northern parts of the Byzantine dominions, and the Emperors had constant wars to wage against enemies on their northern as well as on their eastern frontier. Some of them settled within the Empire, while others simply invaded and ravaged its provinces. Some of these invaders and settlers were Turanians,

but many of them belonged to the race of the Slaves, who play a part in the history of the Eastern Empire something like that which the Teutonic people played in the West. That is to say, they were half conquerors, half disciples. Many of the north-western provinces of the Empire were settled by Slavonic tribes, who have grown into the people of *Servia*, *Dalmatia*, and the other lands now bordering on Hungary, Austria, and Turkey. They also made large settlements in Macedonia and Greece, but from some of these they were afterwards driven out. It is even said that the Macedonian Emperors themselves were really of Slavonic descent. The *Russians*, also a Slavonic people, though their princes were of Scandinavian descent, made several inroads into the Eastern Empire in the ninth and tenth centuries, and even attacked Constantinople by sea. But they were finally defeated by the Emperor John Tzimiskês in 973. Another great enemy was the *Bulgarians*, a people originally Turanian, but who learnt to speak a Slavonic language, and who were so mixed up with their Slavonic neighbours and subjects, that they may pass as one of the Slavonic nations. They founded a kingdom in the north-western part of the Empire, and they were for a long time a great thorn in the sides of the Emperors. With these Bulgarians the Emperors had many wars, till in the end their kingdom was altogether destroyed by *Basil the Second*, who was called the *Slayer of the Bulgarians*, when the Roman frontier was again carried to the Danube. All these invaders and settlers gradually became Christians, getting their Christianity from the Eastern Church, as the Teutons and Western Slaves got theirs from the Western Church. But the Popes and the Patriarchs of Constantinople had long disputes about the obedience of the Bulgarians. It was under Basil the Second, whose sister *Theophanô* married the Western Emperor Otto the Second, that the separate Eastern Empire was at the greatest height of its power, but after his death it greatly fell back again.

6. **England and the Danes.**—England had a good deal to do with the Western Empire during the time of the Saxon Emperors. The daughters of *Edward the Elder* were married to the chief princes of Europe, and one of them named *Eadgyth* or *Edith* was the first wife of Otto the Great. It marks the central position of the German Kingdom that its kings made marriages with England at one end and with Constantinople at the other. Under *Edgar*, who reigned from 959 to 975, England was at the height of its power, but in the reign of his son *Æthelred* the inroads of the Danes and Northmen began again. At one time, in 994, England was attacked at once by *Olaf* King of the Northmen and by *Swegen* or *Sweyn* King of the Danes. Olaf was persuaded to become a Christian and to make peace with England; so he went home to Norway and began to bring in Christianity there. Swegen was the son of that King Harold who had been overcome by Otto the Second; he had been baptized in his childhood, but had fallen back into heathenism. The war with Swegen went on till at last, in 1013, Æthelred was driven out and Swegen was acknowledged King all over England. This was quite another kind of conquest from mere plundering inroads, and even from settlements in parts of the country, like that of Guthrum or that of Rolf in Gaul. A King of all Denmark came against England to make himself King over all England also. Swegen died very soon and Æthelred did not live long after. The war then went on between *Cnut* or *Canute* the son of Swegen and *Edmund* the son of Æthelred. At last, in 1017, Cnut became King over all England; he inherited the crown of his native country *Denmark*, and he also won *Norway* and part of *Sweden*. He was thus lord of all Northern Europe, and was by far the most powerful prince of his time

Though he came into England by force, he ruled well and won the love of the people; but after his death in 1035 the bad government of his sons disgusted the English with the Danish rule, and in 1042 they again chose a native King in the person of *Edward* the son of Æthelred.

7. **Greatness of the Scandinavians.**—The time when Cnut reigned in England was the time when the Danes and the Northmen were at the height of their power. *Denmark*, *Norway*, and *Sweden* were all powerful kingdoms; *England* was under a Danish King, and princes of Scandinavian descent ruled both in *Normandy* and in *Russia*. But wherever the Northmen settled, though they always put a new life into the lands which they made their own, they showed a wonderful power of adapting themselves to the people among whom they settled, and of taking to their manners and language. Thus Cnut, when he reigned in England, became quite an Englishman, and the Northmen who settled in Gaul became quite French, and those who settled in Russia became quite Slavonic. In this way the original lands of the Northmen really lost in strength and importance, and became of less account in Europe than they otherwise might have been. For the best life of Scandinavia went away into other lands to give a new life to them. About the end of the tenth and beginning of the eleventh centuries, all the Northern nations, except the *Prussians* and *Lithuanians*, gradually became Christians. The Scandinavians, like the other Teutonic nations, got their Christianity from the West; but the Russians, like the Bulgarians and the other nations who had to do with the Eastern Empire, got their Christianity from Constantinople and became part of the Eastern Church. To this day they are the only one among the great nations of Europe which remains in the communion of the East, having nothing to do either with the Bishop of Rome or with the Reformed Churches.

8. **Summary.**—Thus, in the ninth century and the beginning of the tenth, the *German kingdom* advanced, and was again united with the *Roman Empire.* The *Eastern Empire* won back much of its power, and drove back its Slavonic invaders. The *Danes* conquered England, and the Scandinavian people generally were at the height of their power. The chief historians of this period were the German writers who recorded the deeds of the Ottos. In England learning had got back from what it was at an earlier time. In Gaul men had already found out that the *Roman*, or the spoken tongue of the people, had grown into a different language from the written *Latin.* But we have no French writings as yet.

CHAPTER IX.

THE FRANCONIAN EMPERORS.

Succession of Kings, Conrad, Henry the Third, Henry the Fourth, Henry the Fifth (1)—*dealings of Henry the Third with the Popes* (1)—*disputes between Henry the Fourth and Gregory the Seventh* (1)—*continued disputes between the Popes and Henry the Fifth* (1)—*causes of the growth of Papal power* (2)—*designs of Gregory the Seventh; disputes about investures and the marriage of the clergy* (2)—*growth of the Duchy of Normandy* (3)—*reign of William the Conqueror; his claims on the crown of England favoured by the Pope* (3)—*election of Harold of England: invasion of Harold of Norway; Norman invasion and conquest of England* (3)—*effects of the Norman Conquest of England; use of the French language; closer connexion of England with other lands* (4)—*relations between France and Normandy* (5)—*effects of the Norman Conquest on France; greatness of Henry the Second in England* (5)—*advance of the Christians in Spain; growth of the kingdom of Arragon* (6)—*Norman Conquest of Sicily; foundation and growth of the king-*

dom (7)—*decline of the Eastern Empire* (8)—*growth of the Turks; their dealings with the Caliphs* (8)—*divisions of the Caliphate* (8)—*wars between the Turks and the Eastern Empire; conquests of the Turks in Asia Minor* (8)—*revival of the Empire under the Komnênian Emperors; decay of the Turkish power* (8)—*causes of the Crusades* (8, 9)—*the Crusade preached by Peter the Hermit and Urban the Second* (9)—*First Crusade; taking of Jerusalem* (9)—*effects of the Crusades* (9)—*Summary* (10).

1. **Succession of Kings.**—On the death of Henry the Second, *Conrad*, a descendant of a daughter of Otto the Great, was chosen King. He was the first of the *Franconian Emperors*. They are so called as coming from the Eastern or Teutonic *Francia*, which, to distinguish it from Latin *Francia* or *France*, is commonly called *Franconia*. He was crowned Emperor in 1027 and reigned till 1039. The chief event of his reign was that in 1032 the Kingdom of Burgundy was united to the Empire on the death of its last King *Rudolf*. Thus three out of the four Frankish Kingdoms were again joined together, France alone, as we must now call it, standing aloof. Conrad's son *Henry the Third* was one of the greatest of all the Emperors. He was crowned King both of Germany and of Burgundy in his father's lifetime. This was often done in those days, in order to make the succession certain, and to avoid the dangers of an *interregnum* or time when there is no King. Henry was called into Italy in much the same way as Otto the Great had been; for there were great disputes at Rome, where three candidates at once all claimed the Popedom. King Henry came into Italy in 1046 and deposed them all. He then gave the Popedom to several German Bishops one after the other, and they ruled the Church far better than the Romans had done. He was himself crowned Emperor in the same year. He did much to restore order and religion both in

Germany and in Italy, and he maintained the authority of the Empire better than had been done for a long time. He was a close ally of the English King Edward, whose half-sister *Gunhild*, the daughter of Cnut, was his first wife. On his death in 1056 he was succeeded by his son *Henry the Fourth*, who was only six years old when his father died, but who had been already crowned King. His childhood and youth was a time of great confusion, and, as he grew up, he ruled at first very ill, and his oppression drove the *Saxons* to revolt in 1073. About the same time there arose long disputes between the Emperors and the Popes, which tore Germany and Italy in pieces. At one time Pope *Gregory the Seventh*, the famous *Hildebrand*, professed to depose the King, and in the beginning of 1077 Henry had to come and crave pardon of Gregory. In the same year the Saxons, and others in Germany who were discontented, chose *Rudolf* Duke of Swabia King instead of Henry. Rudolf was killed in 1080, but, during nearly all the rest of his reign, Henry had to struggle with one enemy after another, among them his own son *Conrad*, and afterwards his other son *Henry*, whom he had crowned King in 1099. Henry himself had driven Gregory out of Rome in 1085, and he had been crowned Emperor by *Clement the Third*, whom he had himself appointed Pope. At last he died in 1106, while still at war with his son King Henry, who now reigned alone. *Henry the Fifth* had nearly the same disputes with the Popes which his father had had, but he was regularly crowned Emperor at Rome in 1111. He married *Matilda*, the daughter of our King Henry the First, but he had no son, and the Franconian dynasty came to an end at his death in 1125.

2. **Growth of the Papal Power.**—The power of the Popes, which has just been mentioned, and their disputes with the Emperors, must be spoken of a little more fully. From the time of Constantine onwards,

the divisions of the Empire and the constant absence of the Emperors from Rome had greatly increased the power of the Popes. They had not, like the Patriarchs of Constantinople, a superior always at hand. Charles the Great had fully asserted the Imperial power over the Church, but, after his Empire broke up, the power of the Popes grew again. It was checked only by their own wickedness and their divisions among themselves, which Kings like Otto the Great and Henry the Third had to step in and put an end to. Things were very different now from what they had been in the old times, when the whole or nearly the whole of the Church was contained within the bounds of the Empire. First of all, there were now two rival Emperors and two rival Churches, and the Empire and the Church of the East in no way acknowledged either the Emperor or the Bishop of the Old Rome. And even in the West, part of the Empire, namely the Kingdom of France, had cut itself off from the main body, while new Christian kingdoms like England, Hungary, and Denmark had risen up beyond the Empire. In this state of things the Bishops of Rome, who were looked up to by so many kingdoms as the chief Bishops of the West, could hardly remain so submissive to the Emperors as they had been when the Emperors were the only Christian princes. The Popes had not as yet any distinct temporal dominion, such as they had in after times; still they were no longer mere subjects of the Emperor, as they had been under Constantine and Justinian and Charles the Great. In truth, it was to this undefined position that the Popes owed much of their power. And now Gregory the Seventh, the greatest of all the Popes, set himself to work to set up the ecclesiastical power as superior to the temporal. To this end he laid down two main rules, one that the clergy might not marry, the other that no temporal prince should bestow any ecclesiastical benefice, as was then commonly done in Germany, England, and most parts of Europe. Hence began the long quarrel between Gregory and Henry the Fourth, and between many Popes and Emperors after them. And we may mark that the quarrel between the Popes and the Emperors was one in which good men might and did take either side. A good Emperor like Henry the Third did much good by clearing away unworthy disputants, and giving to the Church a succession of worthy rulers. But the same power in the hands of a bad prince led to the sale of bishopricks for money and to many other abuses. The great evil was that Popes like Gregory the Seventh, who were really anxious for the purity of the Church, acted too much as if the Church were made up only of the clergy, and strove to make the clergy, with themselves at their head, into quite a separate body from other men. It is hard to say which party won in the end. We may perhaps say that the Popes succeeded in overthrowing the power of the Emperors, but that they had themselves to yield in the end to the power of other temporal princes.

3. **The Norman Conquest of England.**—We have already seen how in 987 the dynasty of the Karlings in the West came to an end, and how Hugh, the Duke of the French, became King of the French. Meanwhile the duchy which had been founded by Rolf had grown up into great power and prosperity, and *Normandy* reckoned among the chief states of Western Euorpe. And Normandy became greater still under its famous Duke *William*, who subdued England, and who is therefore known as *William the Conqueror*. It was now that Britain, which had hitherto been looked on as another world, began to have much more to do with the general affairs of Europe. King *Edward*, the last King of the English of the old West-Saxon dynasty, was, through his mother, a kinsman of Duke William, and it would seem that at one time of his life he made Duke William some kind of

promise that, as he had no children, he should succeed him on the throne of England. But, however this may be, when King Edward died in 1066, the English people, as there was no one in the royal family fit to reign, gave the Crown to Earl *Harold*, who was then the greatest man in the land. Duke William however put forth his claim, and, though he found no one to help him in England, he made most people in other lands believe that he had the right on his side. Especially he persuaded *Hildebrand*, who was not yet Pope, but who already had great influence at Rome, to take his part. So Pope *Alexander the Second* declared in his favour, and blessed his undertaking. This was the way in which the Popes seized every opportunity to extend their power both within the Empire and in other parts of the world. William was thus able to invade England, at the head not only of his own Normans, but of men from all parts, who were taught to look on the enterprise as a holy war. England was just at this time attacked by *Harold Hardrada*, King of the *Northmen*, so that her King Harold had to fight against two foes at once. He defeated Harold of Norway, but was himself defeated and slain by Duke William in the famous battle of *Senlac* or *Hastings*. Duke William was crowned King at Christmas 1066, but the English still withstood him in many places, and it took him about four years to get full possession of the whole kingdom. He gradually found means to give all the greatest estates and highest offices in England to Normans and other strangers, and he handed on the English Crown to his descendants, by whom it has been held ever since.

4. **Effects of the Norman Conquest of England.**—The establishment of Duke William and his followers in Normandy brought about some very great changes both in England and in the rest of Europe. The English were not killed or turned out, as they had themselves done by the Welsh, and they

kept their own laws and language; yet for a long time all the chief men in the land were of Norman or other foreign descent. But it is wonderful in how short a time the Normans in England became good Englishmen. This was partly perhaps because Normans and English were, after all, near kinsfolk, only the English had kept their own tongue, while the Normans had learned to speak French. French remained for a long time the fashionable language in England, and though, in the end, English became once more the speech of all men in the land, yet in the meanwhile it became greatly changed, and a great many French words crept in. Many new ideas came in with the Normans, which gradually made great changes in English laws and manners. The power of the Kings became much greater than it had been before, and William made the whole kingdom far more truly one than it had been up to his time. Since his days no one has ever thought of dividing it. The Norman Conquest also caused far more intercourse than there had been before between England and other nations. Learning flourished more, the art of building greatly advanced, and many reforms were made in the Church; but it must not be forgotten that England from this time was brought much more under the power of the Popes.

5. **Relations between England and France.**—Before the Norman Conquest, England and *France,* meaning thereby the new *Kingdom of Paris*, had hardly anything to do with one another. But France and Normandy often were enemies. Ever since Paris became the capital, the Kings of the French had felt themselves hemmed in by the Dukes at Rouen. And now that the same man was Duke of the Normans and King of the English, the Norman Dukes became still more powerful in Gaul, and were still more dangerous neighbours to their lords the Kings of the French. The King at Paris was in truth shut in on every side by his own vassals, the great Dukes and

Counts, over whom he had no real authority. Just at the time when the Empire was strongest under Henry the Third, the Kingdom of France was weakest under *Henry the First*, the third of the Parisian Kings. From this time there was a distinct rivalry, which we shall constantly come across, between the Kings of the French and the Kings of the English, who were also Dukes of the Normans. This rivalry has gone on almost ever since, and we shall constantly meet with it in one shape or another; and this rivalry had the further effect of keeping up the old connexion between England and Germany, both of them being rivals of France. I have already mentioned that *Henry the First of England*, the son of William and the third of the Norman Kings, gave his daughter in marriage to the Emperor Henry the Fifth. King Henry of England, who reigned from 1100 to 1135, was born in England, and he married *Edith* or *Matilda*, the daughter of *Malcolm* King of Scots. Her mother *Margaret* was the granddaughter of King *Edmund Ironside*, so that Henry's children had some English blood in them. In 1154 *Henry*, the son of Henry the First's daughter, the Empress *Matilda*, by her second husband *Geoffrey Count of Anjou*, came to the Crown of England. The pedigree in this case should be carefully remembered, because with Henry the Second began the *Angevin* Kings of England, who were neither Norman nor English, except in the female line. Henry presently married *Eleanor* the heiress of *Aquitaine;* he thus was master of the greater part of Northern and Western Gaul, holding of the King of the French far greater possessions than the King held himself. Here is quite a new state of things, in which the same man not only held both England and Normandy, but had by far the greatest power in all Gaul. We shall presently see what came of these changes.

6. **Wars with the Mahometans in Spain.**—The time of the Franconian Emperors is also memor-

able as the time when the great struggle between the Christian and Mahometan nations began to spread itself over a much wider field. All this while wars had been going on with the Saracens in all those parts of Europe and Western Asia where they had settled. The Christians of *Spain*, as I have already said, had always kept their independence in the mountainous lands in the north, and the conquests of Charles the Great had been a further check to the advance of the Saracens. As the Western Empire began to be divided, the Western Caliphate grew stronger. The time of the greatest power of the Mahometans in Spain was in the reign of *Abd-al-rahman the Third*, from 912 to 961. The Christian kingdoms however still maintained their independence, and in 1031 the Western Caliphate came to an end, and the Saracen dominion in Spain was cut up into several small states. The Christians were now able to advance, and in 1084 *Alfonso the Sixth*, who had united the two kingdoms of *Leon* and *Castile*, won back the old capital of *Toledo*, and was near making himself master of the whole of Spain. The Mahometans in Spain had now to call in their fellow-believers in Africa to their help. Thus arose the Moorish dynasty of the *Almoravides* in Southern Spain, which put a check for the while to the advance of the Christians. But in 1118, *Alfonso* of Aragon recovered *Zaragoza*, that is *Cæsar-Augusta*, the chief city of Eastern Spain, and from that time the kingdom of *Aragon* also began to grow in importance.

7. **Foundation of the Kingdom of Sicily.**—Meanwhile the Christians were also gaining ground on the Mahometans in the great islands of the Mediterranean. I have said how the Emperor Nikêphoros won back *Crete* for the Eastern Empire, and in the beginning of the eleventh century *Sardinia* was won back by the people of the Tuscan commonwealth of *Pisa*. Soon afterwards, Norman adventurers began to press into the South, and to make conquests at the

expense both of the Saracens and of the Eastern Emperors. Under the famous *Robert Wiscard*, they conquered nearly all the lands which the Eastern Emperors still kept in Italy. They then crossed into *Sicily* in 1062, and founded a county which, in 1130, under its third Count *Roger the Second*, became a kingdom. Thus began the *Kingdom of Sicily*, where at first French-speaking Kings reigned over Arabic-speaking Mahometans and Greek-speaking Christians. All three languages gradually died out, but for a time all nations and religions flourished under the Norman Kings. King Roger afterwards won the Norman possessions in Italy, and the little that was left to the Eastern Emperors. Thus the Kingdom of Sicily took in, not only the island, but all the southern part of the Italian peninsula.

8. **The Eastern Empire.**—We must now look to the affairs of the Eastern Empire in Asia, and the more so because its danger at this time led to the most famous of all the wars between Christians and Mahometans, namely to the *Crusades* or *Holy Wars*. These were the wars which the Christians waged to win back the Holy Land, and especially the tomb of our Lord at Jerusalem, from their Mahometan possessors. After the death of Basil the Second, the Eastern Empire, which, under the Macedonian Emperors, had again become so powerful both in Europe and Asia, began once more to fall back. As a new European enemy had arisen against it in the Normans of Sicily, so a new and terrible enemy arose against it in Asia. These were the *Turks* of the house of *Seljuk*. We may now look on the chief dominion of Asia as being finally handed over from the Saracens to the Turks. This change of power in Asia brought about two memorable results. First, it was the cause of the heaviest blow which the Eastern Empire had undergone since the time of the first Caliphs. Secondly, it was the cause of the *Crusades* which were waged

by men from Western Europe. In the course of the tenth century, the Eastern Caliphate may be looked on as coming to an end as a political power. A third Caliphate arose in *Egypt,* and the Caliphs of Bagdad gradually fell under the control of their own mercenaries and ministers, much as the Merowingian Kings of the Franks had fallen under the control of the Austrasian Mayors. Meanwhile several Turkish dynasties arose in *Persia*, and the Mahometan conquest of *India* began. At last, in 1055, the Caliph *Al Kayem* asked help of *Togrel Beg*, the chief of the Seljuk Turks, much as the Popes had invited Pippin and Charles the Great into Italy. The Caliphs were now left in free possession of Bagdad, but a great Turkish power now arose, which soon took in all Western Asia. War soon arose between this new power and the Eastern Roman Empire. In 1071, at the battle of *Manzikert*, the Turks, under their Sultan *Alp Arslan*, gained a great victory over the Romans, and the Emperor *Rômanos* was taken prisoner, as Valerian had long ago been by Sapor. The result of this was that the Eastern Emperors lost, not only all that had been won back under the Macedonian Emperors, but nearly all their possessions in Asia. The dominions of the Seljuk Turks now reached to the Hellespont. Palestine meanwhile was conquered and conquered again by the different Mahometan powers, and both the Eastern Christians and the pilgrims from Europe who went to pray at Jerusalem were far worse treated than they had been in the days of the first Saracens. Meanwhile a new dynasty arose in the Eastern Empire under *Alexios Komnênos*, a wise prince, whose family kept the throne for about a hundred years, and produced some of the best rulers and bravest warriors among the Byzantine Emperors. Again, in 1092, the Seljuk power, like other Eastern states, was divided. One line of Sultans reigned in Asia Minor, having their capital at *Nikaia*, and, as they ruled over lands which had been won from the Empire, they called themselves Sultans of *Rome.* Thus everything favoured a common enterprise on the part of the Christians. The Mahometans were divided; the Eastern Empire was recovering itself, and men in the West were stirred up by pilgrims who told of all that the Christians suffered in the East. Thus the nations of the West were moved to a great general enterprise to deliver their brethren and the Holy Places from the power of the infidels.

9. **The Beginning of the Crusades.**—The duty of going to deliver the Holy Places was first preached by *Peter*, a hermit of Amiens, though several Popes and Emperors, Gregory the Seventh among them, had already dreamed of such an undertaking. The cause was now zealously taken up by Pope *Urban the Second*, who in 1095 held a Council at *Clermont* in Auvergne, at which the *Holy War* was decreed. This war was called a *Crusade*, because men put a *cross* on their shoulders to show that they were going to fight in a holy war. Neither the Emperor Henry nor any of the Kings of the West took any part in the Crusade, but many of the smaller princes and a vast number of private men set forth on the pilgrimage. Most of those who went on the First Crusade were French-speaking people, from which it has come that the Eastern nations have ever since called all the people of Western Europe *Franks.* The Crusaders passed through Asia Minor into *Palestine*, and at last, in 1099, they took *Jerusalem.* They founded several Christian principalities in Palestine and Syria, of which the head was the *Kingdom of Jerusalem*, of which *Godfrey* of *Boulogne*, Duke of *Lower Lotharingia*,—that is of *Brabant* in the modern kingdom of Belgium,—was the first King. The Crusaders kept Jerusalem for somewhat less than a hundred years; and, though the kingdom was constantly helped by new Crusaders from Europe, it had much ado to hold its ground

against the various Mahometan powers. Meanwhile, as the power of the Turks had been so much weakened by the coming of the Crusaders, the Komnênian Emperors were able to win back a large part of Asia Minor, all the Euxine and Ægæan coasts, and the Sultans of Rome were driven back into the inland parts, and had their capital at *Ikonion,* instead of at Nikaia. The effects of the Crusades were very important in every way. Eastern and Western Christians were brought across one another and across the Mahometans; and, though they commonly met one another as enemies, yet they came to know one another better, and to learn of each other. Both the Saracens and the Romans of the East had much to teach the Western nations in many branches of art and learning. But still more important than this was the general stirring up of men's minds which followed on such great events. From the time of the Crusades a great revival of thought and learning of every kind began throughout Europe.

10. **Summary.**—The time of the Franconian Emperors was thus a time of very important changes. The great struggle between the *Popes* and the *Emperors* began. The *Turkish* power began. The *Crusades* began. The *Norman Conquest* of *England* took place. The Christians began to gain ground again in *Spain.* It was the time when the chief states of modern Europe began to form themselves, and when the literature of the *Romance* languages began. It was also a time when we find many good historical writers in England, Germany, and Normandy. And it was a time of great splendour in building, especially in building churches. But they were still built in the *round-arched* or *Romanesque* style; the use of the *pointed* arch, and what is commonly called the *Gothic* style, did not come in till near the end of the twelfth century.

CHAPTER X.

GENERAL VIEW OF THE MIDDLE AGES.

The Middle Ages; union of Roman and Teutonic elements (1)—the Church and the Empire; how affected by the Teutonic settlements (2)—ideal powers of the Emperor and the Pope; the theory only imperfectly carried out (2)—changes following on the transfer of the Empire to the German Kings (2)—study of the Roman Law (2)—the Western Empire becomes German and the Eastern Empire becomes Greek (3)—condition of the various countries of Europe; extension of the German Kingdom to the East (3)—the old Teutonic constitution; three orders of men, nobles, freemen, and slaves (4)—mixture of Roman and Teutonic ideas (4)—origin of fiefs; Roman grants of land for military service; Teutonic custom of companionship to a personal Lord (5)—distinction of allodial and feudal tenures; change of allodial holdings into feudal (5)—effects of the feudal tenures; growth of the class of serfs (6)—introduction of representative assemblies; growth of the power of the feudal princes (6)—comparison of the political state of England, Germany, and France (7)—Kings commonly chosen out of a single family (8)—origin of the Electors of the Empire (8)—the Crown of France becomes strictly hereditary (8)—uncertainty of succession in the Eastern Empire (8)—spread of Christianity over nearly all Europe (9)—division between the Eastern and the Western Churches (9)—growth of the power of the Popes; tendency of the clergy to act as a distinct class (9)—temporal powers of the clergy; special greatness of the German Prelates (10)—distinction between regular and secular clergy (11)—various orders of monks; the military orders (11)—learning in the West chiefly in the hands of the clergy; contrast in the East (12)—Greek becomes the language of the Eastern Empire; continued use of Latin in the West (12)—early Teutonic literature; growth of the Romance languages (12)—revival of learning in the twelfth cen-

tury (12)—*position of the towns in ancient Greece and Italy; their decline under the Teutonic invasions* (13)—*destruction of Roman towns in Britain* (13)—*growth of the towns in Germany; greatness of the Hanseatic League* (13)—*greatness of the cities in Italy* (13)—*Summary* (14).

1. **General Survey of Europe.**—We have now reached a point at which it will be well to stop and look at the general state of things among the European nations. All the things which distinguish what are called the *Middle Ages*, alike from what we are used to in modern Europe and from the old days of heathen Greece and Rome, have now fully come in. The settlement of the Teutonic nations within the Roman Empire had gradually brought about a state of things in which we may see both Roman and Teutonic elements, but in which the two had, as we may say, so joined together as to make a third thing different from either.

2. **The Church and the Empire.**—The two great powers in Western Europe were the *Church* and the *Empire.* Both of them lived on through the settlements of the German nations, and both in a manner drew new powers from the change of things. Men believed more than ever that Rome was the lawful and natural centre of the world. For it was held that there were of divine right two *Vicars of God* upon earth, the Roman Emperor his Vicar in temporal things, and the Roman Bishop his Vicar in spiritual things. This belief did not interfere with the existence either of separate commonwealths and principalities or of national Churches. But it was held that the Roman Emperor, who was called *Lord of the World*, was of right the head of all temporal states, and that the Roman Bishop, the Pope, was of right the head of all Churches. Now this theory was never carried out, if only because so large a part of Christendom, all the Churches and nations of the East, refused to acknow-

ledge either the Emperor or the Bishop of the Old Rome. But it was much more nearly carried out in the case of the Roman Bishop than it was in the case of the Roman Emperor. For the Popes did really make themselves spiritual heads of the whole West, while the temporal headship of the Emperors was never acknowledged by a large part even of the West. But the continued belief which men still had in the Roman Empire as a living thing is not only most remarkable in itself, but it had a most important effect on the history of the world. Still it is plain that the Roman Empire could not really be the same thing as it had been before the Teutonic nations came into the Roman dominions. Even during the short time that the whole Empire of Charles the Great stayed together, it made a great difference that the Emperor was a German King, living for the most part in Germany, and not at Rome or anywhere in Italy. And afterwards the utter cutting off of France and Spain from the Empire did much to take away from its character as a universal monarchy, and to make the Emperors more like common Kings over a particular nation. They were still Kings of Italy and Burgundy as well as of Germany, but most things were now tending to make the Empire more and more German and less and less Roman. On the other hand, as this was the time of a great new birth of learning, men had begun, among other things, to study the *Civil Law*, the old law of Rome, as it was put together by the Emperor Justinian. This study naturally led men to a respect for the Imperial power, and thus helped to give the claims of the Emperors a new source of strength. We shall see presently the effects of these different tendencies when we come to the history of the Emperors during the twelfth and thirteenth centuries.

3. **The Nations of Europe.**—Nearly all the nations of *Modern Europe* had now come into being.

We may even say that the two Empires themselves had begun to answer to two of those nations. For the Eastern Empire had, through the conquests of the Turks, come to answer pretty nearly to those parts of Europe and of the coasts of Asia where Greek was the prevailing language. That is to say, the *Roman Empire of the East* might be said, speaking roughly, to have become a *Greek* state. And, speaking still more roughly, it might even be said that the *Roman Empire of the West* had become a *German* state. For Germany was now the heart and centre of the Empire, though the possession of the Kingdoms of Italy and Burgundy of course gave the Emperors many Romance-speaking subjects. Southern Italy, it will be remembered, now formed part of the Kingdom of *Sicily*. To the west of Germany and Burgundy, beyond the Rhone, the Saone, and the Maes, lay the Kingdom of *France*, the lands held by the King of the French and his vassals. In the Spanish peninsula the Christian states of *Castile* and *Leon*, *Navarre*, *Aragon*, and *Portugal*, were all growing up, and were gradually driving the Mahometans into the southern part called *Andalusia*. These countries had now so little to do with the Empire that more than one of the Kings of Castile took the title of *Emperor*, as being the chief princes in their own peninsula, just as the West-Saxon Kings had done the like, as being the chief princes in their own island. It was only towards the East, where Germany bordered on the Slavonic nations, that the Empire had much chance of extending itself. The *Wends*, the Slavonic people along the south coast of the Baltic, in *Mecklenburg* and *Pomerania* and the other lands beyond the Elbe, gradually became Christians and were joined on to Germany, and the Low-Dutch language gradually displaced the Slavonic. *Bohemia* became a dependent state, but it kept its own Dukes who afterwards became Kings. So in the other chief Slavonic country, that of *Poland*, the Dukes and Kings had sometimes to submit to the Emperors, but in the end Poland gradually became quite independent, while Bohemia became more and more closely joined on to the Empire. We may say nearly the same of the Kingdom of the *Magyars* in *Hungary*. To the east of Poland and Hungary, *Lithuania*, where the people were still heathens, and *Russia*, where they belonged to the Eastern Church, had very little to do with Western Europe. In Northern Europe, *Denmark*, *Sweden*, and *Norway* were distinct kingdoms. Sweden and Norway had, from their position, very little to do with the rest of Europe, except so far as the Orkneys and the other islands off Scotland were still closely connected with Norway. But Denmark was a very important power, and its Kings made large conquests in various parts of the coasts of the Baltic. *England*, as we have said, had become thoroughly welded into one kingdom under the Norman Kings. *Scotland* was a distinct kingdom, but its Kings were held to be the *men* of the English Kings. And, during the time with which we are now concerned, came the beginnings of the English Conquest of *Ireland*. We thus see that most of the European states which still exist had already come into being. From this point therefore we may, for the most part, leave the internal affairs of each country to be dealt with in its own special History. But we must still go on with our sketch of those events which affected the history of the nations in general, and this will be a good point to say something about the state of government, religion, and other matters during what are called the *Middle Ages*.

4. **Changes in the Old Teutonic Constitution.**—We saw at the very beginning of this book that all the Aryan nations set out, as far as we can see, with very much the same kind of government. There was a *King* or chief as the leader, there was a smaller *Council* of nobles or old men, and there was a general *Assembly* of the whole people. This was the form of

government of the Teutonic nations at the time when they began to settle within the Roman Empire. There were commonly three classes of men in the state, the *nobles*, the common *freemen*, and the *slaves*. And men became slaves in two ways, either by being made prisoners of war or by being condemned to slavery for some crime. And it was also usual, especially in war-time, for men to attach themselves to the service of some particular leader, to become his *companions* or his *men*, who were bound to be faithful to him and who looked to share such rewards as he had to give them. This we may call the old *Teutonic Constitution*, as being at first common to all the Teutonic nations. But our own forefathers, when they settled in Britain, swept away all Roman institutions more utterly than was done in any part of the mainland. Scandinavia too never came under the Roman power at all. It was therefore in Britain and Scandinavia that this old constitution lasted longest on a great scale. In those parts of the mainland which had always belonged to the Empire things went on somewhat differently. As we have already said, Roman and Teutonic institutions influenced one another. As the Roman Empire became something quite different when it began to be held by German Kings, so the Teutonic Constitution was greatly changed by the Roman laws and institutions which were already established. The cities, for instance, kept up something of their Roman constitutions; and, as men learned something of the Roman Law, they began to attribute to the Teutonic Kings something of the great powers of the Roman Emperors. And of course they did this all the more after the Frankish Kings had actually become Roman Emperors. And one institution arose out of the mixture of Roman and Teutonic ideas which has had a most important influence on the world ever since.

5. **Origin of Fiefs.**—It had been very common under the Roman government to grant lands on con-

dition of *military service.* But such lands were held of the Roman Commonwealth or of the Emperor as its head, and their holding did not create any particular personal relation between one man and another. But when this Roman custom was combined with the Teutonic custom of men following a chief as their personal lord, a peculiar relation arose out of the union of the two. The *lord* granted lands to his *man* or *vassal,* on condition of his being faithful to him and doing him service in war. The land so granted was called a *feudum*, *fief*, or *fee;* and land held in this way was said to be held by a *feudal tenure.* Land which was a man's very own, which was not held of any lord but was subject only to the laws of the state, was called *allodial.* But it often happened that men whose estates were small found it better to turn their allodial holdings into feudal, and to agree to hold their land of some powerful lord, in order to get his protection. And the same thing was sometimes done on a great scale, when a prince who was conquered, or who feared that he might be conquered, agreed to hold his dominions in fief of the Emperor rather than lose them altogether.

6. **Effects of the Feudal Tenures.** — The general introduction of these *feudal* or *military tenures* caused some important changes both in political and in social matters. The change was made gradually, and it was slower in England than in most parts of the Continent ; but its general effect was to raise those men who held their lands by these new tenures above all others, and to thrust the poorer freemen lower down. In many countries they gradually sank into the state of *serfs* or *villains ;* that is, men who are not actually slaves to be bought and sold man by man, but who are bound to the land and pass with it. Meanwhile the class of actual slaves was dying out, and the class of villains was increased both by the freemen who fell down to it, and by the slaves who were raised

into it. The smaller freemen also lost power in another way. The old Teutonic Constitution, by which each freeman had a right to appear in the national Assembly, could no longer be fully carried out when the Franks or any other people had got possession of a large country. All men could not come in their own persons, and it was not for a long time, not till the twelfth or thirteenth century, that any one thought of choosing a smaller number of men to speak and act on behalf of all, as is now done in Parliament, and as is done in most of the countries of Europe and America. From all these causes working together two chief results happened. First, in most parts of Europe the old national Assemblies either quite died out, or were attended only by the chief men who could come in their own persons. Secondly, each province or district had a tendency to set up for itself. The *Count* or *Duke*, who was at first merely the governor of a province, often grew into an hereditary prince, acknowledging the Emperor or other King as the *lord* of whom he held his dominions in fief, but acting almost as an independent sovereign in the internal government of those dominions.

7. **Comparison of Different Countries.**— These tendencies were more or less at work in every part of Western Europe, but they were carried out more fully and more quickly in some countries than in others. Scandinavia and England up to the time of the Norman Conquest were less affected by them than other countries. In England the national Assemblies never died out, but, as the *Kings of the West-Saxons* grew into *Kings of the English*, the Assembly of Wessex became the national Assembly of all England. The entering of the Normans greatly strengthened the power of the Crown, and thereby made the nation more thoroughly one. But, on the other hand, it greatly strengthened the feudal ideas, till it was thought that all land must be held of a lord, of the King of

course in the first instance, as the supreme lord. In Germany also the national Assemblies never died out; but the Bishops, Dukes, Counts, and other princes gradually became sovereigns within their own dominions, and the *Diet* or Assembly of the Empire gradually became little more than a meeting of princes. In Italy things took a course so different from other countries that it will be well to speak of it by itself. France for a while fell asunder more completely than any other kingdom. The national Assemblies ceased altogether, and the Kings became mere nominal lords over the great princes who held fiefs of them. But this in the end led to a greater strengthening of the royal power in France than in any other kingdom. For the Kings of the French step by step got into their own hands nearly all the dominions of their vassals, as well as those of many of their neighbours who were not their vassals. Thus, for the very reason that the French Kings had once had much less power than either the Emperors or the English Kings, they came in the end to have much more power than either of them.

8. **Ways of Appointing Kings.**—As for the way in which Kings were appointed, by the old Teutonic Constitution the Kings were chosen by the people, but for the most part out of one particular family. In England this way of choosing Kings lasted till the Norman Conquest, and died out only very gradually afterwards. The Frankish or German Kings, who by virtue of their election in Germany had a right to become Roman Emperors, were always elected. But in the twelfth century the right of election began gradually to be confined to a few of the chief princes of Germany, who were fixed at seven, and who bore the special title of *Electors*. But the Emperors, whenever they could, got their sons to be chosen Kings in their lifetime, as Henry the Third and Fourth both did. In this case, when the young

King's father died, he went on reigning without any *interregnum*, and in due time he was crowned Emperor. In France the crown became more strictly hereditary than anywhere else, because, for more than three hundred years after the election of Hugh Capet, every King of the French left a son ready to succeed him, who had sometimes been crowned in his father's lifetime. Thus in France the male line went on without any break, while, both in Germany and in England, the crown passed several times from one family to another, though the several dynasties were commonly of kin to one another through female descent. All that we have now been saying has to do only with Western Europe. In the East the system of fiefs was never brought in till the Latins began to make conquests at the expense of the Eastern Emperors. And in the East too the Empire went on as it had done from the time of the first Cæsars, often staying in one family for several generations, but being often seized on by any general or leading man who was strong enough. This was a state of things which had quite passed away in the West. In the Eastern Empire too the power of the Emperors remained quite despotic; still their government never became quite like the despotisms of the East, as it was always tempered by some remembrance of the old laws and traditions of Rome.

9. **State of Religion.**—By this time by far the greater part of Europe was Christian. *Poland* and *Hungary* were converted about the end of the tenth century, and the *Scandinavian* countries, as we have already seen, about the same time. Only the *Prussians* and *Lithuanians*, and the *Fins* and *Laps* in the extreme North, remained heathen. In *Spain* the Saracens and Moors were of course Mahometans, and there were still Mahometans in Sicily under the Norman Kings. But, while nearly all Europe thus became Christian, the division between the two great

branches of the Church had become wider than ever. After the eleventh century there seemed no hope of a reconciliation between the Churches of Old and New Rome. In the West the power of the Popes was steadily growing, and it was at its height from the eleventh century to the thirteenth, during which time several Popes followed the example of Gregory the Seventh, in taking upon themselves to depose the Emperors and other Kings, and to give away their dominions. And, while the power of the Popes was thus growing at the expense of civil rulers, it was growing no less fast at the expense of national Churches in each particular country. And, as the rule by which the clergy were forbidden to marry was spreading everywhere, they were becoming a class more and more separate from other men, and more and more obedient to the Popes. In all this there was much that we cannot help blaming, and the Popes and clergy often thought too much of the interests of their own order, and not of the welfare of the Church in general; still we must remember that the Popes and other clergy kept up religion and learning, and a general sense of right and wrong, in very rough and wild times. There was much to blame in their own doings, but they were a great check on the evil passions of men; and, whatever we say of the Popes in particular, the general influence of the clergy was a powerful influence for good.

10. **Position of the Clergy.**—As the Popes were constantly taking to themselves power in temporal matters, so we find that in these times the clergy in general took a part in temporal affairs which we should now think very strange. But this was by no means wholly the fault of the clergy; as things were then, it could hardly be otherwise. The clergy had nearly all the knowledge of the time in their hands, so that it could not fail that they were largely employed in all matters, including many which did not exactly belong

to their own duties. They acted as ministers of Kings and as lawyers, and many of them did not scruple to wear weapons and fight, though this was always held to be a wrong thing and against the laws of the Church. In all parts of Western Christendom the bishopricks and monasteries and other ecclesiastical bodies were richly endowed, and held great lands and lordships. In Germany especially most of the Bishops and Abbots were princes of the Empire, and the three Archbishops of *Mainz*, *Köln*, and *Trier* (called in French *Mayence*, *Cologne*, and *Trèves*) were among the Electors of the Emperor. In other countries they did not rise to such power as this, but they were always high in temporal rank and were chief members of the Parliament or other national Assembly.

11. **The Monastic Orders.** — The distinction between the *regular* and the *secular clergy* was now fully established. The *regular* clergy were those who went out of the world and lived together as *monks* in monasteries; the *seculars* were those who lived in the world as parish priests or as canons of cathedral and collegiate churches. There were many learned men in both classes; but we have on the whole more histories and other books written by the regulars than by the seculars. The oldest monks in the West were the *Benedictines*, who followed the rule of *Saint Benedict*, the great founder of the monastic life in Italy in the sixth century. But, as the Benedictines grew rich and their discipline became less strict, other orders of monks arose, who professed to bring back an older and stricter discipline. Such were the *Cistercians*, an order of which many houses were founded in the twelfth century; and in the thirteenth arose the different orders of *Friars*, as the *Franciscans* and *Dominicans*, called after their founders *Saint Francis* and *Saint Dominic*, who professed more complete poverty than the older orders, and gave themselves much to preaching. All these

different revivals, one after the other, did good at the time, both among the monks and among other men; but each new order commonly came in the end to be rich and corrupt, like those which it had undertaken to reform, and so a new reformation was needed. But the strangest thing of all was that during the Crusades there arose orders of monks who were also soldiers—men who took the vows of monks, but whose further business it was to fight against the enemies of Christianity. Two of these *military orders*, the *Templars* and the *Hospitallers* or *Knights of Saint John*, were the chief defence of the Christian kingdom of Jerusalem. Another order of this kind, called the *Teutonic Knights*, arose in Palestine towards the end of the twelfth century, and in the course of the thirteenth they undertook to convert or conquer the heathens on the coast of the Baltic, in *Prussia* and *Livonia*, where the order held principalities. Thus strangely were religious zeal and the love of fighting mixed up in these times.

12. **Language and Learning.**—In all this it must be remembered that we are speaking wholly of Western Christendom, and more especially when we speak of knowledge being in the hands of the clergy. In the Eastern Empire both the regular and secular clergy play a great part in history, but they neither had all learning to themselves, nor did they fill temporal offices in the same way in which they did in the West. In the East, where the Empire had gone on uninterruptedly without any lasting barbarian conquests, learning had never died out among the laity. The Latin language was now quite forgotten in the East. Greek was the one tongue which men both wrote and spoke, though of course they wrote much better Greek than they spoke. Many of the Histories which were written at Constantinople at this time were written by laymen, often by Emperors and other men of high rank. But in the West there was nowhere any one language com-

mon to all classes of men. The use of Latin was everywhere kept up for all purposes of religion and learning. The Church service was still said in Latin, though Latin was now nowhere the common language of the people. For in Germany, England, and Scandinavia men spoke their own Teutonic languages, and in Italy, Aquitaine, Spain, and France men spoke the Romance tongues, which we must now look on as languages distinct from the Latin. It thus came about that very few books were written by laymen, and that very few books were anywhere written in the speech of the people. Still, more books were written in the speech of the people in the Teutonic than in the Romance countries, because no one could help knowing that High-Dutch, English, or Danish was quite a different language from Latin; while men for a long time looked on the *vulgar tongue*, as it was called, in the Romance countries, simply as bad Latin, which no one would think of writing. Thus we have many Old-English, and some High-Dutch, writings older than anything in any of the Romance tongues. The English have what no other nation has, a History of their own people from the beginning written in their own language. In Scandinavia too men wrote their own legends and histories in their own tongue. We begin to get French verse in the twelfth century, but it is not till the thirteenth century that we get any prose. It is somewhat later that we come to the first great work of Italian literature in the famous poem of *Dante Alighieri.* The first chief writers in both these languages were, as might be supposed, laymen. The twelfth century was a great new birth of learning and science everywhere, partly because men then began to have more dealings with the Greeks and Saracens. Still, even after this time, laymen in Northern Europe were, as a rule, not taught to read and write, though reading and writing gradually became more common, and it must always be remembered that, when a man could not write, it does not at all follow that he could not read.

13. **Growth of the Towns.**—Another thing must here be mentioned, which was of special importance at the time which we have just come to. This was the growing up of the *towns* into greater, in some parts into the very first, importance. In the old state of things, Greek and Roman, the towns had, so to speak, been everything. Every freeman was a citizen of some town or other, and the Roman dominion was throughout a dominion of one city bearing rule over other cities. The Teutonic settlements everywhere drove the towns back; none of the Teutonic nations were used to a town life. They looked on the walls of a town as a prison. In Britain, the inhabitants, who knew nothing of Roman civilization, seem at first to have utterly destroyed the Roman towns, and it was not till some time after the first conquest that new English towns began to arise, very often on the old Roman sites. In the other provinces, the Goths, Franks, and other Teutonic settlers did not destroy the Roman towns; but the towns lost much of their importance and local freedom. But, as civilization began to grow again, new towns began to spring up, and the old towns to win back something of their old greatness. In Germany the Saxon Kings and Emperors were great founders of towns; and, both there and in other parts of the Empire, the old and the new towns alike gradually won for themselves great privileges, which made them almost independent within their own walls. And, as the Imperial power declined and the Dukes and Counts grew into sovereign princes, so in the same way the free Imperial cities grew into sovereign commonwealths, acknowledging only the outward supremacy of the Emperor. And in many cases, like the towns of old Greece and Italy, they joined together in *Leagues* for mutual defence. Thus in Northern Germany, the *Hanseatic League*, the

league of the great trading towns, became a great power in all the Northern seas, and often gave law to the Kings of Denmark and Sweden. But the part of the Empire where the towns rose to the highest pitch of greatness was Italy, especially the northern part. There, from the eleventh century onwards, the towns, as we may say, became everything, just as they had been in old Greece. Here nearly the whole country was parted out among the dominions of the different cities, and the whole land became again an assemblage of commonwealths, independent of any power but that of the Emperor. But, though the freedom of the Italian towns became greater than that of the towns of Germany, it was not so lasting. In Germany a great many of the towns always kept their freedom; and three of them, the *Hanse Towns* of *Lübeck*, *Bremen*, and *Hamburg*, are separate commonwealths even now. But in Italy most of the cities fell, just as those of old Greece did long before, into the hands either of native *lords* or *Tyrants* or into those of foreign princes. Thus it was that Italy became divided, or rather grouped together, into the various principalities which have lately been joined together again into the restored Kingdom of Italy. But a few commonwealths contrived to go on till the end of the last century, and one very small one, that of *San Marino*, remains still.

14. **Summary.**—These are some of the chief characteristics which we may look on as distinguishing the times known as the *Middle Ages* from times earlier and later. It is not easy to say when the Middle Ages begin and end, as the name is nothing more than a convenient way of speaking. But the tendencies of which we have been speaking were about at their height in the twelfth and thirteenth centuries, in the time of the Swabian Emperors. We have now, so to speak, got quite clear of the old Roman times, while we have not yet got into the times which are

more like those in which we now live. In the course of the thirteenth century we shall come across great changes.

CHAPTER XI.

THE SWABIAN EMPERORS.

The Hohenstaufen Kings and Emperors; origin of the names Guelf and Ghibelin (1)—*reign and crusade of Conrad* (1)—*reign of Frederick Barbarossa; his dealings with the Italian cities, with the Popes, with Kings of Sicily, with the Eastern Empire* (2)—*reign of Henry the Sixth; his conquest of Sicily* (3)—*double election of Philip and Otto; reign of Frederick the Second; his dealings with Sicily, Germany, Italy, and the Popes* (4)—*reign of Conrad the Fourth; end of the Swabian dynasty; decline of the Imperial power* (4)—*relations between England and France; dominions of the Angevin Kings; reign of Henry the Second* (5)—*rivalry of Philip Augustus and Richard Cœur-de-Lion* (5)—*reign of John in England; his forfeiture of Normandy* (5)—*victory of Philip at Bouvines; Lewis of France in England* (5)—*reign of Lewis the Eighth* (6)—*reign of Saint Lewis; his dealings with Henry the Third; annexation of Toulouse* (6)—*effects of the reign of Saint Lewis; advance of the French Kingdom* (6)—*growth of the English Constitution; union of Normans and English against foreigners* (7)—*reforms of Simon of Montfort; nature of national assemblies in England and elsewhere* (7)—*the English conquest of Ireland* (8)—*state of the Kingdom of Jerusalem; the Second Crusade; taking of Jerusalem by Saladin* (9)—*Crusade of the Emperor Frederick, and the Kings Philip and Richard* (10)—*Frederick the Second wins back Jerusalem; its final capture by the Chorasmians* (10)—*Crusades of Saint Lewis and of Edward the First; final loss of the Holy Land* (10)—*revival of the Eastern Empire under the Komnênian dynasty; its decline* (11)—*Fourth Crusade; taking of Constan-*

tinople by the Franks and Venetians (11)—*The Latin Empire of Constantinople; Eastern dominion of Venice* (12)—*formation of various principalities in the East; Emperors of Nikaia and Trebizond* (12)—*Constantinople recovered by the Greeks; dynasty of the Palaiologoi* (12)—*the Albigenses; Crusades waged against them; suppression of their sect and of their national independence* (13)—*reign of Manfred in Sicily; Crusades preached against him* (14)—*conquest of Sicily by Charles of Anjou; execution of Conradin; revolt of the island of Sicily* (14)—*state of North-eastern Europe; advance of Denmark east of the Baltic* (15)—*establishment of the Teutonic Knights in Prussia and Livonia* (15)—*new Mahometan dynasties in Spain; victories of the Caliph Jacob* (16)—*advance of the Christian Kingdoms of Castile, Aragon, and Portugal; the Moors confined to Granada* (16)—*rise of the Moguls; reigns of Jenghiz and his descendants* (17)—*invasion of Central Europe by Batou Khan; subjection of Russia* (17)—*overthrow of the Caliphate and of the Seljuk Turks* (17)—*Summary* (18).

1. **Origin of the Guelfs and Ghibelins.**—On the death of Henry the Fifth in 1125, *Lothar*, Duke of Saxony, was elected King, and in 1133 he was crowned Emperor. He submitted more readily to the Popes than most Emperors did, and Pope *Innocent the Second* even gave out that he became his *man* at his coronation. But on Lothar's death the Imperial Crown passed to one of the greatest families which ever held it, that of the *Hohenstaufen* or Dukes of *Swabia*. The first King of that house was *Conrad the Third*, who reigned as King from 1138 to 1152, but who was never crowned Emperor. He was the son of a daughter of the Emperor *Henry the Fourth*, so that the Swabian dynasty did in a manner continue the line of the Franconian Emperors. It might also be said to continue then in their policy; for the Emperors of this family had fully as much to do in disputing with the Popes as the Franconian Emperors had done. This however did not begin

in the time of King Conrad, though the two names of *Guelf* and *Ghibelin*, which presently became so famous in Italy, began during his reign in Germany. For Conrad had several wars with the Saxons and others who disliked his election, and in one of the sieges the war-cry of the rebels was *Welf*, after their leader, *Welf*, brother of Duke *Henry of Saxony*, while the King's men shouted *Waibling*, the name of a village where their leader, Duke *Frederick of Swabia*, the King's brother, had been brought up. These names, written in an Italian fashion, became *Guelfs* and *Ghibelins:* the *Guelfs* meaning those who supported the Popes, and the *Ghibelins* those who supported the Emperors. King Conrad went on the second Crusade to the Holy Land, in which he did not gain much success; and it is a thing to be noted that he made a league with *Manuel*, the Emperor of the East, against *Roger* King of Sicily, who was making himself dangerous to both Empires.

2. **Reign of Frederick Barbarossa.**—But the reign of Conrad was of little importance compared with that of his nephew and successor *Frederick*, who, from his *red beard*, is commonly known as *Frederick Barbarossa*. He was chosen King in 1152; he was crowned Emperor in 1155, and reigned till 1190. The greater part of his reign was taken up with the affairs and wars of Italy. The Italian cities, as has been already said, had grown up into nearly independent commonwealths. They often had wars with one another, and, just as in old Greece, the smaller cities often complained of the oppression of the greater. Thus the great city of *Milan* sought to bring *Como*, *Lodi*, and others of the smaller cities under its power, and the smaller cities in their turn prayed the Emperor to come to their help. Some of the cities, as *Pavia*, which had been the capital in the Lombard times, and the great seafaring commonwealth of *Pisa*, were always strong on the side of the Emperors. But, gradually, most of

the cities of Northern Italy found that it was their interest to join together to defend their independence against the Imperial power. Thus was formed the *Lombard League*, with which Frederick had long wars, which will be best spoken of in the special History of Italy. But, besides the cities, the Western Emperors had other enemies to strive against in Italy. Popes and Emperors never could agree; disputes arose between Frederick and Pope *Hadrian the Fourth*, who had crowned him. When Hadrian died in 1159, a fiercer dispute broke out; for the Popedom was claimed by two candidates, *Victor* and *Alexander*. The Emperor took the side of Victor; therefore the cities which were against him naturally took the other side, and Frederick had to strive against all who followed Pope Alexander. The Kings of Sicily too, *William the Good* and *William the Bad*, were his enemies; and the Emperor *Manuel Komnênos*, who dreamed of winning back Italy for the Eastern Empire, also gave help to the revolted cities. The end was that the Emperor had to make peace with both the Pope and the cities, and in 1183 the rights of the cities were acknowledged in a treaty or law of the Empire, passed at *Constanz* or *Constance* in Swabia. Besides his wars in Italy, the Emperor Frederick had also to strive in Germany with *Henry the Lion*, who was Duke of Saxony and Bavaria at once, and who married Matilda, daughter of Henry the Second of England. Duke Henry lost the greater part of his dominions, and the great duchy of Saxony was broken up. In the last years of his reign, Frederick went on the third Crusade, and died on the way.

3. **Union of Sicily with the Empire.**—Frederick was succeeded by his son *Henry the Sixth*, who had already been chosen King, and who in the next year, 1191, was crowned Emperor. The chief event of his reign was the conquest of the Kingdom of *Sicily*, which he claimed in right of his wife *Constance*, the

daughter of the first King William. He died in 1197, leaving his son *Frederick* a young child. But he had already been chosen King in Germany, and he succeeded as hereditary King in Sicily. The Norman Kingdom of Sicily thus came to an end, except so far as it was continued in Frederick, who was descended from the Norman Kings through his mother.

4. **Reign of Frederick the Second.**—On the death of the Emperor Henry, the election of young Frederick seems to have been quite forgotten, and the crown was disputed between his uncle *Philip of Swabia* and *Otto of Saxony*, the son of *Henry the Lion.* Both Kings were crowned, and, after the death of Philip, Otto was crowned Emperor in 1209. But presently young Frederick was again chosen, and in 1220 he was crowned Emperor, and reigned thirty years till his death in 1250. This *Frederick the Second,* who joined together so many crowns, was called the *Wonder of the World.* And he well deserved the name, for perhaps no King that ever reigned had greater natural gifts, and in thought and learning he was far above the age in which he lived. In his own Kingdom of Sicily he could do pretty much as he pleased, and it flourished wonderfully in his time. But in Germany and Italy he had constantly to struggle against enemies of all kinds. In Germany he had to win the support of the princes by granting them privileges which did much to undermine the royal power, and on the other hand he showed no favour to the rising power of the cities. In Italy he had endless strivings with one Pope after another, with *Innocent the Third, Honorius the Third, Gregory the Ninth,* and *Innocent the Fourth;* as well as with the Guelfic cities, which withstood him much as they had withstood his grandfather. He was more than once excommunicated by the Popes, and in 1245 Pope Innocent the Fourth held a Council at *Lyons,* in which he professed to depose the Emperor. More than one King was chosen in opposition to him

in Germany, just as had been done in the time of Henry the Fourth, and there were civil wars all his time, both in Germany and in Italy, while a great part of the Kingdom of Burgundy was beginning to slip away from the Empire altogether. On Frederick's death, his son *Conrad*, who had been chosen King in Germany in 1237, and who of course succeeded his father in the hereditary Kingdom of Sicily, was reckoned as King by the Ghibelins in Germany and Italy. But he died in 1254, and he was never crowned Emperor. With him ended the line of Swabia as Emperors and as Kings of Germany and Italy. Moreover, from the death of Frederick the Second, we may look on the power of the Empire, as the great leading state of Europe and the centre of all European history, as coming to an end.

5. **England and France.**—While the Swabian Emperors reigned in Germany and Italy, the *Angevin Kings* reigned in England. They began with *Henry the Second*, the grandson of Henry the First through his daughter the *Empress Matilda.* Now came the time when England was part of the dominions of a prince whose greatest power lay on the Continent. The dominions which Henry held through his father, his mother, and his wife, took up nearly the whole of Western Gaul, and he held the mouths of the great rivers Seine, Loire, and Garonne. Thus it came that in England both the native English and the Norman settlers were brought under the rule of a King who was not really either Norman or English. Thus too it came that in France the King was more than ever shut up in his own dominions, when nearly the whole coast was held by a prince who was Duke of Normandy and Aquitaine and King of England all at once. Thus there began in England a more distinct rule of foreigners over all the natives of the land of whatever race, and in France the rivalry between the King and his great vassal is more marked than ever. In France

King *Lewis the Sixth*, who reigned from 1108 to 1137, had done something to strengthen the royal authority, and he had also favoured the growth of the towns. His son *Lewis the Seventh* was often at variance with King Henry of England, but no very great changes happened while they lived. It was quite different in the time of their sons. Lewis died in 1180, and was succeeded by his son *Philip*, called *Philip Augustus;* and Henry died in 1189, and was succeeded by his son *Richard*, called *Cœur-de-Lion* or the *Lion-Heart.* These two Kings joined in a Crusade, of which we we shall say more presently; but enmity went on during the whole of their reigns, and things came to a head in the time of King *John* of England, who succeeded on the death of his brother Richard in 1199. John was lawfully chosen King according to English law, and it does not seem that any party in England thought of raising any one else to the throne. But a party in Richard's foreign dominions wished to have for their Duke young *Arthur*, the son of John's elder brother *Geoffrey*, whose mother was *Constance*, the heiress of *Britanny*. John got Arthur into his power, and he was commonly believed to have murdered him. This of course raised great indignation everywhere, and Philip took advantage of it to cause a sentence to be passed by the peers of his kingdom, by which John was declared to have forfeited all the fiefs which he held of the Crown of France. By way of carrying out this sentence, Philip conquered, with very little trouble, all continental *Normandy* and the other possessions of John in Northern Gaul. But the Duchy of *Aquitaine* and the *Norman Islands* were still kept by the Kings of England. From this time England became the most important part of the King of England's dominions, and all the natives of England, whether of Old-English or of Norman descent, began to draw together as countrymen to withstand the strangers whom the Angevin Kings were constantly bringing into the land.

Meanwhile John contrived to quarrel both with Pope *Innocent* and with his own subjects: and in 1214 Philip won the battle of *Bouvines* in Flanders over the English forces, together with those of the Emperor Otto, who was John's nephew, being the son of his sister Matilda. In this battle the French got the better of three Teutonic nations, Germans, English, and Flemings all together. In 1216, the Barons of England who had revolted against John offered the crown to *Lewis* the eldest son of Philip of France. He came over to England; but as John died before long, the supporters of Lewis gradually left him, and *Henry the Third*, the young son of John, was acknowledged King. Two things strike us in this part of the story. On the one hand, it seems strange that the Normans in Normandy, who had had such long wars with the French, should have allowed themselves to be conquered by Philip almost without making any resistance. On the other hand, it seems strange that the Barons of England, whether we call them Normans or Englishmen, should have offered the crown of England to the eldest son of the King of the French. The truth is that John was felt to be really neither a Norman Duke nor an English King, and men most likely thought that, if they were to have a foreign ruler, Lewis would be better than John.

6. **Saint Lewis.**—After the death of Philip, his son *Lewis the Eighth*, who had failed to get the crown of England, reigned for a few years in France, from 1223 to 1226. Then came his son *Lewis the Ninth*, called *Saint Lewis*, and most rightly so called, for he was perhaps the best King that ever reigned, unless it were our own Alfred. The only evil was that his personal goodness helped greatly to increase the power of the Crown, and so, in the end, to make the Kings of France absolute rulers. And in the like sort it helped greatly to increase the power of France among other nations. While Saint Lewis reigned in France, *Henry*

the Third reigned in England from 1216 to 1272. Henry made some attempts to get back his possessions in France; but in 1259 peace was made, by which Henry kept nothing except his possessions in the South. In Saint Lewis's time also, but while he was still young and under the rule of his mother *Blanche of Castile*, the dominions of the *Counts of Toulouse* were added to the royal possessions by a treaty made in 1229. Thus the Kings of the French, instead of being cooped up in Paris and Orleans, as they had been up to the time of Philip Augustus, had the more part of their kingdom in their own hands. Their dominions now reached to the Mediterranean Sea, and they had havens on all the three seas, the Mediterranean, the Ocean, and the Channel. And, though Provence and the other great fiefs of the Kingdom of Burgundy were not joined to France for a long time to come, still from this time they began to have a connexion with France. The French Kings began to meddle with their affairs in a manner which paved the way for their conquest at a later time. Generally, just as the German Kingdom was getting weaker, and was now in truth splitting to pieces, the French Kingdom was getting stronger and more united; and from this time France was always reckoned amongst the foremost powers of Europe.

7. **The Internal Affairs of England.**—The internal and constitutional affairs of England will be spoken of more at large in the special history of England. But a few words must be given to them, as they are closely connected with the general course of European affairs. The thirteenth century was a time of great changes, a time, so to speak, of beginnings and endings, throughout the world. As both Empires practically came to an end, as the Kingdom of France, in anything like its later extent and importance, may be said to have begun, so now the *Constitution of England* began to put on the shape which it has kept

ever since. Under John and Henry the Third we see how the fondness of the Angevin Kings for foreigners of all kinds drove the natives of England, whether of English or Norman descent, to join together against the strangers. The whole nation joined together to force King John in 1215 to grant the *Great Charter*, by which all the old rights and good laws which he had broken were confirmed. This Great Charter the Kings who followed had to confirm over and over again, because they were always trying to break it; and it has been the groundwork of English freedom ever since. So again, in the time of Henry the Third, the King's misgovernment and his favour to foreigners again drove the Barons and the whole people to rise against him. And, though the Popes again took the side of the King and excommunicated all who rose against him, yet we again find the whole English nation, nobles, clergy, and people, acting firmly together. In this war against Henry the Third the great leader was *Simon of Montfort*, the son of another Simon of whom we shall hear presently. He was, oddly enough, a Frenchman by birth, but he inherited the earldom of *Leicester* through his mother; and when he came to England, he threw in his lot with his new country, and did in everything as a good Englishman. It was by him that the Great Council of the Nation, which was now called by the French name of *Parliament*, was made to take the form which it has borne ever since. Some kind of National Assembly was found in every part of Western Europe. But in most countries the Assembly consisted of *Estates;* that is, representatives of the different classes of freemen in the nation. These, in most countries, were counted as three, *Nobles*, *Clergy*, and *Commons*, the Commons generally being only the citizens of the towns. This kind of constitution was set up in France by *Philip the Fair*, the grandson of Saint Lewis. The States came together in each country to grant money to the King, and to demand such changes in the laws or other reforms as might be needed. But in France the States never met regularly, but only when it suited the King's purposes, or when he could not help calling them together. In England, on the other hand, Parliaments went on far more regularly, so that people have never been without a national Assembly of some kind from the very beginning of things till now. And in England the Parliament took the particular form of an assembly with *Two Houses*. The Earls, Bishops, and other great men, grew into the *House of Lords*, and the *House of Commons* was gradually formed out of the representatives of the people in general. First of all, the freeholders of each *county* were called on to send some of the *knights* of that county to represent them, and at last, when Earl Simon held a Parliament in 1265, he called on the *cities* and *boroughs* to send each two of their *citizens* or *burgesses*. Earl Simon was killed that same year in the battle of *Evesham*, but the system of representation which he had brought in was before long firmly established under King *Edward the First*.

8. **The Conquest of Ireland.**—During this time many things happened between the English Kings and their vassals the Kings of Scots and Princes of Wales, which will be better told in the History of England. But it must be mentioned here that it was in the reign of *Henry the Second* that the English dominion in *Ireland* began. At the very beginning of his reign, in 1155, King Henry got a *bull*—that is, a writing sealed with the Pope's *bulla* or seal—from Pope *Hadrian the Fourth*, who was an Englishman and the only Englishman that ever was Pope, giving him leave to conquer Ireland: thus had the Popes taken upon themselves to dispose of kingdoms. But it was not till 1169 that some nobles and other private adventurers went over into Ireland under pretence of helping a banished Irish king called *Dermot*. Two

years afterwards King Henry went over himself to receive the homage of the whole country. From that time the Kings of England always claimed to be *Lords of Ireland*, and the city of *Dublin* and a greater or less part of the island was always under the English power. But it was not for many ages that English Kings really got possession of all Ireland, and cruel wars long went on between the English settlers and the native Irish.

9. **The Loss of Jerusalem.**—A large part of the history of this time might come under the general head of *Crusades.* The first Crusades or Holy Wars had been undertaken to win back the Holy Sepulchre from the infidels; but after a while both the name and the thing began to be greatly abused, and Crusades were preached against any one with whom the Popes were at enmity. The First Crusade, as we have already seen, led to the establishment of the Christian Kingdom of Jerusalem in 1099. The chief strength of the kingdom lay in the two orders of military monks, the *Templars* and the *Hospitallers* or *Knights of Saint John*, and many warriors from all parts of Christendom went to serve for a while in the Holy Land as a good work. Still the Kings of Jerusalem had much ado to keep their little kingdom from the attacks of the neighbouring Mahometan powers, and several new Crusades had to be made to help them, some of which were led by the greatest princes in Europe. Thus in 1147 the *Second Crusade* was preached by *Saint Bernard*, one of the holiest men of the time, and who is called the last of the *Fathers of the Church. Conrad* King of the Romans and *Lewis the Seventh*, King of the French, both went on this Crusade, but they were not able to do any great things. And there soon arose a power in Egypt which became more dangerous to the Christians of the East than any of the other Mahometan powers had been. We have seen there had been for some time a separate line of Caliphs in Egypt; these were called the *Fati-*

mites, as they profess to be the descendants of Ali and *Fatima*, the daughter of Mahomet. But in 1171 their power was put down by *Joseph* surnamed *Saladin*, who brought back Egypt under the spiritual power of the Caliph of Bagdad, much as if the Eastern Church had been brought under the power of the Bishops of Rome. Saladin became the greatest Mahometan prince of his time, and in 1187 he took Jerusalem and drove the Christians out of the greater part of the kingdom. Thus far all the Crusades since the First had been waged for the purpose of defending the Christian possession of Jerusalem. We have now again to come to Crusades which were waged, as the First had been, to win back the Holy City from the Infidels, as well as to save the small fragment of the kingdom which was left.

10. **The Later Crusades in Palestine.**—The loss of Jerusalem roused the spirit of all Western Christendom. King Henry of England took the cross; but he died two years later, without ever setting out for the Holy Land. But in 1189 the Emperor Frederick set out by land, but was drowned on the way; and in 1190 Philip King of the French and his great vassal Richard, the new King of the English, went to the Holy Land by sea. King Richard did many great exploits; but the princes quarrelled among themselves, so that Jerusalem was not won back; but some parts of Palestine were still left to the Christians, and they were allowed to make pilgrimages to Jerusalem. Of the *Third Crusade* we shall have to speak by itself, as it did nothing for the Holy Land at all. But in 1228 the Emperor *Frederick the Second*, who claimed to be King of Jerusalem in right of his wife, notwithstanding the opposition of Pope *Gregory the Ninth*, really went to the Holy Land, and won Jerusalem by a treaty with the Egyptian Sultan *Kamel*, and was crowned King there. He was the last Christian King who really reigned at Jerusalem. For in 1244

the Holy City was again lost by the Christians, being taken by the Mahometan *Chorasmians*, and it has never been won back again. The Popes, instead of helping the Emperor to win back his kingdom, were always excommunicating him and preaching Crusades against him. The Christians however still kept some small parts of the kingdom, and in 1248 *Saint Lewis*, the King of the French, set out on a Crusade; but, instead of going straight to Palestine, he first attacked *Egypt*, as being the best way of winning the Holy Land. But he was taken prisoner in Egypt; and, though he did afterwards reach Palestine, yet he could not win back Jerusalem. At last he came back to France in 1254, having done little or nothing for the common cause, but having shown his own courage and goodness in a wonderful way. In 1270 he set out on another Crusade; but this time he began by besieging *Tunis*, and died there. In 1270 *Edward* the son of King Henry of England, afterwards the great King *Edward the First*, went on another Crusade, and did something to stop the final overthrow of the Christians in Palestine, though even he could not win back Jerusalem. At last, in 1291, *Acre*, the last town which the Christians held in the Holy Land, was taken by the Mahometans, and the Christian Kingdom of Jerusalem came altogether to an end. But the Emperors called themselves *Kings of Jerusalem* as well as of *Germany*, and the same vain title has been borne and disputed about by several other European sovereigns.

11. **The Latin Conquest of Constantinople.**—No one perhaps would have expected that the *Eastern Empire*, the great bulwark of Christendom against the Saracens and Turks, and which the first Crusaders had professed to go forth to defend, would be actually overthrown by a crusading army. We have seen that the Komnenian Emperors, following in the wake of the first Crusaders, were able to win back a large part of the Byzantine dominions in Asia. The

two Emperors who reigned after Alexios, *John* and *Manuel*, were both great warriors. *John*, who reigned from 1118 to 1143, did much really to restore the strength of the Empire; but *Manuel*, who reigned from 1143 to 1180, was rather a bold knight-errant than either a good ruler or a great general. He had to contend with many enemies both in Europe and in Asia. In his time Greece was several times ravaged by the fleets of the Kings of Sicily; he had to wage wars with Hungary, and at last he was defeated in a great battle against the Turks in 1176. After his time the Eastern Empire again began to decline; there were many internal revolutions; Emperors were set up and put down; the Bulgarians revolted, and a separate Emperor set himself up in the isle of Cyprus. At last, in 1201, several Western princes, among the chief of whom were *Baldwin Count of Flanders* and *Boniface Marquess of Montferrat* in Italy, were setting out on a Crusade, and they came to Venice to ask for ships to take them to the Holy Land. Venice, it will be remembered, had never been part of the Western Empire, but had always kept on its nominal allegiance to the Emperors of the East, till it had gradually become quite independent, as it was now. The three Italian cities, Venice, Genoa, and Pisa, were now the greatest naval powers in Europe. The *Doge* or *Duke* of Venice, *Henry Dandolo*, agreed to let the Crusaders have ships and to go with them himself; only the Crusaders were to conquer for the Venetians the town of *Zara* in Dalmatia, to which they laid claim. Pope Innocent protested against this, as being no part of the business of a Crusade. Yet they not only took Zara, but agreed to help *Alexios Angelos*, the son of an Emperor of the East who had been deposed, in getting back the Empire. This they actually did in 1203. But, as the Romans or Greeks (whichever we are to call them) of Constantinople presently revolted, and slew the Emperors who had been put in by the

Crusaders, the Crusaders in 1204 again took the city; and the Roman Empire of the East may now be said to have come to an end.

12. **The Later Greek Empire.**—When the Crusaders had taken Constantinople, they went on to deal with the whole Eastern Empire as their own. They set up Count Baldwin as Emperor of Constantinople, and they divided among themselves as much of the Empire as they could get. This was the beginning of what was called the *Latin* Empire of Constantinople: the word *Latin* being now often used, as opposed to *Greek*, to mean all those who admitted the supremacy of the Roman Church and who used Latin as their religious and official language. Among the Latin powers which now won settlements in the East, the Venetians got possession of many of the islands and important points of the coast, which was the beginning of their great Eastern dominion. Some of the Venetian and other Latin possessions were never won back by the Greeks, but, on the other hand, the Latins were far from conquering the whole Empire. The Greeks maintained their independence in *Epeiros* and at *Nikaia* and *Trapezous* or *Trebizond* in Asia; in both these latter cities Greek princes reigned with the title of Emperor. Thus the Eastern Empire was cut up into a crowd of small principalities, Greek and *Frank* (the meaning of this last word in the East has already been explained), *Despots* of *Epeiros*, *Dukes* of *Athens*, *Princes* of *Achaia*, and what not; the Latin Emperors at Constantinople being supposed to be lords over all the Frank settlers. But, as the Emperors who reigned at Nikaia, *Theodore Laskarês* and *John Vatatzês*, were very wise and good princes, the Empire of Nikaia, which professed to be the true continuation of the Roman Empire at Constantinople, grew and flourished; and in 1261 the Emperor *Michael Palaiologos* won back Constantinople, and the Empire of the East in some sort began again.

But it never won back its old power, for, besides the provinces which were held by the Mahometans and the new dominions of the Venetians, some of the Greek and Frank princes still went on reigning, and were independent of the Greek Emperor at Constantinople. The Empire of Trebizond especially outlived the restored Empire of Constantinople. In truth this restored Empire of Constantinople was little more than the most powerful of several Greek states which went on from this time till they were all swallowed up by the Turks. Still the Emperors of Constantinople always called themselves *Emperors of the Romans*, and professed to continue the old Roman succession. From this time the Eastern Empire became more strictly hereditary than it had been of old, and the crown remained with very little interruption in the family of Palaiologos, till the Empire was finally destroyed by the Ottoman Turks.

13. **Crusades against the Albigenses.**—We have just seen how a Crusade, which was meant to be a war for the defence of Christendom against the unbelievers, could be turned into an attack made by one body of Christians against another. But when the Fourth Crusade was turned about into an attack on Zara and Constantinople, Pope Innocent at least did what he could to hinder such a falling away from the original design of a Crusade. Yet, before long, Innocent himself caused a Crusade to be preached, no longer against Mahometans, but against Christians who were looked on as heretics. In the South of Gaul, both in those parts which were fiefs of the King of the French and in those which were held of the Emperors as Kings of Burgundy, many men had fallen away into doctrines which both the Eastern and the Western Churches condemned. Those who held these doctrines were commonly called *Albigenses*, from the city of *Albi*. The chief princes in those parts were the *Counts of Toulouse* and the *Counts of*

Provence: each of them held fiefs both of the Emperor and of the King of the French; but the County of Toulouse itself was a fief of France, while the County of Provence was of course a fief of the Empire. The Counts of Provence at this time were of the house of the Kings of Aragon. In 1208 a Crusade was preached against *Raymond Count of Toulouse*, which was carried on at first by *Simon of Montfort*, the father of the Simon who was so famous in English history, and afterwards by *Lewis the Eighth*, King of the French. Simon even defeated *Peter* King of *Aragon* in a great battle, and obtained possession of Toulouse. It looked at one time as if the house of Montfort were going to be established as sovereigns in the South of Gaul; but the end of the matter was that the heresy of the Albigenses was put down by cruel persecutions, and that in 1229 the county of Toulouse was, as we have seen, incorporated with the Kingdom of France.

14. **Crusades against Sicily.**—In this way the Crusades, which had first been preached only against the infidels, next began to be preached against heretics. The next stage was to preach them against any one who was an enemy of the Pope. Thus Crusades were preached against the Emperor Frederick, and, after his death, they were preached against his son *Manfred* King of Sicily, who began to reign in 1258. Manfred was a wise and brave King, and he greatly helped the Ghibelins in other parts of Italy; things almost looked as if a Kingdom of all Italy was about to arise in the House of Swabia. But the Popes were of course the enemies of Manfred. Even while King Conrad was alive, Pope *Innocent the Fourth* had in 1253 professed to give the crown of Sicily to *Edmund* the son of our King Henry the Third. But nothing came of that: so in 1262 Pope *Urban the Fourth* offered the crown to *Charles Count of Anjou*, the brother of Saint Lewis, who was also Count of Provence in right of his wife. Charles got together an army of French

Crusaders, and in 1266 he overthrew and slew Manfred in battle. He then took the kingdom himself; and when, two years afterwards, young *Conradin*, the nephew of Manfred, tried to win back the crown, he was defeated in battle, and was beheaded by order of Charles. Charles was thus *King of Sicily*, both of the island and of the mainland; but in 1282 the island of Sicily revolted against the oppression of him and his Frenchmen, and the Sicilians chose as their King another King *Peter* of *Aragon*, who had married the daughter of Manfred. A long war followed; the end of which was that Charles's descendants kept the kingdom on the mainland, which was commonly called the *Kingdom of Naples*, while the island of Sicily became a separate kingdom in the House of Aragon. But in both kingdoms the Kings called themselves *Kings of Sicily*, so that when the island and the mainland were joined again long afterwards, the kingdom was called the *Kingdom of the Two Sicilies*.

15. **Crusades in the North of Europe.**—Besides the real Crusades against the Mahometans and what we may call the mock Crusades against heretics and other enemies of the Popes, there were also, as we have already seen, Crusades against the heathens in the North of Europe. The people on the east side of the Baltic, in *Prussia*, *Lithuania*, *Livonia*, and *Esthonia*, were still idolaters. *Poland* had become Christian at the end of the tenth century, and the Polish Dukes and Kings had much trouble with their heathen neighbours. Both Poland and Lithuania were much smaller states now than they became afterwards. But *Russia* at this time was a much greater state, and came much further to the west, than it did again till quite late times, for the Poles and Lithuanians made large conquests at the expense of Russia. Both Russia and Poland were at this time often divided between several princes; and one or two of the great cities, especially the famous *Novgorod* in the north,

were able to make themselves into republics. But both Poland and Russia were almost wholly cut off from the sea by their heathen neighbours, and at one time it seemed as if the chief power in those parts was likely to fall into the hands of *Denmark*. For several of the Danish Kings, in the twelfth and thirteenth centuries, made large conquests on the southern and eastern shores of the Baltic. But in the reign of Frederick the Second great changes were made in those parts by the establishment of the *Teutonic Knights*. They were first invited by some of the Polish princes to help them against the heathen Prussians. Under their Grand Master *Hermann of Salza*, they were commissioned by the Emperor Frederick and by Pope *Gregory the Ninth*, who preached a Crusade against the Prussians, to settle themselves in those parts about 1230. They presently conquered Prussia and Eastern *Pomerania*; and in 1237 another order, called the *Knights of the Sword*, who were established in *Livonia*, were joined with the Teutonic Knights. The territories of the Order now quite cut off Poland, Lithuania, and Russia from the Baltic, and hindered any further advance of Denmark in those parts. The wars of the Knights in those lands were looked on as holy wars, and many men came from other parts of Europe to join them in fighting against the heathens, just as they had done against the Saracens in the East. But the government of an order can never be a really good government, and the Knights became quite as dangerous neighbours to the Poles, whom they had at first come to help, as they were to the Prussians and other heathens whom they had come to fight against.

16. **Advance of the Christians in Spain.**—While Crusades against heathens and Mahometans were thus going on in the North and East, the whole history of *Spain* might be called one long Crusade on the part of the Christians who were winning back the land, step by step, from the Saracens and Moors.

The advance of the Christians was still checked by the foundation of new Mahometan dynasties, which passed over from Africa into Spain. As the *Almoravides* passed over in the eleventh century, so the *Almohades*, who were much like a kind of Mahometan Crusaders, passed over in the twelfth. *Alfonso the Eighth*, who, as being the chief prince in Spain, called himself *Emperor*, withstood them for a while; but, after his death in 1159, Castile and Leon were again divided, and the Almohades were able again largely to extend the Mahometan territories. In 1195 *Jacob*, the Caliph of the Almohades, at the head of a kind of general Mahometan Crusade, won the great battle of *Alarcos* over *Alfonso* of Castile, the grandson of the Emperor Alfonso; and as the different Spanish Kings were constantly quarrelling between themselves, it almost seemed as if the Mahometans were going again to get the upper hand. But, when the Caliph Jacob was dead and the Christians began to join together again, the Almohade prince *Mahomet* was utterly defeated in 1212 at the battle of *Tolosa;* and from that time the Mahometan power in Spain steadily went down. *Ferdinand the Third*, called *Saint Ferdinand*, who reigned over Castile from 1217 to 1252, and who in 1230 finally united the kingdoms of Castile and Leon, won back a large territory, including the great cities of *Seville* and *Cordova.* The Kings of *Portugal* and *Aragon* also were pressing their conquests in the West and East of the peninsula. The most famous of the Kings of Aragon was *James the Conqueror*, who reigned from 1213 to 1276. At last nothing was left of the Mahometan power in Spain save only the Kingdom of *Granada* in the South, which began in 1237, and which, having a good barrier of mountains, lasted much longer than any one would have looked for. From this time there were five kingdoms in Spain, *Castile*, *Aragon*, *Portugal*, *Navarre*, and *Granada.* Of these Castile was the greatest and Navarre the smallest: but, as both Castile and Portugal were chiefly employed with their wars with the Mahometans, Aragon was the Spanish kingdom which had most to do with the general affairs of Europe, as we have seen when speaking of the history of Sicily and Southern Gaul.

17. **The Invasions of the Moguls.**—While Christians and Mahometans were thus fighting in various parts of Europe and Asia, a new power, a Turanian power, which was neither Christian nor Mahometan, threatened to overwhelm both alike. These were the *Moguls,* commonly known in Europe as *Tartars*, who in the thirteenth century burst forth from the unknown lands of Asia, beyond either the Saracens or the Turks, much as Attila and his Huns had burst forth eight hundred years before. They began to rise to power under *Temujin* or *Jenghiz Khan*, who reigned from 1206 to 1227. During the whole of the century he and his descendants went on conquering and destroying through the greater part of Europe and Asia. In some parts they only ravaged, and ravaged more cruelly than either the Saracens or the Turks had ever done; in others they founded lasting dynasties. In religion they seem to have been a kind of Deists, acknowledging one God, but not accepting either the Christian or the Mahometan law. But all religions, Christian, Mahometan, and heathen, were freely tolerated among them, and in the end most of them became Mahometans. In Europe *Batou Khan* pressed all through Russia, Poland, and Hungary, as far as the borders of Germany. The furthest point which they reached to the west was *Lignitz* in *Silesia,* the border province of Poland and Bohemia, which had been Polish, but which now was Bohemian. They there, in 1241, gained a battle over the Teutonic Knights and all the princes of those parts. All Europe was naturally frightened at such an invasion, and the Emperor Frederick tried to stir up all the

other Kings to a Crusade against these enemies, who were worse than Saracens or Prussians. But the Moguls pressed no further westwards; they ravaged Hungary and the countries to the north of it, but the only lasting dynasty which they set up in Europe was at *Kasan* on the Volga, whence they held Russia in their dependence. Thus Russia, which had at one time seemed likely to become an important power in Europe, was altogether thrust back for a long time. The Lithuanians conquered all the western provinces, even the old capital of *Kiev*, and the Russian Dukes, first of *Vladimir* and then of *Moscow*, were looked on as mere subjects of the Mogul Khans. In Asia, besides conquests in China and other parts which do not concern us, the Moguls overthrew most of the existing powers, and founded a lasting dynasty in *Persia*. The *Chorasmians*, from the lands east of the Caspian, flying before them, overthrew, as we have seen, the restored Christian Kingdom of Jerusalem. In 1258 *Holagou*, another grandson of Jenghiz, took Bagdad, and put an end to the Abbasside Caliphate, though a line of Caliphs who professed to be the descendants of the Abbassides went on in Egypt, but without any temporal power. The power of the Seljuk Turks was also quite broken up, and the Greek Emperors at Nikaia were greatly frightened, though in the end the invasion of the Moguls helped the Eastern Empire to last a little longer, by destroying the power of the Seljuks. But it was only for a little while, because the overthrow of the Seljuk Turks made a way for the growth of the far more famous Turkish power of the *Ottomans*, whose beginning came a little later than the time which we have now reached.

18. **Summary.**—Thus we see that the time of the Swabian Emperors was a time of still greater changes than that of the Franconian Emperors. In their time much was done towards bringing the various powers of Europe into something like the

state in which they are now. The power of the Western Empire came pretty well to an end, and Germany and Italy began to be collections of separate states, independent or nearly so, as they have been ever since till quite lately. The *Eastern Empire* was broken up; the greatness of *Venice* began; the *Caliphate* perished, and the *Crusades* came to an end. But, while Christendom lost in the East, it gained in the West by the great advances of the Christians in *Spain*. *Castile* now takes the first place in the Spanish peninsula. In the like sort *France* is now fully established as the leading power of Gaul. In *England* Normans and English are fully reconciled; the *Angevin Kings*, by the loss of the more part of their foreign dominions, are driven to become national sovereigns, and that parliamentary constitution is established which has lasted ever since. The north of Europe was further from putting on its present form than the west; but the establishment of the *Teutonic Order*, the check given to the power of *Denmark*, the extension of *Lithuania*, and the subjection of *Russia* to the *Moguls* are all events which had an important effect on later times. This was also a time of great intellectual progress. *Universities* began to arise, among which *Paris* and *Oxford* were two of the most famous north of the Alps. In England there were Latin Historians and other writers, such as *William of Malmesbury*, *John of Salisbury*, and *Matthew Paris*, and the great Friar *Roger Bacon*, who forestalled many of the inventions of later times. In France prose writing began with *Villehardouin*, who wrote an account of the taking of Constantinople. Italian literature began under Frederick the Second, and in Germany this was the time of the *Minnesingers* or love-poets. The pointed or *Gothic* style of architecture also began to come into use in the last years of the twelfth century, and flourished greatly in the thirteenth. Altogether this was, both in Europe and Asia, a time when old systems were falling and new ones were rising, and in most parts we may see the beginnings of the state of things which we see now.

CHAPTER XII.

THE DECLINE OF THE EMPIRE.

Decay of the Empire; the great Interregnum (1) —*double election of Richard and Alfonso* (1)—*election of Rudolf; his grant of Austria to his son* (2)—*reigns of Adolf and Albert* (2)—*reign of Henry the Seventh; his career in Italy* (2)—*history of John of Bohemia* (2)—*reigns of Charles the Fourth, Wenceslaus, and Siegmund* (2)—*reigns of Albert the Second and Frederick the Third* (2)—*new position of the Empire; its connexion with the House of Austria* (2)—*papacy of Gregory the Tenth; of Boniface the Eighth* (3)—*the Avignon Popes; suppression of the Templars* (3)—*the Great Schism* (3)—*the reforming Councils, Pisa, Constanz, and Basel* (4)—*Councils of Ferrara and Florence; reconciliation with the Eastern Church* (4)—*intellectual pre-eminence of Italy* (5)—*study of the Roman Law; revival of classical learning* (5)—*invention of printing and gunpowder* (5)—*growth of the tyrants in Italy; the Visconti at Milan* (6)—*constitutions of Venice, Genoa, and Florence* (6)—*revolution of Rienzi at Rome* (7)—*return of the Popes; their temporal power* (7)—*the Two Sicilies; rivalry of the Houses of Anjou and Aragon* (8)—*dealings of England with Wales and Scotland* (9)—*the Hundred Years' War between France and England* (10)—*claim of Edward the Third to the crown of France; victories of the English* (10)—*Peace of Bretigny; independence and loss of Aquitaine* (10)—*wars of Henry the Fifth; Treaty of Troyes* (10)—*exploits of Joan of Arc; French conquest of Aquitaine* (10)—*growth of France; annexations in the Kingdom of Burgundy; defeat of the French at Courtray* (11)—*beginning of the Swiss League; the three Forest Cantons; battle of Morgarten*

(12)—*the eight Cantons; battle of Sempach* (12)—*relations of the League to the Empire, France, and Austria* (12)—*beginning of the Valois Dukes of Burgundy; acquisition of Flanders* (13)—*reigns of John the Fearless and Philip the Good; advance of the Burgundian power within the Empire* (13)—*reign of Charles the Bold; his rivalry with Lewis the Eleventh* (13)—*his schemes and conquests; his war with the Confederates; battles of Grandson, Morat, and Nancy* (13)—*effects of the Burgundian War on the Confederates* (13)—*the Greek Empire of Constantinople; its advance and decline* (14)—*rise of the Ottoman Turks; their conquests in Asia* (14)—*their advance in Europe; institution of the Janissaries* (14)—*rise of Timour; he defeats Bajazet at Angora* (15)—*reign of Mahomet the Second; fall of Constantinople* (16)—*conquest of Greece and Trebizond; taking of Otranto; death of Mahomet* (16)—*civil war in Castile; battle of Najara* (17)—*wars of Aragon with Provence and France* (17)—*maritime discoveries and conquests of the Portuguese* (17)—*union of Castile and Aragon; conquest of Granada; beginning of the greatness of Spain* (17)—*state of the Scandinavian Kingdoms; Union of Calmar* (18)—*the House of Oldenburg in Denmark; affairs of Sleswick and Holstein* (18)—*conversion of Lithuania; its union with Poland; partition of Prussia* (19)—*deliverance of Russia from the Moguls* (19)—*the Angevin Kings in Hungary; reign of Siegmund; his defeat at Nikopolis* (20)—*exploits of Huniades; defeat of Wladislaus at Varna* (20)—*reign of Matthias Corvinus; designs of Austria on Hungary* (20)—*growth of Universities* (21)—*writers of history and poetry* (21)—*final triumph of the English language* (21)—*theology and philosophy* (21)—*levelling doctrines taught; condition of the villains* (21)—*use of infantry in war* (21)—*state of architecture* (21)—*Summary* (22).

1. **The Great Interregnum.**—After the death of Frederick the Second the power and dignity of the Western Empire greatly declined. Italy now began quite to fall away. Many of the Kings who were chosen in Germany never went to Rome to be crowned

Emperors at all, and those who did so, though their passing through the country always made some changes at the time, could not keep any lasting hold on the Italian Kingdom. The Kingdom of Burgundy quite broke in pieces; some of its princes and commonwealths still kept on their nominal connexion with the Empire, but others passed, one by one, by one means or another, under the power of France. Thus began that growth of France at the cost of the kingdoms belonging to the Empire, of which we had a sort of foreshadowing in the battle of Bouvines, and which has gone on ever since, till it was stopped only yesterday. In fact, after the death of Frederick the Second, his successors, though they were still called Kings and Emperors of the Romans, were really very little more than Kings of Germany, and even in Germany their power was always growing less and less. The time from the death of Conrad in 1254 to the year 1273 is commonly called the *Great Interregnum*, because, though more than one King was chosen during that time, there was no King really acknowledged by all Germany, much less by the other parts of the Empire. In 1256 some of the Electors chose *Richard* Earl of Cornwall, brother of King Henry the Third of England, and others chose *Alfonso* King of Castile. Alfonso never came to Germany at all. Richard came and was crowned King, but he never was crowned Emperor, and he kept very little power in Germany, and spent most of his time in England, where we often hear of him in English history. He died in 1271, the year before his brother King Henry. This long *Interregnum* was a time of great confusion in Germany. The Empire quite lost its hold over the neighbouring countries, and the princes in Germany itself greatly enlarged their own powers while there was no King to keep them in check. In short, every sort of lawlessness and wickedness was rife through the whole land. At last men felt that an end must be put to such a state of things, and in 1273 a King dwelling in the land was once more chosen.

2. **Kings of the Houses of Habsburg and Lüzelburg.**—The King who was now chosen was not one of the great Princes of the Empire; he was *Rudolf* Count of *Habsburg*, a castle in *Aargau* in the south of Swabia. He reigned till 1292, and was a brave and wise man, who did much to restore peace and to subdue *Ottocar* King of Bohemia and other enemies. He was the founder of the *House of Habsburg* or of *Austria*, from which so many Kings and Emperors were afterwards chosen. For the old Margraves and Dukes of Austria had come to an end, and the Duchy was granted by Rudolf to his son *Albert*, from whom the later Dukes, Kings, and Emperors of the Austrian House all sprang. Neither Rudolf nor either of the two next Kings, *Adolf* of *Nassau* and Rudolf's son *Albert*, was ever crowned Emperor. Albert was the first Austrian King, and there were no more for some time to come; for, when he was murdered in 1308, the Electors chose *Henry* Count of *Lüzelburg* or *Luxemburg*, who reigned as *Henry the Seventh*. In his time it seemed as if the Empire were going to win back again all its old power. For he went into Italy, and was crowned King at Milan and Emperor at Rome in 1312; but in the next year he died, by poison as was thought, and his great schemes died with him. He was however able to provide for his own family as Rudolf had done, for he got the Kingdom of Bohemia for his son *John*, by marrying him to the daughter of the last King *Wenceslaus*. This King John figures a good deal in the history of the time, but not so much either in his own kingdom or in Germany as in going about as a kind of knight-errant in Italy and France. At last he died in the battle of *Crecy* between the French and the English, of which we shall speak presently. He was never Emperor or King of the

Romans himself, but several of his descendants were, as we shall soon see. On the death of Henry the Seventh, there was a double election between *Lewis* Duke of *Bavaria* and *Frederick* Duke of *Austria*, the son of King Albert. But Lewis reigned in the end, and in 1328 he was crowned Emperor. He had great quarrels with Pope *John the Twenty-second*, and each professed to depose the other, just as Gregory the Seventh and Henry the Fourth had done. Lewis was again declared deposed in 1346 by Pope *Clement the Sixth,* and then John of Bohemia persuaded the Electors to declare the Empire vacant and to elect his son *Charles*, who reigned as *Charles the Fourth.* He was crowned Emperor in 1347, and, what one would hardly have expected, he was crowned King of Burgundy at Arles in 1365. Charles made a good King in his own kingdom of Bohemia, but he sadly lowered the Empire both in Germany and in Italy. He is chiefly remembered for granting a charter known as the *Golden Bull*, by which the way of choosing the Emperor was finally settled, but by which the powers of the Empire were still further lessened in favour of the princes. Then followed several Kings who were never crowned Emperors, and on whom we need not dwell long. One of them, *Wenceslaus,* son of the Emperor Charles, so far from taking heed to Italy, took none to Germany, and kept always in Bohemia. At last, in 1410, his brother *Siegmund* was chosen King, and he was crowned Emperor in 1433. He was already Margrave of Brandenburg and King of Hungary, and he afterwards became King of Bohemia. The truth is that the Empire by itself was growing so weak and so poor that it was found needful to choose some prince for Emperor who had dominions of his own which would enable him to keep up his dignity. And in Siegmund we get the beginning of that special connexion between the Empire and the Kingdom of Hungary which afterwards became of great importance. Siegmund was specially zealous in the attempts for reforming the Church of which we shall hear presently. He died in 1437. Then came his son-in-law *Albert Duke of Austria*, who died in 1439, and was succeeded by another Austrian Prince, *Frederick* Duke of *Steiermark* or *Styria*. His was a very long reign, lasting from 1440 to 1493, but he himself did nothing memorable. In 1452 he was crowned Emperor at Rome, being the last Emperor who was crowned there. From the time of Siegmund we may look on the Empire as putting on quite a new character. Neither as Emperor nor as King of Germany, was the Emperor any longer the chief prince of Europe. But the Empire was now held by princes who were powerful through their dominions both in and out of Germany, Kings of Hungary, Dukes of Austria, and so forth. And, from the time of Albert the Second, though the Emperors were still always elected, yet the Electors always chose a member of the House of Austria, and most commonly the head of that House. Thus from this time the Emperors were again very powerful princes, though it was not from the Empire that they drew their chief strength. The House of Austria lent its strength to the Empire, and the Empire lent its dignity to the House of Austria, and, before the death of Frederick the Third, the German Emperor was again the only Emperor. How this came about we shall see presently.

3. **The Popes at Rome and Avignon.**—We left the Popes disputing and waging war against the Emperor Frederick the Second and his descendants, both in Germany and in Sicily. There were however some Popes who gave their minds to better things. Thus, nearly about the same time that Rudolf was chosen King, a very good Pope, *Gregory the Tenth*, was chosen in 1271. Indeed Gregory had a good deal to do with the election of Rudolf; for his great wish was to put an end to all the strifes and confusions

which were going on in Germany, Italy, and elsewhere, and to make all Western Europe join together in an attempt to win back the Holy Land. He even brought about for a moment the reconciliation of the Eastern and Western Churches; and, between him and King Rudolf and King Edward in England, it almost seemed that the whole world was going to start afresh with a good beginning. But Gregory only reigned a little while; he died in 1276, and the real power and glory of the Popes died with him. *Boniface the Eighth*, who reigned from 1294 to 1303, tried to get back all the powers which any of the earlier Popes had ever made use of. But the times were no longer fitted for this. The more Europe began to settle down into a system of distinct nations, and the more the Popes began to put on the character of Italian princes, the less were they able to act as rulers of the whole world, even in purely ecclesiastical matters. Boniface the Eighth quarrelled with *Philip the Fair*, the King of the French, and in the end Philip sent and seized him, and he died soon after. The next Pope but one, *Clement the Fifth*, was a Pope of Philip's own choosing, and was quite at his beck and call. He left off living at Rome, and moved his Court to *Avignon* on the Rhone, just outside the French border. Avignon had been one of the free commonwealths in the Kingdom of Burgundy; but it had come under the power of the Counts of Provence, so that it now belonged to the French King of Naples. The new Pope was thus more within the power of his master the King of the French. For seventy years the Popes lived at Avignon instead of in their own place at Rome, a time which men called the *Babylonish Captivity*. Of course this greatly weakened their power. Presently Clement and Philip joined together to destroy the order of the *Templars*, which had done such great things in the Holy Wars. We can well believe that many corruptions had come into the order, but no one can believe the monstrous tales which the Pope and the King got up against them, as if they had cast aside all religion and morals altogether. It was no doubt the wealth of the knights which Philip wished to seize; so the order was suppressed throughout Europe, and in France many of its members were cruelly put to death. The next Pope, *John the Twenty-second*, had, as we before said, great disputes with the Emperor Lewis, and he was also thought to have gone wrong in some hard points of theology. This is one of many things which show how much men's minds were now stirred on the subject of religion, as we shall presently see. The Popes did not finally go back to Rome till 1376, in the time of *Gregory the Eleventh;* and, when he died two years afterwards, there was a double election. *Urban the Sixth*, an Italian, was the first chosen, and afterwards *Robert of Geneva*, who called himself *Clement the Seventh.* So the Church was divided. Urban lived at Rome and Clement at Avignon, and some nations followed one and some the other; France of course took the side of the Pope at Avignon, and England therefore took that of the Pope at Rome. There were thus two opposition Popes, for, when Urban and Clement died, their several parties chose others to succeed them; and this state of things went on till men got weary of their disputes, and tried to settle them in another way.

4. **The General Councils.**—Ever since the time of Constantine, *General Councils*, that is meetings of Bishops and divines from all parts, had been summoned, first by the Emperors and afterwards by the Popes, whenever there were matters to be discussed concerning the whole Church. Such Councils were always held to have greater authority than the Popes. But of course, after the separation of East and West, they could not really represent the whole Church, but only the Western part of it. So now a series of

Councils were held to settle the affairs of the Church, especially the disputes between the Popes. The first was held at *Pisa* in 1402. This Council deposed both the Popes and chose a third, *Alexander the Fifth,* who was succeeded by *John the Twenty-third.* But as the other two, *Benedict the Thirteenth* and *Gregory the Twelfth,* would not give in, this only made three Popes instead of two. At last in 1415 another Council was held at *Constanz,* chiefly by the help of King Siegmund, who worked very hard to bring about the peace of the Church. This Council deposed all the three Popes, and very rightly; for John the Twenty-third, whether he were rightly chosen or not, deserved to be deposed, for his wickedness reminded men of the old times of John the Twelfth. The Council then elected *Martin the Fifth,* who was acknowledged everywhere as the true Pope. But the Council did some other things which were less to its credit. The religious controversies at the time, and the abuses of the Papal dominion, had led everywhere to much thought on religious matters and to the putting forth of many new doctrines. In England *John Wickliffe,* a doctor of Oxford, had written against many things in the received belief and practice of the times, especially against the *Begging Friars,* that is the *Franciscans* and *Dominicans,* who professed to live upon alms. He made many followers, and his opinions spread, especially in Bohemia. Two of the chief Bohemian preachers, *John Huss* and *Jerome of Prague,* were brought before the Council and were burned, to the great shame of King Siegmund, who had plighted his word for the safety of Huss. The followers of Huss in Bohemia now rebelled, and a fearful civil war followed. In 1431 there was another Council held at *Basel,* which professed to depose Pope *Eugenius the Fourth,* and which lasted from 1431 to 1439. This Council, had its decrees taken effect, would have greatly lessened the powers of the Popes and increased those of the

Bishops and the national Churches, bringing things in short more to the state in which they were in early times. But the Council of Basel gradually fell into discredit, and it died out. The Popes never liked these Councils which were held in places north of the Alps, like Basel and Constanz; and meanwhile Pope Eugenius held a Council of his own in Italy, first at *Ferrara* and then at *Florence*, where in 1439 another nominal reconciliation with the Eastern Church was made. This was because the Eastern Empire was just then at its last gasp, and was glad to get help from the West on any terms. For the rest of this century the Popes must be looked on as little more than Italian princes, and we will speak of them again as such.

5. **The Revival of Learning in Italy.**— During all this time we may look on *Italy* as being in some sort the central nation of Europe. It had indeed no kind of political power over other nations, for the power of the Emperors was gone, and this time, when the Popes were so much away in Gaul, was just the time when they were less Italian, and had less power both in Italy and elsewhere, than at any time before or after. And Italy, cut up as it was into many principalities and commonwealths, was in no state to bear rule over other nations. Still it might be called the centre of Europe, as being the country which had more to do with the rest of the world than any other one country. It was the country to which others looked up as being at the head in arts, learning, and commerce, and it was the country too where, just as in old Greece, there was the greatest political life among the many small states. But of course, as in old Greece also, this was bought at the cost of constant wars between the different cities and of many disturbances within them. The two nations which had been the most civilized in Europe, the Greeks in the East and the Saracens in the West, were now falling before the Turks and the

Spanish Christians. The Italians in some sort took their place. Ever since the twelfth century there had been a great movement of men's minds in the way of learning, and this turned more and more towards the study of the ancient Latin writers, and after a while the Greek also. And studies of this kind also had an important political effect. Thus men in the twelfth century began to study the old *Roman Law*, and this study disposed them much in favour of the Swabian Emperors. So again, somewhat later, the study of the old Latin poets, and what they said about the old Cæsars, led men to welcome Henry the Seventh and the Emperors who came after him. The great poet *Dante Alighieri* was strong on the Imperial side, both in his poems and in his prose writings, and he reproaches King Albert for staying away from Italy and not taking heed to the garden of the Empire. But, on the other hand, the study of the ancient republican writers, and the praises which they give to the killers of tyrants, several times stirred up men in the fifteenth century to conspiracies against the Popes and other princes. Towards the end of the time with which we have to do printing was invented; and though it was not invented in Italy but in Germany, by *Gutenburg* at *Mainz*, yet it was in Italy, where there were more learned men and writers than elsewhere, that it was for a long while of the most importance. Gunpowder too, an invention as important in war as printing was in peace, gradually came into use in the fourteenth and fifteenth centuries. It quite changed the manner of warfare; the old style of armour and the old style of fortification, both of which had in Italy been carried to such perfection that men could not be wounded, and castles could not be taken, by any arms then known, now became of little use, and a new order of things in warfare began.

6. **The Commonwealths of Italy.**—Meanwhile the political state of Italy greatly changed. The

separate cities, which had in the twelfth century been independent commonwealths, were gradually grouped together into larger states. Sometimes the lord or tyrant of one city got possession of several cities, so as to form a large continuous dominion. In such cases a ruler generally tried to give some show of lawfulness to his power by getting the Pope or the Emperor to invest him with his dominions as a fief, and to give him the title of *Duke* or *Marquess* as an hereditary prince. Thus, in the course of the thirteenth century, the chief power at *Milan* gradually came into the hands of the family of the *Visconti.* Then, in 1395, *Gian-Galeazzo Visconti*, who was *Lord* of Milan and held Pavia and other cities of Lombardy, bought a charter from King Wenceslaus making him *Duke of Milan.* The Dukes of Milan, through the wealth and industry of the cities over which they ruled, became far richer and more powerful than many princes who had much wider dominions, but, now that their dominions were made hereditary, they were laid open to the usual disputes and wars as to the right of succession to the duchy. When *Filippo-Maria*, the last of the Visconti, died in 1447, the Milanese tried to set their ancient commonwealth up again. But they were obliged to admit *Francesco Sforza*, the son-in-law of the late Duke, as his successor. He was one of a class of men of whom there were then many in Italy, mercenary generals who went about with bands of soldiers, hiring themselves out to fight for any prince or commonwealth that would pay them. It was by the help of such leaders that most of the princes and commonwealths of Italy in the fourteenth and fifteenth centuries waged their wars. Thus there was a new dynasty at Milan, that of the *Sforza.* Meanwhile, as some of the cities of Northern Italy thus fell under the power of the Dukes of Milan, so others came under the power of the commonwealth of Venice. For it was in Italy at this time just as it was long before in old

Greece; one city bore rule over another. Venice, as we have seen, had gained the first position in the world as a maritime power, holding large possessions in the East. But in the fifteenth century she was tempted to become a land power also, and she won a large dominion over the cities in the north-east of Italy. The government of Venice had by this time grown into a narrow oligarchy. The chief power was in the hands of the noble families, quite shutting out the people and leaving very little power to the Doge. But, though Venice was an oligarchy, yet it was a prudent and moderate oligarchy, which never failed to supply wise statesmen and brave commanders by sea. For the fleets of Venice were always manned by her own citizens and subjects, though by land mercenary troops were commonly used. Genoa also remained a republic, and kept up a great deal of her old maritime power. At one time, in 1379, she seemed almost on the point of conquering Venice. But at Genoa, unlike Venice, there were constant internal revolutions, and the city had several times to submit to the Dukes of Milan and the Kings of France. The other great maritime commonwealth, Pisa, lost nearly all her power after a sea-fight with the Genoese in 1284, and at last in 1406 Pisa became subject to Florence. This last commonwealth, which had not been prominent in the twelfth century, gradually became, in the course of the thirteenth century, one of the chief states of Italy. As Venice was the greatest example in later times of an aristocratic commonwealth, so Florence was the greatest example of a democracy. In this way the two in some sort answer to Sparta and Athens in the old Greek times. At Florence the old nobles were quite put down in 1292, but, in the course of the fifteenth century, a kind of new nobility gradually arose. Among these, one family in particular, that of the *Medici*, gradually rose to have the chief power in the state, though without disturbing the forms of the commonwealth, or taking any particular title to themselves. Such were *Cosmo de' Medici*, called the *Father of his Country*, and his grandson *Lorenzo*. Their power was of a different kind from that of the lords or tyrants, either in old Greece or in other cities of Italy. Nor was it such a power as that of Periklês at Athens, for it passed on from father to son. It was more like the power of Augustus and the other Roman Emperors who respected the forms of the commonwealth. On the whole, Florence, though the greatest and most famous democratic state in later times, was by no means so pure and regular a democracy as Athens was. Still there was no part of Europe where there was so much life, political, intellectual, and commercial. Dante, the greatest of all Italian poets, was born at Florence in 1265, and died in banishment in 1321. Many other of the chief artists and men of letters also belonged to Florence; the commerce of the city was famous, and its bankers lent money to Kings in England and elsewhere. And in the time of the Medici there was no city in Italy where greater encouragement was given to the men who were engaged in reviving the old Greek and Roman learning.

7. **Rome and the Popes.**—Rome meanwhile, forsaken as the city was for so long both by the Emperors and by the Popes, quite lost its old place in Italy, and did not begin to win it back again till the affairs of the Popes became more settled after the Council of Constanz. The Romans never forgot the old greatness of their city, and, as men's minds were constantly falling back on old times, one *Cola di Rienzi* in 1347 set up again for a short time what he called *the Good State*, and ruled himself by the title of *Tribune*. So again, after the Popes came back to Rome, there were one or two conspiracies to set up the old commonwealth; but from the Council of Constanz onwards we may look on the Popes as undoubted temporal princes of Rome. They were gradually able to bring

under their power all that part of Italy, stretching from one sea to the other, over which they professed to have rights by the grants of various Kings and Emperors. The latter Popes of the fifteenth century must be looked on as little more than Italian princes, and many of them were among the very worst of the Italian princes. Some of them, like *Nicolas the Fifth*, did some good in the way of encouraging learning; and *Pius the Second*, who reigned from 1458 to 1464, and who is famous as a writer by his former name of *Æneas Silvius*, tried, like Gregory the Tenth, to get the Christian princes to join in a Crusade for the deliverance of the East. But *Sixtus the Fourth* and *Innocent the Eighth* were among the worst of the Popes, men who thought of nothing except increasing their temporal power and advancing their own families.

8. **The Two Sicilies.**—The *Two Sicilies* meanwhile remained divided. The Kingdom of Sicily on the mainland, often called the Kingdom of *Naples*, was in extent the greatest state in Italy, and some of its Kings, especially *Robert*, who reigned from 1309 to 1343, played an important part in Italian affairs. But it shows how much greater was the life of the separate cities, even when they were not under a free government, when we see how this large kingdom lagged behind the rest of Italy, and how, even in political power, it was not more than on a level with the principalities and commonwealths of Northern Italy which were not above half its size. This Kingdom of Sicily was much torn in pieces by civil wars arising out of disputed successions to the Crown. Two bad Queens, *Joanna the First* (1343 to 1382) and *Joanna the Second* (1419 to 1435), caused much confusion by their different marriages and adoptions of successors. During the greater part of the fifteenth century the crown was disputed between a branch of the *House of Aragon*, who for the most part kept possession, and the *Dukes of Anjou*, a branch of the royal house of France, who

ever and anon tried to make their own claims good. At last the claims of the Angevin princes passed to the Kings of France themselves, and then many important events followed. Meanwhile in the Island of Sicily the other branch of the house of Aragon went on reigning. The first King *Frederick*, who established the independence of the island, ruled bravely and wisely, but after him the island kingdom became of no account at all. At last Sicily became united to the Kingdom of Aragon, another step towards the great events of the next period.

9. **England, France, and Scotland.**—A great part of the history of the lands beyond the Alps during this time is taken up by the long wars between England and France. These had now become thoroughly national wars, and before long they grew into attempts at a complete conquest of France on the part of England. And the wars between England and France are a good deal mixed up with the wars of the English Kings with Scotland, and even with Wales. For, when England and France became constant national enemies, it was the natural policy of the French Kings to raise up enemies to their rivals within their own island. It was the object of Edward the First, like that of his namesake Edward the Elder in old times, to join all Britain, as far as might be, under one dominion. That part of *Wales* which still kept its own princes was joined on in 1282. Wales was never again separated from England; but once or twice, when there were revolts in Wales, those who were discontented with the English rule tried to get help from France. How *Scotland* was for a moment united with England, how, after the death of Edward the First, it was again separated under its King *Robert Bruce*, how in 1328 Scotland was acknowledged by England as an independent kingdom, but how constant rivalries and wars went on between the two kingdoms in one island, must be told more fully in our Histories of England

and Scotland. The point to be borne in mind now is that, from this time, we find a steady alliance between France and Scotland against England. This began as early as the time of Edward the First. In the long wars of the fourteenth and fifteenth centuries we now and then find French troops serving in Scotland, while the Scots soon learned to take service in France, and in the later wars we find them serving against the English in every battle. Through this close connexion with France, Scotland came to hold a higher place in Europe than she could otherwise have had from her size and position.

10. **Wars between England and France.**—During the reigns of Edward the First and of his son *Edward the Second*, who reigned from 1307 to 1327, the rivalry between England and France did not lead to any great war. Philip the Fair got possession of the Duchy of Aquitaine in the year 1294, but he had soon to give it up again. It was in the reign of *Edward the Third*, from 1327 to 1377, that the great war began which the French writers call the *Hundred Years' War*. It was something like the Peloponnesian War in Greece in old times; for, though there was not actual fighting going on for the whole time, yet there was no firm or lasting peace between the two countries for more than a hundred years. Edward the Third professed to have a claim to the Crown of France through his mother *Isabel*, who was a daughter of Philip the Fair. But the French held that no right to the Crown could pass through a woman. And Edward might very likely not have pressed his claim, had not the French King, *Philip of Valois*, driven him into war by his attempts to get possession of Aquitaine. A long war followed, which was famous for the taking of *Calais* and for the great victories of the English at *Crecy* in 1346 and at *Poitiers* in 1356. Edward, as was natural, was an ally of the Emperor Lewis and of the Flemish cities, which were now beginning to rise

into great importance, though they never won the same complete independence as those of Italy. The feudal superiority over Flanders belonged to France; the Flemings were therefore better pleased when King Edward took the title of *King of France*, so that they might seem to be fighting for, and not against, their over-lord. As King Edward was an ally of the Emperor Lewis, it came about that King John of Bohemia took the French side, so that he and his son *Charles*, who had just been chosen King of the Romans, were both at Crecy, and King John was killed there. At Poitiers another King John, the French King himself, was taken prisoner, and, as *David King of Scots*, the son of Robert Bruce, was taken prisoner in 1346, there were two captive Kings in England at once. This first part of the war with France was ended by the *Peace of Bretigny* in 1360, by which Edward gave up his claim to the Crown of France, but kept his possessions in Aquitaine, together with Calais and some other small districts, and that no longer as a vassal of the French King, but as an independent sovereign. Edward then granted his dominions in the south to his son *Edward*, called the *Black Prince*, who ruled at Bourdeaux as *Prince of Aquitaine*. Before long the Peace of Bretigny was broken by the French King *Charles the Fifth*, and, before the end of the reign of Edward the Third, the English had lost nearly all their possessions in Aquitaine except the cities of Bourdeaux and Bayonne. The cities commonly stuck to the English rule, under which they were less meddled with, while the nobles were mostly for a union with France. After the peace was broken, King Edward again took up his title of *King of France*, which was borne by all the Kings of England down to the year 1800. Then came a time which was neither war nor peace. Many truces were made, and now and then there was some little fighting, but it was not until the reign of *Henry the Fifth* in England that the war began again on a great scale. He took advantage of the dissensions by which France was torn in pieces during the reign of the weak, or rather mad, King *Charles the Sixth.* He won the *Battle of Agincourt* in 1415, took Rouen in 1419, and in 1420 concluded the *Treaty of Troyes*, by which Henry was to succeed to the crown of France on the death of Charles, and the crowns of England and France were to be ever after united. Both Charles and Henry died in 1422, but a large part of France refused to acknowledge the treaty; so, after their deaths, the war went on between *Charles the Seventh*, who reigned at *Bourges*, and *John Duke of Bedford*, who was Regent of France for his nephew *Henry the Sixth.* Now comes the great story of the waking up of France under the famous *Maid of Orleans, Joan of Arc.* She came from the borders of Lorraine, but she was called the Maid of Orleans, because she relieved that city when it was besieged by the English. By her means Charles the Seventh was crowned at Rheims, the old crowning-place of the French Kings, in 1429. He thus got the start of his English rival, who had not yet been crowned, but who was now crowned at Paris in 1431. The war now went on for a long time, and, after the death of the Duke of Bedford, it was for the most part badly managed on the English side. The English were gradually driven out, not only from France, but from Aquitaine also, till at last, in 1453, Bourdeaux and Bayonne were finally taken by the French, and the English kept nothing on the continent except the territory of Calais. The *Hundred Years' War* was now over. The Kings of England still kept on their claim to the Crown of France, and they now and then professed to make attempts to recover it. But, though there were for a long time many wars between England and France and long enmity between the two nations, the notion of conquering France was never again seriously taken up after the time of Henry the Sixth.

11. **The Growth of France.**—The long wars of the English were a great check to the growth of the Kingdom of France, yet it was growing all this time, both by uniting the territories of the great vassals to the Crown and by annexations at the expense of its neighbours. These were of course mainly made at the expense of the Empire; but, as Aquitaine had become an independent state by the Treaty of Bretigny, its conquest also may be looked on rather as a foreign conquest than as the union of a great fief to the Crown. And it was during this time that the French Kings began the process which has gone on ever since, that of joining the states which made up the Kingdom of Burgundy one by one to the Kingdom of France. Even before this they had taken the little County of *Venaissin*, but that had been given up to the Popes. But now they began in earnest. In 1314, Philip the Fair took advantage of the disputes which the citizens of the Imperial city of *Lyons* had with their Archbishops, and annexed the city to his own dominions. In 1349, in the thick of the English wars, the last of the princes of *Vienne* on the Rhone, who from their arms bore the title of *Dauphin* or *Dolphin*, sold his dominions to *Charles* the eldest son of King John of France, and from this time it became the rule that the eldest son of the King of France bore the title of *Dauphin*. The County of *Provence* also, though not part of the Kingdom of France, was, from the time of Charles of Anjou onwards, held by French princes. And so it came about that, somewhat after our present time, in 1481, *Lewis the Eleventh*, the son of Charles the Seventh, was able to add Provence also to France. The French Kings also more than once got hold of the *County of Burgundy* or *Franche Comté*, of which Dôle is the capital. But this they were not able permanently to keep till long afterwards. Still, before the end of the fifteenth century, the acquisition of Provence, Lyons, and the Dauphiny of Vienne had

given the French Kings a good half of the Burgundian kingdom. The only princes of any great power left in that part of the world were the *Counts*, afterwards *Dukes*, of *Savoy*, who ruled on both sides of the Lake of Geneva, and who had also possessions in the north-west corner of Italy. In other parts of the Empire also, even where the French Kings did not make conquests, they were winning influence. To the north of their own dominions they often had wars with the stout people of the Flemish cities, over whom they sometimes won victories, but by whom they were sometimes defeated. The battle of *Courtray* in the time of Philip the Fair is famous as the first great victory north of the Alps won by townsmen over nobles. On the whole, notwithstanding the long wars with England, the kingdom of France had greatly grown in power and in extent in the times between the middle of the thirteenth century and the middle of the fifteenth.

12. **Beginning of the Swiss League.**—While the three kingdoms which belonged to the Empire were thus getting weaker and more divided, and while the kingdom of France to the west of them was growing stronger and stronger, two new powers gradually arose in what we may call the border-land of all these kingdoms. One of these lasted but a short time, but the other has lived on to our own day. These are the *Duchy of Burgundy* and the *League of the Swiss Cantons*. This last began among three small mountain districts on the borders of Germany, Burgundy, and Italy, called *Uri*, *Schwyz*, and *Unterwalden*. They were German-speaking members of the Empire, and there was nothing to distinguish them from other German-speaking members of the Empire, except that they had kept far more of the freedom of the old times than most other lands had. Like many other districts and cities of the Empire, they joined together in a League for mutual defence. This they had doubtless

done from earlier times, but the first written document of their union belongs to the year 1291. The *Counts of Habsburg*, who had now become *Dukes of Austria*, and who had estates within the three lands themselves, were now very dangerous neighbours, and the Confederates had to keep close together in order to guard their freedom. This they made safe by the battle of *Morgarten*, which they won over Duke *Leopold of Austria* in 1315. Presently several of the neighbouring cities, *Luzern*, *Zürich*, and *Bern*, joined their alliance, as also did the smaller towns of *Zug* and *Glarus;* so that in the course of the fourteenth century they formed a league of eight states. Its name was the *Old League of High Germany*, and its members were called the *Eidgenossen* or *Confederates;* but the name of the Canton of *Schwyz* gradually spread over the whole League, and they came to be commonly called *Swiss* and their country *Switzerland*. But it is only in quite late times that those names have come into formal use. Such a league was of course much dreaded by the neighbouring nobles, but it was for a long time favoured by the Emperors. The three lands had been specially loyal to the Swabian Emperors, and they were no less favoured by Henry the Seventh and Lewis of Bavaria. Charles the Fourth was their enemy, but they were again favoured by his son Siegmund. But the Dukes of Austria were their constant enemies, and therefore, when the Empire passed into the Austrian House, the Confederates had to be on their guard against the power which had hitherto been friendly. But they did not throw off their allegiance to the Empire, and, during all the time of which we speak, the Confederates remained a purely German body, although some parts of their territory, including Bern, which was the most powerful member of the League, lay within the bounds of the Kingdom of Burgundy. The Confederates had to wage several wars for the defence of their freedom, as when in 1386 they won the battle of *Sempach* over another Duke *Leopold of Austria* and a great confederacy of the nobles, and when in 1444 they were attacked by the Dauphin *Lewis*, afterwards Lewis the Eleventh. They had also some disputes and even civil wars among themselves; but on the whole the League steadily advanced and made many alliances with its neighbours. And these commonwealths also, like those of old Greece and of Italy, conquered, or sometimes bought, various towns and districts, which they held as their subjects. Thus, by the middle of the fifteenth century the Confederates had grown into a new power in Europe, and one which was getting more and more independent of the Empire. But they in no sort formed a nation, because all the members of the League were still purely German. They were simply one of many German Leagues, which circumstances allowed to become more independent than the others, and, as it turned out, to survive them. We must now speak of the other power which was growing up meanwhile in the border-lands, and with which the Confederates presently had a great deal to do.

13. **The Dukes of Burgundy.**—It must be always borne in mind that the name *Burgundy* has several meanings. Thus, besides the *Kingdom of Burgundy*, which, in the times of which we are now speaking, quite fell to pieces and was almost forgotten, there was the *Duchy of Burgundy*, which was a fief of the Crown of France, and the *County of Burgundy*, which was part of the Kingdom, and therefore a fief of the Empire. A power now began to arise, which took in more than one of these Burgundies, and which seemed not unlikely to bring back the old times when there was a *Middle Kingdom* of *Burgundy* or of *Lotharingia* lying between Germany, Italy, and France. This came about in this way. The French Duchy of Burgundy fell in to the Crown in 1361, and *Philip* the son of King John of France became the first of a new

line of Dukes, that of *Valois*. He married *Margaret* the heiress of Flanders, and thus united two of the greatest fiefs of the Crown of France. Of these two, Flanders, where the great cities were always quarrelling with the Counts, was almost an independent state. After Philip there reigned three Dukes of his family, *John the Fearless* from 1404 to 1419, *Philip the Good* from 1419 to 1467, and *Charles the Bold* from 1467 to 1477. All these Dukes, as French princes, played a great part in the affairs of France. They also were always winning, in all kinds of ways, by marriage, by purchase, or by conquest, large territories within the Empire, including the greater part of the *Netherlands* or *Low Countries*, taking in nearly all both of the present *Kingdom of the Netherlands* and the present *Kingdom of Belgium*, besides much which has now gone to France. They thus were vassals at once of the Emperor and of the King of France, and they were really more powerful than either of their lords. For their position as a border power gave them great advantages, and their possession of the great cities of the Low Countries, turbulent as their citizens often were, made them the richest princes in Europe. Duke John the Fearless was murdered by the Dauphin Charles, afterwards Charles the Seventh, and this threw his son Duke Philip into the arms of the English. Philip supported the English in France for a long time, and, after he forsook their side at the *Treaty of Arras* in 1435, the English power in France fell away very fast. Duke Philip reigned very prudently, and increased the power of his Duchy in every way. But under his son, Charles the Bold, his great power fell to pieces. There was a constant rivalry between him and Lewis the Eleventh. He also kept all the world in alarm by endlessly planning one scheme after another, and by annexing such of the territories of his neighbours as he could get hold of. One great object of his was to annex the *Duchy of Lorraine*, that is the southern part of the old Lotharingia, the capital of which is *Nancy*. This would have joined his dominions in the Netherlands with the Duchy and County of Burgundy. But he also dreamed of getting Provence, and of making himself King of all the lands which had ever formed part of any of the old Burgundian and Lotharingian kingdoms. In this way he got into disputes with the cities on the Rhine, with Duke *Siegmund of Austria*, and lastly with the Confederates. And the King of France, of course, took care to stir up all his enemies against him. A war now followed between Duke Charles and the Confederates, which was carried on in the dominions of the Duke of Savoy north of the Lake of Geneva. Charles was overthrown in two great battles at *Granson* and at *Murten* or *Morat* in 1476. At last he was defeated and killed in 1477 in a third battle at *Nancy*, whither the Confederates had gone to help *René Duke of Lorraine* to win back his Duchy from Charles. This war had two great results. The great power of the Dukes of Burgundy was broken up. Charles' daughter Mary kept his dominions in the Low Countries and, after a while, got back the *County of Burgundy*. But the *Duchy of Burgundy* was joined to the Crown of France, and the scheme of a great power lying between Germany and France came to an end. On the other hand, the great victories of the Confederates raised their reputation to the highest pitch. They now began to take a part in general European affairs, and to count as a distinct power. They also now began to win dominions in the Romance-speaking lands to the west and south of them. But their successes did much to corrupt them; the *Swiss*, as they now began to be called, were such good soldiers that all the princes of Europe, especially the Kings of France, were glad to have them in their armies, and thus began the practice of serving for hire, which was the disgrace of the Swiss League till quite lately.

14. **The Eastern Empire. Rise of the Ottomans.**—While the *Western Empire* was quite changing its character, sinking into a German Kingdom, or rather into a Confederation of German States, the *Eastern Empire*, which had now become practically Greek, came to an end altogether. After the Greeks had won back Constantinople from the Latins in 1260, their dominion, under the last dynasty of the *Palaiologoi*, was but a shadow of the old Empire. Yet, as had so often happened before, there was for a while a time of revival, and the Emperors of Constantinople, *Emperors of the Romans* as they still called themselves, were able to join on to their dominions many of the little states, both Greek and Frank, which had sprung up at the time of the Latin Conquest. During these last days of the Eastern Empire there was more intercourse than before between the Greeks and the Western nations, especially the Venetians and Genoese. And, whenever the Greeks were in any trouble, their Emperors always made a show of putting an end to the division between the Eastern and Western Churches. But schemes of this sort never really took root, as the Greeks were fully determined never to admit the authority of the Pope. These applications for Western help were commonly made when the Eastern Emperors were hard pressed by an enemy which seemed likely to swallow up, not only the Eastern Empire but all Christendom. These were the *Ottoman Turks*, so called from their early leader *Othman*. They arose in the middle of the thirteenth century, being first heard of about 1240. This branch of the Turks produced a succession of greater rulers than any other Eastern dynasty, and their power has lasted till our own time. They gradually swallowed up the provinces of the Empire in Asia, and most of the other powers, Christian and Mahometan, in those parts, and Turkish pirates began to ravage the coasts of Europe. About 1343 they got a firmer footing in Europe during some

of the dissensions within the Empire, and they were never again driven out. In 1361 their Sultan *Morad* or *Amurath* took *Hadrianople*, which became the Ottoman capital. What remained of the Eastern Empire was now altogether hemmed in; all was lost, except Constantinople itself and a small territory round it, and some outlying possessions, chiefly in Peloponnêsos. Meanwhile the Turks were spreading themselves to the north, and were overcoming the Slavonic lands which had learned their Christianity from the Eastern Empire, *Servia*, *Bulgaria*, and other states in those parts. This brought them into contact with *Hungary*, and thus led to wars of which we shall speak presently. The successes of the Turks were largely owing to their taking a tribute of children from their Christian subjects, the strongest and bravest of whom were brought up as soldiers, and formed a well-disciplined body of infantry which overcame all enemies. These were called *Janissaries* or *New Soldiers*. During the reign of *Bajazet*, surnamed the *Thunderbolt*, who reigned from 1389 to 1402, things seemed as if the Eastern Empire and all the Christian states of South-eastern Europe were about to be destroyed at once. But they gained a respite in a strange way from the appearance of a new Mahometan power in Asia.

15. **Rise of Timour.**—The great *Mogul Empire* which had been founded by *Jenghiz* had long ago fallen to pieces; but dynasties rising out of it reigned for a long time in Persia, and for a still longer time held Russia in bondage. In the latter half of the fourteenth century a prince called *Timour* arose in Central Asia, whose descendants are commonly spoken of as the *Moguls*, but who seems in truth to have been Turkish rather than Mongolian. He was a Mahometan of the *Shiah* sect, those who hold the divine right of *Ali* the son-in-law of Mahomet, and who look, not only on all the Ommiad and Abbasside Caliphs, but

on the first three Caliphs, Abou Bekr, Omar, and Othman, as usurpers. They had always existed as a religious sect, but most of the great Mahometan nations were *Sonnites* or orthodox Mahometans, who look on all the first four Caliphs as lawful successors of Mahomet. Timour therefore made religious zeal an excuse for attacking the whole world, whether Christians, heathens, or such Mahometans as he looked on as heretics. At last he came into Western Asia to attack the Ottoman Sultan Bajazet, whom in his letters he addressed as the *Cæsar of Rome*. Bajazet was utterly defeated and taken prisoner in the battle of *Angora* in 1402; but Timour never crossed into Europe. He died in 1405, and his great dominion, like other great dominions of the kind, broke in pieces.

16. **The Fall of Constantinople.**—The little that was left of the Eastern Empire got a breathing space through the overthrow of Bajazet by Timour. A civil war arose among his sons, and the Ottoman monarchy was not again united till 1421 under Sultan *Amurath the Second*. He besieged Constantinople in 1422, but the Empire still dragged on a feeble existence till the accession of his son *Mahomet the Second*, called the *Conqueror*, in 1451. All the Ottoman Sultans hitherto had been great warriors, and, according to the Eastern standard, wise rulers. Mahomet was perhaps the greatest of them all. He presently besieged Constantinople: the last Emperor of the East, *Constantine Palaiologos*, made another of those reconciliations with the Western Church of which we have already heard; but he gained no real help from the West except a few volunteers, who came chiefly from Venice and Genoa. The great siege of Constantinople began, one of the first great sieges in which cannon, which had been gradually coming into use in war for about a hundred years, played a great part. The Emperor did all that man could do in such a strait, but at last, on May the 29th, 1453, Constantinople was taken by storm. Con-

stantine died sword in hand, and the Roman Empire of the East came to an end. Constantinople now became the capital of the *Ottoman Empire*, and Justinian's great church of Saint Sophia became a Mahometan mosque. In a few years Mahomet conquered Peloponnêsos and the greater part of Greece, and in 1461 he conquered the Greek Empire of *Trebizond*, which thus outlived that of Constantinople. He had thus got possession of nearly the whole mainland which had belonged to the Eastern Empire at any time since the first Saracen conquest. But the Venetians still kept several points on the mainland, besides *Crete* and *Corfu* and some smaller islands. Some of the other islands were still kept by Latin princes, and *Rhodes* was held by the Knights of Saint John. *Cyprus* too remained a Latin kingdom, though before long the Venetians gained that also. Mahomet went on to plan the invasion of Western Europe, and the Turks actually took *Otranto* in Southern Italy; but the West was delivered by the death of Mahomet in 1481, for his successor *Bajazet the Second* was not a conqueror like his father.

17. **The Spanish Kingdoms.**—The two ends of Europe, the Scandinavian and the Spanish peninsulas, played a less important part in general history during this time than they did either before or after. Their history is chiefly confined to dealings within their own bounds. In Spain the Saracens or Moors were now shut up in the one kingdom of Granada, and, though there were often wars between them and their neighbours of Castile, yet the Spanish history of this time is much more taken up with wars and disputes among the several Christian kingdoms. The history of Castile is connected with that of England, because the Black Prince, Edward, Prince of Wales and Aquitaine, was persuaded in 1366 to lead an army into Spain to restore King *Pedro* or *Peter*, surnamed the *Cruel*, who had been driven out by his brother

Henry of Trastamara. In this war Edward won his third great battle of *Najara* or *Navarete*, and restored Peter, who was however before long killed by Henry. Aragon again was closely connected with the Two Sicilies. The island kingdom was united to Aragon in 1409, and *Alfonso the Fifth*, who was King from 1416 to 1458, was, during part of that time, in possession of Naples. But, as he was succeeded in Naples by his natural son *Ferdinand* and in Aragon by his brother *John*, the two kingdoms were again separated for a while, and the crown of Naples was all the while disputed by the Angevin princes. At one time, in 1467, the war was carried into Spain by *John, Duke of Calabria*, son of *René, Count of Provence* and *Duke of Anjou*, who called himself *King of Sicily*. This John came to help the *Catalans*, who were in revolt against John of Aragon. John had also wars with Lewis of France for the possession of the border county of *Roussillon*, which changed hands several times between the two crowns. *Portugal* meanwhile was doing great things. Under *John the Great*, who reigned from 1385 to 1433, the Portuguese began to take revenge for the long possession of Spain by the Saracens of Africa by conquests in Africa itself. And at the same time, under the *Infant* or prince *Don Henry*, they began a course of navigation and discovery along the western coast of Africa and among the islands of the Atlantic, which went on during the whole of the fifteenth century. At last the great discovery of the Cape of Good Hope in 1486 opened for Portugal a yet wider dominion in *India* and other parts of the East. In this work of exploring, conquering, and colonizing distant parts of the world, other nations soon followed, but it was the Portuguese who first showed the way. Meanwhile a change took place in the Spanish peninsula, which led to great changes in Europe generally. This came about through the marriage in 1471 of *Isabella Queen of Castile* with *Ferdinand* the *Infant of*

Aragon, who soon after succeeded to the Aragonese crown. The Crowns of Aragon and Castile were ever afterwards, except for a very short time, held together. In 1481 the *Catholic Kings*, as Ferdinand and Isabella were called, began a war with Granada, whose King had invaded the Castilian territory. In 1492 they took Granada itself and united the kingdom to Castile. The Mahometan dominion in Spain, which had lasted through so many ages, was now at an end, and the recovery of Granada might almost seem to make up in Christendom for the loss of Constantinople at the other end of Europe. *Spain*, as the united dominions of Ferdinand and Isabella were commonly called, soon became the greatest power in Europe.

18. **Northern Europe.**—In the Scandinavian peninsulas, the power of Denmark gradually sank in the course of the thirteenth century. Towards the end of the fourteenth, in 1397, the three kingdoms were united by the famous *Union of Calmar*, under *Margaret Queen of Norway* and daughter of *Waldemar the Third King* of Denmark. This union, with some interruptions, went on through the fifteenth century. In 1448, under *Christian the First*, the House of *Oldenburg* began to reign, which has gone on in Denmark till our own time, and which held Norway also within the present century. During all this time the Northern kingdoms had many wars with the *League of the Hansè Towns*, and the shifting relations began between the Kings of Denmark and the Duchies of *Sleswick* and *Holstein* which have gone on till our own days. *Sleswick*, the land north of the Eyder, was the southern part of Denmark, which had become a separate Duchy, but which was not a fief of the Empire. Its people were partly Danish and partly Low-Dutch. *Holstein*, on the other hand, that part of Saxony which lay between the Elbe and the Eyder, always was a fief of the Empire, and its people were wholly Low-Dutch.

19. **Russia and Poland.**—Great changes took place in the lands to the east of the Baltic during this period. The *Lithuanians*, the last Aryan people in Europe to accept Christianity, were converted towards the end of the fourteenth century. Their Duke *Jagellon* married *Hedwig Queen of Poland* in 1386, and was baptized and brought about the conversion of his people. He was the founder of the dynasty of Kings of Poland of the house of *Jagellon*. The union of Poland and Lithuania under one sovereign formed one of the greatest states in Europe. The dominions of the Jagellons stretched far to the east and south, taking in a large part of Russia and reaching to the new conquests of the Ottoman Turks. And in 1466 *Casimir the Fourth* finally got the better of the Teutonic Knights, annexing the western part of Prussia to Poland, and so cutting Prussia off from Germany. *Russia* meanwhile, while cut short by the Poles and Lithuanians to the west, was held in bondage by the Moguls to the east. But, after *Moscow* became the capital in 1328, Russia began to recover itself somewhat, and at last, in 1477, *Ivan Vasilovitz* completely freed the country from the Mogul supremacy. Still Russia was altogether hemmed in, and it had no means of taking any part in European affairs for some time to come.

20. **Hungary and the Turks.**—Meanwhile *Hungary* shifted about from one dynasty to another. Towards the end of the thirteenth century the Hungarian crown passed by marriage into a branch of the Angevin house of Sicily. The greatest King of this line was *Lewis*, who reigned from 1342 to 1382, and who was also King of Poland. He was the father of Hedwig who married Jagellon. Her sister *Mary* married Siegmund, who was afterwards Emperor, and who also became King of Hungary. In his time the Turks became dangerous to Hungary, and both Hungary and Poland soon became special bulwarks of

Christendom by land, as the commonwealth of Venice was by sea. In 1396 King Siegmund and a large body of Western allies were overthrown by Sultan *Bajazet* at *Nikopolis.* In the next century a famous captain, *John Huniades, Waiwode* or prince of *Transsilvania,* greatly distinguished himself against the Turks; but in 1444 *Wladislaus* the son of Jagellon, who was King both of Hungary and Poland, after driving back Sultan Amurath for a while, was defeated and slain by him at *Varna.* After this John Huniades was regent, and in 1456 he drove back Sultan Mahomet from Belgrade. His son *Matthias Corvinus* was King from 1458 to 1490. He did much to civilize his kingdom, and valiantly kept off the Turks, while on the other side he won great victories over the House of Austria, who were striving to get the kingdom of Hungary into their own hands.

21. **Language, Science, and Art.**—The progress of learning has been already spoken of with regard to Italy, as it was there that it had most effect on the political history of the country. But men's minds were at work in other parts of the world also. Men were eager after knowledge in many ways. Many of the *Universities* in different countries were now of great importance, and in England *Colleges* began to be founded in them. History was in most countries still written in Latin. In the thirteenth century there were good writers of history in England, especially *Matthew Paris,* who spoke out boldly against both the Pope and the King. But in England the writing of history went down a good deal in the fourteenth and fifteenth centuries. There was, on the other hand, a series of historical writers in French from the thirteenth century onwards, and in the fourteenth and fifteenth we learn much about the different stages of the Hundred Years' War from the French-speaking writers *Froissart* and *Monstrelet.* In England the English tongue had in the fourteenth century again

quite driven French out of use, except for some legal and formal purposes. And now lived such poets as *Geoffrey Chaucer*, whose works did much towards fixing the standard of the English language. There were many divines and thinkers in various ways, some of whom, as we have already seen, began, especially in England and in Bohemia, to teach doctrines different from those which were commonly received in the Church. And the general stirring of men's minds led some into speculations about the natural equality of mankind which led to revolts of the peasants both in France and England in the course of the fourteenth century. The people called *Lollards* in England, the followers of Wickliffe, often mixed up the religious and the social movement together. But in England villainage was on the whole dying out, while in many other countries it was getting harder and harder. In war, up to the invention of gunpowder, the knights and gentlemen who fought on horseback still despised all other troops, though the Scots, the Swiss, the Flemings at Courtray, and the English archers at Crecy, all showed what a good infantry could do. These centuries also, the thirteenth, fourteenth, and fifteenth, were the ages when architecture reached its height in Europe, and when the finest churches and castles were built. But it was only towards the end of this period, as times grew quieter and law grew stronger, that we find many great houses strictly so called, except within the walls of the cities.

22. **Summary.**—During this time then the *Empire of the West* dwindled into insignificance, and the *Empire of the East* was destroyed altogether. A great Mahometan power was settled in the East of Europe, while the last Mahometan kingdom was overthrown in the West. *Spain* became a great power. In *Italy* learning revived, but the freedom of the cities was in most cases destroyed, and the corruptions of the *Popedom* grew greater and greater. *England* and *France*

waged a long war, in which France was nearly conquered, but she gained in the end, and won a large increase of territory both from England and from other powers. The *Swiss League* and the *Duchy of Burgundy* became important powers, but the advance of the latter was cut short. The three *Scandinavian kingdoms* were united, though not very firmly. *Poland* became a great power, and *Russia* laid the foundation of her greatness by throwing off the yoke of the Moguls. The defence of Christendom against the Turks, though endlessly talked about by Popes and Emperors, really fell in the main on Poland, Hungary, and Venice.

CHAPTER XIII.

THE GREATNESS OF SPAIN.

Characteristics of modern Europe; formation of the existing powers and nations (1)—*progress of arts and inventions; falling back of political freedom* (1)—*increase of the royal power; introduction of standing armies* (1)—*all Western Europe now Christian* (2)—*chief causes of the Reformation of Religion; practical abuses; the power of the Popes; disputes on points of theology* (2)—*different forms taken by the Reformation in different countries; the Reformation, as a rule, accepted by the Teutonic nations and refused by the Romance* (3)—*no real toleration on either side* (3)—*names given to the different parties* (3)—*growth of the power of Spain; acquisition of various kingdoms by conquest and marriage* (4)—*succession of Charles the First of Spain; his election as the Emperor Charles the Fifth; the Austrian Kings in Spain* (4)—*reign of Philip the Second; annexation of Portugal* (5)—*reigns of Philip the Third and Fourth; wars with France and loss of territory; persecution and expulsion of the Moriscos* (5)—*rivalry of France and Spain in Italy* (6)—*conquest of Naples by Charles the Eighth* (6)—*conquest of Milan by Lewis the Twelfth, and of Naples by Ferdinand* (7)—*League of Cambray against Venice; the Holy League; restoration of the Medici at Florence* (7)—*rivalry of Charles and Francis; battle of Marignano; captivity of Francis at Pavia* (8)—*sack of Rome; peace between Charles and Francis; coronation of Charles* (8)—*dominion of Charles throughout Italy; subjugation of Florence* (9)—*Wars of Venice with the Turks; loss of Cyprus; battle of Lepanto* (9)—*the Popes; their purely worldly policy at the beginning of the period* (10)—*improvement under the later Popes; Council of Trent; foundation of the Jesuits* (10)—*reign of Maximilian* (11)—*the Emperors after Charles the Fifth; the Empire becomes purely German* (11)—*beginning of the Reformation in Germany; preaching of Luther* (12)—*religious wars and persecutions; invasion of the Turks* (12)—*growth of France; annexation of Brittany* (13)—*reign of Francis the First; Henry of England takes Boulogne* (13)—*reign of Henry the Second; seizure of the Theee Bishoprics; Peace of Câteau-Cambresis* (13)—*the Reformation in France; teaching of Calvin* (14)—*persecutions and civil wars in France; reign of Henry the Fourth* (14)—*revolt of the Netherlands against Spain; William the Silent* (15)—*formation of the Republic of the United Provinces* (16)—*growth of the Swiss Confederation; the Reformation under Zwingli and Farel* (17)—*conquests of Bern from Savoy; Savoy loses in Burgundy and gains in Italy* (17)—*civil wars in England; reign of Henry the Eighth* (17)—*the Reformation in England; Henry throws off the Papal power; religious changes under Edward* (18)—*restoration of the Pope's power under Mary; final settlement under Elizabeth* (18)—*relations between England and Scotland; reign of Mary in Scotland* (19)—*war between Elizabeth and Philip* (19)—*union of England and Scotland under James; civil wars of England* (19)—*final separation of Denmark and Sweden under Gustavus Vasa* (20)—*the Reformation in Denmark and Sweden; advance of Sweden under Gustavus Adolphus* (20)—*greatness of Poland; humiliation of the Teutonic Order; foundation of the Duchy of Prussia; its union with Brandenburg* (21)—*disputes about Livonia* (21)—*growth of Russia; accession of the house of Romanoff; the Polish crown becomes purely elective* (21)—*beginning of the modern kingdom of Persia* (22)—*reigns of Selim the Inflexible and Suleiman the Lawgiver; Turkish conquests in Hungary* (22)—*conquest of Cyprus and battle of Lepanto* (22)—*disputes in Bohemia; the Elector Palatine chosen King; beginning of the Thirty Years' War* (23)—*career of Gustavus Adolphus* (23) —*interference and advance of France* (23)—*Peace of Westphalia; degradation of the Empire; acquisitions of Sweden and France* (24)—*continued war between France and Spain; Peace of the Pyrenees* (24)—*European colonies and settlements; different kinds of settlements* (25)—*Portuguese settlements in Africa and India* (25)—*discovery of America* (26)—*Spanish settlements in America* (27)—*French, English, and Dutch settlements in America* (28)—*progress of learning, art, and science; use of the national languages* (29)—*Summary* (30).

1. **Characteristics of Modern Europe.**—We are now gradually passing into a new state of things. Nearly all the nations and powers of Europe which now remain have been already formed; the independent states are fewer and larger than before, and things are beginning to be in many ways more like what they are now than they have been hitherto. The great advance of learning and science in the fifteenth century altogether changed the face of the world, and three great inventions, printing, gunpowder, and the mariner's compass, were now fully in use and gave a wholly new character to all matters both of war and peace. The general stirring of men's minds, and the spirit of thought and enterprise which began to be abroad, took various forms. It led to the great changes in religion which are spoken of as the *Reformation*, and it led to the discovery of new lands beyond the sea, and to the establishment of colonies by the chief European nations in distant parts of the

world. In all matters of intellectual progress, and in all the arts of ordinary life, the time to which we have now come is a time of wonderful advance. But, for a long time after the beginning of what we may call modern history, political freedom did not go forward, but rather fell back. It was a time of much deeper and more far-seeing policy than earlier times, and it was a time when governments grew stronger, when laws could be more regularly carried out, and when much of the turbulence and disorder of earlier times came to an end. But it was also a time when, in most parts of Europe, Kings contrived to get all power into their own hands; it was a time of wars which Kings waged for their own purposes, and in which the nations which they governed had very little interest. To wage these wars they had to keep standing armies, that is, armies of soldiers who are always under arms and who always receive pay. A standing army need not be an army of mere mercenaries, like those which served in Italy for any prince or commonwealth that would hire them. Still, where there are standing armies, things are very different from what they are when a lord calls on his vassals, or when a commonwealth calls on its citizens, to fight when they are wanted to fight and then to go home again. A standing army makes the government which employs it far stronger; and it was by means of these standing armies that the Kings in most parts of Europe were able to overthrow those free institutions of earlier times which many countries have only quite lately won back again. But the main outward difference between these times and the times that went before them is that the old ideas of the *Church* and the *Empire* now passed away for ever. The Eastern Empire was gone; the Western Empire survived in name only. The Emperors were often very powerful princes, but it was not by reason of their being Emperors that they were so. We have now very largely to deal, not so much with nations, or even with particular states, as with collections of states and nations in the hands of particular families. And we now come to that great revolution in religion by which the Churches of Western Europe have ever since been still more widely divided among themselves than in former times the whole Western Church was from the Eastern. The Eastern Church meanwhile remained for a long time as it were hidden, as most of the nations which belonged to it were in bondage to the Turks. It is only in later times that the Eastern Church has again become politically important, as being the religion of the great Empire of Russia.

2. **Causes of the Reformation.**—At the beginning of the sixteenth century we may say that the whole of Western Europe was in communion with the Western Church. And, though all men did not think exactly alike as to the authority of the Pope or Bishop of Rome, yet all looked on him as being at least the head Bishop of the whole Church. There was no nation in the West which was not Christian. The Lithuanians had been converted, and the Moors in Spain had been conquered. If there were any heathens left anywhere, it would be a few Laps in the extreme North. Nor was there any Christian nation in the West which refused submission to the See of Rome. The Albigenses had been put down long ago, and the revolt of the followers of John Huss in Bohemia had, after much hard fighting, been put down also. There had all along been religious discontents among particular men, and both in England and elsewhere many men had been burned as heretics. Still no whole nation had as yet set up any new ecclesiastical system for itself. But early in the sixteenth century there began to be a much greater stir about religious matters in most parts of Western Europe. This was owing, partly to the general stir in men's minds caused by the revival of learning, and partly to the exceeding wickedness of the Popes of those times. There were

three things at which men were specially offended. First, there were many practical abuses in the Church which could have been done away with without either casting off the authority of the Pope or making any changes in doctrine. Many of these things the Councils of the fifteenth century, at Constanz, Basel, and elsewhere, honestly tried to mend; but the Popes always stood in the way. The Popes themselves in after days tried to mend many things, but not till it was too late. Secondly, the authority of the Popes was itself felt to be a great grievance, partly because it was often so badly used, but also because, even when it was well used, it interfered with the rights both of civil governors and of national Churches. The truth is that the power of the Bishops of Rome had grown up from the same causes as the power of the Emperors of Rome, that is, because Rome was the head city of the world. And now men were beginning to be discontented with the power of the Popes through the same causes which had made the power of the Emperors die away. That is to say, Christendom was split up into separate nations and kingdoms, and Rome no longer kept its place as the centre of all. But, as the power of the Popes was held to be a matter of religious belief, it was not so easy to get rid of it as it was to get rid of the power of the Emperors. Lastly, besides all this, many men held that not a few of the doctrines which were believed, and of the ceremonies which were practised, in the Church were wrong in themselves, and had no ground in Scripture or in the practice of the first Christians. Disputes arose about the *Mass* or sacrament of the Lord's Supper, about the use of images and the practice of praying to saints, about the state of men after death, about the necessity of confessing sins to a priest, about the laws which forbade the clergy to marry, and about the practice of saying the Church service in Latin now that Latin was nowhere the tongue commonly understood. Some of these disputes were about points which the Popes might have yielded without giving up their general system, and which indeed they have sometimes yielded in distant parts of the world. But others were about points of doctrine strictly so called, which those who held the received belief to be true could not give up so easily. Thus the early part of the sixteenth century was a time, above all others, of religious controversies, and these controversies led to the most important events, both religious and political.

3. **The Reformation in different Countries.**—The end of all these disputes was that a large part of Western Europe gradually became separated from the communion of the See of Rome. This gradual change is commonly called the *Reformation*. And, as in old times, Christianity took different forms in the Latin, the Greek, and the Eastern provinces of the Empire, so nearly the same thing happened now. Allowing for a good many exceptions, it may be said that the Teutonic nations accepted the new teaching, while the Romance nations clave to the See of Rome. And there were great differences in the way in which the Reformation arose and was carried out in different countries. In some countries the change arose among the people and was rather forced upon the governments, while in others it was chiefly the work of Kings and rulers. And change went much further in some countries than in others. In some countries quite new forms of worship and Church government were set up, while in others men cast off the authority of the Pope and changed what they thought wrong in doctrine and practice, but let the general order of the Church go on much as it did before. The extremes each way might be seen in England; for, of all the countries which made any reformation at all, England changed the least and Scotland the most. And in Ireland the great mass of the people have always withstood all change, partly no doubt because their

English rulers tried to force it upon them. And, though the stirring of men's minds, and the habit of thinking for themselves which led to the Reformation, did in the end lead men in most countries to see that they ought not to persecute each other for differences in religion, yet they did not find this out for a long time. For a long time men on both sides held it to be a crime to allow any kind of worship except that which they themselves thought right. Thus the Reformation gave rise to civil wars wherever the two parties were nearly equally balanced, and to persecutions wherever one side was much stronger than the other. Those who clave to the old teaching thought it their duty to hinder the spread of the new, and those who adopted the new teaching thought it their duty to hinder the practice of the old. It was only in a few cases, where neither side was strong enough to do much mischief to the other, that the old and new worship went on for any time side by side. Those who accepted the Reformation were commonly called *Protestant* or *Reformed*, two names which at first had different meanings, but which are now commonly used without much distinction. Those who clave to the Popes called themselves *Catholics*, as claiming to be the whole and only true Church. The other side called them in contempt *Papists* and *Romanists*. Perhaps it is safest to use the name *Roman Catholics*, a name which is not very consistent with itself, but which avoids disputes either way, and which in England is the name known to the law.

4. **Growth of the power of Spain in Europe. Charles the Fifth.**—From the latter part of the fifteenth century onwards the power of Spain grew fast, and during the greater part of the sixteenth century we may fairly call it the greatest power in Europe. The marriage of Ferdinand and Isabella had united Aragon and Castile; they had conquered Granada, and, after Isabella's death in 1504, Ferdinand,

in 1512, conquered nearly all the Kingdom of *Navarre*, that is all south of the Pyrenees. The whole peninsula, except Portugal, was thus joined together. Ferdinand also held Sardinia and the island of Sicily, and in 1501, by wars which we must speak of presently, he also got possession of the continental kingdom of Naples. Isabella was succeeded in Castile by her daughter *Joanna*, who had married *Philip* of Austria. He was the son of *Mary* of *Burgundy* the daughter of Charles the Bold, and of *Maximilian* the son of the Emperor Frederick, who was chosen King of the Romans in his father's lifetime. Each chain in this pedigree ought to be remembered, because each marriage brought with it some fresh dominion, and so helped to build up the great fabric of the Spanish power. Mary, after her father's death, kept the Low Countries and the *County* of Burgundy, while Lewis of France seized the *Duchy*. Her son Philip was thus sovereign of the Low Countries. By his marriage with Joanna came the strange union of those distant provinces with the kingdoms of Castile and Aragon. Thus *Charles*, the son of Philip and Joanna, succeeded to all the possessions of the Houses of Castile, Aragon, and Burgundy. In 1516 he succeeded one grandfather *Ferdinand* in his Spanish dominions, and in 1519, on the death of his other grandfather *Maximilian*, he was elected to the Empire. In Spain he was *Charles the First*, but, as he was the fifth Emperor of the name, he is always spoken of in history as *Charles the Fifth*. Thus the Emperor was again the greatest prince in Europe; but this was not because he was Emperor, but because of his dominions in Spain and the Netherlands. Charles could hardly be said to belong to any nation in particular, but in the male line he came of the House of Austria, and the Kings of Spain of his dynasty are called the *Austrian Kings*. He also obtained possession of the County of Burgundy and of the Duchy of Milan, and all these dominions he gave up to his son *Philip* in 1555.

5. **Successors of Charles the Fifth.**—After Charles the Fifth came three Kings of Spain called *Philip*. *Philip the Second* reigned from 1556 to 1598. He was a most bigoted Catholic, yet almost the first act of his reign was a war with the Pope, *Paul the Fourth*, in his character of a temporal prince. In Philip's time began the war in the Netherlands by which the northern provinces threw off the Spanish yoke, of which we shall speak more presently. It was he also who sent the famous *Armada* against England in 1588, and he also interfered largely in the affairs of France. On the other hand, in 1571 his fleet, in alliance with that of the Commonwealth of Venice, won the sea-fight of *Lepanto*—the ancient *Naupaktos* in the Corinthian Gulf—over the Turks. This was the first great check which their power met with. In 1580 he got possession of the Kingdom of *Portugal*, so that the whole Spanish peninsula was for a while joined together under one ruler. As long as Philip lived, Spain outwardly kept its place as the leading power of Europe; but under the two following Kings, *Philip the Third*, who reigned from 1598 to 1621, and *Philip the Fourth*, from 1621 to 1665, the Spanish power greatly decayed. The war in the Netherlands went on till the independence of the seven northern provinces was acknowledged, and in 1639 the Portuguese threw off the Spanish yoke, and set up the dynasty of *Braganza*, which has reigned in Portugal to our own times. In the reign of Philip the Fourth there was a long war with France, which was ended in 1659 by giving up to France part of the Spanish dominions at the two ends of Gaul, *Roussillon* and part of *Artois*. The Spanish dominions were thus lessened in various places, though Spain still kept her distant possessions of the Two Sicilies, Milan, the County of Burgundy, and the Southern Netherlands. In its internal govern-

ment, Spain was, during all this time, the most despotic and intolerant country in Europe. The old liberties of Castile were overthrown by Charles the Fifth, and those of Aragon by Philip the Second. Nowhere were Jews and heretics of all kinds more cruelly persecuted, so that in Spain the Reformation made no progress. The Moors too, who, at the conquest of Granada, had been promised the free exercise of their religion, were shamefully oppressed. A revolt under Philip the Second was put down with great cruelty, and at last under Philip the Third, the remnant of them, called *Moriscos*, was driven out of the country. This was a great loss to Spain, as the Moors were a sharp-witted and hard-working people, and the provinces where they lived were the most flourishing parts of the peninsula.

6. **French Invasion of Italy.**—During the first half of the sixteenth century, no part of Europe is brought more constantly before our notice than *Italy*. But this is no longer a sign of the greatness of Italy, but of its decay. Italy had now become the battle-field on which most of the princes of Europe fought out their quarrels. During all this time there was a long rivalry between France and Spain, which was in some sort a continuation of the dispute between the Houses of Anjou and Aragon for the kingdom of Sicily, as that was a continuation of the older dispute between Guelfs and Ghibelins. But now that the two sides were represented by the great kingdoms of France and Spain, the quarrel was carried out on a much greater scale, and, between the two, Italy was torn to pieces and utterly trampled under foot. What the Italians called the invasion of the *Barbarians* began in 1494, when *Charles the Eighth* of France took it into his head that he had a right to the Kingdom of Naples. In two years he marched all through Italy, conquered the kingdom with very little trouble, and, as soon as his back was turned, lost it again. Great confusion was caused throughout Italy by

Charles' march, and one result of it was that the Florentines were able to get rid of the Medici, and that Pisa was able to throw off the yoke of Florence, and remained independent till 1509. Presently, when the next King of France, *Lewis the Twelfth*, again set up a claim to the Kingdom of Naples and also to the Duchy of Milan, Ferdinand did not scruple to make a treaty by which Naples was to be divided between the two Kings of France and Aragon. Lewis won the Duchy of Milan in 1499, but, before the division of Naples was fully carried out, he and Ferdinand quarrelled over their spoil; and the end of it was, that in 1504 Ferdinand got possession of the whole kingdom, and was thus *King of the Two Sicilies*. In these wars the Spanish infantry won a renown which they long kept.

7. **The League of Cambray.**—Spain had thus gained a footing on the mainland of Italy, and Ferdinand now went on to meddle still more with its affairs. In 1508 he and Lewis of France, the reigning Pope *Julius the Second*, and the Emperor-elect *Maximilian*, all joined together in a league, called the *League of Cambray*, to despoil the commonwealth of Venice. For each of these princes pretended that some part of its territories rightly belonged to himself. Venice now seemed on the point of ruin, when again the spoilers quarrelled among themselves, but this time it did not happen as it had done in the case of Naples. For Venice got back nearly all that she had lost, though the commonwealth was never again so powerful after this war as it had been before. The cause of the division among the enemies of Venice was that Pope Julius, when he had got all that he himself wanted from the republic, made what he called the *Holy League* to drive the *Barbarians* out of Italy. To this end he joined with Ferdinand against Lewis. In 1512 the French defeated the Spaniards in a great battle at *Ravenna*, but Pope Julius leagued himself

with the Swiss, and by their means the French were altogether driven out of Italy. Florence had all along been in alliance with France, and, now that the French were driven out, the commonwealth was obliged to receive the Medici again. Milan also went back to its own Dukes of the House of Sforza. Lewis and Ferdinand both died before long, Lewis in 1515, and Ferdinand in 1516.

8. **Wars of Charles and Francis in Italy.**—Lewis and Ferdinand were succeeded by two young Kings whose rivalry led to more wars. Lewis was succeeded in France by *Francis the First*, and Ferdinand, as we have seen, by his grandson Charles. Both Charles and Francis sought for the Empire on the death of Charles' other grandfather Maximilian in 1519, when Charles was elected. Thus the rivalry between France and Spain was yet further heightened by the personal rivalry between the two Kings. Francis had by far the most compact and united kingdom; but Charles united the power of Spain, the wealth of the Netherlands, and the dignity of the Empire. But before Charles began to reign either in Spain or in the Empire, Francis had begun his reign by another invasion of Italy. He had first to overcome an army of *Swiss* in the battle of *Marignano* in 1515, and he presently won back the Duchy of Milan. Then in 1521 Pope *Leo the Tenth*, who was of the House of the Medici, joined with the Emperor, and another war began, which may be said to have gone on till 1530. The armies of the rival princes fought at both ends of Italy, both in the Duchy of Milan and in the Kingdom of Naples. In 1525 Francis himself was taken prisoner at the *battle of Pavia*, and was only released after consenting to a treaty (which he did not keep), by which he yielded many things to the Emperor. Amongst other things, those parts of the Netherlands which were held in fief of the Crown of France, namely the Counties of *Flanders* and *Artois*,

were set free from all homage, just as the Duchy of Aquitaine had been by the Peace of Bretigny. In all these wars the princes and commonwealths of Italy, the Popes among them, were dealt with as something quite secondary. The Duke of Milan was set up and put down again, as happened to suit the Emperor who professed to be his protector; and in 1527, when *Clement the Seventh*, who was also of the House of the Medici, was Pope, Rome itself was taken and sacked by the Imperial troops, and suffered far more from them than it had ever suffered in old times from the Goths or even from the Vandals. The Florentines took advantage of the taking of Rome again to get rid of the Medici. But at last, in 1529, the Pope, the Emperor, and the King of France all came to terms. Francis betrayed all his allies, while Charles stuck by his. In 1530, Charles was crowned King of Italy and Emperor, but instead of taking the two crowns, one at Milan and the other at Rome, he took both crowns together at Bologna. All Italy was now completely under his power. Charles was more powerful than any Emperor since Charles the Great, and it might have seemed that the old days of the Empire were come again. But after the time of Charles his power in Italy passed, not to the next Emperor, but to his son who reigned in Spain, so that it was plain where his real strength had lain.

9. **The States of Italy.**—The end of these wars thus was that the power of the Emperor, or rather of the King of Spain, was established throughout Italy. Charles was himself King of the Two Sicilies, and, on the death of the last Duke of Milan, he granted the Duchy to his son Philip, so that the Kings of Spain ruled at both ends of Italy. The other states of Italy too were really under his power, much as, in the old days of Rome, the kingdoms and commonwealths of Greece and Asia had been before they were actually made into provinces. But there was one Italian state

which at least did not yield without a struggle. This was the commonwealth of Florence. The Pope and the Emperor agreed that the Florentines should be obliged again to take back the Medici, but they did not do so till after a long and terrible siege. Then princes of the house of the Medici began to reign as *Dukes of Florence*, and in 1557 Duke *Cosmo* added to his dominions the territory of the commonwealth of *Sienna*. Some time after this he got from the Pope and the Emperor the title of *Grand Duke of Tuscany*, and the memory of the old republic was quite wiped out. Of the other commonwealths, Venice, Genoa, and Lucca, besides the little San Marino, still went on. But their governments were aristocratic, and the only one of them which played any part in European affairs was Venice, which was still the bulwark of Christendom by sea, as Poland and Hungary were by land. But, in the course of the sixteenth century, the Turks won from the Venetians many of their possessions both in the islands and on the few points which they held on the mainland of Peloponnêsos. And, notwithstanding their share in the great victory of Lepanto, the Venetians had in 1570 to give up the island of *Cyprus*, which the Turks had conquered, but they still kept *Crete* and *Corfu* and some of the smaller islands.

10. **The Popes.**—The Popes must, especially in these times, be looked at in two lights, as Italian princes and as the heads of those of the Western Churches which still clave to them. In their temporal character the Popes were much mixed up in the wars of Italy, and they had the great advantage of being able to call on men to support their political schemes under pretence of helping the cause of the Church. During the sixteenth century the Popes greatly extended their temporal dominion, joining on to it many principalities and cities which, as they gave out, were held in fief of them, so that, if their holders rebelled or if their families became extinct, they would

fall to the Pope as superior lord. In this way the Popes came to be, even as temporal princes, the greatest power in Italy after the Kings of Spain. At the latter end of the fifteenth and the beginning of the sixteenth centuries, the corruption of the court of Rome, and the personal wickedness of the Popes, was at its height. Some of them were men of most scandalous lives, as was *Alexander the Sixth* of the Spanish family of *Borgia*, who was Pope when Charles the Eighth came into Italy. And even those who were not so bad as this were thoroughly worldly men, who thought more of increasing their dominions and exalting their own kinsfolk than of doing their duty as the chief Bishops of the Church. Such was *Julius the Second*, the great fighting Pope, and *Leo the Tenth* and *Clement the Seventh*, the two Popes of the house of Medici. Between them came *Hadrian the Sixth*, a native of the Netherlands, an honest man who was anxious to reform practical abuses, but who had no kind of love for Italian ways, or for the revival of ancient learning, of which Leo the Tenth was a great promoter. Hadrian however reigned only a very little time. It was in the time of Leo the Tenth that the Reformation began to be preached by *Martin Luther* in Germany, but the Popes for some time took but little heed of what was going on. But towards the middle of the century things began to change. The Reformation, as a system of doctrine, made but little progress in Italy, and it never became the religion of any Italian state. But there were many men, even high in the Roman Church, who would gladly have yielded to the Reformers on some points, and there were still more who, without wishing to change any of the received doctrines, were eager to reform practical abuses and get rid of scandals. In this way there came to be a marked change between the Popes at the beginning of the century and those towards its end. These later Popes were often fierce bigots, ready to persecute and to approve of crimes done in the cause of the Church; but they were almost always men of good lives in their own persons, and eager to do what they thought their duty. One famous Pope at this time was *Sixtus the Fifth*, who reigned from 1585 to 1590; he was wonderfully active in bringing his temporal dominions into good order. In 1545 a General Council came together at *Trent*, which went on, with some stoppages, till 1563. This Council reformed many practical abuses, but it fixed the Roman Catholic doctrines and practices in a much more rigid shape than they had ever been put forth before. Its decrees were not received by the Churches which accepted the Reformation, and therefore the holding of the Council only made the breach wider and more hopeless. During this time too new religious orders were formed for the special purpose of advancing the doctrines of the Church and converting heretics and heathens. The chief of these was the famous *Society of Jesus*, or *Order of the Jesuits*, founded by the Spaniard *Ignatius Loyola*. This order was for a long time the chief support of the Papal dominion; and the Jesuits won back a large part of Europe to the communion of Rome, but in most countries, Roman Catholic as well as Protestant, they contrived to make themselves obnoxious to the civil power.

11. **The Emperors.**—Frederick the Third was the last Emperor who was regularly crowned at Rome. His son Maximilian, who married Mary of Burgundy, was never crowned either at Milan or at Rome, but he took the new title of *Emperor-elect* instead of merely *King of the Romans*. No later Emperor except Charles the Fifth was crowned in Italy at all, and Charles, as we have seen, was not crowned at Rome. Maximilian also took the title, which had never before been formally used, of *King of Germany*, and all the Kings after him were called in formal language *Kings of Germany and Emperors-elect*. But they were commonly spoken

of as *Emperors*, which before was never done unless they had been crowned at Rome. Maximilian was always trying to do greater things than he was able to do, but, as King of Germany, he certainly did something to restore the royal power, and much more to bring the country into greater peace and order. In his time Germany was divided into *Circles*, and a supreme court called the *Imperial Chamber* was set up. These changes did not do all that they were wished to do, but still they did something. Then came the reign of Charles the Fifth, and the great power of the Emperor, though not of the Empire, in Italy and the world generally. After Charles' abdication, his brother *Ferdinand*, who was already King of the Romans, succeeded. In his time and in that of his successors *Maximilian the Second*, *Rudolf the Second*, and *Matthias*, we may say that the Empire was purely German and had nothing to do with the affairs of Italy or of the world in general. In the next reign, that of *Ferdinand the Second*, things began to change somewhat.

12. **The Reformation in Germany.**—In the reign of Charles the Fifth came the beginning of the Reformation. Nowhere was reformation more needed than in Germany, where the Bishops and Abbots had grown into powerful temporal princes, and quite neglected their spiritual duties. Towards the end of Maximilian's reign attempts began to be made in the Diet for the reformation of practical abuses, and about the same time the famous *Martin Luther* began to attack, first the practical abuses, and then the established doctrines, of the Church. This he began to do in 1517, and he was greatly followed by many people, though little notice was at first taken of him in high places. Luther was protected by his own sovereign, *Frederick Elector of Saxony*; and, when in 1520 a bull was put forth against him by Pope Leo the Tenth, Luther ventured to burn it. By this time Charles the Fifth had been elected Emperor, and in

1521 Luther was condemned in a Diet of the Empire at *Worms*. But Luther was still protected by the Electors of Saxony, and gradually many of the princes and cities of Germany, especially in the north, embraced his doctrines. Germany was further disturbed by a revolt of the peasants in various parts, but all that came of it was to make their bondage harder than it had been before. There were also revolts of the *Anabaptists*, fanatics who not only preached wild doctrines in religion, but tried to upset all government and society. Against all movements of this kind, Luther set himself quite as strongly as the Catholics did. His own reformation meanwhile went on. At the Diet of *Speyer* in 1529 the Emperor and a majority of the Diet passed a decree against all ecclesiastical changes. Against this the princes who followed Luther *protested*, and thus arose the name of *Protestants*, a name which originally meant the German followers of Luther, as distinguished, not only from the Roman Catholics, but from the other Reformers who did not agree with Luther on all points. In 1530 the Lutherans or Protestants drew up a statement of their doctrines, which was called the *Confession of Augsburg;* in the next year the Protestant princes and cities joined together in a confederacy for mutual defence, which was called the *Smalcaldic League.* But, when some of them tried to get help from France, Luther protested against such treason, and a kind of reconciliation was patched up with the Emperor. There was no time when Germany more needed to be at peace, for, besides France on the one hand, the Turks were threatening on the other, and Sultan *Suleiman* or *Solomon* in 1529 actually besieged Vienna, and ravaged the country as far as *Regensburg* or *Ratisbon.* In 1546 Luther died, and in the same year a war broke out between the Emperor and the Catholics on one side and the Protestant princes on the other, which went on with some stoppages till in 1555, by the *Peace of Augsburg*, the two religions were put on terms of equality throughout the Empire. But this was no real toleration; it simply meant that the government of each German state might set up which religion it pleased, Catholic or Protestant; nothing was done for those persons in any state who might be of a different religion from the Government. Thus, for instance, in Austria, where a large part of the people had become Protestants, the Catholic religion was brought back, chiefly by the help of the Jesuits. And in the same way Protestants of one sect did not scruple to persecute Protestants of another; for in some parts of Germany men had followed the doctrines of the French reformer *Calvin*, and they and the Lutherans drove one another out. During Ferdinand's time and that of the following Emperors, religious disputes went on, till, in the reign of Ferdinand the Second, came the beginning of a more fearful religious war than had ever happened before between Christian and Christian.

13. **The Advance of France.**—The power of *France* was meanwhile advancing, and the jealousy between the French Kings and the House of Austria, both in Spain and in the Netherlands, was getting stronger and stronger. The Kings of France were getting more and more absolute in their own dominions, and they were still increasing their dominions at the expense of their neighbours. In their Italian wars they failed; for they were never able to keep either the Duchy of Milan or the Kingdom of Naples. But the only great fief of the Crown of France which still kept its own princes was now added to the royal dominions. This was the *Duchy of Britanny*, which passed to an heiress, *Anne*, who married two Kings of France in succession, Charles the Eighth and Lewis the Twelfth. From this time Britanny has been reckoned part of France, but to this day a large part of the people do not speak French, but still use their old Celtic tongue, akin to the Welsh of Britain. Lewis the

Twelfth, though he did so much harm in Italy, made a good King in his own kingdom, and was called the *Father of the People.* The next King, Francis the First, was thoroughly bad in every way, except that he was a promoter of art and learning. All these Kings were of the *House of Valois;* but, as neither Charles the Eighth nor Lewis the Twelfth left any sons, the Crown did not again pass from father to son till the death of Francis in 1547, when it passed to his son *Henry the Second.* There were some wars between France and England at this time, but they were of small moment compared with those either earlier or later. At one time, in 1544, *Henry the Eighth* of England took *Boulogne*, but in 1557 the French got back *Calais*, which the English had kept ever since the time of Edward the Third. But these wars with England were nothing compared with the long wars which Francis and his son Henry waged with the Emperor Charles and his son Philip. These may be said to have gone on from 1520 to 1558. For, though peace was made several times, it never was well kept or lasted long. The French Kings, while cruelly persecuting the Protestants in their own kingdom, did not scruple to help the Protestants in Germany in their wars with the Emperor, nor were they ashamed to encourage the Turks, the common enemies of Christendom, to attack the Empire and its allies by land and sea. In 1537 Francis got hold of the greater part of the dominions of *Charles Duke of Savoy*, but this conquest was not kept very long. Thus far the French Kings had mainly sought after Italian dominion; they now began more directly to attack the Empire on the side of Germany. In 1552 Henry the Second got hold of three Bishopricks of the Empire, *Metz*, *Toul*, and *Verdun*, which, though they lay apart from the Kingdom of France and were surrounded by the Duchy of Lorraine, were kept by France ever after, till Metz was won back in our own times. Indeed, from this time, though Lorraine remained a fief of the Empire, yet it began to come very much under the power of France, and the family of *Guise*, who were of the ducal House of Lorraine, began to play a great part in French affairs. After Charles had abdicated, the war still went on, though of course it was now a war between France and Spain, and no longer between France and the Empire. At last the French underwent two great defeats at *St. Quentin* and *Gravelines*, on the borders of France and the Netherlands, so the *Peace of Câteau-Cambresis* was made in 1558, and the advance of the French power was stopped for a time.

14. **The Civil Wars of France.**—From the Peace of Câteau-Cambresis till the end of the sixteenth century, the history of France is mainly taken up with the religious wars between the Catholics and Protestants within the country. These lasted, with stoppages now and then, from 1562 to 1595. The French Protestants were not Lutherans, but followers of *John Chauvin*, or *Calvin*, a Frenchman by birth, who settled at Geneva. His teaching went further away from that of the Roman Church than that of Luther. It was followed by all who accepted the Reformation in the Romance-speaking countries, and also in part of Germany. The name *Protestant* therefore did not properly belong to the Calvinists in France, who called themselves the *Reformed*, and who were commonly known as *Huguenots*. They were cruelly persecuted under Francis and Henry the Second. After Henry three of his sons reigned in order, *Francis the Second* from 1559 to 1560, *Charles the Ninth* from 1560 to 1574, and *Henry the Third* from 1574 to 1589. The mother of these three Kings, *Catharine of Medici*, of the House of Florence, had great power, which she used very badly, during the reigns of all her sons. The religious wars began in 1562, and in the latter part of them the chief part on the Reformed side was taken by *Henry of Bourbon*, King of *Navarre*. He was the

next heir to the Crown of France after the sons of Henry the Second, though the kindred between them in the male line was very remote, as they were descended from different sons of Saint Lewis. Henry had inherited from his mother the title of *King of Navarre*, and with it the possession of that small part of the kingdom which lay north of the Pyrenees, and which had been kept by its own Kings when all the rest had been conquered by Ferdinand of Aragon. He had also large fiefs in the South of France, which was the part where the Huguenots were the strongest, like the Albigenses in the old times. The two parties were always going to war, and always making peace again; but, when peace was made, it never gave any real toleration. The Reformed religion was allowed to be practised in particular towns and places,—*La Rochelle* especially became something like a separate Calvinist commonwealth—but men were not allowed to follow what religion they pleased everywhere. Philip of Spain meddled as much as he could, of course helping the Catholics. The most famous event of these times was the massacre of the Huguenots at Paris on Saint Bartholomew's Day, 1572, which was called the *Massacre of Saint Bartholomew.* At last, when Henry the Third died in 1589, the Crown came of right to Henry of Navarre, but he found that, as long as he remained a Huguenot, Paris and the greater part of the kingdom would not acknowledge him. So in 1593 he turned Catholic, and then he soon obtained possession of the whole land. Instead of the old title of *King of the French* (in Latin *Rex Francorum*), he called himself *King of France and Navarre.* Henry was murdered in 1610, and was succeeded by his young son, *Lewis the Thirteenth*, who reigned till 1643. Under his famous Minister *Cardinal Richelieu*, the royal power was greatly strengthened, and, though the Huguenots were not persecuted, they lost their special privileges in particular places. Under him too the House of

Bourbon began to take the first place in Europe instead of the House of Austria.

15. **The Revolt of the Netherlands.**—Meanwhile a deadly blow was dealt to the power of Spain in her outlying possessions, and a new commonwealth arose in Europe. It will be remembered that the Netherlands had been brought together under the Dukes of Burgundy, and that they had now passed to Philip of Spain as their successor. They were a most important part of his dominions, for nowhere else north of the Alps were there so many great and rich cities near together; but the bad government of Philip, especially his religious persecutions, and above all the cruelties of his Lieutenant the *Duke of Alva*, led to a revolt. This began in 1568, and the war went on till 1609. The great leader of the revolt was *William Prince of Orange*, called the *Silent*. His principality of *Orange* was one of the small fiefs of the Kingdom of Burgundy which had not been swallowed up by France, though it was now almost wholly surrounded by French territory. In this he was something like Henry of Bourbon, with his little kingdom of Navarre, for the Prince of Orange had private estates in the Netherlands which were really worth much more than his principality. His wisdom and endurance led to the deliverance of all the northern part of the Netherlands from the Spanish yoke. At the beginning of the revolt the Southern provinces were the most zealous; but after a while, as their people were mainly Catholics, they fell back under the power of Spain, and they remained dependencies of one power after another, till such parts of them as escaped being swallowed up by France became the present *Kingdom of Belgium*.

16. **The United Provinces.**—Meanwhile the Northern provinces, *Holland*, *Zealand*, and others, where the people were mostly of the Reformed religion, stuck by the Prince of Orange, and called in help from England, France, and the German branch

of the House of Austria. But none of these foreign helpers did them much real good; so at last they formed themselves, in 1581, into the *Federal Commonwealth* of the *Seven United Provinces.* In 1584 the Prince was murdered; for Philip, who stuck at no crime in what he thought the cause either of the Crown or of the Church, had offered rewards to any one who would kill him. After William's death the war was continued by his son *Maurice,* and it went on after Philip's death till peace was made in 1609. The peace was in name only a truce for twelve years, because Spain was too proud to acknowledge the independence of her revolted subjects, but the war now really came to an end, and the *United Provinces,* answering nearly to the present *Kingdom of the Netherlands,* were firmly established as an independent power. This was one of the most famous wars in all history, for never did so small a power so long and so successfully withstand a great one. Some of the greatest generals of the age were brought against the Provinces. There was the Duke of Alva first, and then *Don John of Austria,* Philip's half-brother, who had won the battle of Lepanto, his nephew the famous *Alexander Duke of Parma,* and lastly the *Marquess Spinola,* whose great exploit was the siege of *Ostend,* in the latter years of the war. The *Dutch,* as the people of Holland and the other United Provinces are now commonly called in a special way, did everything for themselves; for they got very little real help from those who professed to be their allies in England and France. Thus a new state and a new commonwealth was formed in Europe. In strictness the Provinces were still members of the Empire, but their allegiance was quite nominal, and in 1648 their absolute independence of the Empire was formally acknowledged. Owing chiefly to the daring and activity of their people in all things to do with trade and the sea, the United Provinces, small as their territory was, reckoned during the whole of the seventeenth century as one of the chief powers of Europe. They came afterwards to defy France, as they had before defied Spain, and things so turned about that, before the end of the century, they were helping Spain against France.

17. **Switzerland and Savoy.**—Meanwhile the older Federal commonwealth which had grown up at the other end of the Empire, the Old League of High Germany or of Switzerland, was playing an important part in European affairs. From the middle of the fourteenth century till after the war with Charles of Burgundy, the Confederates had made many conquests and alliances, but they did not admit any new Canton into their own body. But in the latter years of the fifteenth and the beginning of the sixteenth century five new Cantons were made, *Freiburg*, *Solothurn*, *Basel*, *Schaffhausen*, and *Appenzell*. These made up the *Thirteen Cantons*, which lasted till the end of the eighteenth century. All these were purely German, but now begins the connexion of the League with the Romance lands. About the end of the fifteenth century the Confederates won a small territory in Italy, and we have seen that they played a great part in the wars of that country. And, ever since the Burgundian War, they had been making their way to the West, in the lands of the now pretty well forgotten Kingdom of Burgundy. The history of the *Dukes of Savoy* now becomes of great importance. For, whereas they had lands both in Burgundy and in Italy, they have ever since been losing their lands north of the Alps and winning new lands to the south. At last, in our own day, they have lost all their old Burgundian dominions, but have become Kings of all Italy. But at this time it seemed as if the power of Savoy was going to be wiped out altogether. We must remember that the territories both of the Confederates and of the Dukes of Savoy were still parts of the Empire, though their real connexion with

it was very slight. As in Germany, religious and political affairs had much to do with one another; but Switzerland had its own Reformation distinct from that of Germany. The new doctrines were first preached at Zürich in 1519, by *Ulrich Zwingli*, whose teaching in many things went further away from the received faith than that of Luther. He also did good by speaking against the custom of men hiring themselves out as mercenary soldiers. Zürich, Bern, and several other Cantons accepted his teaching, while others remained Catholic and some were divided. A civil war followed, and Zwingli was killed in battle in 1531. Meanwhile the Reformation was preached by *William Farel* in the lands bordering on the Confederates to the west, and especially in the free city of *Geneva*. That city was hemmed round by the dominions of the Dukes of Savoy, who were always wishing to get hold of it. Now that Geneva had embraced the Reformed religion, there was a further pretext for attacking it, and in 1534 Duke Charles of Savoy besieged the city. But Geneva was in alliance with Bern and with some others among the Confederates; so a Bernese army marched to deliver Geneva, and at the same time took the opportunity of conquering a large part of the dominions of Savoy on both sides of the Lake of Geneva. Other parts were seized by the Canton of Freiburg, though it remained Catholic, and by the little Confederation of *Wallis* or *Valais*, which was in alliance with the Swiss. Bern not long after also annexed the *Bishoprick of Lausanne*—the Bishop of Lausanne, like other Bishops of the Empire, being a temporal prince—but in 1564 she restored to Savoy her conquests south of the Lake. The result of all this was that the Confederates, themselves a purely German body, became the head of a large body of Romance-speaking subjects and allies, which in later times have been made Cantons alongside of the original German states. Geneva from this time remained a free city, though the Dukes of Savoy still sometimes tried to seize upon it. And presently the great French Reformer, *John Calvin*, came there, and became the real ruler of the city, which thus grew into a kind of centre for men of all lands who followed his doctrines. After this time the affairs of the Confederates had but little to do with the general state of things in Europe, but it should be noticed that in 1648 they were, like the United Provinces, acknowledged to be quite independent of the Empire. As for Savoy, almost as soon as Bern had conquered the northern districts, the whole of the Duke's dominions were overrun by France, but they were gradually won back by the next Duke *Emmanuel Filibert*. From this time the Dukes of Savoy began to look more to their Italian than to their Burgundian dominions. Thus a dispute with France about the marquisate of *Saluzzo* was ended by the Duke *Charles Emmanuel*, who reigned from 1580 to 1630, keeping *Saluzzo* and giving up the district of *Bresse* to France. These are but small districts, but they show the way in which France was winning the old Burgundian lands bit by bit, while Savoy was losing territory north of the Alps and gaining it in Italy.

18. **The Reformation in England.** — The affairs of the countries of which we have thus far spoken were all closely connected with one another. England meanwhile was constantly mixed up with the general course of affairs, but she did not engage in any such great wars on the Continent as she did in either earlier or later times. After the ending of the great war with France, England was torn in pieces by the Civil Wars between the different claimants of the Crown of the *Houses of York* and *Lancaster*, and there was no King whose title was altogether undisputed till the accession of *Henry the Eighth* in 1509. He was always mixed up with foreign affairs; and when the Empire was vacant, in 1519, he had some notion of

getting chosen himself, and there was talk more than once of his famous minister, *Cardinal Wolsey*, being chosen Pope. But in truth nothing very great was done by England on the Continent at this time, except that, as we have seen, the English conquered *Boulogne* and kept it for a short time. The Reformation in England is commonly said to have begun under Henry the Eighth, but in truth Henry changed very little either in doctrine or in ceremony. What was done in his time was to restore and enlarge the authority which the old Kings had in ecclesiastical matters, and to declare that the Pope had no jurisdiction in England. All through his reign men who taught the Reformed doctrines were burned as heretics. It was only when Henry's son, *Edward the Sixth*, succeeded in 1547 that any strictly religious changes were made. Then, in 1553, came Henry's daughter *Mary*. She was, through her mother *Katharine of Aragon*, a cousin of the Emperor Charles, and she married his son *Philip*, afterwards Philip the Second of Spain. Thus England was in close alliance with Spain and at enmity with France. Now it was that England lost *Calais*, and so had no longer any possessions on the Continent. Mary also undid all that had been done by her father and brother; not only were the old doctrines and ceremonies restored, but the authority of the Pope was set up again. Under her sister *Elizabeth*, who began to reign in 1558, the English Reformation was finally settled. The Pope's authority was again thrown off, such changes as were thought needful were made in doctrine and worship, but the general system and government of the Church went on. But the reign of Philip and Mary, under which many men were burned for their religion, had thoroughly set Englishmen against anything that had to do with either Spain or the Pope, and many men in England wished that change had gone further in religious matters than it had gone.

19. England and Scotland.—Meanwhile the relations between England and the neighbouring kingdom of Scotland were very important. The old wars often began again, and, when *James the Fifth* of Scotland died in 1541, leaving only a young daughter called *Mary*, there was talk of joining the two kingdoms by marrying her to Henry the Eighth's son Edward, afterwards Edward the Sixth. But all that came of this was more wars, and the throwing of Scotland still more thoroughly on the side of France. Queen Mary was brought up in France and she married the Dauphin *Francis*, who was afterwards King for a little while. She was thus Queen regnant of Scotland and Queen consort of France, and she claimed to be Queen of England also, because, according to the extreme views of the papal power, she had a better right to the English Crown than Elizabeth. After the death of Francis she went back to Scotland, but about this time the greater part of the people of Scotland embraced the Reformation in a very extreme form, while Mary stuck to the old religion. She was afterwards driven out of her kingdom for her personal crimes, and took refuge in England, where she was kept in ward for many years. She thus naturally got to be looked on as a Catholic saint and confessor, and she became a centre of conspiracies against Elizabeth at home and abroad. At last, in 1587, she was beheaded for her share in a plot against Elizabeth's life. The indignation of the Catholic party everywhere was great, and now the quarrel between England and Spain broke out on a great scale. Elizabeth and Philip had for many years been doing harm to each other in a small way, but now, in 1588, Philip sent his great *Armada* against England, which came to nothing. Elizabeth now came to be looked on as the head of the Reformed party throughout Europe, and she gave some help at different times to the Reformers both in France and in the Netherlands. The war between England and

Spain went on during all Elizabeth's reign; but when, on her death in 1603, the Crowns of England and Scotland were united in Mary's son *James, Sixth* of Scotland and *First* of England, the policy of England altogether changed. For James truckled to Spain, and England for a long time lost the position which she had before held in Europe. The reign of his successor *Charles the First* was mainly taken up with internal affairs, and the latter years of it with the great *Civil War*, which lead to the King's beheading in 1649. All this time is one of the most important parts of the history both of England and Scotland, but it is mainly taken up with the internal affairs of the two countries, which have comparatively little to do with the general course of things in Europe. But the union of England and Scotland under one King had this effect, that Scotland was no longer the enemy of England, nor could it any longer be an ally of France in wars between France and England.

20. **Northern Europe.**—It was in the beginning of the sixteenth century that the attempt to join together the three Scandinavian kingdoms of Denmark, Norway, and Sweden, which had never been carried out for any long time together, came wholly to an end. *Christian the Second*, called *Christian the Cruel*, who became King of Denmark and Norway in 1513, became King of Sweden also in 1520; but his oppression provoked revolts in all his dominions. In 1523 he was driven out of both Denmark and Sweden. The Swedes chose as their King the famous *Gustavus Vasa*, who had been their leader in driving out Christian. He brought in the doctrines of Luther, but less change was made in the order and government of the Church in Sweden than anywhere else except in England. Under Gustavus Sweden began to rise to a much higher position in Europe than it had ever held before. He died in 1560, and the Kings who followed him were of no great account till the famous *Gustavus*

Adolphus, who began to reign in 1611. Of him we shall hear more in the history of the great wars in Germany. On his death in 1632 came his daughter *Christina*, in whose time a part of Norway, namely the province of *Jamteland*, with other districts, and the isle of *Gotland*, were won from Denmark. All this while Denmark and Norway remained under the same King. Under *Frederick the First*, who reigned from 1523 to 1533, the Lutheran religion was established in Denmark; but after his death there were disputes about the succession to the Crown, and wars with the city of *Lübeck*. Under *Frederick the Second*, who reigned from 1559 to 1588, the free people of *Ditmarschen*, who had all this time kept on their old freedom at that end of Germany just as the Forest Cantons did at the other end, and who had more than once defeated the Counts of Holstein and Kings of Denmark, were at at last conquered. His son *Christian the Fourth* reigned from 1588 to 1648, and we shall hear of him again.

21. **Russia and Poland.** — In Poland and Lithuania the descendants of Jagellon went on reigning till nearly the end of the sixteenth century. Under them Poland was at the height of its power, and it formed one of the greatest states of Europe. Its territory now stretched far to the east, and took in large countries which had once been part of Russia, and which have since become part of Russia again. In the course of the sixteenth century, when the Russian power began to rise again, parts of these territories were won back again, and from that time the Polish frontier has commonly gone back. But before this, as we have seen, the Teutonic Order was greatly humbled in 1466, when the Knights had to give up the western part of Prussia to Poland, and to hold the eastern part as a fief of the Polish Crown. This led to a further change in 1525. The Grand-Master *Albert* of *Brandenburg* had become a Lutheran. By a

treaty with *Sigismund the First* of Poland, the Teutonic order was abolished as a sovereign power, and Albert became hereditary *Duke of Prussia*, holding his duchy, which took in *East Prussia* only, as a fief of Poland. After a few generations the Duchy of Prussia and the *Mark* or *Electorate* of *Brandenburg* were, in 1611, joined together. Thus began the power of the *House* of *Hohenzollern* as sovereigns of Brandenburg and Prussia, which has gone on so greatly growing to our own times. In 1657, under *Frederick William the First*, who was called the *Great Elector*, the Duchy of Prussia became independent of the Crown of Poland, just as the Duchy of Aquitaine three hundred years before became independent of the Crown of France. In 1701, to go on some way beyond our present time, the Great Elector's son *Frederick* took the title of *King of Prussia* instead of *Duke*. Thus the Electors of Brandenburg, besides their possessions in Germany, held the Duchy or Kingdom of Prussia, which was cut off from their Electorate by that part of Prussia which had been given up to Poland. The other possessions of the Order to the North were treated in nearly the same way. In 1561 the Grand-Master of Livonia, *Gotthard Kettler*, who had also turned Lutheran, gave up all the dominions of the Order to Poland, except *Curland*, which was made into a Duchy for himself, just as Prussia was for Albert. But in the one case, out of the treaty with Albert arose one of the great states of Europe, while out of the treaty with Kettler nothing came but long wars between Sweden and Poland for the lands east of the Baltic, till in the end they were all swallowed up by Russia. But long before this Russia was making great advances. *John* or *Ivan the Fourth*, known as *Ivan the Terrible*, reigned from 1533 to 1584, and his doings towards his own subjects were among the strangest in history. But, besides wars with Sweden and Poland waged with various success, he altogether overthrew the power of the Moguls or

Tartars of Kasan, who had once held Russia in bondage; he took *Astrakhan* also, and so extended the Russian dominions to the Caspian Sea. He was the first of the Russian princes who took the title of *Czar.* Some say that this name is simply a Slavonic word meaning *King*, while according to others it is the Russian form of *Cæsar;* anyhow it is certain that the sovereigns of Russia, who have latterly been called *Emperors*, have always wished, as the most powerful princes belonging to the Eastern Church, to be looked on as successors of the Eastern Emperors. Russia was now a powerful state, but it was cut off from the Baltic by the Poles and Swedes, and from the Black Sea by the Tartars of *Crim* or *Crimea*, so that Russia had no havens except on the Caspian and the White Sea. It was by the White Sea, from the port of *Archangel*, that Russia now began to have trade with England and the other nations of the West. In 1589 the old line of Ruric came to an end, and great confusions followed, among which the Poles were able in 1605 to place a pretender, who professed to be the true heir, on the Russian throne. But in 1613 the Russians chose *Michael Romanoff*, from whom the present royal family springs in the female line, and Russia began to flourish again, though it had to wage wars with Sweden and Poland with various success to the end of the century. In 1573 the Poles made their crown purely elective, instead of choosing, as before, from the royal family. Sometimes they chose a native Pole, sometimes a foreign prince; but from this time all power came into the hands of the nobles, to the loss both of the King and of the people, and Poland began to go down both at home and abroad.

22. **Turkey and Hungary.**—Under *Bajazet the Second*, the successor of Mahomet the Conqueror, the Ottoman power did not advance, but in some parts rather fell back. In his time a new Mahometan

enemy rose to the east of him. This was the modern kingdom of Persia, which rose again, very much as Persia had risen again under Artaxerxes in the third century, by the preaching of a national religion. Only this time it was not the preaching of the old Persian religion, but that of the *Shiah* sect of Mahometanism. Thus the Turks and Persians were not only political enemies, but they looked upon each other as heretics. The new dynasty, which began with *Shah Ismael* in 1501, was known as that of the *Sophis*. Endless wars now followed between the Turks and the Persians; meanwhile *Selim the Inflexible*, who reigned from 1512 to 1520, added Syria and Egypt to the Ottoman Empire, and obtained a surrender of the Caliphate from the nominal Abbasside Caliph at Cairo. Then came *Suleiman*—that is, *Solomon*—the *Lawgiver*, who reigned from 1520 to 1566, and was one of the greatest of the Sultans. It was in his time that Francis of France made alliance with the Turks against the Empire. Under him the Ottomans made great conquests. In 1521 he took *Belgrade;* in 1522 the Knights of Saint John were driven off the island of Rhodes, after which the Emperor Charles gave them the isle of *Malta*, which they successfully defended against the Turks in a great siege in 1565. But meanwhile Suleiman conquered a large part of Hungary. In 1526 *Lewis the Second*, King of Hungary, was killed at the battle of *Mohacs*, after which the crown passed in the end, though not without a good deal of opposition, to Lewis's brother-in-law, *Ferdinand Archduke of Austria*, who was afterwards Emperor. But the greater part of the country fell into the hands of the Turks, and *Buda* became the seat of a Turkish Pasha. The Hungarian Crown has ever since been held by the Archdukes of Austria. It was in the course of these Hungarian wars that Suleiman made his way into Germany, and besieged Vienna. He had also wars with the Empire in other parts, as along the coast of

Africa, where the Emperor Charles at one time took *Tunis*. And in 1543 the Turkish fleet was actually brought by the Most Christian King into the waters of Italy and Provence, where *Nizza* or *Nice* was in vain besieged by the Mahometans. Suleiman was the last of the great line of Sultans who had raised the Ottomans to such power. After his death, though the Turks still made some conquests, they no longer threatened the whole world as they had done before. In the reign of the next Sultan, *Selim*, the Turks gained the island of Cyprus and lost the battle of Lepanto; and from this time they had constant wars with the Persians to the east, and with the Poles and with the Emperors, in their character of Kings of Hungary, to the north.

23. **The Thirty Years' War.**—We now come to the great war which took up all the later years of this period, which had Germany for its centre, but in which most of the nations of Europe had more or less share. This is called the *Thirty Years' War*. It began in *Bohemia*, where the intolerance of the King, the Emperor *Ferdinand the Second*, provoked a revolt. In 1619, just about the time that Ferdinand was crowned Emperor, he was deposed in Bohemia, and the *Elector Palatine Frederick*, a Protestant Prince, was elected in his place. It was like the old wars of the Hussites beginning again. The next year Frederick was driven out of Bohemia, and he presently lost his own dominions as well. Meanwhile, at the other end of Ferdinand's dominions, the Protestants of Hungary revolted, and for a while turned him out of that kingdom also. But the great scene of the war was Germany, where it was first of all carried on between the Catholic and Protestant princes within the country; but gradually, as the Emperor, with his famous generals *Tilly* and *Wallenstein*, seemed likely to swallow up all Germany, other powers began to step in. The first was Christian the Fourth King of Den-

mark, who was himself a Prince of the Empire for his German dominions. In 1625 he became the chief of the Protestant League, but he was soon driven out and obliged to make peace. Presently, in 1630, a greater power stepped in from the North. This was the famous *Gustavus Adolphus* King of Sweden, who became for two years the head of the Protestants, and carried on war with wonderful success for a short time till he was killed in the battle of *Lutzen* in 1632. In this war Gustavus showed himself one of the greatest leaders that ever commanded an army. By this time other nations were beginning to take part in the war. England never formally joined in it, but there was, as was natural, a strong feeling in England on behalf of the Protestant cause, all the more so as Frederick's wife *Elizabeth* was a daughter of James the First, and many Englishmen and Scotsmen served in the Swedish army. France too, under *Cardinal Richelieu*, began to meddle, first making a treaty with Gustavus and helping him with money, and afterwards, in 1635, joining openly in the war. Richelieu had put down the special privileges of the Protestants in France; yet he did not scruple to make a league with the Protestants in Germany and with the Protestant powers of Sweden and Holland, in a war which had begun as a war for religious liberty in Bohemia and Germany. From this time it changed into a war for the aggrandizement of France, all the more so as most of the Protestant states of Germany made peace with the Emperor in 1635. Meanwhile the Emperor Ferdinand died in 1637, and was succeeded by his son *Ferdinand the Third.* The war went on for a while in most parts of Europe with various success, the chief leader in Germany on the Protestant side being Duke *Bernhard of Weimar*. In 1642 the great minister of France, Cardinal Richelieu, died, and his power passed to another Cardinal, *Mazarin.* In 1643 Lewis the Thirteenth died, and then began the long reign of *Lewis the*

Fourteenth, who was only five years old when he came to the crown. Thus the latter part of the war went on under a different Emperor and different sovereigns both of France and of Sweden from those under whom it had begun. In this latter part of the war the French arms, under their great leaders *Turenne* and the *Prince of Condé*, began to be decidedly successful. At last, after long negotiations, peace was made in 1648.

24. **The Peace of Westphalia.**—The peace that was now made, which is known as the *Peace of Westphalia*, made some important changes in Europe. In Germany the two religions were put quite on a level, that is to say, the government of each state might establish which religion it chose. But the country had been utterly ruined by the long war, and whatever traces were left either of authority in the Empire or of freedom in the people quite died out. From this time Germany long remained a mere lax confederation of petty despotisms and oligarchies, with hardly any national feeling. Its boundaries too were cut short in various ways. The independence of the two free Confederations at the two ends of the Empire, those of Switzerland and the United Provinces, which had long been practically cut off from the Empire, was now formally acknowledged. And, what was far more important, the two foreign kingdoms which had had the chief share in the war, France and Sweden, obtained posesssions within the Empire, and moreover, as *guarantors* or sureties of the peace, they obtained a general right of meddling in its affairs. Sweden received territories in northern Germany, both on the Baltic and on the Ocean, part of *Pomerania*, the city of *Wismar*, and the Bishopricks of *Verden* and *Bremen*. The free Hanseatic city of *Bremen* remained independent, as well as *Lübeck* and *Hamburg;* but these were now the only remnants of the famous Hanseatic League which had once been so great. But for

these possessions the Kings of Sweden became Princes of the Empire, like the Kings of Denmark and Hungary, the Elector of Brandenburg, and any other princes who had dominions both in the Empire and out of it. But the territories which were given to France were cut off from the Empire altogether. The right of France to the Three Lotharingian Bishoprics, which had been seized nearly a hundred years before, was now formally acknowledged, and, besides this, the possessions and rights of the House of Austria in *Elsass*, the German land between the Rhine and the Vosges, called in France *Alsace*, were given to France. The free city of *Strassburg* and other places in Elsass still remained independent, but the whole of South Germany now lay open to France. This was the greatest advance that France had yet made at the expense of the Empire. Within Germany itself the Elector of Brandenburg also received a large increase of territory. The war in Germany was now over, but the war between France and Spain still went on, till 1659. Then France gained *Roussillon*, and a few places in Lorraine and the Netherlands, and *Dunkirk* was given to England, much as England had at other times held Calais and Boulogne and afterwards Gibraltar. In the next year Lewis the Fourteenth seized the little principality of *Orange*, but this was afterwards given back.

25. **European Settlements in the East.**—We have now come to the time when European history begins to spread beyond Europe itself and those parts of Asia and Africa which had immediate dealings with Europe. In the last years of the fifteenth century new worlds were opened, both in the East and in the West, and gradually all those European nations which had any power by sea began to trade, to conquer, and to make settlements, in parts of the world which were never before heard of. In this way England, France, Spain, Portugal, and Holland have all,

like the old Greek commonwealths, planted colonies in various parts of the world. But there has been a great difference between the ways of colonizing in the two times. An old Greek colony was an independent state from the beginning; it owed a certain respect to the mother city, but it was in no way subject to it; but the colonies planted by European kingdoms have been looked on as parts of the dominions of the mother country, and have been held as dependent provinces. The colonists therefore, when they have got strong enough, have commonly thrown off the yoke of the mother country, and have made themselves into independent states. Then again we may make some distinctions among the different kinds of colonies. In some places the European settlers have gradually killed or driven out the native inhabitants, much as the English did with the Welsh when they first came into Britain. This has been the case with most of the colonies of England. The English settlers have often been largely mixed with settlers of other European nations and even with slaves from other lands, but they have hardly mixed at all with the natives. In other cases, as has happened in most of the colonies of Spain, the Europeans and the natives have mixed a great deal, and things have been somewhat as they were in the time of the conquests of Rome; that is to say, large bodies of men speak Spanish who are not Spaniards by blood. Then there is a third class of European possessions in distant lands, where Europeans bear rule over the natives, but neither drive them out nor mix with them, and indeed cannot be strictly said to settle or colonize at all. Such is the great dominion of England in *India*, which is something quite different from her colonies in *America*, *Africa*, and *Australia*. Possessions of both sorts began in the times with which we have now to do. The colonies strictly so called were chiefly planted in America, while dominions of the other kind were chiefly gained in the distant parts of Asia and Africa. The first European state which began this course of distant dominion was *Portugal;* of this we have seen the beginning in the time of Don Henry. Before the end of the fifteenth century Portugal had made a great number of settlements along the west coast of Africa as far south as the Equator. Then, when *Vasco da Gama* found out the passage to India round the *Cape of Good Hope*, the Portuguese carried on their discoveries and settlements along the eastern coast of Africa, along the coast of the Persian Gulf, and on into Southern India and into the peninsulas and islands beyond India. This quite changed the course of trade with India and the far East generally. Hitherto trade had gone by way of Alexandria and Venice; now it went by the longer but easier way round the Cape. Throughout the sixteenth century the Portuguese had a far greater Eastern dominion than any other European power; indeed they could hardly be said to have any European rivals in Asia at all. The Spaniards held only the *Philippine Islands*, and the settlements of the English and Dutch and other nations did not begin till the seventeenth century. *Russia* indeed, after she had overthrown the Tartar dominion, went on to win a vast territory in Northern Asia, the great land of *Siberia.* But this was not gained by sea; it was the mere extension of European Russia by land to the east, and the cold and profitless country of Siberia could never be compared with the rich possessions of other European nations in Asia and Africa.

26. **Discovery of America.**—But the land of European colonization, as distinguished from mere dominion, the land in which European settlers have grown up into independent nations, is the New World, *America.* It was in the last years of the fifteenth century that this New World began to be opened to the men of the old. It has been thought that the old Northmen who settled in Iceland touched

on some parts of the coasts of North America, and it is quite certain that they made a settlement in *Greenland*, which lasted till the fourteenth century. But, if they ever found out any of the lands in which the great Spanish and English colonies were afterwards planted, they certainly made no lasting settlements in them. The New World was first found out in 1492 by *Christopher Columbus*, a Genoese in the service of Ferdinand and Isabella, who was not seeking a world to the west, but, now that the earth was known to be round, was trying to find a westward road to India. Thence the lands which he first discovered came to be called the *West Indies*. These were the islands in the Gulf of Mexico, and one of the first of those on which he landed he called *Hispaniola* or *New Spain*. It is also called *Saint Domingo* or *Hayti*. But Columbus did not land on the continent till 1498, and before that time *Sebastian Cabot*, a Venetian in the service of Henry the Seventh of England, had made his way to the mainland of North America much further to the north. Thus America was discovered by citizens of the maritime commonwealths of Italy, though they were acting, not in the service of their own cities, whose fleets never got beyond the Mediterranean, but in that of the Kings who commanded the Ocean. This marks how the course of trade and of dominion was now changing. And the new continent took its name of *America* from a third Italian, *Amerigo Vespucci*, who at one time was thought to have reached the mainland before Columbus. He too was in the service of Spain: thus it was that, though Italy had no part in the discovery of America, yet Italians had the chief part in it.

27. **The Spanish Colonies.**—Thus the New World was found out, and all Europeans then held that they had a perfect right to seize upon any countries beyond the bounds of Christendom, and to do pretty much as they pleased with the people. The

Spaniards in this way conquered the rich lands of *Mexico* and *Peru*, where they found gold, much as in old times the Phœnicians had found gold in Spain itself. Those lands had reached a high degree of civilization and regular government without any dealings with the civilized nations of Europe and Asia. And they were without many things, such as iron, horses, and the use of alphabetic writing, without which no Christian or Mahometan people would have thought it possible to get on. They were of course heathens, and the idolatry of the Mexicans was of a specially horrible and bloody kind. The Spaniards dealt with the natives in a way not unlike that in which the first Saracens had dealt with Christians and heathens, mixing up the notions of conquest and conversion in a strange way. But it is certain that no Mahometans ever treated their Christian subjects so badly as the Spaniards did the natives in America. At last, when it was found that they could not do the hard work of the mines, negro slaves from Africa were brought in to work in their place. The Portuguese in their African settlements had made many negro slaves, and thus the slavery of the black man in the New World began, which went on for a long time in all the European colonies, and which still goes on in Brazil and the Spanish Islands. And thus too began, what was yet worse than slavery itself, the trade in slaves, the stealing men and bringing them over from Africa, which is now forbidden by all civilized nations. *Mexico* was conquered by *Hernando Cortez* between 1519 and 1521, and *Peru* by *Francisco Pizarro* between 1532 and 1536. And, shameful as was the greediness and cruelty shown by the Spaniards, there was something very wonderful in the overthrow of such great powers by such small bodies of men. But a wide difference must be made between the conquest of Mexico and that of Peru. For Cortez, though he did several very cruel deeds, really tried to convert and civilize the countries which he conquered, while Pizarro seems to have had no objects of this kind. Thus began the great Spanish dominion in America, which has grown up into several independent nations speaking the Spanish tongue.

28. **French, English, and other Colonies.**—The next people after the Spaniards who began to settle in North America were the French, and the next were the English, and the settlements of both nations had a good deal to do with the religious dissensions at home. The first attempt at a French settlement was made by Huguenots in 1562, in the land to which they gave the name of *Carolina*, but it was not till 1607 that any lasting French settlements were made in America. From that time the French gradually occupied, or laid claim to, a vast territory in North America, taking in a great deal of the western part of the present *United States* and of the lands to the north of them. These lands were called *Canada* and *Louisiana*, but in a much wider sense than those names bear now. These settlements of the French in North America have all passed either to England or to the United States, but some of their colonies in the West Indies, and their small possessions in South America at *Cayenne*, remain French still. The English sailors, *Gilbert*, *Drake*, and others, kept making discoveries and waging war with the Spaniards during the whole reign of Elizabeth, and in 1585 *Sir Walter Raleigh* tried to begin the colony of *Virginia*, but it was not really settled till 1606. This was the beginning of the English colonies in North America, which have grown up into the United States. *New England* was next colonized, and afterwards *Maryland:* both of these were largely peopled by those men in England who were dissatisfied with the state of religion, and who were often persecuted for not conforming to the law in such matters. For no one as yet thought of allowing perfect freedom to all religions; each country, Catholic or Protestant or

whatever it was, punished with penalties, greater or less, all those who did not conform to the established religion. So men tried to get more freedom by settling in distant lands. Thus the French Huguenots tried to settle in America; and thus, amongst the English colonies, New England was largely peopled by *Puritans*, that is, zealous Protestants who thought that reform in the Church of England had not gone far enough. Maryland, on the other hand, was largely settled by Roman Catholics, who followed the Pope and the Council of Trent, and held that the Church of England had gone wrong in having any Reformation at all. The English colonies in America were all held to be parts of the English dominions; but most of them had free constitutions, and they were able to do much as they pleased in their own local affairs. Meanwhile the Dutch, who, having freed themselves from Spain, were fast driving the Portuguese out of the commerce of the East Indies, settled in North America also, and founded a colony called *New Netherland* between Maryland and New England. In South America, besides the French, the English and Dutch had some small possessions. But the other great South American power besides Spain was Portugal. For the Portuguese founded the great colony of *Brazil*, after some opposition from the English, Dutch, and French. The Portuguese began to settle in those parts about 1531, and after 1660 they had Brazil wholly to themselves.

29. **Learning, Art, and Science.** — All this time the mind of man was making great progress in all parts. The revival of learning in the fifteenth century did something to check original genius in Italy, for all men took once more to writing in Latin. But in the sixteenth century there were again great Italian writers both in prose and verse, and the time from the later part of the fifteenth century till that of the sixteenth was the great time of Italian painting. Learning also spread through all parts of the West, and there

were great scholars in most countries, in none more than in the United Provinces after they had won their freedom. There too men began to give special heed to the *Law of Nations*, that is, to the rules by which different countries hold themselves to be bound in their dealings with one another. In this time also men began to have truer notions on matters of physical science; to learn, for instance, that the earth goes round the sun, instead of the sun going round the earth. In religious matters too the endless controversies, both between the Roman Catholics and the Protestants and between the different sects of Protestants, brought out a great number of learned and zealous theological writers on all sides. And this was not only a time of learning, but also of original genius, for, besides Italy, it was the age of the greatest poets of England, Spain, and Portugal. France perhaps lagged a little behind in poetry, but she had many good writers in prose. Generally throughout Europe, men were taking to their own languages for poetry and history, though some great histories were still written in Latin, and Latin was still the common language of learning and science. Men also began to learn more of each other's languages, and the Italian language especially was much admired and studied in other countries. In Germany the standard of language was fixed by Luther's translation of the Bible, which had this effect, that the *High-Dutch* in which he wrote it became the received tongue of Germany, while the *Low-Dutch*, though the natural tongue of so large a part of the country, came to be looked down on as a mere vulgar dialect. But, after the wretched times of the Thirty Years' War, both learning and native literature sadly went down. Altogether, the time from the latter years of the fifteenth century to the middle of the seventeenth was one of the most fertile times, both in great scholars and in great writers of their own tongues, but it would be endless to try to set their names down here. It will be better done in the histories of their particular countries.

30. Summary.—In this period we see the *Empire* practically come to an end. In strictness there was no Emperor after Charles the Fifth, and the Imperial title no longer carried with it any authority in Italy, and not much in Germany. It had become little more than a title of honour in one branch of the *House of Austria*, while the greatest power in Europe had really passed away to the other branch of the House of Austria which held *Spain* and its dependent states. At the beginning of the period Spain decidedly held the first place, but before the end of it, the Spanish power greatly lessened, and *France*, by the result of the *Thirty Years' War*, became the leading power instead of Spain. *Italy* sank into a mere dependency of Spain, except so far as *Venice* still fought the battles of Christendom against the Turks. *Germany*, after taking the lead in the Reformation, was utterly ruined and divided by the Thirty Years' War. *Switzerland* held a high position at the beginning of the period, and the dominion of its Cantons in the *Romance* lands began. But, before the end of the period, the reputation of the Confederates greatly sunk through the practice of mercenary service. *Hungary* had sunk, partly into a Turkish province, partly into a possession of the House of Austria. On the other hand, several old powers greatly advanced and some new ones came into being. *England* and *Scotland*, though not yet united into one kingdom, became one power as regards other nations. *Sweden* suddenly grew into a first-class power. *Poland* both gained and lost, but *Russia*, her neighbour to the East, grew in a manner which, in her own part of the world, might almost be set against the growth of Spain in the West. But she was not as yet of any importance in European affairs generally. The power of the *Turks* rose to its height, but it met with its first great check and began

to go down. *Savoy*, losing territory to the north of the Alps, gained territory to the south, and thus had its course marked out for it as an Italian power. The revolt of the *Netherlands* against Spain gave birth to the new commonwealth of the *United Provinces*, which at once rose to the rank of a great power. The treaty of Poland with the *Teutonic Knights* gave birth to the new power of *Prussia*, though Prussia did not become great till the United Provinces had begun to go down again. And, besides these shiftings of territory and risings and fallings of various powers, we have in this period the *Reformation* and all its results, and we have the great stirring of men's minds which partly caused it and partly followed it. And we have the discovery of *New Worlds* both in the East and in the West, and the conquests and settlements of all the seafaring powers of Europe in those distant lands.

CHAPTER XIV.

THE GREATNESS OF FRANCE.

Growth of the power of France; accession of Lewis the Fourteenth; his character and absolute dominion (1)—*his aggressions on Spain and the United Provinces; league against France; defence of the United Provinces by William of Orange* (1)—*Peace of Nimwegen; acquisitions of France* (1)—*Lewis at the height of his power; seizure of Strassburg* (2)—*devastation of the Palatinate; second league against Lewis; Peace of Ryswick* (2)—*schemes for the partition of the Spanish dominions; War of the Spanish Succession* (3)—*Lewis's persecution of the Protestants; losses of France by his reign* (3)—*England under the Parliament and the Protectorate; her greatness under Cromwell; wars with the United Provinces* (4)—*degradation of England under Charles and James the Second; wars with the United Provinces; election of William of Orange* (4)—*different effects of the Revolution in England, Scotland, and Ireland; union of the Kingdoms of England and Scotland* (5)—*share of Great Britain in the wars with France; accession of the Hanoverian dynasty* (5)—*reign of the Emperor Leopold; growth of Brandenburg under the Great Elector; Prussia becomes a kingdom* (6)—*affairs of Hungary; siege of Vienna by the Turks; the Hungarian Crown becomes hereditary; Peace of Carlowitz; reigns of Joseph the First and Charles the Sixth; advance of the Austrian power; Peace of Passarowitz* (6)—*decay of the Spanish power* (7)—*affairs of Italy; advance of Savoy* (8)—*wars of Venice with the Turks; war of Candia; conquest and loss of Peloponnêsos* (9)—*great position of the United Provinces; changes in their form of government; Stadholdership of William the Third* (10)—*greatest extent of the power of Sweden; Denmark and Sweden become absolute monarchies* (11)—*exploits of Charles the Twelfth* (11)—*loss of territory and lessening of the royal power in Sweden; comparison of Sweden and Savoy* (11)—*decline of Poland; reigns of John Sobieski and Augustus the Strong* (12)—*decline of the power of the Turks; the tribute of children no longer levied; advance of the subject nations* (13)—*English and Dutch settlements in India; beginning of the East India Company* (14)—*the Mogul Emperors* (14)—*English settlements in Madras, Bombay and Calcutta* (14)—*English settlements in North America; annexations of the Swedish and Dutch colonies* (15)—*French colonization in Louisiana* (15)—*Summary* (16).

1. Conquests of Lewis the Fourteenth.—We have now come to the time when *France* takes the same place among the nations of Europe which had for a while been held by Spain, and becomes in the like sort the object of fear to most other nations. We have seen that the power of France was confirmed, as against the Empire, by the *Peace of Westphalia* in 1648, and, as against Spain, by the *Peace of the Pyrenees* in 1659. Thus the House of Bourbon had humbled both branches of the House of Austria. The reigning King was now *Lewis the Fourteenth*, who came to the crown as a child in 1643, and reigned seventy-two years, till 1715. The earlier part of his reign was a time of great confusion and rebellion, but from the time of his taking the government on himself, on the death of Cardinal Mazarin in 1661, till the end of his long reign, no King of any country ever kept things more wholly in his own hands. He was served by very able ministers and generals, but his own will gave the law to France, and thereby to a great part of Europe. His common saying was, "I am the State;" and he made himself so; for, besides greatly advancing the power of France in Europe, he greatly advanced the royal authority in France. The States-General were never summoned; he humbled the *Parliament of Paris*, the chief court of law, which had hitherto put some check on the King's will; in short, he made France still more thoroughly an absolute monarchy than it was before. He married *Maria Theresa*, an *Infanta* or Princess of Spain, and at the marriage all rights to any part of the Spanish dominions which might thus pass to himself or his children were solemnly given up. Notwithstanding this, when Philip the Fourth of Spain died in 1665, Lewis gave out that by an old law of the Netherlands certain parts of those provinces ought to pass to his Queen rather than to the next King, *Charles the Second*. This frightened the United Provinces, who feared that the claim would extend to them. Presently, in 1667, he invaded the Netherlands, and in the next year, he, for the first time, conquered the County of Burgundy, now called *Franche Comté*, which still belonged to Spain, and the Imperial city of *Besançon*, which had now become a part of the County. These last conquests he gave up the same year by a treaty at *Aachen*, but he kept his conquests in the Netherlands. Next in 1672, he attacked the United Provinces, and both

England and several German princes were, to their great shame, on his side. But after a while the English Parliament compelled the King, Charles the Second, to make peace. The war now became general; the Emperor Leopold and King Charles of Spain made a league with the United Provinces, so strangely had things turned about since they first threw off the Spanish yoke. The Empire, as a body, was neutral, but some of the German princes, among them the *Great Elector* of Brandenburg, Frederick William, joined the league against France; so did Denmark, while Sweden took the French side, so that there was a kind of separate war going on in the North. It was in this war that *William Prince of Orange*, the descendant of William the Silent, and who was afterwards King of England, first made himself famous. At last peace was made at *Nimwegen* in 1678 and 1679, by which France kept most of her new conquests in the Spanish Netherlands, with the County of Burgundy and the city of Besançon, and some Imperial towns in Elsass which had not been given up by the Peace of Westphalia. In all this war Lewis had been spreading his influence far and wide, and making alliances everywhere. Just as other Kings of France had done, though he was a cruel persecutor of the Protestants in France, he helped the Hungarian Protestants against their King the Emperor, and even allied himself with the Turks, as Francis the First had done.

2. **Lewis the Fourteenth and William of Orange.**—Lewis was now at the height of his power, and his flatterers called him *Lewis the Great.* But, even after these great successes, he never could keep quiet; he went on annexing small places in Elsass, and at last, in 1681, he seized on the free Imperial city of *Strassburg* in time of peace. Then he began to meddle in Italy, and, among other things, he picked a quarrel with the commonwealth of *Genoa*, bombarded the city, and made the Doge come and ask

humbly for peace. Other smaller wars with Spain followed, and in 1688 Lewis seized *Avignon*, which belonged to the Pope, and directly afterwards he began a new war, because he could not get a candidate of his own chosen to the Archbishoprick of Köln. But by this time one very important change had taken place. *James the Second* of England, who, like his brother Charles, had been in the pay of Lewis, had been driven out, and his nephew and son-in-law William Prince of Orange, the *Stadholder* of Holland, had been chosen King of England in his stead. England was now therefore against France, and King William was the very soul of the general league called the *Grand Alliance*, which was now made to keep Lewis from bringing all Europe under his yoke. But William found it hard to manage many of his allies, for both Spain and the German princes were often anxious to throw the burthen of the war on England and the United Provinces, and towards the end of the war Lewis contrived to detach the Duke of Savoy from the Alliance. This war went on almost everywhere at once. The thing by which it is best remembered is the cruel ravaging of the dominions of the Elector Palatine by Lewis's orders at the beginning of the war. Many battles were fought and towns taken on both sides, especially in the Netherlands; and at last peace was made at *Ryswick*, by which most of the conquests on both sides were restored. France especially gave up the places which had been seized in Germany, except the great city of Strassburg, which she was allowed to keep.

3. **War of the Spanish Succession.**—Another war began in 1700, on the death of Charles the Second of Spain. This is called the *War of the Spanish Succession*. As Charles had no children, there was much doubt who should succeed to his dominions, and several treaties had been made between England and the United Provinces, France, and

the Empire, to hinder the whole of the Spanish dominions from being any longer united. By the last treaty they were to be divided among the several claimants, and the Crown of Spain itself was to pass to the *Archduke Charles of Austria*, the son of the Emperor Leopold. But when King Charles of Spain died, it was found that he had left the whole of his dominions to *Philip of Anjou*, the grandson of the King of France. *Philip the Fifth* therefore succeeded to the Crown of Spain. But war broke out in 1701; the Emperor, England, the United Provinces, Brandenburg or Prussia (whichever we are now to call it), and afterwards Savoy, all took part in it. This was the war in which the *Duke of Marlborough* carried on his great campaigns in the Netherlands, and in which England got possession of *Gibraltar*. The war went on in all parts with various success till 1713 and 1714, when it was ended by the Treaties of *Utrecht* and *Rastadt*. By these treaties the great Spanish monarchy was divided, in a way of which we shall say more when we come to the several countries which were concerned in the division. But Philip kept Spain and *the Indies*, that is, the distant possessions of Spain in America and elsewhere, so that Lewis succeeded so far that he had established his grandson on the throne of Spain. But in this last war he had made no such conquests for his own kingdom as he had made in his earlier wars. And these constant wars, and his despotic government at home, had greatly weakened and impoverished his kingdom. It was weakened above all by Lewis's persecutions of the Protestants. In 1685 he revoked the *Edict of Nantes*, which had been granted in their favour by Henry the Fourth. A most cruel persecution followed, chiefly in the South, where the Protestants were most numerous. This was a great blow for France, as crowds of skilful and industrious men left the country, and carried their skill to England and elsewhere. But, as far as mere military glory went, there had as yet been no time when France had had so large a share of it as during the reign of Lewis the Fourteenth.

4. **England.**—It marks the great position which France held during this time, that, in telling the history of France, we have to tell so large a part of the history of all Western Europe. But this was a most important time, both in England and in other countries. From the execution of *Charles the First* in 1649 to the Restoration of his son *Charles the Second* in 1660, England was a commonwealth. During the first years after the King's death, the Long Parliament, which had overthrown him, kept the government in its own hands. But in 1653 the great general of the Parliament, *Oliver Cromwell*, took on himself the chief power by the title of *Lord Protector*, for, like Cæsar at Rome, he did not dare to call himself King. He kept his power till his death in 1658, and then came a time of confusion till the *Restoration* of *Charles the Second.* Under the government of the Parliament and of the Protector, England rose again to the place, or more than the place, in Europe which she had held under Elizabeth, and which she had lost under the first two Stewart Kings. Scotland, where Charles the Second had been acknowledged King after his father's death, was now united with England. Ireland was conquered as it had never been conquered before. A war was waged with the United Provinces, in which the great admirals of the two commonwealths, *Blake* on the English side, and *De Ruyter* and *Van Tromp* on the Dutch, won victories over each other. The Island of *Jamaica* in the West Indies was won from Spain; the Protector interfered to protect the Protestants in Savoy, who were persecuted by their Duke, and he made favourable treaties with most of the powers of Europe. All this was changed after Charles the Second came to the Crown; for he had no care for the honour of the

nation, and he actually was in the pay of Lewis of France. The secret object of their schemes was to set up absolute power and the Roman Catholic religion in England. Charles first made men angry in 1663 by selling *Dunkirk* to the French King. Then followed a war with the United Provinces from 1664 to 1667, just at the time when the *Plague of London* happened in 1665, and the *Great Fire* in 1666. In this war the Dutch fleet sailed up the Thames, a thing which no enemy's fleet had done since the old times of the Danes. In this war Lewis professed to be on the side of the Dutch, but intrigues were going on between him and Charles. Though in 1668 a *Triple Alliance* was concluded between England, Sweden, and the United Provinces, to check the advance of France; yet, when Lewis invaded Holland in 1672, Charles joined him, and another naval war between England and the United Provinces followed. Peace however was made the next year, and after a while *Mary*, the niece of Charles and daughter of *James Duke of York*, was married to her cousin *William, Prince of Orange.* In 1685 James came to the throne. He had openly become a Roman Catholic, and his illegal doings in favour of those of his own religion at last obliged him to leave the country, and *William* and *Mary* were chosen King and Queen.

5. **Great Britain.**—The effects of the *Revolution* which placed William and Mary on the throne were different in the three kingdoms of England, Scotland, and Ireland. In England the old laws and liberties were restored after a time of misgovernment. In Scotland, which, at the restoration of Charles the Second, had again become a separate kingdom, the Stuart Kings had tried in vain to force the rites and government of the English Church on a people who preferred a system departing further from that of Rome. William and Mary were therefore gladly chosen in Scotland, and the Presbyterian Church was finally

established. But in Ireland, where the mass of the people were Roman Catholics, the cause of James was maintained for a while. But in the end Ireland was more thoroughly conquered than ever, and the native Roman Catholic inhabitants were ground down for a long while under the dominion of the Protestant English. Thus the Scots gained their freedom and the establishment of their own religion by the same revolution which enslaved Ireland. In 1707, in the reign of Queen *Anne*, who succeeded William, *England* and *Scotland* were joined together into one kingdom, with one Parliament, called the *Kingdom of Great Britain*, while Ireland remained a separate and dependent kingdom. Meanwhile, after the election of William and Mary, now that the same man was King of England and Stadholder of Holland, England took a leading part, as we have already said, in the last two wars against Lewis. By the *Treaty of Utrecht*, England, or we should now rather say *Great Britain*, gained the fortress of *Gibraltar*, which we have kept ever since, and the island of *Minorca*. This was the English share in the partition of the Spanish monarchy, and it was our first possession in the Mediterranean. *Tangier* had been an English possession during the reign of Charles the Second, but Tangier lies outside the Strait. In all these ways England became more mixed up with continental affairs than she had been before, and this was still more the case when, just before the death of Lewis the Fourteenth, the Crown of Great Britain passed to a foreign prince who was actually a reigning sovereign, which William was not, except in his little principality of Orange. This was *George Elector of Hanover*, a descendant of James the First in the female line, who, as neither William nor Anne left any children, was chosen by Parliament to succeed, as being the next Protestant heir. Thus England had again, after so many years, a King who could not speak English.

6. Germany and Hungary. — We have seen how utterly the power of the Emperors came to an end by the Peace of Westphalia; and the next Emperor, *Leopold*, who succeeded Ferdinand the Third in 1658 and reigned till 1705, was not a man likely to set it up again. The German princes now did much as they pleased, and many of them did not scruple to become the allies of Lewis. In fact, in a great part of Germany the King of France was much more truly the head than the Emperor. The most famous German prince of this time was the *Great Elector* of Brandenburg, *Frederick William*, who has been already spoken of as taking a part in the war against Lewis. It was under him that the House of Hohenzollern began to rise to greatness. He inherited and gained several fresh territories in Germany, and, as we have seen, he made his Duchy of Prussia independent of Poland. His son *Frederick*, the first *King of Prussia* took part against France in the War of the Spanish Succession; he also inherited a possession at a great distance, namely the Principality of *Neufchâtel* in the old Kingdom of Burgundy. This small state was in close alliance with the Canton of Bern, and it has since become a part of Switzerland. The next King, *Frederick William the First*, who succeeded in 1713, received some further additions to his territories in western Germany by the Peace of Utrecht. Thus *Prussia*, as it must now be called rather than *Brandenburg*, was advancing step by step to the position of a great power in Europe. The Emperor Leopold meanwhile, besides the wars with France, had much to do in his kingdom of Hungary, both with the wars against the Turks and with the revolts of the Hungarians themselves, who were stirred up by his cruel persecutions of the Protestants. The Protestants did not scruple to join with the Turks, and we can hardly wonder at them; for the Christian subjects of a Mahometan power, though they are dealt with as an inferior people, are not denied the free exercise of their religion. In 1683 the Turks besieged Vienna, which was delivered by *John Sobieski, King of Poland*, and *Charles Duke of Lorraine*. After this the war went on, and the Turks were gradually driven out of the part of Hungary which they held, and peace was made at *Carlowitz* in 1699. In the midst of all this the crown of Hungary, which, though it had been so long in the Austrian family, was still by law elective, was made hereditary in 1687. Leopold then gave up the kingdom to his son *Joseph*, who in 1690 was chosen King of the Romans, and succeeded his father as Emperor in 1705. He took a leading part in all the affairs of Europe during his time. The war with France went on, and so did the civil wars in Hungary, till 1711, after which we hear of no more revolts for a long while. In that year Joseph died, and was succeeded by *Charles the Sixth*. He it was whom the Allies had wished to make King of Spain, and now the fear of uniting Spain with the dominions of the House of Austria helped to incline the Allies to peace. By the terms of peace the House of Austria got, as its share of Spanish dominions, all that remained of the Spanish Netherlands, the Kingdoms of Naples and Sardinia, and the Duchy of Milan, except some parts which were given to the Duke of Savoy. In 1715 another war began with the Turks, which was ended in 1718 by the *Peace of Passarowitz*, by which more territory was won, including *Belgrade* the capital of Servia. Thus the House of Austria, whose archdukes were so regularly chosen emperors, gained a great increase of territory during this period, but it all went to the advantage of the House of Austria, not at all to the advantage of what was still called the Roman Empire.

7. **The Spanish Peninsula.**—The history of Spain during this time has pretty well been told already. The power which had been so great

been so great under Charles the Fifth and Philip the Second had now sunk to nothing, and Spain was disputed about by other powers without their asking the consent of its own people. But of the competitors for the Spanish Crown the Spaniards certainly preferred the French candidate to the Austrian, except in *Catalonia*, where the people took the other side. They had been deceived by the French in earlier wars. *Portugal* during this time has hardly any general history. At first it took the side of the French, and afterwards that of the allies. And we must not forget that, besides the loss of its possessions in different parts of Europe, Spain itself suffered dismemberment. For, as we have seen, England got, not only the island of Minorca, but also the fortress of Gibraltar on the mainland of Spain itself.

8. **Advance of Savoy.**—Italy also has very little history during these times. From this time onwards we shall find both Italy and the Netherlands used as a kind of battle-field for the wars of other nations. We have seen how, by the *Treaty of Utrecht*, several parts of Italy were again made to change masters, and how, for the first time since Charles the Fifth, the *Emperor*, though we can no longer say the *Empire*, again became an important power in Italy. But there are two independent states in Italy of whose history some account must be given. The *House of Savoy* was steadily making its way. From the beginning of the seventeenth century the Dukes of Savoy had sought to add to their dominions the possessions of the commonwealth of Genoa, and also whatever they might be able to win in Lombardy, which was then divided between the commonwealth of Venice and the Kings of Spain as Dukes of Milan. Genoa they were not to win for a long time; but, by taking a part dexterously, and not very scrupulously, in every war, they always contrived to gain something by each treaty of peace. Thus Duke *Victor Amadeus the Second* took a part in

both the wars of the Allies against France. He gained in some campaigns and lost in others; he changed sides more than once; but he gained an increase of territory both by the Peace of Ryswick and by the Peace of Utrecht. His gains by this last peace were very great; he gained a part of the Duchy of Milan, and, more than this, he became a King. The Dukes of Savoy had for a long time claimed to be *Kings of Cyprus and Jerusalem*, but these were mere nominal kingdoms. But now Victor Amadeus became really King of the *Island of Sicily*, while the kingdom on the mainland went to the Emperor. The *Two Sicilies* were thus again divided, as they had been in the fourteenth and fifteenth centuries. The Dukes of Savoy in all this show a marked contrast to the other princes of Italy, and the corruption which had spread itself over most parts of Italy under the Spanish domination had hardly touched their dominions. They were thus able to do great things; and, though their policy as yet was purely selfish, they were really laying the foundation of the power which in our own time has grown into the restored Kingdom of Italy.

9. **Wars of Venice.**—The other Italian state of which some account must be given during this time was the commonwealth of Venice, which was still nobly playing its part as the champion of Christendom against the Turks. Cyprus had been lost, but the Venetians still kept Crete. But in 1645 the Turks attacked the island, and a war in its defence went on for twenty-four years. This war, as the greater part of it was taken up by the siege of the town of *Candia*, was commonly called the *War of Candia*. The Venetians were helped, just as in the old times of the Crusades, by volunteers and others from various parts of Europe, from France, Spain, England, and Savoy; but at last, in 1669, Candia could no longer hold out, and the whole island passed to the Turks. In 1684 the Venetians joined the Emperor Leopold and the

Poles in their war with the Turks, and presently *Francesco Morosini*, who had commanded at Candia, conquered the whole of *Peloponnêsos*, and was afterwards elected Doge. It was in this war that the *Parthenôn*, the great temple at Athens, which had become a church under the Eastern Emperors and a powder-magazine under the Turks, was finally broken down when Morosini was besieging Athens. Peloponnêsos was confirmed to Venice in the *Peace of Carlowitz* in 1699, but it was won back by the Turks in 1715, as well as all that Venice still kept in the East, except the *Ionian Islands* and one or two points on the west coast of Epeiros. In 1716 the Turks in vain tried to take Corfu, but in 1718 the Emperor Charles forsook Venice just when there was a chance of winning back Peloponnêsos. With the *Peace of Passarowitz* in that year the history of the wars of Venice in the East, which had gone on ever since the taking of Constantinople in 1204, came to an end.

10. **The United Provinces.** — During all this time the Seven United Provinces, as what we have already said will show, held a much higher position in Europe and the world in general than could have been looked for from the extent of their territories. And they did this notwithstanding an awkward constitution in which each of the states of which the Confederation was made up kept nearly all the rights of sovereignty. In *Holland*, which was the leading province of the seven, there was a chief magistrate called a *Stadholder*, who often held the same office in other provinces also. This office had passed on for some generations, almost as if it had been hereditary, in the family of the Princes of Orange. But, when *William the Second*—as it is most convenient to call him, though he was really the *Ninth* in his own principality of Orange—died in 1650, his son *William the Third* was not yet born, and the office of Stadholder was formally abolished in 1667. At this time the States

were chiefly led by a famous statesman of Holland, *John de Witt*, but in 1672 there was a revolution; De Witt and his brother were murdered, and the Prince was appointed Stadholder. It was he who carried on the great defence of the Provinces against France, but after his death the office of Stadholder was again abolished for a long while.

11. **The Northern Kingdoms.**—Sweden, like the United Provinces, held during all this time a greater position in Europe than it was really able to keep. Queen Christina abdicated in 1654; the wars went on during the time of the next King, *Charles the Tenth*, and in 1660 *Charles the Eleventh* concluded the Treaties of *Oliva* and *Copenhagen*, by which Sweden gained almost all *Livonia* from Poland, and obtained from Denmark all that part of Denmark which lay within the northern peninsula, so that Denmark now kept only Jütland and the islands. Sweden now had greater territories than it had at any time before or since, and in this King's reign, in 1682, the royal power was made absolute by law. The same had been done in Denmark in 1660, in the reign of *Frederick the Third*. Then, in 1697, came the famous *Charles the Twelfth*. He was presently attacked by Denmark, Poland, and Russia all at once. He first beat the Danes, and then the Russians in the famous battle of *Narva;* then he passed on into Poland, where he deposed one King and set up another; then he passed on into Russia, where at last he was defeated at *Pultowa*, and had to take shelter in the Turkish dominions at *Bender*. There he stayed in a kind of captivity for a while, but in 1714 he made his way almost alone to *Stralsund* in his Pomeranian dominions, where he was besieged by the forces of Denmark, Prussia, and Saxony. In 1718 he was killed in attacking *Frederickshall* in Norway. His sister *Ulrica* succeeded him. Absolute monarchy was now again abolished, and the royal powers were made very small

In 1720 and 1721 peace was made by Sweden with her various enemies, and the Swedish dominions were cut short in all parts. Livonia and the neighbouring land were given up to Russia, whose territories now reached to the Baltic. *Bremen* and *Verden* were given up to Hanover, and part of Swedish *Pomerania* to Prussia. So of the fruits of the German victories of Gustavus Adolphus nothing was left except part of *Pomerania* and the town of *Wismar;* but the Scandinavian territories which had been won from Denmark in the last century were still kept. Charles the Twelfth had won victories which astonished the whole world, but he taxed the resources of his kingdom beyond its strength, and since his time Sweden has never been what it was during the whole of the seventeenth century. But, on the other hand, Sweden now reached to the extreme south of her own peninsula, and was no longer cut off by Denmark from the western seas. In fact Sweden has to some extent, like Savoy, gained territory at one end and lost it at the other, though the gains have been greater in the case of Savoy and the losses in the case of Sweden.

12. **Russia and Poland.**—We need say but little about the history of Russia in this chapter, because its wonderful advances towards the end of this time will come better as a connected story in the next chapter. Poland meanwhile had, as we have seen, to give up her new territory of Livonia to Sweden, and presently, in 1672, she had to give up the border province of *Podolia* to the Turks, and to submit to pay a tribute. But in 1674 the Poles chose as their King their own famous general, *John Sobieski*, the same who delivered Vienna in 1683. Both before and after he became King, he won several victories over the Turks. He got back part of the lost territories, and for a time joined *Moldavia* and *Wallachia* to Poland; these are the two *Danubian principalities* of which there has been much talk of late years. These con-

quests were not long kept. Sobieski died in 1696, and the Poles did not choose a new King for more than a year. Then they chose *Frederick Augustus, Elector of Saxony*, who turned Catholic to receive the Crown, since which time the Electors and Kings of Saxony have been Catholics, while their people have remained Protestant. This King is called *Augustus the Strong*. He won back the strong town of *Kaminiec* from the Turks; but, having joined the league against Charles the Twelfth of Sweden, he was utterly overthrown in 1702. Charles called on the Poles to depose Augustus and choose a new King; so in 1704 they chose one of their own nobles, *Stanislaus Leszczynski*. But he reigned no longer than Charles could help him, and, after Charles's defeat at Pultowa and after a civil war in Poland, Augustus was brought back. Poland was now falling very fast from the high place which it had once held in Europe.

13. **The Turks.**—The chief events in the history of the Turks have already been told when we spoke of their wars with Venice and in Hungary. Though they conquered Crete and recovered Peloponnêsos, yet on the whole the power of the Ottomans was going down. Some of the Sultans, like *Mahomet the Fourth*, in whose time Vienna was besieged, were men of spirit, and Mahomet sometimes commanded his own armies, but some were very weak men indeed, and none were like the great series of Sultans who had founded the Ottoman dominion. One great reason for the decline of the Ottoman power was that the tribute of children was no longer regularly levied on the subject nations. The Janissaries had become a kind of hereditary caste, and their old spirit was quite gone. In former times all the best servants of the Sultans, both in war and peace, had come from among the tribute children. Now that the tribute was no longer levied, the Sultans had no longer the same succession of able and faithful servants, and the subject nations

were no longer deprived of the men who were most fitted to be their leaders. As long as the tribute was levied, we may say that the subject nations could not revolt. As it was, we do not hear of any revolts for some time to come, but the subject nations now began to gain strength and their masters became weaker.

14. **European Settlements in India.**—The English dominion in India began during this time. The great sailors of Elizabeth's time had made their way into the Indian seas as well as into those of the West, and a systematic trade with India, carried on, as was usual in those days, by a *Company*, began in the times of James the First. The English merchants had at first to withstand the opposition of the Dutch in the islands, and of the Portuguese on the mainland. The Dutch had got possession of the islands called the *Spice Islands*, which form part of the great group of islands which lie beyond the two peninsulas of India, and in 1623 great indignation was caused by what was called the *Massacre of Amboyna*, when several Englishmen were put to death by a sentence of the Dutch Court in the island. With India itself the English began to trade in a regular manner about 1613, when they received a charter from the reigning Emperor *Jehangir*. The great power in India was now the *Mogul Empire*, which was ruled by Mahometan princes, sprung from *Baber*, a descendant of *Timour*, who established himself in India in 1526. His grandson *Akbar*, in whose time the Mogul dominion was spread over the greater part of India, was the greatest and best of all Mahometan rulers. But in truth he gave up Mahometanism, and set up a new religion of his own. Jehangir was his son. The first settlements in India were merely factories for trade, but in those distant seas it was needful for merchants to fortify their factories, and to have ships which could withstand an enemy. Commercial enterprises thus gradually changed into political and military enter-

prises, and the Company, which was at first merely a company of traders, came to have its dominions and armies like a sovereign prince or commonwealth, and in the end to have rule over nearly all India. These times however are yet to come; but the story of the English power in India is something like the history of Rome; wherever the English merchants settled and fortified their factories, their dominion really began. Their first settlement was at *Surat;* one which became of more importance began at *Madras* in 1640; and in 1662 the King of England, as distinguished from the English trading Company, first became possessed of a dominion in India. This was *Bombay*, which was given to England by Portugal on the marriage of Charles the Second to the Portuguese Infanta Katharine. But this new dominion was before long granted by the King to the Company. In 1698 began the English settlement at *Calcutta*, and these three, Madras, Bombay, and Calcutta, remained the chief seats of the British dominion in India. During all this time there were many disputes between different sets of merchants about the right of trading with India, till at last, in 1708, the *East India Company* was put on the footing which it kept long after, and under which it gradually obtained either sovereignty or commanding influence in most parts of India. By this time the Mogul Empire was much weaker than it had been at the time when the English first settled. *Shah Jehan*, the son of Jehangir, who reigned from 1627 to 1658, was a great prince, but under his son *Aurungzebe*, who reigned from 1658 to 1707, being thus nearly contemporary with Lewis the Fourteenth, the Empire, though outwardly at its highest pitch of splendour, was really falling to pieces. For Aurungzebe was a bigoted Mahometan, and his intolerance led to a revolt of the *Mahrattas*, a Hindoo people who founded a great dominion in Central India. And presently the rulers of the different provinces under the Mogul Emperors began to grow into independent princes, keeping up only a nominal submission to the *Great Mogul*, as he was called. This is the same thing as we have seen so often in other parts of the world, in the Caliphate and in the Empire and in the kingdom of France. By these means the progress of the English in India was much helped. But we must remember that during all this time there was no sign at all that the English were likely to come to be the head power in India. There were as yet nothing more than one set of traders and settlers among others, Portuguese, Dutch, French, and Danish. Some of these settlements of other nations remain still, though the English have so greatly outstripped them. But with the islands—except *Ceylon*, which lies close to the peninsula, as Sicily does to Italy—the English have had but little to do. They have always chiefly belonged to the Dutch and Spaniards.

15. **European Colonization in America.**—During all this time colonization was going on briskly. The two great maritime and commercial powers, England and the United Provinces, now took the lead in it. It was now that England was rising to her great position by sea, and her new power led both to the foundation of new colonies and to the conquest of the colonies of other European nations. The Spaniards and Portuguese kept their great possessions in America, though the Spanish power had utterly gone down in the New World as well as in the Old. The Dutch colony of *New Netherland* was flourishing, though the Dutch and English often had quarrels. In 1638 the Swedes also, now that Sweden had become a great power, set up a colony on *Delaware Bay*, but in 1655 this colony was conquered by the Dutch, and was joined to their own New Netherland. But New Netherland itself did not last very long, for it was conquered during the first war between the Dutch and the English in Charles the Second's time, and several

English colonies were made out of parts of it. The chief town, *New Amsterdam*, changed its name to *New York*, in honour of the king's brother, James Duke of York. Other colonies were planted during Charles the Second's time, as *Carolina* and *New Jersey*, and especially *Pennsylvania*, which was planted by the famous Quaker *William Penn*, who made laws for his colony, and established greater toleration in religion than was to be found anywhere else. Meanwhile the French claimed to hold all the vast regions to the north and west of the English colonies, and, whenever there was war between France and England in Europe, there was also war between the French and English colonies in America. By the Peace of Utrecht in 1713 the French colony of *Acadie* was given up to Great Britain, and became the colony of *Nova Scotia*. But, on the other hand, the French were really colonizing at the mouth of the Mississippi, in their province of *Louisiana*, and in 1718 they founded the city of *New Orleans*. The last of the English colonies in these parts was *Georgia*, which was founded in 1723. This made up the number of the thirteeen colonies in North America, which still remain as the thirteen oldest States of the American Union.

16. **Summary.**—Thus, during this period, France gained a great increase of territory, and more than once she caused great alliances to be formed to withstand her. The great Spanish monarchy was divided, all its outlying possessions in Europe being separated from Spain. England and Scotland were more firmly joined together, and began to take a leading part in all continental affairs, and Great Britain for the first time won a footing in the Mediterranean. In Germany the Emperors became mere Austrian princes: but, as Austrian princes, they gained a great increase of power, both in Italy, from which they had so long been shut out, and in South-Eastern Europe as Kings of Hungary. In Northern Germany also we see the

beginning of a great and more strictly German power in the growth of *Brandenburg* or *Prussia.* In Italy, Savoy advanced, and Venice still maintained a gallant, though on the whole a losing, fight against the Turks. In Northern Europe Sweden had, by the end of the period, quite lost the great position which it held at the beginning, though it had gained some territory at the expense of Denmark. Poland was fast sinking, while the greatness of Russia was beginning. The power of the Turks was now much less to be feared, and, if they gained territory from Venice, they lost their possessions in Hungary and the neighbouring lands. In India the Dutch drove the Portuguese from the Islands, and the English settlements in India itself began. Colonization went on steadily in North America, and the English colonies were decidedly getting the upper hand. In the way of learning and literature, the United Provinces still produced great scholars and political writers; but for literature in their own tongues England and France certainly stood at the head. Many of the most famous writers of both those languages, and also some of the chief philosophers, belong to this time. Spain and Italy had greatly sunk; and Germany had not thoroughly recovered from the Thirty Years' War, though it is impossible not to mention the great scholar and philosopher Leibnitz. Generally, French influence had too much power in Germany just now for anything very original to be done.

CHAPTER XV.

THE RISE OF RUSSIA.

Character of the period (1)—*rivalry of Austria and Prussia* (2)—*revival of the power of Spain; reign of the Emperor Charles the Sixth; exchange of the Kingdoms of Sardinia and Sicily* (2)—*War of the Polish Election* (2)—*the Pragmatic Sanction* (2)—*War of the Austrian Succession; Prussian conquest of Silesia; election of Charles the Seventh* (3)—*Maria Theresa; her husband Francis elected Emperor* (3)—*Frederick the Great; the Seven Years' War* (3)—*reign of Joseph the Second* (3)—*the Hanoverian Kings in England; attempt of the Pretender; dealings with France, Spain, and Sweden* (4)—*War with Spain; share of England in continental wars; administration of Pitt* (4)—*revolt of the American colonies; war with France and Spain* (4)—*independence of Ireland* (4)—*reign of Lewis the Fifteenth; annexation of Corsica and Lorraine* (5)—*improved state of things in Spain; the Family Compact; administration of Pombal in Portugal* (6)—*changes in Italy; advance of Savoy; revolution in Genoa and Corsica* (7)—*the Popes* (7)—*Reign of Peter the Great in Russia; his conquests from Sweden and other powers; rise of Russia* (8)—*reigns of women in Russia; Catharine the Second; conquest of Crim Tartary* (8)—*affairs of Poland; the three partitions* (8)—*loss of power and territory by Sweden; state of Denmark and the Duchies* (9)—*affairs of the Netherlands; the Stadholders in the United Provinces made hereditary; revolts in the Austrian Netherlands* (10)—*success of the Turks against Austria* (11)—*their wars with Russia; successive losses of territory; dealings of Russia with the Christian nations* (11)—*growth of the English power in India; career of Clive; relation of England to the native states; trial of Warren Hastings* (12)—*the English Colonies in America; conquest of Canada* (12)—*revolt of the colonies; foundation of the United States* (13)—*cession of Florida* (13)—*Summary* (14).

1. **Character of the Period.**—The greatest change which took place in Europe during the time to which we have now come was undoubtedly the growth of the great power of *Russia*. No other state in Europe changed in anything like the same degree till quite the last years of the eighteenth century. Still Russia did not come to at all the same kind of rank which had been held by France, and, before that, by Spain. Nor did Russia rise to its greatness by displacing France in the way in which France rose by displacing Spain. Therefore, though this chapter is called after the greatest event of the period, still Russia will not be the centre of our story in the same way that the Empire was for so long, and afterwards Spain and France. In fact there is not during this time any one power in Europe which stands out in any marked way above all others. There are several great powers which are much more nearly on a level than before, and among them one very important one is growing up in the form of Prussia. Indeed a great part of this period is taken up with rivalries between France and England, and between Prussia and Austria. And it is specially characteristic of this time that France and Spain, the two great *Bourbon* powers are commonly allied against England. In short, no power in Europe held a higher place at this time than Great Britain. Without exercising any general dominion or making any general conquests, England had a hand in nearly everything that went on. But we must, in this chapter, make the Imperial House of Austria the centre of our story, as hardly anything

happened during this whole time in which that House had not a direct share.

2. **The Reign of Charles the Sixth.**—The greater part of the German history of this period is taken up with the rivalry between the Austrian House, the family of the Kings of Hungary and Archdukes of Austria, out of whom the Emperors were now chosen almost as a matter of course, and the *House of Hohenzollern*, the House of the Kings of Prussia and Electors of Brandenburg, who had begun to rise into greatness under the Great Elector. But this did not begin till some time later, not till after the death of the Emperor Charles the Sixth. The first disturbance came—what we should hardly have expected—from Spain. The new French King of Spain, Philip the Fifth, under his minister, *Cardinal Alberoni*, tried to get back the lands which Spain had lost, especially the kingdom of Sardinia, which had passed to the Emperor, and that of Sicily, which had passed to the Duke of Savoy. The Spaniards actually conquered Sardinia, and went some way towards conquering Sicily. But France, England, and the United Provinces presently joined the Emperor in the *Quadruple Alliance* against Spain, and the end of it was that Spain had to give up her projects, and the Emperor and the King of Sicily exchanged their two Italian kingdoms. Thus the Emperor Charles the Sixth became *King of the Two Sicilies*, like Frederick the Second, and the Dukes of Savoy became *Kings of Sardinia*, the title by which they were known till the present King became *King of Italy*. This was in 1720, and in the same year the Emperor made what is called a *Pragmatic Sanction*, which was guaranteed by the chief powers of Europe, and by which all his hereditary dominions, Hungary, Sicily, Austria, and the rest, were to pass to his heirs female, in case he left no son. Presently this Emperor got entangled in a series of unsuccessful wars. On the

death of Augustus the Strong, in 1733, there was a double election to the crown of Poland between *Frederick Augustus Elector of Saxony*, the son of the late king, and *Stanislaus*, who had before been made King by Charles the Twelfth. The Emperor and Russia supported Augustus, but, as Lewis the Fifteenth had married the daughter of Stanislaus, he took upon him to make war on the Emperor, and he was joined by *Charles Emmanuel the Third*, King of Sardinia, and by Philip of Spain, or rather by his wife *Elizabeth of Parma*, both of whom had designs on the Austrian possessions in Italy. Thus a war took place, in which the two Bourbon Kings were joined against the Emperor, and in which for once England took no part. The end of this war, called the *War of the Polish Election*, was that the House of Austria lost the greater part of its Italian dominions. There was, as usual, a good deal of shifting among the smaller duchies, but the important changes were that the Two Sicilies were given to a younger son of the King of Spain—making a third Bourbon kingdom in Europe—and part of the Duchy of Milan was given to the King of Sardinia, whose frontier, as usual, thus advanced a little. And not only the House of Austria, but the Empire also lost, for it was settled that the Duchy of Lorraine, a fief of the Empire, should pass to Stanislaus—who gave up his claim to the crown of Poland—for life, and should be joined to France at his death. Thus France again advanced at the expense of Germany. The Duke of Lorraine, *Francis*, who had married *Maria Theresa*, the daughter of the Emperor Charles, got the succession to the Grand Duchy of Tuscany, where the line of the Medici was dying out, instead of his own Duchy of Lorraine.

3. **The Wars of Austria and Prussia.**—It was in this way settled that the hereditary dominions of the House of Austria should pass to the *House of Lorraine*, as representing the House of Habsburg in the

female line. And it was no doubt expected that the Empire and the Kingdom of Germany would pass quietly along with the hereditary states. And all this did happen in the end, but not till after much disputing and fighting. When the Emperor Charles died in 1740, all his hereditary dominions, the Kingdoms of Hungary and Bohemia, the Archduchy of Austria, and the rest, passed, according to the Pragmatic Sanction, to his daughter Maria Theresa, who was of course called by her highest title, that of *Queen of Hungary*. The Empire of course was at the disposal of the Electors, and there was an interregnum of two years. But, notwithstanding the Pragmatic Sanction, various princes began to lay claim to the whole, or to particular parts, of the dominions of the House of Austria. Above all, *Charles Elector of Bavaria* gave himself out as the rightful heir, and his claim was supported by France. Meanwhile *Frederick the Second of Prussia*, commonly called *Frederick the Great*, who had just succeeded his father Frederick William, and had inherited from him a well-disciplined army, put forth a claim to the greater part of the *Duchy of Silesia*, and presently took possession of it by force. The next year the French and Bavarians overran Austria; and in 1742 the Elector of Bavaria was elected Emperor as *Charles the Seventh.* Maria Theresa had now to take refuge in Hungary, where, notwithstanding all that the Hungarians had suffered from her predecessors, she found great zeal in her cause. Presently England and Sardinia came to her help, and the war went on in Germany till 1745, when Charles the Seventh died, and Maria Theresa's husband Francis was elected Emperor. From this time she was called the *Empress-Queen*, being Queen of Hungary in her own right and Empress as wife of the Emperor Francis. The war went on between the Empress-Queen, England, and the United Provinces on one side, and France and Spain on the other, till 1748, when Silesia was formally given up to the King of Prussia. It was under Frederick the Great that Prussia, the growth of which had begun under the Great Elector, rose to be one of the chief powers of Europe. He was a philosopher and writer, and, when he was not at war, he did much to make things better within his kingdom. But there was a good deal more fighting to come before the end of his reign, for in 1756 another war broke out between him and the Empress-Queen. This was called the *Seven Years' War.* Now things turned about, for not only Russia, Poland, and Sweden, but even France was on the Austrian side, and Frederick was surrounded by enemies and left alone on the continent. England however joined him, and in 1762 *Peter the Third of Russia*, who was a great admirer of Frederick, changed sides. The way in which Frederick bore up for so long against so many enemies was one of the greatest triumphs of military skill on record. There was another smaller war in Germany in 1777 about the succession of *Bavaria*, between Frederick and the *Emperor Joseph the Second.* Joseph had been elected King of the Romans in 1764, and he succeeded his father in 1765, being also made by his mother fellow-sovereign of her hereditary dominions. In 1780 Maria Theresa died, and Joseph reigned alone. Joseph had great schemes of reform in all his dominions, but he was too fond of putting everything to rights according to his own notions, without regard to the old laws of his different kingdoms, so that in the end he did more harm than good. In this way he tried to sweep away all the old institutions of Hungary, but just before his death in 1790 he restored them. He was succeeded by his brother, *Leopold the Second*, and he in 1792 by the last Emperor, *Francis the Second.* By this time quite a new state of things was beginning throughout Europe.

4. **Great Britain.**—For a great part of this time during which *Great Britain* was so much mixed

up with the affairs of the continent, she had herself a foreign King. *George the First* could not even speak English, and he thought much more of his Electorate than of his Kingdom. The same may be said of *George the Second* also, though he had got so far as to speak English. Thus England got mixed up in several wars with which she had not much to do. At the beginning of George the First's reign, Lewis the Fourteenth, just before his death, abetted an attempt made in 1715 by the son of James the Second, who called himself *James the Third*, to win the crowns of England and Scotland, for of course he did not acknowledge the Union of the two kingdoms. This attempt failed, and England was on good terms, and even in alliance, with the *Duke of Orleans*, who was Regent for the young King *Lewis the Fifteenth*. This was the time when England joined with France and the Emperor Charles to withstand Spain. This time England really was threatened, for Spain now took up the cause of the Pretender, as did Charles of Sweden, who was angry because the King of Great Britain, as Elector of Hanover, had got his possessions in north-western Germany. In George the Second's reign we had another war with Spain, which began in 1739, and which was forced on the King and his Minister, *Sir Robert Walpole*, by the general wish of the people, who were stirred up by tales of wrongs done to Englishmen by the Spaniards in America. But little came of this war, except some additions to geographical knowledge in the shape of the famous voyages of *Lord Anson*. Then, from 1741 to 1748, England plunged into a war on the continent about a matter with which she had nothing to do at all, namely the war of the *Austrian Succession*, in which, as we have seen, England took the side of the Queen of Hungary, and France that of the King of Prussia and the Emperor Charles the Seventh. Nothing came of this war either, as the English and French gave back their conquests to each other at the end of it; but it should be remembered that in 1745 the son of the old Pretender, *Charles Edward*, with French help, made an attempt to gain the British crowns for his father. Scotland he actually did hold for a while, and he kept court at Edinburgh and even held Carlisle, but this rebellion was quelled, like the earlier one, at the *Battle of Culloden.* Then a war with France arose out of the quarrels between the colonists of the two nations in America, and this war got mixed up with the Seven Years' War in Germany. The war, as far as England was concerned, was chiefly waged by sea and in America; and under the administration of *Mr. Pitt*, afterwards *Earl of Chatham*, many victories and conquests were made, especially in the year 1759. The war went on into the reign of George the Third, which began in 1760, and it was ended in 1763 by the *Peace of Paris*, by which England got back much that had been lost by the war, and greatly enlarged her American possessions. But presently, in the reign of George the Third, the greater part of those possessions were lost altogether. An attempt to impose taxes on the colonists led to resistance. The thirteen colonies, from New England to Georgia, revolted, and in 1776 they declared themselves independent, and thus made the beginning of the great Federal Republic of the *United States.* The French stepped in during the war to help the colonists, and they were presently joined by Spain and the United Provinces; and, when peace was made in 1783, Great Britain had to acknowledge the independence of the States and to give back Minorca to Spain. But Gibraltar, her other Spanish possession, was kept, and its defence during this war against the forces of France and Spain is one of the exploits of which Englishmen are most proud. In 1782 Ireland, which had hitherto been a kingdom dependent, first on England and then on Great Britain, became independent, the two kingdoms of

Great Britain and Ireland now having the same King, but distinct and independent Parliaments. It was also during this time that the English power vastly extended itself in India, but that will be better spoken of in a separate section. During all these wars Great Britain commonly kept herself to her position as an insular power. She made no attempt at winning continental dominion, as she had done in the times of the old wars with France. Her only outlying possessions in Europe were Gibraltar and Minorca; on the other hand, though foreign powers gave help to pretenders to the British Crown, there was no serious attempt on the part of any enemy to get possession of any part of the British islands. The true object of these wars was dominion in distant parts of the world, and the great gains and losses of England and France were not made in Europe, but in America and India. It marks quite a new state of things that this should be so. Europe had now ceased to be the only world of European nations. The great maritime powers held dominions in the East and West greater than they possessed at home; and the colonies which England lost have grown into a great English-speaking nation in the New World.

5. **France.**—The long reign of Lewis the Fourteenth was followed by the reign, nearly as long, of his great-grandson Lewis the Fifteenth, who also came to the crown in his childhood, and reigned till 1774. Lewis the Fourteenth, with all that is to be said against him both as a man and as a King, was at least a ruler with a strong will, who had objects, and who largely carried those objects out. But Lewis the Fifteenth, though not without capacity, wilfully gave himself up to vice and idleness and the dominion of unworthy favourites. Yet France, as we have already seen, kept up her position as a great power throughout his reign, and she even gained some increase of territory. We have already seen how France took a

leading part in all the chief wars of this time—how, except in the first war, she was always in alliance with Spain, and opposed to England, and how her wars with England were mainly carried on by sea, and among the colonial possessions of the two countries. In Europe France extended herself in two places during this time, namely in *Lorraine*, where the Duchy, which had been given to King Stanislaus for life and which had greatly flourished under him, was joined to France at his death in 1766. And, as by this time nearly the whole of Elsass had been annexed bit by bit, the lands which France had taken from the Empire since the first seizure of the Three Bishopricks now formed a large and compact territory. The other gain of France at this time was in quite another part of Europe, namely the Italian island of *Corsica*. This had been for a long time subject to the commonwealth of Genoa. But the Genoese government was oppressive, and the Corsicans revolted more than once. Their chief leaders were the two *Paoli*, father and son, of whom the second is by far the better known. The Genoese called in the French to help them, and at last, in 1768, they gave up their rights to France, and the French presently conquered the island. These annexations happened during the reign of Lewis the Fifteenth, during which time the internal state of the kingdom was getting worse and worse. His grandson Lewis the Sixteenth tried to make things better as well as he could; but he was quite unfit for such a task, and he had in the end to suffer for the misgovernment of his forefathers, and for the despotism under which they had brought their own kingdom and so many lands which they had added to it.

6. **Spain.**—We have already seen that Spain under the new Bourbon dynasty, showed, perhaps because her dominions were now so much smaller,

much more of life than she had shown during the latter part of the seventeenth century. This was shown both in a marked improvement in her government at home and in a vast advance in her European position. If her attempts to win back her lost territory failed, she was able to set up Spanish princes on more than one throne in Italy. In the time of Alberoni we have seen that France and England were united against Spain; in the later wars it was the other way, and the Bourbon kingdoms of France and Spain were united, by what was called the *Family Compact*, against England and the allies of England on the continent. Presently they both set upon *Portugal*, as being an ally of England. The reigning King of Portugal was *Joseph*, who had an able minister called the *Marquess of Pombal*. By the brave resistance of the Portuguese and the help of the English, the French and Spanish invaders were driven back. During this period the *Jesuits* were driven out of both Spain and Portugal, having been found, as they were in most countries, to be dangerous to the civil power.

7. **Italy.**—During this period Italy again gained some show of independence as compared with its state in the seventeenth century. It still formed a collection of distinct principalities and commonwealths, of which the commonwealths were oligarchies and the principalities despotisms, and most of the princes were members of foreign royal families. Little room was thus left for any real national feeling. Still the whole country was not utterly under the power of one foreign King, as it had been in the days of the Spanish dominion. On the other hand, the commonwealth of Venice, which had done such great things in the sixteenth and seventeenth centuries, seemed to lose all strength and life after the loss of Peloponnêsos. For a moment indeed after the Peace of Utrecht, and still more after the exchange of Sicily

and Sardinia, it might seem that Italy was as completely held down by the *German* branch of the House of Austria as it had before been by the *Spanish* branch. Among the other states there were constant changes during the several wars, but things were at last settled by the Peace of 1748. One Bourbon prince from Spain, *Charles*, who afterwards succeeded to the Crown of Spain, was settled in the Kingdom of the Two Sicilies, another became Duke of *Parma and Piacenza*, and the Emperor Francis was Grand Duke of Tuscany, where he was succeeded in 1765 by his son Leopold, who afterwards was Emperor. Leopold did a vast deal for his duchy, and was as good a ruler as a despotic prince can be. But the only really national princes in Italy were those of the House of Savoy, who were now Kings of Sardinia, *Victor Amadeus* the Second and *Charles Emmanuel* the Third. They took a part in every war, and were not very scrupulous about changing sides, but they always gained something in the end. This time, by the Peace of 1748, they gained another part of the Duchy of Milan, while the rest was left to the House of Austria. In all these changes the people were handed over from one master to another without their wishes being thought of at all. The only parts of Italy where any life remained among the people at this time were Genoa and Corsica. In the war of the Austrian Succession Genoa took the side of France, so in 1746 it was occupied by the Austrians. But the people, without any help from the oligarchical government, rose up and drove the Austrians out, a revolution which had a good deal of effect on the course of the war in those parts. And we have seen that, as the people of Genoa rose against the yoke of Austria, so the people of Corsica rose against the yoke of Genoa, till they were handed over to France. The Popes of this time, especially *Benedict the Fourteenth* and *Clement the Fourteenth*, were mostly very good men, but they had ceased to be of any importance as temporal princes, and the best of them were unable to make any thorough reform in their own dominions. Clement the Fourteenth, who is perhaps better known by his family name of *Ganganelli*, altogether put down the Order of the Jesuits in 1773, but it was afterwards set up again.

8. **Russia and Poland.**—We now come to what is really the greatest event during this time, namely, the wonderful rise of Russia. For this we must go some way back to an earlier period, so as to tell the story straight on. Russia was already a powerful state in its own part of the world, but it was quite cut off from any dealings with Europe in general till the reign of *Peter the Great*. He began to reign together with his brother *Ivan* in 1682, and alone in 1689. During their joint reign Poland finally gave up to Russia a great deal of the Russian territory which she had formerly held. Presently Peter began to turn his mind to naval affairs. He improved his one haven of *Archangel*, and presently, in 1696, he conquered *Azof* from the Turks, so that he now had a haven on the Black Sea. Then he twice travelled in various countries, especially Holland and England, to learn such things as might be useful for his own people. Between his two journeys came his war with Charles the Twelfth of Sweden, which in the end turned to the greatest advantage of Russia. For Peter got Livonia and the other possessions of Sweden east of the Baltic, and so he had a footing on a third sea. Within this newly-gained territory he founded his new capital of *Saint Petersburg*, which thus supplanted Moscow, as Moscow had supplanted the earlier capitals. Later in his reign he extended his borders on the other Russian sea, the Caspian Sea, at the expense of Persia. He took the title of *Emperor of all the Russias*, which amounted to a claim over the Russian provinces held by Poland, and which besides gave great offence to

the German Emperors of the West. He made many changes in the internal state of his dominions, bringing the clergy under the control of the civil power, and making improvements in many ways, though it must be remembered that improvements of this kind, when made by the single will of a despot, do in fact only make his despotism stronger. Still Peter is entitled to the honour of having raised his country from a very low position in Europe to a very great one. His policy was carried on by his widow *Catharine*, who succeeded him in 1725: for the crown of Russia passed, like the old Roman Empire, sometimes by will and sometimes by revolution, without any very certain rule of succession. During the greater part of the eighteenth century the throne was filled by women, *Anne* the niece of Peter, *Elizabeth* his daughter, and lastly *Catharine the Second*, who succeeded in 1762 by the murder of her husband *Peter the Third*, and reigned till 1796. With some checks, *Azof* for instance being twice or thrice lost and won again in the wars with the Turks, Russia, notwithstanding its internal revolutions, went on advancing in the face of other nations. Under Catharine the Second the great conquest of *Crim Tartary* or *Crimea* was made. Russia now got rid of the last trace of the old Tartar dominion, and she again had free access to the Euxine, as when Russian fleets threatened Constantinople in the ninth and tenth centuries. This conquest on the part of Russia was very much like the conquest of Granada by Ferdinand and Isabel. But the chief advance of Russia towards Western Europe was made by her share in the successive partitions of *Poland*. The internal government of that country was so bad, both the King and the people being subject to a tumultuous nobility, that the state grew weaker and weaker. The last two Kings, *Augustus Elector of Saxony*, son of Augustus the Strong, and *Stanislaus Poniatowski*, a native Pole were forced on the country by Russia, and attempts at internal reform, as being likely to make the kingdom stronger, were always checked. At last, in 1772, the Empress Catharine of Russia, Frederick the Great of Prussia, and the Empress-Queen, as Queen of Hungary—though the last very unwillingly—joined together to *partition* Poland, each taking certain provinces. In 1793 another partition was made by Russia and Prussia only, and in 1795 Poland was altogether destroyed as an independent nation, and its remaining territory was divided among its three neighbours. What was then understood by *Poland* took in both the old Kingdom of Poland, the Duchy of Lithuania, and the Russian provinces which were held by Poland. Of this, Russia got back most of her old territory, and she took also the greater part of Lithuania. Prussia took West Prussia, the greater part of old Poland, and a small part of Lithuania. Austria or Hungary (whichever we are to call it) took the rest of old Poland, and some territory which had been Russian. In the Russian provinces the mass of the people were still Russian, and they had often suffered persecution from Poland for cleaving to the Eastern Church. This however does not justfy the breach of the law of nations, and the other two powers, which divided Poland itself, had not even thus much of excuse to make. By this partition, Russia, which had hitherto stood on the confines of Europe, was brought into the middle of the continent and into the thick of European affairs.

9. **Northern Europe.**—During this time the Scandinavian Kingdoms, especially Sweden, were of much less account than they had been in the period before it. Neither of them now took much share in the general affairs of Europe. Sweden had had more than one war with Russia, and in 1743 she had to give up the district called *Carelia* on the Gulf of Finland, and this time without gaining any territory to the West.

The history of the country is mainly remarkable for its internal revolutions. After the changes of 1720 the government became almost wholly aristocratic; but in 1772 the royal power was set up again. In Denmark meanwhile the government remained an absolute monarchy, but the country was on the whole well governed and prosperous, and its naval power especially was greatly increased. During this time too the ever-shifting Duchies of *Sleswick* and *Holstein* were at last wholly united with the Danish Crown. Holstein was held as a fief of the Empire, while Sleswick was not.

10. **The Netherlands.**—During this time those provinces of the Netherlands which had belonged to Spain were held by the House of Austria, while the Seven United Provinces remained independent; but, like Sweden, their importance in Europe in the eighteenth century was very much less than it had been in the seventeenth. In the war of the Austrian Succession, the United Provinces supported the Queen of Hungary, and the Austrian provinces were overrun by the French. But when, in 1747, the Dutch territory also was invaded, a change in the internal constitution followed, by which the Prince of Orange, *William the Fourth*, was made *hereditary Stadholder*. His own principality of Orange had before this been annexed by France. During the war between England and France which arose out of the revolt of the American colonies, there was a short war between England and the United Provinces, but both the grounds of quarrel and the terms of peace had almost wholly to do with the colonial possessions of the two countries. Presently there were disturbances in the country and dissatisfaction with the Stadholder, *William the Fifth*, which gave both the King of Prussia and the Emperor Joseph the Second excuses for interfering. By the end of this time, about 1790, the United Provinces had sunk into utter insignificance, being almost wholly

under the control of Prussia. In the *Austrian Netherlands* also the changes made by Joseph the Second led to revolts.

11. **The Turks.**—The power of the Turks during this time had altogether ceased to be dreaded by Christian nations. The advances of Russia during this time form the greater part of the European history of Turkey, but it was not till the reign of Catharine the Second that the advantage set steadily in on the Russian side, and in the early part of the period Turkey was decidedly successful on the side of Austria. During the reign of *Mahmoud the First*, who reigned from 1730 to 1754, in a war which began in 1737, the Turks, by the *Peace of Belgrade* in 1739, recovered from Austria the city of *Belgrade*, and all that had been given up by the Peace of Passarowitz. And by this treaty Russia was not to keep any fleet in the Black Sea. But in the war between *Catharine the Second* and *Mustapha the Third*, which began in 1769, the advantages were wholly on the Russian side. The loss of territory by Turkey during the reign of Catharine was great. By the *Peace of Kainardji*, in 1774, the Sultans gave up their superiority over the Tartar Khans of Crimea. The Khan was then recognized as an independent power, but the country was soon afterwards conquered by Russia. By the next war, which was ended by the *Treaty of Jassy* in 1792, the Turkish frontier fell back to the Dniester. But still more important than these losses of territory was the system of interference in the internal concerns of the Sultan's dominions which went on from this time on the part of Russia. As the Turkish government grew weaker, and as the tribute of children was no longer levied, the Christian nations, Greeks, Slaves, and others, which were under the Turkish yoke, began to revolt whenever they had a chance. In so doing they were always encouraged by Russia, though they seldom really gained anything by

Russian meddling in their affairs. Still this tendency of the Christian nations to revolt, and the encouragement given to these revolts by Russia, all mark the beginning of a new state of things in Eastern Europe, and one which is going on still. It should specially be noticed that by the treaty of Kainardji Russia obtained certain rights of interference in the Danubian Principalities of *Moldavia* and *Wallachia*, which were under the superiority of the Sultans, without forming part of their immediate dominions. In these wars, Russia, which sixty years before had had no European haven except on the White Sea, was able to send fleets into the Mediterranean. She was now fully established, not only as one of the chief powers of Europe, but as the ruling power in the south-east as well as in the north-east. The Eastern Church, which had been so long kept down under Mahometan bondage, now again begins to be of importance, as being the religion both of the greater part of the Christian subjects of the Turks and also of Russia, which professed to be their defender.

12. **The English Power in India.**—It was in the course of this period that the great English dominion in India grew up out of the mercantile settlements of the East India Company. But this was not till after a hard struggle with the French, who at one time seemed likely to gain the greatest power in the peninsula. In 1746, during the war of the Austrian Succession in Europe, *Labourdonnais*, the French governor of Mauritius, seized *Madras*, which was kept till the end of the war. But meanwhile *Dupleix*, the governor of *Pondicherry*, the chief French settlement in India, formed great schemes of French dominion in the East, and wars went on between the French and the English in India, under cover of supporting different native princes. These wars did not stop even when France and England were at peace, in the time between the two wars of

the Austrian Succession and the Seven Years' War. In 1756 the English settlement at *Calcutta* was taken by *Suraj-ad-dowla*, the Nabob of *Bengal*, one of the princes who owed a nominal vassalage to the Great Mogul. Now it was that many Englishmen died in what was called the *Black Hole*. But now came the great advance of the English power under *Clive*, and the battle of *Plassy* in 1757, in which the Nabob, with a vast native army and with a small body of French auxiliaries, was utterly overthrown by Clive's little army of English and of natives under English discipline. This battle laid the real foundation of the English dominion in India. But the war with France still went on in Southern India with varying success till the Peace of 1763, when *Pondicherry*, which had been taken by the English, was restored to the French. Since then it has been commonly taken and given back whenever there has been any war between England and France. But neither the French power in India nor that of any other European nation has, since the days of Clive, been able to stand up against that of England. Since that time the English dealings with India have been much like those of ancient Rome in the Mediterranean lands. One state after another has first become dependent and then has been incorporated, just as when a kingdom or commonwealth was made a Roman province. It must be remembered that all this time the English dominion in India was not in the hands of the King's Government, but was still in those of the Company. It was only in 1784 that the affairs of India were at all brought into the hands of the Home Government by the institution of the *Board of Control*, a body acting in the King's name, to control in certain cases the management of affairs by the Company. After Clive, the most famous name in the history of British India was that of the Governor-General *Warren Hastings*, who was impeached and tried before the House of Lords on various charges of oppression and misgovernment, and was acquitted after a trial which lasted many years.

13. **The Independence of the United States.**—*Georgia* was the last English colony that was founded in North America during this time. The English colonies lay wholly along the east coast; the French possessions in Canada and Louisiana hemmed them in to the north and west, and the Spanish colony of *Florida* to the south. The colonies of the different European nations took a large share in the several wars of the century. In 1759 Canada was conquered by the English troops, British and colonial; this war was memorable for the victory and death of *General Wolfe* at *Quebec.* A large French-speaking population in Canada was thus handed over to English rule, and the French settlements now no longer stood in the way of the growth of the English colonies to the west. By the same treaty of 1763 Florida was given up by Spain to England, and Louisiana was divided between England and Spain, the Mississippi being the boundary. The French were thus quite shut out of North America. Then came the attempt on the part of Great Britain to tax the colonies, their revolt, and the assistance given them by France, and afterwards by Spain. When the colonies in 1776 declared themselves independent, each colony formed an independent State, joined together only by a very lax Confederation. But, when the war was over, a closer union was found necessary, and in 1789 the constitution of the *United States of America,* as a perfectly organized Federal commonwealth, remarkably like the constitution of the Achaian League in old times, was fully established. Each *State* kept its independence in its own affairs, but the *Union* formed one nation in all dealings with other powers. The first President of the new commonwealth was *George Washington,* who had been the great leader of the colonists during the war. This constitution was gradually accepted by all the

States. By the treaty of 1783 Florida was given back to Spain, and the late British conquest of Canada, with the colonies of *New Brunswick*, *Nova Scotia*, and *Newfoundland*, remained part of the British dominions. The States were thus hemmed in to the north, and for a while to the south also; but they had free power of growth to the west, where new settlements were quickly founded and were admitted into the Union as independent States on the same terms as the first thirteen.

14. **Summary.**—The greatest events during this period are thus to be found in the furthest parts of the civilized world. The rise of Russia in Eastern Europe, the foundation of the English dominion in India, and the establishment of the United States in America, are the three greatest events of the time. They are more than mere common conquests or acquisitions of territory. Each one of them is the real beginning of a new state of things. The English now fairly took their place as the leading people of the earth in colonization and distant dominion. The British Empire in India is the greatest example of distant dominion, as distinguished from proper colonization, on the part of any European power; and the establishment of the United States as an independent power has given to a people of English birth and speech the means of growing to far greater extent and power than they could have done if they had remained dependent on the mother country. Geographical knowledge was also greatly increased by the more thorough survey of the islands of the Eastern Ocean, including the vast island, or rather continent, of *Australia*, which just at the end of the period with which we are now dealing, opened another field for English colonization. France was now altogether driven out of the world of distant dominion, and the other colonizing powers, Spain, Portugal, and Holland, could at most keep what they had got. None of the changes which happened in

Western Europe at this time were at all on the same scale as these, for the gains and losses of the maritime powers had been made much less in Europe than in their distant possessions. In Europe, the three Western powers, England, France, and Spain, kept nearly the same position at the end of the period which they had held at the beginning. The United Provinces and the Scandinavian kingdoms had fallen from their momentary greatness, and Italy hardly existed, except as the battle-field for other powers, and as a land in which the younger branches of ruling families might be provided for. But the House of Savoy was still pushing its way, and it gained some increase of territory by nearly every fresh treaty of peace. But in Eastern Europe the advance of Russia, at once against Sweden, Poland, and Turkey, the way in which, from having been cooped up inland, she made her way into both the Baltic and the Mediterranean, and became a great and even threatening power, was the greatest European change of the time. Russia, after having been thrown back for so many ages, at last won the place which she had tried to win when she attacked Constantinople in the old times. Her advance is also remarkable as bringing into prominence a race and a religion which had long been kept in the background. The Slavonic nations with whom we have hitherto had most to do, the Poles, Bohemians, and others, belonged to the Western Church, and were more or less closely connected with the Western Empire. But with the rise of Russia, a Slavonic country which got its Christianity and civilization wholly from Constantinople, both the Slavonic race and the Eastern Church again rise into special importance. And so in some sort does the Eastern Empire also, by means of the influence which the Russian princes, as the most powerful princes of the Eastern Church, were able to exercise on those nations of their own Church, both Greek and Slavonic, which were still in bondage to the Turks. The advance of Prussia during the same time was very important, but it was not so important as this. The change was not so sudden, and it was not so great in itself. A new German power came to the front in Germany, and it has gradually grown to be the head of Germany, much in the same way as Wessex grew in England, Castile in Spain, and France in Gaul. But its rise did not, like the rise of Russia, bring a race and a religion from the background to the front. The partition of Poland, in which Russia and Prussia had the chief share, stands pretty well by itself in history ; disputed and tributary dominions have often been divided between several claimants, but there is no other case of a great and independent country being cut up in this way among its neighbours. These political changes and the rise of these new powers were very great events in themselves, and they were also closely connected with the stir in men's minds which went on during this time. During the eighteenth century men were speculating on religion, government, and society in a more daring way than they had ever speculated on so great a scale before. French and French-speaking writers, *Voltaire*, *Rousseau*, and others, were leading on men's minds towards that general crash of existing things, good and bad together, which marks the next period in so large a part of Europe. And rulers like the Emperor Joseph, Frederick of Prussia, and Catharine of Russia helped to the same end. For, though they ruled as absolute princes, yet the great changes which they made, both good and bad, tended to unsettle men's minds, and to make them more ready to break with the past altogether. This whole period then was one of very great importance, but it was mainly in the way of preparation for what was coming. It was a time of great advance in both physical and moral science, and one of great mechanical discovery. But in most branches of art, learning, and original composition the eighteenth century was below either the times before or the times after it. It seemed as if the world needed to be stirred up by some such general crash as was now near at hand.

CHAPTER XVI.

THE FRENCH REVOLUTION.

Character of the time (1)—*reign of Lewis the Sixteenth; the States-General of* 1789; *they become the National Assembly* (2)—*Constitution of* 1790; *abolition of monarchy; National Convention; execution of the King* (2)—*Reign of Terror; Robespierre; establishment of the Directory* (2)—*foreign wars of the Republic; rise of Napoleon Buonaparte* (2)—*annexations in Germany, Italy, and the Netherlands; wars in Switzerland and Egypt* (2)—*Buonaparte seizes the chief power as Consul; character of his rule; treaties of Luneville and Amiens* (2, 3)—*Buonaparte calls himself Emperor of the French and King of Italy* (3)—*conquests of Buonaparte; his dependent kings* (3)—*he invades Russia; liberation of Germany* (3)—*fall of Buonaparte; his return from Elba; battle of Waterloo; his final overthrow* (3)—*effects of the French Revolution in Germany; abolition of the Empire; title of Emperor of Austria; the new Kings; the Confederation of the Rhine* (4)—*Buonaparte's victories over Prussia and Austria; greatest extent of Buonaparte's dominion in Germany* (5)—*formation of the German Confederation* (5)—*changes in Italy; its resettlement at the Peace* (6)—*dealings of Buonaparte with Spain; Joseph Buonaparte made King; campaigns of the Duke of Wellington; return of Ferdinand the Seventh* (7)—*King John of Portugal goes to Brazil; liberation of Portugal* (7)—*changes in the Netherlands; union of the whole Netherlands into one Kingdom* (8)—*the French in*

Switzerland; the Helvetic Republic; the Act of Mediation; formation of the Swiss Confederation (9)—*share of England in the general War; bombardment of Copenhagen* (10)—*rebellion in Ireland; Union of Great Britain and Ireland* (10)—*war with the United States; settlement at the Peace* (10)—*Russian conquest of Finland; election of Bernadotte in Sweden; union of Sweden and Norway* (11)—*affairs of Denmark* (11)—*reigns of Paul and Alexander in Russia* (12)—*Peace of Tilsit; wars with Sweden, Turkey, and Persia* (12) *French invasion of Russia; Kingdom of Poland united with Russia* (12)—*decay of the Turkish Empire; independence of Servia, Egypt, and other provinces; Turkish wars with France and Russia; accession of Mahmoud* (13)—*English conquests in India; colonization of Australia* (14)—*revolutions of Hayti* (14)—*growth of the United States; purchase of Louisiana; abolition of slavery in the Northern States* (15)—*Summary* (16).

1. **Character of the Time.**—We have now come, we may almost say, to our own times, to times which a few old people still living can remember. And these times are so full of matter that it would be vain to try to do more here than to point out the general effect which the events which then happened had on the relations of the states of Europe to one another. It was a time which saw such an upsetting of the existing state of things everywhere as had never happened before in so short a space of time. The centre of everything during this time is *France;* and in France at this time men did what had never been done before; that is, they went on the fixed principle of changing everything, whether it were good or bad, wherever their power reached, both in their own country and elsewhere. There was a general change of everything, often out of a mere love of change, and there was in particular a silly way of imitating old Greek and Roman ways and names, even when they were nothing to the purpose. But in this general crash the evil of

the older times was largely swept away as well as the good, and means were at least given for a better state of things to begin in our own time.

2. **The French Republic.**—The events of the French Revolution must be told in the special History of France. It is enough to say here that *Lewis the Sixteenth*, the grandson of Lewis the Fifteenth, who succeeded him in 1774, had to pay the penalty of the misgovernment of so many Kings who had gone before him, and above all of the last two. Now that there was such a spirit of thought and speculation about in the world, men could no longer bear the abuses of the old French system of government, the absolute power of the King and the monstrous privileges of the nobles and clergy. The finances of the country too were in utter disorder, and generally there was need of reform in everything. Lewis the Sixteenth, an honest and well-intentioned man, but not strong enough for the place in which he found himself, tried hard to make things better, though perhaps not always in the wisest way. At last, in 1789, the *States-General* were called together, which had not met since 1614. They were presently changed into a *National Assembly*, which made the greatest changes in everything, abolishing all the old privileges, and giving all things as it were a fresh start. Among other things, they wiped out the old *provinces*, so many of which had once been independent states, and divided the whole country into *departments*, called in a new-fashioned way after rivers and mountains. The small part of Elsass which remained independent, and the territories of Venaissin and Avignon in the old Kingdom of Burgundy, which belonged to the Popes, were now finally swallowed up by France. Then came a time of great confusion and rapid changes. In 1790 a new constitution was made, by which the King's power was made very small indeed, and the old title of *King of the French* was revived. In 1792 monarchy was abolished,

and France became a Republic under the *National Convention;* in the next year the King was beheaded, and religion and everything else was swept away. Now came the *Reign of Terror;* one party after another as it rose to power put its enemies to death. Among the men who had the chief hand in this general destruction was the famous *Robespierre.* He was a native of *Arras* in Artois, but, owing to the conquests of Lewis the Fourteenth in the Netherlands, his country was now French. But, before long, a time of rather more quiet began under the *Directory.* Meanwhile France was at war with many of the powers of Europe; for Kings began to be afraid of the example of France spreading. In 1790 war began with the Emperor and the King of Prussia, and, directly after the King's beheading in 1793, war was declared against England also. Thus began the long *Wars of the French Revolution,* in which every part of Europe had a share at one time or another, and which went on, with some stoppages, till 1815. The first part of the war may be looked on as lasting till 1797. It went on in the Austrian Netherlands, along the Rhine, and in Italy, and it was in the Italian part of the war that *Napoleon Buonaparte* began to make himself famous. He too, like Robespierre, was a Frenchman only through the annexations of France, being an Italian of Corsica who had to learn the French language. His victories in Italy forced the Emperor Francis to give up the Austrian Netherlands to France, and Piedmont and Savoy were also annexed. This was the way in which things went on during the whole time; sometimes territories were actually added to France; sometimes they were made into separate states, nominal republics, which were altogether dependent on France. But for the old republics of Europe, whether aristocratic or democratic, no more respect was shown than for Popes or Kings. As the Emperor had given up so large a territory to France, that he might get something in exchange, he joined the French in destroying the ancient commonwealth of Venice, and they divided its dominions between them. France wished to get power in the east of Europe, and therefore took the Ionian Islands as part of her share. Then, in 1798, Buonaparte planned an expedition to Egypt, and, to get money, the Directory attacked Switzerland, because Bern was known to have a large treasure. Presently, in 1799, another war began against the Emperor, who was helped by Russia; this war chiefly went on in Switzerland. At home the Directory greatly mismanaged things, and, when Buonaparte came back the same year, he was easily able to upset it and to take all power into his own hands. An old Greek would have said that he made himself *Tyrant;* but, after the fashion of calling everything by Roman names, he first called himself *Consul* and then *Emperor;* he had a Senate and what not, being in truth a still more absolute ruler than ever Lewis the Fourteenth had been.

3. **Napoleon Buonaparte.**—Buonaparte was now master of France, and he came nearer to being master of Europe than any other one man had done before. For fifteen years the whole continent was in confusion, Kings and kingdoms being set up and put down again pretty much as it pleased him. But in France itself, though his rule was altogether despotic, and though in the end he made himself hateful by draining all the resources of the country for his endless wars, there can be no doubt that the land gained by having a time of quiet after the disorders of the Revolution. He restored the Christian religion, and, like Justinian, put out a code of laws for his dominions. During the time when he called himself Consul, peace was made with the Empire at *Luneville* in 1801, and with England at *Amiens* in 1802. By the former peace all Germany left of the Rhine was given up to France. The Rhine was in the Roman times the boundary between independent Germany and the Roman province of *Gaul;*

but the modern kingdom of *France* had never come anywhere near the Rhine till the annexations began in Elsass. But now France got the Rhine frontier from Basel to its mouth, or we might say, from its source to its mouth; for Switzerland was now merely a French dependency. In 1804 Buonaparte called himself *Emperor of the French,* and he crowned himself at Paris, having sent for the Pope to anoint him. In this his object was to give himself out as the successor of Charles the Great, not merely as the successor of any of the local Kings of France. For it was of course part of his plan that men should look, as Frenchmen commonly do, on the great German Emperor as a Frenchman. It shows how thoroughly the old notion of the Empire had died out, when such a pretence could have any effect on men's minds. Since Buonaparte's time the title of *Emperor*, which once meant so much, has ceased to have any particular meaning. Everybody that chooses now calls himself an Emperor; the title has even been borne by several adventurers in Mexico and the West Indies. But, besides calling himself Emperor of the French, Buonaparte made part of Northern Italy into a kingdom, and called himself *King of Italy* in imitation of the old Emperors. No King of Italy had been crowned since the Emperor Charles the Fifth was crowned at Bologna, but now Buonaparte was crowned again the next year at Milan. Before he had taken up these titles, he was again at war with England, and he planned an invasion of that country, which he never carried out. For the power of France by sea was broken by the English under Lord *Nelson* at the great battle of *Trafalgar.* From this time Buonaparte did much as he pleased by land, but the smallest arm of the sea stopped him everywhere. Meanwhile his great land campaigns spread with little stoppage over the years from 1805 to 1809. He now brought the greater part of Western Europe more or less under his power. He set up his brothers and other dependents as Kings of Spain, Naples, Holland, and elsewhere, and he moved them from one kingdom to another, or joined their dominions on to France, just as he thought good. He cut short the dominions both of Prussia and Austria, and made himself really master of the rest of Germany, joining what he pleased to France, and calling himself *Protector* of the rest. In 1811 his power stood at its height. What he called the *French Empire* took in France with all its old conquests, Germany west of the Rhine, the Netherlands and the United Provinces, and North-west Germany also, so that the French frontier took in Hamburg and Lübeck, and reached to the Baltic. At the other end it took in all Western Italy, including Rome; the rest belonged to the *Kingdom of Italy*, of which Buonaparte called himself King. Beyond the Hadriatic a large territory made up of the former possessions of Austria and Venice and the Republic of *Ragusa* was also part of the French Empire. The Kingdom of Naples was held by his brother-in-law *Joachim Murat*, but Sicily and Sardinia were still held by their own Kings, because they were islands, and the British fleet could help them. Denmark was his ally, and Spain was under his brother. But presently deliverance began to come from two quarters. In 1812 Buonaparte thought good to invade Russia, but the climate fought against him as well as the people, and he had to come back the next year, for the first time, utterly discomfited. The next year, 1813, Germany began to rise against him, rather by a common impulse of the people than by any act of the German governments. But Austria, Prussia, Sweden, and most of the smaller German states, gradually joined against him. Germany was now set free in the great battle of *Leipzig*. Meanwhile, ever since 1808, when *Joseph Buonaparte* had been sent to be King of Spain, the British troops had been engaged in the deliverance of the peninsular kingdoms. Now it was that the *Duke of Wellington* won his great victories over several of Buonaparte's best generals. In 1814 the Allies entered France on both sides, the English from the south, the other powers from the east. Several battles were fought at both ends of the country. At last Paris was taken, Buonaparte abdicated, and he was allowed to hold the little island of *Elba*, keeping the title of Emperor. The French people were now quite weary of him, and they gladly welcomed the restoration of the old royal family in the person of the last King's brother, who called himself *Lewis the Eighteenth.* But in the next year, 1815, Buonaparte came back; he was received by the army, and reigned again for a few months, till the Allies again gathered their forces, and he was overthrown for ever by the English and Prussians at *Waterloo.* He now abdicated again; but this time he was not trusted to stay anywhere in Europe, but was kept in ward for the rest of his days in the island of *Saint Helena*, a British possession in the Atlantic between Africa and America. The wars of the French Revolution were now over. By a series of treaties made at *Paris* and *Vienna*, the boundaries of the different states of Europe were settled afresh, and France had to give up the conquests which she had made during the republic and in the time of Buonaparte. The boundaries of the restored kingdom did not greatly differ from what they had been before the wars of the Revolution began.

4. **The Fall of the Empire.**—The part of Europe which, next to France itself, was most affected by the French Revolution was *Germany.* The changes in Italy were in themselves equally great, but Italy had already been partitioned out over and over again, while Germany had never before fallen under a foreign dominion. It was during this time that the old state of things, and the old ideas which had lasted so long, came altogether to an end. The *Roman Empire* and the *Kingdom of Germany* were now abolished, even in name. First of all, as we have seen, the

Austrian Netherlands, which were now pretty well separated from the Empire, and all Germany west of the Rhine, including the three great archbishopricks of *Mainz*, *Köln*, and *Trier*, and the old royal city of *Aachen*, were all added to France. Meanwhile the princes who lost their dominions by the *Peace of Luneville* were allowed to make up for it at the cost of the bishopricks and free cities east of the Rhine, and a new electorate of *Hessen-Cassel* was made, whose Elector, as it turned out, never had any one to elect. In 1804, as soon as Buonaparte began to call himself Emperor of the French, *Francis the Second*, King of Hungary and Archduke of Austria, being Emperor-elect of the Romans and King of Germany, began to call himself *Hereditary Emperor of Austria*, whatever that meant. And in 1805, after the war had begun again, and after the Austrians and Russians had lost the great battle of *Austerlitz*, the Emperor made a treaty with Buonaparte at *Pressburg*, which was drawn up between the *Emperor of Germany and Austria* and the *Emperor of the French and King of Italy*. It was time that the Empire should come to an end, when its chief had in this way forgotten who he was. And so it happened within two years. Many of the German princes had by this time joined Buonaparte. They declared themselves independent of the Empire, and they began to call themselves by higher titles, *King of Bavaria*, *King of Würtemberg*, and so forth. They then made themselves into the *Confederation of the Rhine*, which was put under the protection of Buonaparte, and they added to their dominions such of the remaining free cities and smaller principalities as they thought good. This was in 1806, and in the same year the Emperor Francis formally resigned the Empire altogether, and no Roman Emperor has since been chosen. Thus the old Kingdom of Germany, which had gone on ever since the division of the dominions of Charles the

Great, and the Roman Empire, which had gone on in one shape or another ever since Augustus Cæsar, came at last to an end. The Kingdom of Burgundy was now wholly forgotten, and all of it was now either annexed to France or, being part of Switzerland, was quite under French influence. As for the third kingdom, that of Italy, we have seen that Buonaparte called himself King of it, though by the Treaty of Pressburg he promised that France and Italy should not be joined again after his time. Thus all traces of the old state of things passed away. But the former Emperor Francis still went on calling himself *Emperor of Austria*, and his successors in the Kingdom of Hungary, the Archduchy of Austria, and his other hereditary dominions, have gone on doing so ever since.

5. **The Settlement of Germany.**—The union of the German States, which had been so lax ever since the Peace of Westphalia, thus quite passed away. Buonaparte had now to deal with the separate states which had not submitted to him. Prussia had made a separate peace long before, and now, in 1806, the King *Frederick William the Third* made a league with France by which he obtained the Electorate of Hanover, which belonged to the King of Great Britain. But the yoke of the French alliance was too hard to bear, and a war broke out between France and Prussia, in which Prussia was supported by Saxony. Now came the great battle of *Jena*, in which the Prussians and their allies were utterly defeated. Saxony now gave way, and the *Elector* was made *King*, and joined the Confederation of the Rhine. In the next year Prussia was cut short at the *Peace of Tilsit;* her western dominions and some other districts were made into a *Kingdom of Westphalia*, of which Buonaparte made his brother *Jerome* King, while the lands which Prussia had taken from Poland, except West Prussia, were made into a *Grand Duchy of Warsaw*,

which was given to the new King of Saxony. Austria meanwhile, having again ventured on war in 1809, was overthrown at *Wagram*, and had to yield her south-western dominions to France and Bavaria, being thus quite cut off from Italy and the Hadriatic. Lastly, North-western Germany, including the free cities of *Lübeck*, *Bremen*, and *Hamburg*, was altogether joined on to France. To crown all, the German states were made to send men to help in Buonaparte's attack on Russia. Then, in 1813, came the uprising of the German people, which the German governments had to join one after another. And lastly, in 1815, at the *Congress of Vienna*, the state of Germany was finally settled as it stayed till a few years back. There was no longer an Emperor or a King of Germany; but the German princes and free cities, of which last four only, *Lübeck*, *Bremen*, *Hamburg*, and *Frankfurt*, were left, formed themselves by a lax Federal tie into the *German Confederation*. Many of the small states were swallowed up, and the boundaries of all were settled afresh. And it should be marked that several of the chief princes who were members of the Confederation joined it for parts of their dominions, but not for all. Francis of Austria, who had been Emperor, and his successors, were to be *Presidents of the Confederation;* they joined it for the Kingdom of Bohemia, the Archduchy of Austria, the County of Tyrol, &c., but not for the Kingdom of Hungary or their other dominions out of Germany. So the greater part of the Prussian dominions were within the Confederation, but the Kingdom of Prussia itself, that is, East Prussia and the Polish provinces, lay out of it. So too the Kings of Great Britain, Denmark, and the Netherlands—a new kingdom to be presently spoken of—were members of the Confederation for *Hanover* (which was now called a kingdom), *Holstein* and *Lauenburg*, and *Lüzelburg* severally. The German princes whom Buonaparte had set up as

Kings, those of Bavaria, Württemberg, and Saxony, kept their titles; but, as the King of Saxony had stuck to Buonaparte as long as he could, a large part of his kingdom was added to Prussia. All the princes promised free constitutions to their people, but most of them forgot to give them.

6. **Italy.**—Italy was as much tossed to and fro during these times as Germany. It is hardly worth while to mention all the little commonwealths and principalities which were set up and put down. The first conquests from Austria and Venice were made into the *Cisalpine Republic*, which was afterwards changed into Buonaparte's *Kingdom of Italy*. A large part, at last taking in Rome itself, was, after many shiftings, a *Ligurian Republic*, a *Kingdom of Etruria*, and what not, joined on to France, and the Pope, *Pius the Seventh*, was got into Buonaparte's power. In the South, first Buonaparte's brother Joseph and then his brother-in-law Murat held the Kingdom of Naples. When things were settled in 1815, the princes who had lost their dominions came back again. The King of the Two Sicilies, who had all along kept the island, got back the continental kingdom also. So the King of Sardinia got back Piedmont and Savoy, and the Grand Duchy of Tuscany and the lesser principalities were set up again, and the Pope again held Rome and his old temporal dominions. But the commonwealths were not set up again. Lucca became a Duchy; Genoa was joined on to Piedmont, and the Duchy of Milan and the Venetian dominions, which had changed their names so often, were made into the *Kingdom of Lombardy and Venice*, and joined on to Austria. Only little San Marino kept its freedom. Thus Germany and Italy both remained disunited, cut up among a number of absolute princes. But there was this difference between them: the German princes were Germans, and the country had a certain unity, however lax, in

the Confederation. But Italy was altogether cut up. A large part was held by Austria and by the Pope, and the other Kings and Dukes were not real Italian princes, but all looked to Austria as their chief. Piedmont indeed was held by a native prince, but its government still was despotic. This was the third time—under Charles the Fifth, under Charles the Sixth, and again under Francis the Second—that the House of Austria had the chief power in the Italian peninsula.

7. **Spain and Portugal.**—Under *Charles the Third*, who had been King of the Two Sicilies, Spain went on greatly recovering herself, as she had done before under Philip the Fifth. In the reign of *Charles the Fourth*, under the administration of *Godoy*, when the French Revolution began, Spain at first acted against France; but afterwards in 1796, she joined France against England and Portugal, as she did again when war broke forth once more in 1803. Buonaparte presently began to meddle in Spanish affairs, and he caused the King to abdicate in 1807. He then moved his brother Joseph from Naples to Spain, but the patriotic Spaniards proclaimed *Ferdinand the Seventh*, the son of the late King, though he was actually in Buonaparte's hands. Then came the great struggle in which the French were finally driven out of the Peninsula by the English victories. In 1814 the lawful King Ferdinand came back, but he overthrew the free constitution which had been made during his captivity, and reigned as an absolute monarch. Meanwhile *Portugal*, the old ally of England, was overrun by the French, and *John the Sixth*, the King, or rather Regent for his mother *Maria*, left Portugal for the great Portuguese colony of *Brazil*, where he went on reigning, and did not go back to Portugal till after the peace. The Portuguese at home meanwhile shared in the war of independence along with the English and Spaniards.

8. **The Netherlands.**—The *Austrian Netherlands*, as we have seen, were conquered and joined to France, with which they remained united till the Peace. The *Seven United Provinces* were in 1795 turned into a dependent commonwealth called the *Batavian Republic*, which in 1806 was turned into a kingdom for Buonaparte's brother *Lewis*. But in 1810 Buonaparte took his brother away, and joined Holland and the other provinces to France. At the Peace the whole Netherlands, except the districts which had been conquered by Lewis the Fourteenth, which France was allowed to keep, were formed into a *Kingdom of the Netherlands*, under *William Prince of Orange*, who also held the Grand Duchy of Lüzelburg or Luxemburg within the German Confederation.

9. **Switzerland.**—The old state of things in Switzerland, the Confederation of the Thirteen Cantons surrounded by their allied and subject states, went on till 1798, when the French came to seize the treasure at Bern. Their coming had the good effect of releasing the Romance-speaking people of *Vaud* from the yoke of Bern, but the French went on to invade the democratic cantons also. They now set up what they called the *Helvetic Republic*, which took in the old cantons and most of their allies and subjects. But they were no longer to be a Federal state, in which each member is independent in its internal affairs; the Helvetic Republic was a single commonwealth in which the cantons were no more than departments. Geneva and some other of the allied districts were added to France, some now, and some afterwards in Buonaparte's time. But, as the new republic did not suit the Swiss people, who were used to a Federal constitution, Buonaparte in 1803, by the *Act of Mediation*, gave them a better constitution, in which the old cantons and several new ones were joined together as separate states, but on equal terms, without the old distinction of confederates, allies, and

subjects. Now for the first time there were independent Romance-speaking *cantons* as distinguished from *allies* and *subjects*. Buonaparte kept Switzerland altogether dependent on France, but on the whole he treated it somewhat better than he did other countries. At the Peace, Geneva and the other districts which had been joined on to France were set free, and the *Swiss Confederation* of twenty-two cantons was formed, though with very lax union among themselves. The neutrality of the Confederation was acknowledged, as was also that of the northern part of Savoy, which had once belonged to Bern. This, with the rest of Savoy, went back to the King of Sardinia, and it was not to be given by him to any power except Switzerland.

10. **Great Britain and Ireland.**—The external history of this nation chiefly consists of the long war with France, with the short stoppage after the *Peace of Amiens*. England was the one enemy whom Buonaparte could never cajole or win over, as, at one time or another, he did all the powers of the continent. She was the object of his special hatred, and he did all that he could to ruin her trade, by forbidding, when he was at the height of his power after the Peace of Tilsit, all dealings between England and any continental state. But England kept her power by sea, and, except the great campaigns of the Duke of Wellington in Spain and Portugal, it was by sea that the English share in the war was carried on. The great victories of Nelson, at the mouth of the Nile in 1798 and at Trafalgar in 1805, altogether broke the naval power of France, and of Spain, which at Trafalgar was joined with France. Equally successful, but less righteous, were the two attacks on Denmark in 1801 and 1806, in which latter Copenhagen was bombarded. Meanwhile there was a rebellion in Ireland in 1798, the suppression of which was followed by the union of the Kingdom and Parliament of Ireland with that of Great Britain in 1800, when the

title of *King of France*, which had been borne by every King since Edward the Third, was at last dropped. Towards the end of the great war with France there was unhappily a war with the United States from 1813 to 1815. By the final Peace England, as usual, kept large distant conquests, but she gained no territory in Europe, except the island of *Malta*, which, up to the French Revolution, had belonged to the *Knights of Saint John*, and of the Frisian island of *Heligoland*, a possession of Denmark. The *Ionian Islands* also, part of the old Venetian dominion in Greece, were made into a Republic, under a protectorate on the part of England which did not differ much from actual sovereignty.

11. **The Scandinavian Kingdoms.**—At the beginning of the French Revolution the reigning King of Sweden, *Gustavus the Third*, was engaged in a war with Russia, which led to no change on either side. He also increased the royal power, but he was murdered in 1792. The next King, *Gustavus the Fourth*, was more zealous than anybody else against Buonaparte and the French; but he had no means of doing any great things, and he contrived to offend all other powers and his own subjects as well. Russia now conquered all *Finland*, and in 1809 the King was deposed, and the free constitution was restored, without either the despotism or the oligarchy which had of late prevailed by turns. As the new King, *Charles the Thirteenth*, had no children, the Swedes chose *Bernadotte*, one of Buonaparte's generals, to be *Crown Prince*, and to succeed to the kingdom at the King's death. In 1813 Bernadotte joined in the war of liberation in Germany, and led the Swedish troops against his old master. As Sweden had taken the part of the Allies, while Denmark had been on the side of France, it was settled at the Peace that Norway, which had all this time had the same king as Denmark, should be joined to Sweden, to make up for the loss of Finland, which

was kept by Russia. But the Norwegians withstood this arrangement; they chose a Danish prince for their King, and they made themselves the freest constitution of any state in the world that has a King at all. They were so far conquered that they had to accept the union with Sweden, but they joined it only as a perfectly independent kingdom, keeping its new constitution. Meanwhile Denmark still remained an absolute monarchy. When the Empire came to an end, the King of Denmark incorporated his German duchy of *Holstein* with his kingdom. At the Peace Denmark obtained the small piece of *Pomerania* which was held by Sweden; but this was presently given up to Prussia in exchange for the Duchy of *Lauenburg*, and the King of Denmark became a member of the German Confederation for the Duchies of *Holstein* and *Lauenburg*.

12. **Russia and Poland.**—After the death of Catherine the Second in 1796, her son *Paul* succeeded. In his time the Russian armies acted with those of Austria in the campaigns of Italy and Switzerland, but Paul soon afterwards made a separate peace with Buonaparte. Paul seems to have been quite mad, and he was murdered in 1801. His son *Alexander* remained at peace with France till 1805, when he again joined with Austria, but, after the overthrow of both Austria and Prussia, he made peace with Buonaparte at *Tilsit*, and a small part of the Lithuanian possessions of Prussia was added to Russia. Alexander and Buonaparte seemed to have pretty well agreed to divide Europe between them, as if they were to be the Eastern and Western Emperors. Russia and France remained at peace for six years, during which time Finland was conquered from Sweden and a war was waged with the Turks. In this last the Russian frontier was advanced to the Danube, much as, long before, the French frontier had reached the Rhine. By another war which went on at the same time with *Persia*

Russia gained a large territory in the land between the Euxine and Caspian Seas. At last, in 1812, came the French invasion of Russia, which led to the fall of Buonaparte, and Russia took a leading part in the last wars in which he was overthrown. At the general Peace the *Grand Duchy of Warsaw*, which Buonaparte had formed out of the Polish provinces of Prussia, and to which the Polish territory gained by Austria at the last partition had been added, was taken away from the King of Saxony. The *Grand Duchy of Posen* was given back to Prussia. The rest of the Duchy of Warsaw was made into a *Kingdom of Poland*, with a constitution of its own, which was united with Russia as a separate state, like Sweden and Norway, or like Great Britain and Ireland just before the union. The city of *Cracow*, the old capital of Poland, which stood at the meeting of the dominions of the three powers, Russia, Prussia, and Austria, was made into a separate commonwealth, under the protection of all of them. The new Kingdom of Poland did not differ very much in extent from the old kingdom before its union with Lithuania and its conquests from Prussia. It did not take in all that had belonged to the old Poland, but it took in some other lands which had not been part of it.

13. **The Turks.**—Sultan *Selim the Third* came to the throne in 1789, while Turkey was engaged in the war with Russia and Austria which was ended by the *Peace of Jassy*. He had to struggle against enemies on every side. The Turkish power had now got very weak, and many of the subject nations, Christian and Mahometan, were seeking for independence. Many of the distant Pashas in Europe and Asia seemed likely to set up for themselves, just as happened at the breaking up of the Caliphate and of the Mogul Empire. Especially the Christians of *Servia* revolted in 1806 under *Czerni George* (that is, *Black George*). Servia was conquered again in 1813, but in 1815 it again revolted under *Milosh Obrenowitz*, and it was after a

while acknowledged as a separate, though in some degree dependent, state, as it still remains. And in *Czernagora* or *Montenegro*, the small mountain land on the borders of the old Venetian and Turkish possessions, the Christians had never submitted, and they kept up a constant warfare with the Turks. So did the Christians of *Souli* in Epeiros and their Mahometan neighbour *Ali Pasha* of Joannina; and the *Mamelukes* in Egypt were practically independent. In the midst of all this came the successive French and Russian wars, and it was of course the interest of Russia to stir up discontent everywhere among the subject nations, and especially to put herself forward as the protector of all who belonged to the Eastern Church. In the war with France both Russia and England naturally took the Turkish side, and it was by English help that the French were driven out of Syria and Egypt. In the war with Russia, equally naturally as things stood then, England was on the Russian and France on the Turkish side. But Selim, who was a reformer, was deposed in 1807 and presently murdered. Then came *Mahmoud the Second*, whose reign lasted till 1839, taking in great events which will come in the next chapter.

14. **British Possessions abroad.**—It was during this time that the English dominion was practically spread over nearly all India. During the administrations of the *Marquess Cornwallis* and the *Marquess Wellesley* as Governors-General, the greater part of the country was either annexed to the English dominions or brought wholly under British influence. In the course of the war large conquests were also made among the French, Dutch, and Spanish possessions, and by these means England acquired *Ceylon*, the great colony of the *Cape of Good Hope*, the *Mauritius* or *Isle of France*, several of the *West India islands*, and a small territory in South America. Colonization was also beginning in *Australia* and in the neighbouring

island of *Tasmania* or *Van Dieman's Land.* Meanwhile we may mention, though it did not happen in any British colony, that in the island of *Saint Domingo*, *Hispaniola*, or *Hayti*, which, at the beginning of the Revolution, was held partly by France and partly by Spain, the negroes in both parts set up for themselves. A number of revolutions followed in imitation of those in Europe; sometimes republics were set up, while sometimes a successful negro called himself *Emperor* in Hayti, just as Buonaparte did in France.

15. **The United States.**—The new Constitution of the *United States* came into force in the same year that the French Revolution began, and, for about forty years, a remarkable succession of able rulers filled the office of President. The republic grew and prospered, and a great number of new States arose, especially in the lands to the West. But one territory was added in a different way. Spain had now given up her possessions in *Louisiana* to France, and in 1803 the whole of the French possessions in North America were bought by the United States. The States thus gained, not only the territory which forms the present State of Louisiana, but a claim to all the lands beyond the Mississippi which lay south of the British and north of the Spanish settlements. Out of this territory a great number of new States have gradually been made. During this time too negro slavery was done away with in the Northern States of the Union, but not in the Southern. Out of this difference mainly came the disputes between the *Northern* and *Southern* States which had been so important in late years.

16. **Summary.**—Thus, in the space of about five-and-twenty years, Europe was more changed than it had ever been before in the same space of time. The great wonder of these times was that, in France itself and in all the countries which were brought altogether under French influence, old ideas and old institutions

were utterly swept away in a way that had never happened before. It followed of course that much that was good and much that was bad perished together. France itself, since the Revolution, has never had a government of any kind that could last for any time. But, on the other hand, none of the ever-shifting French governments have brought in anything like the abuses and oppressions of the old monarchy. So in other countries, where the old governments went on or where the kings came back again at the general peace, the restored princes mostly forgot their promises and went on reigning as despots; yet men in general had learned lessons which they never forgot, and which bore fruit afterwards. Even where there was no great political change, there was a wide social change; and we may say generally that, since the French Revolution, there has been no part of Europe where the people have been so utterly down-trodden as they were in many parts before. Thus *serfage*, answering to *villainage* in the old times in England, has been abolished wherever it still went on, though in Russia this has been done only quite lately by the present Emperor. And, though no man ever did more than both Buonaparte himself and the Allies who overthrew him in parting out nations to this and that ruler without asking their leave, yet during all this time ideas were growing up which have taught men that such things should not be done. So again, though the union both of Germany and of Italy was not to happen at once, yet the wars of Buonaparte led men in both countries in different ways to feel more strongly than they had ever felt before that all Germans and all Italians were really countrymen, and that they ought to be more closely joined together. As for particular changes, *France* came out at the end of the war with nearly the same boundaries and under the same dynasty which she had at the beginning, but with her internal state utterly changed. *England* had raised her own position in Europe to the highest pitch; her European territory had been increased only by one or two small islands, but she had vastly increased her colonial dominions. *Germany* had changed in everything; the *Empire* was gone, and after the time of confusion, a lax *Confederation* had at last arisen, in which it could not fail that the two great states of *Austria* and *Prussia* would strive for the mastery. *Italy* was still cut up into a crowd of small states; Austria held a large part of Northern Italy, and had a commanding influence in the whole peninsula. *Spain* had got back her old dynasty. *Portugal* might be said to have become a dependency of *Brazil*, instead of Brazil being a dependency of Portugal; this is the only case of a state of the Old World being governed from the New. *Switzerland* had got rid of the old distinctions, and a Confederation on equal terms had been made. The whole of the *Netherlands*, less happily, were joined into a single kingdom. *Sweden* finally withdrew from the lands east and south of the Baltic, but the whole of the greater Scandinavian peninsula came under one ruler, though its two parts remained distinct kingdoms, *Norway* keeping her new and very free constitution. *Russia* had grown at all points, and *Poland* had been restored in a kind of way, though not in a way at all likely to last. In the *New World* the great English-speaking commonwealth was fast advancing. And this time, as commonly happens in times of great general stir, was a time of great inventions and of great writers in various ways. *Germany*, above all, now thoroughly awoke, and both her learned men and her original writers began to take the place which they have ever since kept.

CHAPTER XVII.

THE REUNION OF GERMANY AND ITALY.

Character of the present time; stronger feeling of nationality; change in the nature of wars (1)—*revolutions in France; reign of Lewis the Eighteenth; illegal acts and deposition of Charles the Tenth; Revolution of July* (2)—*reign of Louis-Philippe; attempts of Louis-Napoleon Buonaparte* (2)—*Revolution of February; Louis-Philippe driven out; the second Republic; administration of Cavaignac* (2)—*Louis-Napoleon Buonaparte chosen President; he seizes absolute power and calls himself Emperor* (2)—*his wars with Russia and Austria; Savoy and Nizza taken from Italy* (3) —*he attacks Prussia; Prussia supported by all Germany; victories of the Germans; Buonaparte taken prisoner; Paris taken; Elsass recovered by Germany* (3)—*the third Republic; the* Commune *of Paris; administration of M. Thiers* (3)—*steps towards the union of Germany; the* Zollverein—*revolutions of* 1848 (4)—*war between Prussia and Austria; formation of the North-German Confederation; Austria shut out of Germany* (4)—*union of Germany against France; the southern states join the Confederation; King William chosen Emperor* (4)—*disturbances in Italy; dominion of Austria; reign of Charles-Albert in Sardinia* (5)—*reign of Pius the Ninth; revolutions and wars of* 1848; *the new republic suppressed* (5)—*constitutional reign of Victor Emmanuel in Sardinia; his second war with Austria; help given by France; French attempts to divide Italy* (5, 6)—*the Italian States join Sardinia; exploits of Garibaldi; Victor-Emmanuel chosen King of Italy; the Pope kept at Rome by the French* (6)—*Italy joins Prussia against Austria; recovery of Venice* (6)—*recovery of Rome* (6)—*reign of Ferdinand the Fifth of Hungary; revolutions in Hungary and Austria;*

Hungary conquered by Russian help (7)—*reforms after the war with Prussia; Francis Joseph King of Hungary* (7)—*weakness of the Turks; Greek War of Independence; battle of Navarino; kingdom of Greece* (8)—*wars between Turkey and Russia; independence of Egypt* (9)—*Crimean War; affairs of the Danubian Principalities* (9)—*union of Russia and Poland, revolts of the Poles under Nicholas and Alexander the Second; serfage abolished; suppression of the republic of Cracow* (10)—*reign of Ferdinand the Seventh in Spain; revolts on behalf of the Constitution; intervention of France* (11)—*civil war on the death of Ferdinand; reign and deposition of Isabel; election of Amadeus of Italy* (11)—*revolutions and civil war of Portugal; reign of Donna Maria* (11)—*separation of Belgium and the Netherlands; affairs of Luxemburg* (12)—*changes of government in the Swiss Cantons; war of the Catholic and Protestant Cantons; establishment of the Federal Constitution* (13)—*Denmark becomes a constitutional state; disputes between Denmark and the Duchies; Sleswick and Holstein joined to Prussia* (14)—*affairs of Sweden and Norway; reforms in Sweden* (15)—*affairs in Great Britain; less interference in continental affairs than before; extension and increased independence of the British Colonies; abolition of slavery* (16)—*wars and mutiny in India; the government transferred from the Company to the Crown* (16)—*firm union of all Great Britain; troubles in Ireland; measures for its benefit* (16)—*revolt of the Spanish colonies in America; revolutions of Mexico* (17)—*separation of Brazil from Portugal* (18)—*advance of the United States; secession and reconquest of the South States; abolition of slavery* (19)—*Summary* (20).

1. Character of the Time.—We have now come altogether to our own times, and there is so much to tell that we must cut our tale very short indeed. A long time of peace has been followed by a time full of wars. And there is much to mark in these latest wars. Military science has greatly advanced, and the means of getting about have been greatly improved. It has therefore followed that wars have been, on the one hand, carried on with much greater armies, but that, on the other hand, they have been brought to an end in a much shorter time than formerly. There has been no Thirty Years' War, not even a Seven Years' War, in our time. There has also been a much stronger feeling of *nationality* than there ever was before. Some nonsense has been talked about this matter, because it is not always easy to say what makes a nation. For, though language proves more than any other one test, it will not always do by itself. Thus in Switzerland four languages are spoken: yet the Swiss certainly make one nation. But, when men thoroughly feel themselves to be one nation, when they wish to come together as such and to get rid of the dominion of foreigners, it is clearly right that they should be able to do so. Now this is what in different parts of Europe men have been striving to do in our own time more than they ever did before: and this feeling has been shown above all things in the joining together of the great nations of Germany and Italy, which had been so long split up into a number of small states. This change is the greatest event of our times; but it will perhaps be better understood if we first run through the changes that have happened in France, as they have had so much to do with the history of the other countries, but we must tell the tale in as few words as may be.

2. **Revolutions in France.**—After the final overthrow of Buonaparte, *Lewis the Eighteenth* came back again, and reigned as a constitutional King, but many of those who came with him would gladly have had the old state of things back again, when the King ruled as he pleased, and when the nobles and clergy were set up above the rest of the nation. Of this sort was his brother, the next King *Charles the Tenth*, who was the last who was crowned at Rheims, and

the last who called himself *King of France.* For when, in 1830, he put out some ordinances which were wholly against the law, the people of Paris rose, and King Charles was driven out in the *Revolution of July.* We may mark in all these changes how the one city of Paris always acts, and how the rest of France accepts what it does. This time, when the King was driven out, his cousin *Louis-Philippe Duke of Orleans* was made King, with the old title of *King of the French*, and with a freer constitution. France was not engaged in any great wars during the time of these three Kings; only in Africa the piratical power of *Algiers* was put down, and all that part of the coast of Africa became a French dominion. After some revolts at Lyons and Paris early in his reign, Louis-Philippe reigned quietly till 1848; only twice in his reign *Louis-Napoleon Buonaparte*, a nephew of the first Buonaparte, tried to make a disturbance. The first time he was allowed to go free; the second time he was imprisoned, but he escaped. But in 1848 the King's government had become unpopular, and in February of that year he was driven out, as Charles the Tenth had been. This time a Republic was set up, and in June there was a second revolt in Paris of the more extreme republicans, which was put down by General *Cavaignac.* But when the President of the Republic was to be chosen, Louis-Napoleon Buonaparte, who had been allowed to come back, was chosen by many votes over Cavaignac. He was chosen President for four years, and he swore to be faithful to the republic. But at the end of the third year, in December 1851, with the help of the army, he seized upon the government, as his uncle had done, and called himself President for ten years with nearly absolute power. The National Assembly, which passed a vote to depose him, was dissolved by force; many men were killed, and others were sent to the unhealthy colony of Cayenne, while most of the chief men of the country were imprisoned for a while. A year after, in December 1852, he called himself *Emperor*, as his uncle had done before him.

3. **The Wars of France.**—When Louis-Napoleon Buonaparte took the title of Emperor, he gave out that the Empire should be peace; but there have been wars in Europe ever since, in which France has taken the chief part. In 1854, when a quarrel again arose between Russia and Turkey, France and England both joined in the war against Russia and shared in the victories over the Russians in the *Crimea*. In 1859, when there was a dispute between Austria and Sardinia, France made war upon Austria, and it was given out that France would free Italy from the Alps to the Hadriatic. But, when the French armies reached the strong fortress of Verona, all that was done was to make a peace with Austria, by which Italy was freed only as far as the Mincio. At the same time, the two provinces of *Nizza* and *Savoy*, the remaining Burgundian possessions of the King of Sardinia, were given to France. This new possession took in the districts whose neutrality had been guaranteed, and which, according to old treaties, if they ever passed from Sardinia, were to pass to Switzerland. Lastly, in 1870 France declared war upon Prussia, the reason given being that there had been talk of giving the Crown of Spain to a distant kinsman of the King of Prussia. But Prussia was supported by all Germany. The French crossed the German frontier, but they were driven out in a few days, and then the German armies entered France, and won a series of victories. Buonaparte himself became a prisoner: afterwards he went to England and died there. Meanwhile he was declared deposed, and a Republic was again set up in Paris. Paris was besieged, and surrendered to the Germans, and a treaty was made by which, besides the payment of a large sum of money, nearly all *Elsass*, together with that part of *Lorraine* where

German is spoken, and also the strong fortress of *Metz*, were given back to Germany. Thus *Strassburg* and the other German places which had been gradually taken by France have become German again, and the French frontier, which first reached the Rhine in 1648, is now kept quite away from it. Soon after the peace with Germany, Paris was held by the *Communists* or extreme Republicans, and the city had again to be besieged and taken by the Government of the new Republic under the President *M. Thiers*, who was at one time chief minister under King Louis-Philippe. Since then M. Thiers has resigned, and the present President, *Marshal Macmahon*, was chosen. In the year 1875 a regular republican constitution was made; but ever since the fall of Buonaparte there have been different parties in France, some wishing to bring back his son, and others wishing for a King, either *Henry* the grandson of Charles the Tenth or one of the princes of the House of Orleans.

4. **The Union of Germany.**—The German princes, when they were set up again at the Peace, mostly forgot their promises of setting up constitutional governments; still the national spirit largely tended towards progress and union. And one great step towards it was taken, as Prussia gradually, from 1818 onwards, became the centre of a commercial union among the German states, the members of which agreed to levy no duties on merchandise passing from one state to another, but to levy them only at the common frontier. This union, called the *Zollverein*, was gradually joined by most of the German states. In 1848 there were revolutions over the most part of Europe, and among them in Prussia, Austria, and most of the German states; an attempt was made at the same time to join Germany together under an Emperor and a common Parliament, instead of the lax Confederation which had gone on since 1815. But, before long, things came back much as they were

before, till in 1866 a war broke out between Prussia and Austria, in which the German states took different sides. Prussia got the better in so short a time that it has been called the *Seven Weeks' War*. By the peace which was now made Austria was shut out from Germany altogether, the Kingdom of Hanover and some smaller states, among them the free city of *Frankfurt*, were annexed to Prussia, and the Northern states were formed into the *North-German Confederation*, under the presidency of Prussia, with a common constitution and assembly. When France made war on Prussia in 1870, the Southern states took part in the war as well as the Northern. They soon joined the Confederation, Bavaria, the largest of them, keeping some special privileges to herself. Thus all Germany, except Austria, Tyrol, and the other German dominions of the House of Austria, has been joined together much more closely than it had ever been since the Thirty Years' War, or indeed since the great Interregnum. And, while the German siege of Paris was going on, King *William* of Prussia, being in the great hall of Lewis the Fourteenth at Versailles, received the title of *German Emperor* from the princes and free cities of Germany. And presently the German lands held by France were, as we have seen, joined again to the new Empire. Of course, in the old use of words, this was a restoration, not of the *Empire*, but of the *Kingdom of Germany;* for in old times, as we know by this time, the title of Emperor could be held only by one who was, or claimed to be, sovereign of either the Old or the New Rome. But now that several of the German princes are called Kings, it would have been hard to find a better title than *Emperor* for the chief of a Confederation which has Kings among its members.

5. **The Revolutions of Italy.**—Italy can hardly be said to have had any history from 1815 to 1848. There were many conspiracies, and some in-

surrections, in different parts of Italy, especially in 1831. But the Austrian power was strong enough, not only to hold the Austrian possessions of Lombardy and Venice, but to keep the smaller princes on their thrones. Meanwhile the movement for the liberation and union of Italy was growing up in its north-western corner. In 1831 a new branch of the house of Savoy, that of *Carignano*, succeeded to the Sardinian crown in the person of *Charles Albert*. In the early part of his reign he ruled harshly, but he was an enemy of Austria. Then, in 1846, the present Pope, *Pius the Ninth*, was chosen, and for a while it seemed as if he were going to do great things for Italian freedom; so much so that his dominions were partly occupied by Austria in 1847. In the course of 1847 and 1848, most of the Italian princes gave their people constitutions. Milan and Venice rose against Austria, and now the King of Sardinia entered the Austrian dominions in Italy at the head of an allied army from various parts of the peninsula. But he was finally defeated at *Novara* in 1849, and he abdicated, and was succeeded by his son *Victor Emmanuel the Second*. Meanwhile Venice, which had again become a republic, was recovered by Austria. Rome, whence the Pope had fled and where a republic had been set up, was overcome by troops sent by the new republic of France, and the constitutions in the other Italian states were withdrawn. Thus, after 1849, Italy was left in much the same case in which she had been before the insurrections. The Pope was maintained in his dominions by French help; Austria had recovered her possessions; but Sardinia remained a constitutional and advancing state, for King Victor Emmanuel steadily kept his word to his people.

6. **The Union of Italy.**—And now, after ten years, came the beginnings of the great movement which has at last made Italy one. In 1859 there came the war between Sardinia and Austria, in which

France took a part: by the peace Austria gave up *Lombardy*, but kept *Venetia*. France now tried to make what was called an *Italian Confederation*, but, as Austria was to have been a member of it, it could have been no real Confederation at all, and the Italians settled the matter themselves by willingly joining themselves to the kingdom of Victor Emmanuel. Now it was that *Garibaldi*, who had before defended Rome against the French, wonderfully delivered the Two Sicilies, and joined them also to the kingdom of Victor Emmanuel. The King of Sardinia thus had possession of all Italy, except the part held by Austria, and Rome, where the French still kept the Pope in possession. In 1861 Victor Emmanuel was made *King of Italy* by the Italian Parliament, and in 1865 the capital was removed to Florence till Rome could be had. The kingdom had hardly been established in 1861 when *Count Cavour*, who had had the chief hand in bringing about the new state of things, died. When the war broke out in 1866 between Prussia and Austria, Italy joined Prussia, but the Italians were defeated by the Austrians both by sea and land. But at the peace, Austria gave up *Venice* and *Verona*; but she kept, not only the old Venetian possessions in *Dalmatia*, but *Istria*, *Aquileia*, and *Trent*, Italian-speaking places which formed part of the ancient Kingdom of Italy. Lastly when the war between France and Germany caused the French troops to be withdrawn from Rome, Rome was at last joined on to the Italian kingdom, and it now of course is the capital of Italy. The Pope's spiritual position remains unchanged, though he is no longer a temporal prince.

7. **Hungary and Austria.**—*Francis the First of Hungary*, who till 1806 had been the *Emperor Francis the Second*, went on reigning in Hungary, Austria, and his other states till 1836. Then came *Ferdinand the Fifth.* In 1847 and 1848 there were revolutions in

Austria and Hungary as well as elsewhere. The Hungarians stood up for their ancient constitution with certain reforms, and, when Ferdinand abdicated, they refused to acknowledge *Francis Joseph*, who succeeded him in Austria, because the abdication was not lawful according to the laws of Hungary. Afterwards they set up a republic under the famous *Kossuth*. But feuds had unluckily arisen between the Magyars and the other races in Hungary, and this greatly helped the reconquest of the country by Austria, which however was not done without the help of Russia. Hungary now remained crushed till after the war between Austria and Prussia. Then the government was put on a better and more lawful footing; Austria and Hungary became two distinct states under a common sovereign, and Francis Joseph was lawfully crowned *King of Hungary* in 1867. Since then Hungary and Austria have agreed well together; but difficulties have arisen through the other states, Bohemia and the rest, asking for more or less distinct governments. The *Austro-Hungarian Monarchy*, as it is called, is in fact a mere joining together of various nations without any natural connexion; but this is the general character of South-Eastern Europe, and Hungary seems marked out to be the leading state among the Christian nations in those parts.

8. **The Deliverance of Greece.**—We have seen that the Ottoman power had been growing weaker and weaker, while the subject Christian races were growing stronger. *Servia* had won back her freedom, and *Montenegro* had never lost hers. In 1821 the Greeks revolted. The War of Independence began, strangely enough, in the Danubian Principalities of *Wallachia* and *Moldavia*, but presently the Greeks revolted in all parts of the Ottoman dominions where they were strong enough. In some parts they were put down with cruel massacres, but in the greater part of old Greece the inhabitants, Greek and Albanian, with

some little help from the other subject races and much more from volunteers from Western Europe, were able to hold their ground against the Turks. But in 1826 Sultan Mahmoud called in the help of the Pasha of Egypt, *Mahomet Ali*, who had a better disciplined army than his own. His son *Ibrahim*—that is *Abraham*—brought the Greeks almost to destruction, and Peloponnêsos might have been altogether wasted had not the three powers, England, France, and Russia, stepped in and crushed the Ottoman fleet at *Navarino*, the old *Pylos*, in 1827. The French troops afterwards drove the Egyptians out of Peloponnêsos. The end of this was the establishment of the *Kingdom of Greece.* It has had two Kings, *Otho of Bavaria*, who was turned out in 1862, and the present King, *George of Denmark.* The kingdom has also been increased by England, in 1864, giving up the protectorate of the *Ionian Islands*, which became part of the kingdom of Greece. But the new state has not been so prosperous or well governed as it was once hoped that it might have been. It has been cooped up within a bad frontier, and moreover the Greeks have had their heads too full of the memories of the old times, and they have been too fond of copying the institutions of Western countries which are not suited to them.

9. **Turkey and Russia.**—Meanwhile great changes went on in the Ottoman dominions themselves, and the Turks had several wars with Russia and other powers. In 1826 Sultan Mahmoud destroyed the *Janissaries*, who had now become a turbulent and useless body. In 1828 a war with Russia followed. The next year the Russians got as far as Hadrianople, and a treaty was made by which Russia gained some advantages at the mouth of the Danube and made some stipulations on behalf of the Christians in Turkey. Then followed wars with *Mahomet Ali*, the Pasha of Egypt, in which several of the European powers took part, and which were ended in 1841 by Egypt

becoming a nearly independent state, though under the superiority of the Porte. Lastly came the war with Russia in 1854, in which France, England, and Sardinia took part on the Turkish side. It ended in 1856 by Russia agreeing to certain terms which lessened her power in the Euxine and giving up a small territory, which kept her away from the Danube, much as France has since been kept away from the Rhine. Meanwhile, as Greece has been altogether cut off from the Ottoman dominions, and as Servia and Egypt had been made practically independent, so also the Principalities of Moldavia and Wallachia, dependent states whose position was very anomalous, and which formed a constant excuse for disputes between Russia and Turkey, have been formed into a separate principality, whose connexion with Turkey is purely nominal. But the Roumans, like the Greeks, have been too fond of imitating Western forms of government for which they are not fit.

10. **Russia and Poland.**—We have seen that, by the Peace of 1815, Poland, in the latest sense of the word, became a separate constitutional kingdom, to be held by the Russian Emperor. Such a state of things may last between two constitutional kingdoms like Sweden and Norway, where, though Sweden is the greater, it is not so very much greater; but it could not last between a huge despotic empire and a small constitutional kingdom. Disputes therefore naturally arose, especially after the accession of *Nicholas* in 1825; the constitution was not carried out; so in 1831 the Poles revolted, declared the throne vacant, and held out for several months against the Russian power. But they were crushed and very harshly treated, and the Polish constitution was taken away. The wars between Russia and Turkey have been already spoken of; during the great war with France and England, Nicholas died, and was succeeded by the present Emperor *Alexander the Second.* In his time the *serfs*

have been set free, but in 1863 another Polish revolt was put down as harshly as the other, and the Polish kingdom has been quite swept away. In 1846 too the commonwealth of *Cracow*, which still went on as a kind of representative of Poland, was added to the Austrian dominions.

11. **Spain and Portugal.**—In Spain *Ferdinand the Seventh* came back and refused to abide by the constitution which had been set up during the war with Buonaparte. Several risings on its behalf took place, and, in 1820, it was restored. A civil war followed, and in 1822 French troops entered Spain to restore the King's authority. This was done, but not till after much fighting, and the French did not leave Spain for seven years. In 1833 Ferdinand died. The Spanish law as to the succession of females had been altered backwards and forwards several times, so on Ferdinand's death there was a civil war between the partisans of his daughter *Isabel* and those of his brother *Charles* or *Don Carlos.* The Carlist party was strong only in the Basque provinces in the North, but the war went on a long time, and was not fully put an end to till 1840. Spain was now ruled as a constitutional state, but it has been constantly disturbed by insurrections of the army, and at last the misgovernment and bad life of the Queen caused her to be deposed in 1868, like Mary Stuart in Scotland. Spain now remained for some time without a King or a settled government of any kind; several candidates for the crown were proposed, and some wished for a commonwealth. At last, in 1870, a son of the King of Italy, *Amadeus Duke of Aosta*, was chosen King. Presently he abdicated, and, after another time of confusion, the son of Isabel was brought back in 1875 by the title of *Alfonso the Twelfth*, though in the north a war has still gone on with the partisans of *Don Carlos*, a grandson of the old Carlos. Owing to all these confusions, the position of Spain has been

much lower in Europe than it was of old, besides the loss of its American possessions. In *Portugal* a constitution was proclaimed in 1820, at the same time as in Spain, the King, *John the Sixth*, being in Brazil. From this time till 1832 there was a time of great confusion and civil war between the absolute party under Don *Miguel* or *Michael*, the King's younger son, and the constitutional party under his eldest son *Don Pedro* or *Peter*, who succeeded in 1826 and who presently abdicated in favour of his daughter *Maria*. In 1828 Don Miguel assumed the crown; but he was at last driven out, and the Queen was acknowledged. The strangest thing of all was that Pedro, after giving up the crown himself, acted as regent for his young daughter. Since then there have been some disputes and risings in Portugal, but there has been no revolution or serious change.

12. **The Netherlands.**—By the peace of 1815 all the provinces of the Netherlands had been made into one kingdom, but as the Northern and Southern provinces differed in religion and other things, they did not well agree together; so in 1830 the Southern provinces revolted. Then the Kingdom was divided: the Northern part, which had been the *United Provinces*, went on as the *Kingdom of the Netherlands* in the House of Orange; while the formerly Spanish, and afterwards Austrian, Netherlands became the *Kingdom of Belgium* under the *House of Coburg*, the first King being *Leopold*, who had been husband of the Princess *Charlotte* of England. This arrangement has gone on since, only there have been disputes about the Duchy of *Lüzelburg* or *Luxemburg*, which was held by the King of the Netherlands as a member of the German Confederation, and which since the fall of the Confederation has been declared neutral.

13. **Switzerland.**—Switzerland has remained a Federal state ever since the Peace in 1815, and since that time it has not been engaged in war with any

other power. But there have been great changes in its own constitution, and at one time there was even a civil war. About 1831 there were disputes in most of the Cantons, which ended in their governments being made much more popular, but nothing was done to the Federal Constitution. In 1847 a war broke out between the Catholic and Protestant Cantons, in which the Protestants had the better. It was now seen that the tie between the Cantons needed to be made much stronger, and in 1848 a new *Federal Constitution* was made, in many things very like that of the United States, only, instead of a single President, there is a Council of Seven, with much smaller powers. Further changes were made in 1874, by which many of their powers were taken away from the several Cantons and given to the Federal body.

14. **Denmark and the Duchies.**—Denmark remained an absolute monarchy till the accession of *Frederick the Seventh* in 1848, who at once gave his people a constitution. Since then there have been endless disputes about the two Duchies held by the Danish Kings, of which *Holstein* undoubtedly was part of Germany, while *Sleswick* was not a member of the German Confederation, and its people were partly German and partly Danish. A war went on from 1841 to 1851, but this time Denmark kept both Duchies. But in 1864, under the present King *Christian the Ninth*, disputes arose again; a war followed, and the Duchies were given up by Denmark to Prussia and Austria, and again in 1866 by Austria to Prussia alone. The northern or Danish part of Sleswick was to have been given back to Denmark, but this has not yet been done.

15. **Sweden and Norway.**—At last we come to those countries in which during all these years there has been no revolution or great disturbance. One is Great Britain; the other is the two Scandinavian kingdoms of Sweden and Norway. *Bernadotte*, who

had been already chosen Crown Prince of Sweden, succeeded to both kingdoms as *Charles the Fourteenth*, and the two crowns have since stayed in his family. On the whole the two kingdoms have gone on well side by side, having the same king, but each keeping its own constitution. A wish has sometimes been shown to encroach on the independence of Norway, but the Northmen have always been able to hold their own. During the reign of the late King *Charles the Fifteenth*, improvements were made in the Swedish constitution also, and greater liberty was given to people of other religions than the Lutheran.

16. **Great Britain and Ireland.**—No time has been more important in English history than this last time of which we are now speaking, but its events have been mainly of a kind which will be best spoken of in a separate History of England. It has been a time of great advancement in every way, both politically and socially, and it has also been a time of many inventions and of great progress in men's minds. England has also had something to do in some way or another with most of the affairs of the continent of Europe, but she has been engaged in only one great war, namely that with Russia from 1854 to 1856. Nor has she gained or lost any European territory, unless we reckon it a loss that she has withdrawn from the protectorate of the Ionian Islands. But this time has been a time of great changes and great advance in the British possessions in distant countries. The trade in negro slaves was finally forbidden in 1807, and slavery itself was abolished throughout the British dominions in 1833. The colonial dominions of England have vastly extended themselves, especially in Australia and North America. And most of them have received constitutions which have made them altogether independent in their internal affairs. In *Canada* alone has there been any serious disturbance. There was a rebellion in 1837 among the French

Canadians, but the colony has since been made almost independent, and it is now highly prosperous. In *India* we have had to wage several wars, and several provinces have been annexed. Here the British dominion was altogether shaken for a time by the *Mutiny* of the native soldiers in 1857. After its suppression, the government of India was taken from the Company and given to the Crown, and the phantom of the *Great Mogul* came at last to an end, as the last nominal Emperor had been concerned in the mutiny. There have also been wars with *China*, *Persia*, *Abyssinia*, and the *Ashantees* in Africa; and generally England has come more and more to the position of an insular power, withdrawing from any great interference with the affairs of the continent of Europe, but keeping up trade and colonization in all parts of the world, and being therefore ever and anon engaged in distant wars. The whole island of Great Britain has long been firmly joined together, notwithstanding the differences of race and speech in different parts which have still not wholly died out. But the remembrance of ancient misgovernment has constantly kept up the spirit of disaffection in Ireland, which has broken out into more than one conspiracy and rising, though none on any great scale. Every care has been taken by a succession of measures to do justice to Ireland, by the admission of the Roman Catholics to equal rights with Protestants, by the disestablishment of the dominant Protestant Church, and by laws for the benefit of the occupiers of land. But it would seem that the memory of old wrongs is even now stronger than the feeling of recent benefits.

17. **The Spanish Colonies in America.**—If this period has been one of great change in the Old World, it has been one of equal change in the New. The example of the British colonies, which have given birth to the great commonwealth of the United States, has been followed by the Spanish Colonies also.

But it must be remembered that there is this great difference between the Spanish and the English colonies, that, though in the United States the people are not of purely English blood, yet the mixture has been with other European nations, or with slaves brought from Africa, and not at all with the natives of America. But in the Spanish settlements the Europeans and the natives have been largely mixed, and in truth the native blood prevails. When the national government in Spain was upset by Buonaparte, the Spanish colonies began to set up for themselves in 1810. *Mexico* was recovered, but it revolted again in 1820. A certain *Iturbide* for a while called himself Emperor, as people did in other places, but after a while a Federal Commonwealth was established. But the country has never been quiet for any long time, and it has lost the great province of *Texas* to the United States. In 1862 a quarrel arose with *England*, *France*, and *Spain;* from this England and Spain soon withdrew, but *France* went on, and in 1863 the Austrian Archduke *Maximilian* was set up under French influence as yet another Emperor; but he was not acknowledged by the whole country, and in 1867 he was overthrown and shot by the native President *Juarez*. *Chili* also separated from the Spanish dominion in 1810, and *Peru* in 1820, and now Spain has no dominions on the continent of America; and in the Spanish island of *Cuba* there have been endless disturbances.

18. **Brazil.**—The great Portuguese settlement in South America has had a somewhat different history from either the English or the Spanish colonies. It separated from the mother-country, but it is the only state in the New World which, instead of becoming a republic, has remained under a prince of the old royal family. King *John the Sixth*, as we have seen, reigned in Brazil when he had to leave Portugal, and he called himself *King of Brazil* as well as of Portugal.

In 1822 Brazil was declared independent with a free constitution, under *Dom Pedro* as *Emperor.* The crowns of Brazil and Portugal have since remained distinct, as on Pedro's abdication he was succeeded by his daughter *Maria* in Portugal, and by his son *Pedro* in Brazil. Brazil has had fewer disturbances, and has been more prosperous, than any other South American state.

19. **The United States.**—But neither in the Old nor the New World has this period made more important changes than it has in the commonwealth of the United States. Many new States have been founded towards the West, and the great dominion of Texas, which had been part of Mexico, first became a separate commonwealth, and was afterwards joined on to the Union. But the greatest event in the history of America has been the war which began in 1861 between the *Northern* and *Southern States.* There were many causes of difference between them, the chief being the allowance of slavery in the South, while it had long died out in the North. On the election of *Abraham Lincoln* as President, in 1860, *South Carolina* seceded from the Union, and the rest of the Southern States presently followed her. They called themselves the *Confederate States*, and set up a Federal constitution, nearly the same as that of the United States, under *Jefferson Davis* as President. Then followed the war which lasted till 1865, when the Confederate States had to submit. About the same time President Lincoln, having just been chosen President a second time, was murdered. The result of the war has been the reconstitution of the Union, and the final getting rid of slavery throughout all parts of the North American continent. In Brazil and in the Spanish and Dutch colonies it still goes on, but in Brazil it will come to an end before many years.

20. **Summary.**—Thus, in our own days, France has

again, for the third time, tried to get the chief power in Europe, and a third time she has been beaten back, and has been driven to give up part of her former conquests. The rest of Europe has been completely changed by the union of Italy into one kingdom, and by the union, though less close, of nearly all Germany under the leadership of Prussia. Austria has withdrawn from both German and Italian affairs, and has become a state joined with Hungary, something in the same way as Sweden and Norway. The last traces of Polish independence have been trampled out, and Denmark has been cut short by the complete loss of the Duchies. Two new kingdoms have arisen, namely Belgium and Greece, of which the former has prospered much more than the latter. The whole East of Europe has during the whole time been more or less unsettled, as it doubtless always will be, as long as a Mahometan power rules over Christians. On the whole Europe has greatly gained in freedom and good government since the end of the wars of the French Revolution. But on the other hand, the keeping up of vast standing armies by nearly all the governments of the continent makes peace at all times uncertain, and the tendency of later times has been to lessen the importance of the smaller states and to group Europe under a few great powers. Still, both in Great Britain, in most other parts of Europe, and in the United States, men may be very glad that they live in our own day and not in any of the times which have gone before us.

INDEX.

A.

Aachen ; French annexation of, 334
Abbas, forefather of the dynasty of the Abbassides, 125
Abbassides, dynasty of, overthrow the Ommiads, 125 ; end of, 197
Abdal-rahman founds the Ommiad dynasty at Cordova, 126
Abd-al-rahman III., Caliph, greatness of the Mahometan power in Spain under, 154
Abu-Bekr, first Caliph, 117, 119 ; his wars with the Empire, 117
Abyssinian war, the, 364
Acadie, French colony of, acquired by Britain, 301. *See* Nova Scotia.
Achaia, later importance of, 44 ; beginning of the League of, 45 ; extension of, *ib.* ; war of, with Sparta, 46 ; helped by Antigonos Dôsôn, *ib.* ; resigns Corinth to him, *ib.* ; in alliance with Philip, *ib.* ; helps him against Rome, 64 ; becomes the ally of Rome, *ib.* ; extension of the League, 65 ; war with Rome, *ib.* ; dissolution of the League, 66 ; Principality of, 190
Act of Mediation, 339
Acre taken by the Mahometans, 188
Adolf of Nassau, King, 202
Aetius, Roman general, commands at Châlons, 102
Ælfred, *see* Alfred
Æneas, 53
Æneas Silvius, *see* Pius II.
Æquians, their wars with Rome, 56
Æschylus, 34
Æthelberht, King of Kent, Bretwalda, 133 ; converted by Augustine, *ib.*
Æthelred the Unready, Danish invasions of England in his reign, 144 ; driven out by Swegen, *ib.*
Ætolia, rise of its people, 42 ; League of, 45 ; war with the Achaians and Macedonians, 46 ; alliance with Rome, 64 ; Roman conquest of, 65
Africa, its geographical character, 10 ; Roman province of, 63 ; settlement of the Vandals, 104 ; recovered to the Empire by Belisarius, 114 ; Saracen conquest of, 118
Agathoklês, Tyrant of Syracuse, 59
Agêsilaos, King of Sparta, his campaigns in Asia, 36 ; returns to Greece, 37
Agincourt, battle of, 217
Agis, King of Sparta, attempts to throw off the Macedonian yoke, 42
Agricola, his conquest of Britain, 87
Agrippina, wife of Germanicus, death of, 85
Agrippina, wife of Claudius, poisons him, 85
Aigos-potamos, defeat of the Athenians at, 35
Aix, *see* Aquae Sextiae
Akarnania, League of, 46 ; helps Philip against Rome, 64
Akbar, Mogul Emperor, 298
Aktion, battle of, 79
Alarcos, battle of, 195
Alaric, King of the West-Goths, takes Rome, 101
Alberoni, Cardinal, minister of Philip V. of Spain, 305
Albert I., King, son of Rudolf of Hapsburg, grant of Austria to, 202 ; murder of, *ib.*
Albert II., King, 204
Albert of Brandenburg, Duke of Prussia, 266
Albigenses, crusades against, 191, 192
Alexander the Great succeeds Philip, 39 ; takes and destroys Thebes, *ib.* ; his victories at the Granikos, Issos, and Arbêla, 40 ; takes Tyre, *ib.* ; conquers Egypt and founds Alexandria, *ib.* ; death of, *ib.* ; effects of his conquests, *ib.*
Alexander Severus, Emperor, takes the name ot Antonnius, 89 ; his wars with Persia, 90

Alexander I. of Russia, his relations with Buonaparte, 352
Alexander II. of Russia, abolition of serfage under, 359
Alexander II., Pope, sanctions Norman invasion of England, 151
Alexander V., Pope, chosen by the Council of Pisa, 207
Alexander VI., Pope, 249
Alexander Farnese, Duke of Parma, 258
Alexandria, foundation of, 40; becomes the seat of Greek learning, 71
Alexios Angelos, restored to the Eastern Empire by the Crusaders, 189
Alexios Komnênos, Eastern Emperor, 156
Alfonso of Aragon recovers Zaragoza, 154; growth of the kingdom under, *ib.*
Alfonso V. of Aragon, 228
Alfonso VI. of Castile, union of Leon and Castile under, 154; recovers Toledo, *ib.*
Alfonso VII. of Castile takes the title of Emperor, 195; his wars with the Almohades, *ib.*
Alfonso VIII. of Castile defeated by the Caliph Jacob at Alarcos, 195
Alfonso X. of Castile, his election to the Empire, 201
Alfonso XII. of Spain, 360
Alfred, King of the West-Saxons, his wars with the Danes, 135; his treaty with Guthrum, 136
Algiers, French conquest of, 351
Ali, Caliph, 125
Ali Pasha of Joannina, 344
Ali Kayem, Caliph of Bagdad, asks help of Togrel Beg, 156
Allia, Gauls defeat the Romans at the, 56
Allodial tenure, origin and nature of, 165
Almohades, growth and decline of their power in Spain, 195
Almoravides, dynasty of in Spain, 154
Alp Arslan, Sultan, defeats the Emperor Romanos at Manzikert, 156
Alphabet, originally Phœnician, 23
Alsace, *see* Elsass
Alva, Duke of, his government in the Netherlands, 257
Amadeus, Duke of Aosta, chosen King of Spain, 360; abdicates, *ib.*
Ambrose, Saint, Archbishop of Milan, submission of Theodosius to, 101
America, discovery of, 275; origin of its name, *ib.*; Spanish settlements in, 276; French, English and Dutch settlements in, 277, 278, 300; American War of Independence, 310; revolts of the Spanish colonies, 365
Amerigo Vespucci gives his name to the new world, 275
Amiens, Peace of, 330, 340
Amphiktionic Council, 39; Philip made member of, *ib.*
Amurath I., Sultan, takes Hadrianople, 225
Amurath II., Sultan, union of the Ottoman monarchy under, 226; besieges Constantinople, *ib.*; defeats Wladislaus of Poland, 231
Anabaptists, revolts of in Germany, 252
Andriskos heads the Macedonian revolt against Rome, 65; defeat of, *ib.*
Angevin dynasty in England, 153
Angles, a Low-Dutch tribe, 109; give their name to England, *ib.*
Angora, battle of, 226
Anne, Empress of Russia, 316
Anne, Queen of England, union of England and Scotland under, 289
Anne of Britanny, her marriages, 253
Anson, Lord, 309
Antalkidas, Peace of, 37
Antigonos Dosôn, King of Macedonia, helps the Achaians, 46
Antigonos Gonatas, King of Macedonia, 43
Antioch, its foundation, 40; capital of the Seleukid kingdom, 67; won back to the Eastern Empire, 143
Antiochos the Great, helps the Ætolians, 65; defeated by the Romans at Thermopylai, *ib.*; at Magnêsia, 66
Antipatros, Macedonian general, takes Athens, 42
Antoninus, *see* Alexander Severus
Antoninus, *see* Caracalla
Antoninus Pius, Emperor, 87
Antonius, Marcus, Triumvir, 79; civil war of with Brutus and Cassius, *ib.*; makes war on the Parthians, *ib.*; influence of Kleopatra on, *ib.*; his civil war with Cæsar, *ib.*; his defeat and death of, *ib.*
Apennines, the, 49
Apollôn, Philip of Macedonia declares himself champion of, 38
Apollônia, submission of to Rome, 63
Aquæ Sextiæ, Roman colony of, 69; defeat of the Teutones near, 70
Aquitaine, early inhabitants of, 69; part of the Spanish kingdom of the West-Goths, 103; conquered by the Franks, 104; Romance speech of, 106; part of the dominions of Charles the Great, 127; duchy of, 131; seized by Philip the Fair, 215; rule of the

Black Prince in, 216; French conquest of, 216, 218
Arabs, a Semitic nation, 7; *see* Saracens
Arados, *see* Arvad
Aragon, kingdom of, its growth, 154; House of, reigns in Sicily, 193; conquests of her kings over the Mahometans, 195; union of Sicily with, 214, 228; relations of, with Naples, *ib.*; war of, with Provence and France, *ib.*; union of Castile with, 229, *see* Castile and Aragon
Aratos, frees Sikyôn, 45; leader of the Achaian League, *ib.*
Arbêla, battle of, 40
Arcadius, Emperor in the East, 101
Archangel, port of, 267, 315
Architecture in the 11th century, 152, 158; in the 12th and 13th centuries, 198; in the 13th, 14th, and 15th centuries, 232
Ardeshir, *see* Artaxerxes
Argos, its early greatness, 26; joins the Confederacy against Sparta, 37; besieged by Pyrrhos, 43; joins the Achaian League, 45
Aria, *see* Iran
Aristeidês the Just, 33
Aristocracy, meaning of the word, 28
Aristophanês, comic poet, 34
Arkadia, League of, 38
Arius, doctrine of, 97; Teutonic nations become followers of, 99, 100
Arles, *see* Burgundy
Armada, the Spanish, 243, 263
Armies, standing, beginning and cause of, 237
Arminius, victory of over the Romans, 83
Armorica, British settlement in, 127; called Britanny, *ib.*
Arnulf, King of the East-Franks and Emperor, 130
Arpinum, birth-place of Marius, 73
Arras, treaty of, 222
Arsakês, founds the kingdom of Parthia, 66
Art, highest development of found in the Aryan nations of Europe, 2; Roman, 83; state of in the 13th, 14th, and 15th centuries, 231; influence of, on modern Europe, 236; in the 16th and 17th centuries, 278
Artaxerxês, King of Persia, helps the Athenians against Sparta, 37
Artaxerxês founds the Sassanid dynasty, 90
Arthur of Britanny, son of Geoffrey, death of, attributed to John, 181
Artois, part of the county of, annexed to France, 243; freed from homage, 246
Arts, mechanical state of among primitive Aryans, 4
Arvad, a Phœnician city, 22
Aryan, use of the word, 3; its orign, 8.
Aryan nations of Europe, 2, 3; connexion among their languages, 4; early state of, before their dispersion, *ib.*; their advances in religion and government, 5, 6; movements of, in Europe and Asia, 9; order of their coming into Europe, 12, 16; encroached on by the Turanians, *ib.*; struggle between them and the Turanians in Europe, 102
Ashanti war, the, 364
Ashk, *see* Arsakês
Asia, south-western, chief seat of the Semitic nations, 7; extent of the Turanians in, 8; Aryan settlements in, 9, 20; its geographical character, 10; Greek colonies in, 27, 30, 32; conquests of Alexander in, 40; Macedonian kingdoms, 41, 64; Gaulish settlement in, 42; first Roman Province in, 63; spread of Mahometanism in, 117; Saracen conquests in, 118; extent of the Eastern Empire in, under the Macedonian Emperors, 142; power of the Seljuk Turks in, 155; ravages and conquests of the Moguls in, 196, 197, rise of the Ottomans in, 224; rise of Timour in, 225; Russian dominion in, 274
Asia Minor, Greek colonies in, 24, 30; Persian dominion in, 32; submission of the Greek cities in, to Xerxês, 33; the Persians driven out of, *ib.*; latter part of the Peloponnesian war carried on in, 35; campaigns of Agêsilaos of Sparta in, 36; cession of the Greeks in to Persia, 37; Macedonian kingdoms in, 41; Roman dominion in, 66, 67; Seljuk power in, 156
Assembly, national, common among Aryan peoples, 6, 27, 54, 71; Roman, becomes too large, 72; effects of the feudal tenures on, 166; nature of in France, 184, 185; in England, 185
Astolf, king of the Lombards, 121
Astrakhan, taken by Ivan the Fourth, 267
Athaulf, King of the West Goths, begins the Gothic kingdom in Gaul and Spain, 101
Athens, commonwealth of, 26; tyranny of Peisistratos, 29; reforms of Solôn, 30; expulsion of Hippias, 32; head of the League against Persia, 33; greatness of under Periklês, 34; wars

with Persia, *ib.*; war with Sparta, *ib.*; expedition to Syracuse, 35; surrenders to Lysendros, *ib.*; government and expulsion of the Thirty, *ib.*; second war with Sparta, 37; partial restoration of her power, 38; war with Philip, 39; surrenders to Antipatros, 42; in alliance with Rome, 84; Duchy of, 190
Attalos the First, King of Pergamos, helps Rome against Macedonia, 64; Attalos the Third, leaves his kingdom to the Romans, 67
Attila, King of the Huns, defeated at Châlons, 102
Augsburg Confession, 252; Peace of, *ib.*
Augustine, Saint, his mission to Britain, 133
Augustus, title of, given to Roman Emperors, 79, 116
Augustus Cæsar, (Caius Julius Cæsar Octavianus) Triumvir, 79; defeats Antonius and Kleopatra, *ib.*; his special title of Augustus, *ib.*; his reign, 82; literature and art under, 83
Augustus the Strong, Elector of Saxony and King of Poland, wins back Kaminiec from the Turks, 297; his deposition and restoration, *ib.*; death, 306
Augustus III., King of Poland, 316
Aurelian, Emperor, 89; overthrows the kingdom of Palmyra, 90
Aurelius Marcus, Emperor, 87; his wars with the Germans, 88; his writings, *ib.*
Aurungzebe, Mogul Emperor in India, decline of the Empire under, 299; revolt of the Mahrattas from, *ib.*
Austerlitz, battle of, 334
Australia, beginning of colonization in, 323; English in, 344
Austria, origin of the Duchy, 139; grant of to Albert of Habsburg, 202; many of its Dukes chosen Emperors, 204; early dealings with Swiss League, 220; dynasty of in Spain, 242; its Archdukes Kings of Hungary, 268; its power, 291; rivalry with Prussia, 304; loss of Italian dominions, 306; wars under Charles the Sixth, 305; with Prussia, 307, 308; Genoese revolt against, 314; share of, in the final partition of Poland, 317; wars with Buonaparte, 332, 334, 336; dominion of in Italy, 338, 355; war with France, 352; with Prussia, 354; final loss of her Italian dominions, 355, 304; relations with Hungary, 357
Austrian Succession, War of the, 307 309
Avars, wars of the Empire with, 115, 128
Avignon, become the seat of Popedom, 205; seized by Lewis XIV., 285; French annexation of, 328
Azov, conquered by Peter the Great, 115

B.

Baber, his reign and descendants, 298
Babylon, taken by Cyrus, 32; death of Alexander at, 40
Babylonish Captivity, meaning of the name, 205
Bagdad, capital of the Abbassides, 125; taken by the Moguls, 197
Bajazet the Thunderbolt, Sultan, growth of the Turkish power under, 225; defeated by Timour, 226; defeats Siegmund at Nikopolis, 231
Bajazet II., Sultan, 227 267
Baldwin, Count of Flanders, goes on the Fourth Crusade, 189; made Emperor of Constantinople, 190
Baltic Sea, answers to the Mediterranean in Northern Europe, 10
Barbarians, meaning of the name, 25; settlements of within the Empire, 99
Barcelona, County of, 131
Bartholomew, Saint, massacre of, 256
Basel, Council of, 207, 208
Basil I., Eastern Emperor, reign of, 142
Basil II., Eastern Emperor, 142; power of the Empire under, 143; overthrows the Bulgarian kingdom, *ib.*
Basques, remnant of the non-Aryan people of Europe, 8, 13
Batavian Republic, 339
Batavians, revolt of, against Rome, 86
Batou Khan, Mogul invasions of Europe under, 196
Bavaria, under Charles the Great, 127; war of succession to, 308
Begging Friars, preaching of Wycliffe against, 207
Belgium, kingdom of, 257, 361, *see* Netherlands
Belgrade, Mahomet II. repulsed from, 231; taken by Suleiman, 268; ceded to Austria, 291; restored to Turkey, 319; Peace of, *ib.*
Belisarius, his Persian campaigns, 114; ends the Vandal kingdom in Africa, *ib.*; his wars with the Goths in Italy, *ib.*
Bender, Charles XII. takes shelter at, 295

Benedict, Saint, founder of western monasticism, 170
Benedict XIII., Pope, 207
Benedict XIV., Pope, 315
Beneventum, Pyrrhos defeated at, 59
Berengar, King of Italy, submits to Otto the Great, 140
Bern joins the Confederates, 220; follows the teaching of Zwingli, 260; her alliance with Geneva, *ib.*; her conquests, *ib.*
Bernadotte, chosen Crown Prince of Sweden, 341; *see* Charles XIV. of Sweden
Bernard Saint, preaches the Second Crusade, 186
Bernhard of Weimar, his share in the Thirty Years' War, 270
Besancon, annexed by Lewis XIV., 283
Bithynia, kingdom of, 42
Blake, Admiral, 287
Bœotian League, character of, 44
Bohemia, origin of, 127; its relations to the Empire, 139, 162, 163; Hussite war in, 207; Frederick, Elector Palatine, King of, 269
Bombay, English settlement of, 299
Boniface, Apostle of Germany, 133
Boniface, Marquess of Montferrat, goes on the Fourth Crusade, 189
Boniface VIII., Pope, reign and death of, 205
Boulogne, English conquest of, 254, 262
Bourdeaux, rule of the Black Prince at, 216
Bourges, 217
Bouvines, battle of, 182
Braganza, Portuguese dynasty of, 243
Brandenburg, Electorate of, 266, 272, 290, *see* Prussia
Brazil, Portuguese colony, 278; its separation from Portugal, 366
Bremen, Commonwealth of, 174; Bishoprick of, annexed to Sweden, 271; to Hanover, 296
Bresse, annexed to France, 261
Bretigny, Peace of, 216
Bretwalda, meaning of the name, 133
Britain, its inhabitants, 77, 108; campaigns of Cæsar in, 77; Roman conquest of, 85–87; Picts and Scots invade the Roman province, 108; first Saxon invasion, 109; Roman troops withdrawn from, *ib.*; English conquest, *ib.*; settlement of the English in, 132; of the Northmen, 134; the English kings become Lords of, 136; destruction of Roman towns in, 173
Britain, Lesser, *see* Britanny.
Britanny, origin of the name, 127; Duchy of, annexed to France, 253 popular speech of, *ib.*
Bruce, Robert, separation of Scotland from England under, 214
Brutus, Marcus Junius, conspires with Cassius and kills Cæsar, 78; defeated at Philippi, 79
Buda, Turkish pashalic at, 268
Building, knowledge of, among primitive Aryans, 4
Bulgaria, kingdom of, 143; conquered by Basil II., *ib.*; converted to Christianity, 145; revolts against the Empire, 189; conquered by the Turks, 225
Buonaparte, Napoleon, rise of, 329; his wars in Italy, *ib.*; in Switzerland and Egypt, 330; Consul, *ib.*; reigns as Emperor of the French and King of Italy, 331; his war with England, *ib.*; his dependent kings, 332; invades Russia, *ib.*; general alliance against, *ib.*; his fall, 333; his return from Elba and final overthrow, *ib.*
Buonaparte, Louis Napoleon, his early career, 351; chosen President of the Republic, *ib.*; reigns as President for ten years, *ib.*; as Emperor, 352; his wars with Russia and Austria, *ib.*; his dealings with Italy, *ib.*; his war with Prussia, *ib.*; his death, *ib.*
Buonaparte, Jerome, King of Westphalia, 335
Buonaparte, Joseph, King of Spain, 332
Buonaparte, Lewis, King of Holland, 339
Burgundians, settlement of, in Gaul, 103
Burgundy, County of, temporary annexation of, by France, 218; part of the dominions of Charles the Bold, 223; of Charles V., 242; conquered by Lewis XIV., 283
Burgundy, Duchy of, 131; beginning of the Valois Dukes of, 221; growth of their power within the Empire, 222; united to France, 223;
Burgundy, Kingdom of, 129, 130; its union with the Empire, 147; relations of, with France, 183; broken up, 201; the greater part annexed to France, 335
Burgundy, various meanings of the name, 221
Byzantion, 42; keeps its independence, *ib.*; the capital of Empire removed to, 96

C.

Cabot, Sebastian, discovers the main land of America, 275

Cadiz, *see* Gades.
Cæsar, title of, 79, 93
Cæsar, Caius Julius Octavianus, *see* Augustus Cæsar.
Cæsar, Caius Julius, his birth and character, 76; his conquests in Gaul, *ib.*; his campaigns in Germany and Britain, 77; his civil war with Pompeius, 77, 78; his dictatorship and death, 78; his writings, 84
Caius Cæsar, surnamed Caligula, Emperor, 85
Calais, English conquest of, 215; retaken by the French, 254, 262
Calcutta, English settlement at, 299; taken by Suraj-ad-dowla, 321
Caliph, meaning of the word, 117
Caliphate, Eastern, beginning of, 117; division of, 119, 125; decay of, in 10th century, 156
Caliphate, Western, beginning of, 126; end of, 154
Calmar, union of, 229
Calvin, John, his German followers, 253; teaching of, 255; his settlement at Geneva, 261
Cambray, League of, 245
Camillus, Marcus Furius, Dictator, takes Veii, 56
Canaanites, native name of the Phœnicians, 22
Canada, French settlement of, 277; English conquest of, 322; French rebellion in, 363
Candia, war of, 293
Cannæ, battle of, 64
Canute, *see* Cnut
Cape of Good Hope, Portuguese discovery of, 228; ceded to England, 344
Capitoline Hill, Sabine settlement on, 53
Caracalla, Emperor, 88, 89; extension of Roman citizenship under, 89
Carelia, Russian annexation of, 307
Carlist wars in Spain, 360
Carolina, first colonized by Huguenots, 277; English settlement of, 301; South, secession of, from United States, 366
Carlowitz, Peace of, 291, 294
Carthage, Phœnician colony of, 23, 59; treaty of Rome with, 56; extent of her power, 59; difference between her warfare and that of Rome, 60; her naval superiority, *ib.*; her wars with Rome, 60–63; her fleet defeated by the Romans, 61; her Sicilian possessions ceded to Rome, *ib.*; her dominion in Spain, 62, 68; becomes dependent on Rome, 62; taken and destroyed by younger Scipio, 63; restored as a Roman colony by Cæsar, 81; capital of the Vandal kingdom in Africa, 113; taken by the Saracens, 118
Casimir IV. of Poland, annexes Western Prussia, 230
Cassius, Caius, conspires with Brutus against Cæsar, 78; defeated at Philippi, 79
Castile, united with Leon under Alfonso VI., 154; separated from Leon, 195; reunited, *ib.*; campaign of the Black Prince in, 227; union of, with Aragon, 229
Catalans, revolt of against John of Aragon, 228
Câteau-Cambresis, Peace of, 254
Catharine of Medici, her influence over her sons, 255
Catharine I., Empress of Russia, 316
Catharine II., Empress of Russia, succeeds Peter III., 316; her conquest of Crim Tartary under, *ib.*; her share in the partitions of Poland, 317; death of, 342
Cato, Marcus Porcius, 76
Catullus, Roman poet, 84
Catulus, Caius Lutatius, defeats the Carthaginians by sea, 61
Cavaignac, General, administration of, 351
Cavour, Count, his share in the union of Italy, 356
Cayenne, French colony of, 277, 351
Celts, the earliest Aryan settlers in Western Europe, 13; remains of their languages, 13, 127; their place in history, 16; their settlements in Spain, 68; in Britain, 103
Ceylon, 300; acquired by the English, 354
Chairôneia, victory of Philip at, 39; victory of Sulla at, 75
Chalkêdôn, Persian armies encamp at, 115
Chalkidikê, peninsula of conquered by Philip, 39
Châlons, battle of, 102
Charlemagne, *see* Charles the Great
Charles Albert, King of Sardinia, reign and abdication of, 355
Charles, Duke of Lorraine, delivers Vienna from the Turks, 291
Charles Edward Stuart, (the Young Pretender) attempt of, 310
Charles Emmanuel, Duke of Savoy, 261
Charles Emmanuel the Third, Duke of Savoy and King of Sardinia, his exchange of kingdoms with Charles VI., 305; his share in the war of the Polish succession, 306

Charles Martel defeats the Saracens at Tours, 119; mayor of the palace, 122
Charles of Anjou, conquers the kingdom of Sicily, 192, 193; loses the island, 193
Charles the Bold, Duke of Burgundy, his rivalry with Lewis XI., 222; his schemes and conquests, *ib.*; his war with the Confederates, 223; death of, *ib.*
Charles the Great, conquers Lombardy, 122; his titles, *ib.*; elected Emperor, *ib.*; extent of his empire, 127; his death, 128
Charles the Bald, King of the West Franks and Emperor, 128; his kingdom, 129
Charles the Fat, Emperor, union of the Frankish kingdoms under, 129; deposed, *ib.*
Charles the Simple, King of the West Franks, his grant to Rolf, 137
Charles IV., Emperor, crowned King of Burgundy, 203; his Golden Bull, *ib.*; present at the battle of Crecy, 216
Charles V., Emperor (the First of Spain), his pedigree, 242; extent of his possessions, *ib.*; abdication of, 243; overthrows the liberties of Castile, 244; his wars in Italy, 246; makes peace with Francis, 247; crowned at Bologna, *ib.*; his dealings with the reformers, 251; gives Malta to the Knights of Saint John, 268; takes Tunis, 269
Charles VI., Emperor, 291; becomes King of the Two Sicilies, 305; his Pragmatic Sanction, *ib.*; his wars, 306; death of, 307
Charles VII., Emperor (Elector of Bavaria), disputes the claims of Maria Theresa, 307; his election and death, *ib.*
Charles I. of England, execution of, 264, 287
Charles II. of England, restoration of, 287; his intrigues with Lewis XIV., 288; joins with him against Holland, *ib.*
Charles V. of France, breaks the Peace of Bretigny, 216; his title of Dauphin, 218
Charles VI. of France, 217
Charles VII. of France, crowned at Rheims, 217; murders John the Fearless, 222
Charles VIII. of France, his conquest and loss of Italy, 244; marries Anne of Britanny, 253
Charles IX. of France, 255
Charles X. of France, illegal acts and deposition of, 350
Charles I. of Spain, *see* Charles V., Emperor
Charles II. of Spain, part of his dominions claimed by Lewis XIV., 283; his alliance with the United Provinces, 284; death of, 285
Charles III. of Spain, King of the Two Sicilies, 314; rise of Spain under, 338
Charles IV. of Spain, 338; abdication of, *ib.*
Charles X. of Sweden, 295
Charles XI. of Sweden, greatest extent of the power of Sweden under, 295; Sweden becomes an absolute monarchy under, *ib.*
Charles XII. of Sweden, exploits and death of, 295; abets the attempt of the Old Pretender, 309
Charles XIII. of Sweden, 341
Charles XIV. of Sweden, 363
Charles XV. of Sweden, 363
Charlotte, Princess of England, 361
Charter, the Great, wrested from John, 184
Chatham, William Pitt, Earl of, 310
Chaucer, Geoffrey, influence of his works on the English language, 232
Chauvin, *see* Calvin
Chili separates from Spain, 365
Chilperic, King of the Franks, deposition of, 122
Chlodwig, King of the Franks, 103; made Roman Consul, 113; his descendants, 121
Chorasmians, Jerusalem taken by, 188, 197
Chosroes, or Nushirvan, greatness of Persia under, 114
Chosroes II., his conquests from the Empire, 115
Christian I. of Denmark, 229
Christian II., his reign in Norway, Denmark and Sweden, 264; driven out of, *ib.*
Christian IV. of Denmark and Norway, 265; his share in the Thirty Years' War, 269, 270
Christian IX. of Denmark, 362
Christina, Queen of Sweden, annexations under, 265; her abdication, 295
Christianity, origin of, 91, 116; its growth and persecutions, 92; its establishment in the Empire, 97; various forms of, 98; early disputes, 97, 98, 115; conversion of European nations to, 143, 145; spread of, in the 10th century, 168
Chrysostom, *see* John

Church, General Councils of, 97, 112; Eastern, condition of, 111; Iconoclastic controversies in, 121; Eastern and Western, disputes between, 141, 143; Western, how affected by the Teutonic settlements, 160; theory of the ideal powers of the Popes, *ib.*; Eastern and Western, further division between, 168, 169; reconciliation between Eastern and Western, 208; changed relations between the Church and the Empire, 237; Eastern, modern importance of, 238, 320
Cicero, Marcus Tullius, 76, 84
Cimbri, invade Gaul, 70; defeated at Vercellæ, *ib.*
Cimbric Chersonêsos, *see* Jütland
Cisalpine Republic, 337
Cistercians, order of, 170
Cities, greatness of, in Italy, 174
Citizenship, 53, 58
Civil Law, Origin of, 87; Code of, compiled by Justinian, 113; study of, in Middle Ages, 161, 164, 209
Claudii, Emperors of their house, 84
Claudius, Emperor, chosen by the army, 85
Claudius Gothicus, Emperor, 89, 91; his victory over the Goths, 91
Clement III. Pope, crowns Henry IV., Emperor, 148
Clement V., Pope, his subservience to Philip the Fair, 205; moves his Court to Avignon, *ib.*; joins with Philip to destroy the order of the Templars, *ib.*
Clement VI., Pope, deposes Lewis of Bavaria, 203
Cisalpine Gaul, 49; Roman conquest of, 67, 68
Clement VII., Anti-Pope, *see* Robert of Geneva
Clement VII., Pope, 247; makes peace with Charles V., *ib.*; his policy, 249
Clement XIV., Pope, suppresses the Jesuits, 315
Clergy, marriage of, forbidden by Gregory VII., 249; position of, in Middle Ages, 169, 170; distinction between regular and secular, 170; learning in the West chiefly in their hands, 171; one of the three Estates, 184
Clermont, Council of, 157
Clive, Lord, career of, 321
Clovis, *see* Chlodwig
Cnut, his conquest of England, 144; his northern dominion, *ib.*
Cola di Rienzi, *see* Rienzi
Colleges founded in English Universities, 231
Cologne, *see* Köln
Colonies, Phœnician, extent of, 22, 23, 68; Geeek, extent of, 23, 24, 68; their relation to the mother cities, 26, 273; their early prosperity, 27, 31; their difference from European colonies, 273, *see* European Colonies
Columbus, Christopher, his discovery of the New World, 275
Commodus, Emperor, 88
Commons, one of the three Estates, 184; House of, *see* Parliament
Commons of Rome, *see* Plebeians
Commonwealths, German, 173, 174; Italian, 174, 209, 212
Commune of Paris, 353
Como, oppressed by Milan, 177; seeks help of Frederick Barbarossa, *ib.*
Condé, Prince of, his share in the Thirty Years' War, 271
Confederate States of North America, 367
Confederates, *see* Swiss League
Conrad II., Emperor, first of the Franconian dynasty, 147; unites Burgundy with the Empire, *ib.*
Conrad, son of Henry IV., war of, with his father, 148
Conrad III., King, 176; goes on the Second Crusade, 177, 186; makes a League with the Emperor Manuel, 177
Conrad IV., King, son of Frederick II., 180
Conradin, attempts to win back Sicily, 192; his defeat and death, *ib.*
Constance, *see* Constanz
Constance of Britanny, mother of Arthur, 181
Constance, wife of Henry VI., Emperor, 178
Constantine the Great, first Christian Emperor, 94; union of the Empire under, *ib.*; moves his capital to Byzantion or New Rome, 96; his changes in the government, *ib.*; division of his dominions, *ib.*; his baptism, 97; calls the Council of Nikaia, *ib.*
Constantine Koprônymos, Emperor, reign of, 120
Constantine VI., Emperor, deposition of, 122
Constantine Palaiologos, last Eastern Emperor, his reconciliation with the Western Church, 226; his defence of Constantinople, and death, 227
Constantinople, becomes the capital of the Empire, 96; Greek influence in, *ib.*; Saracen sieges of, 118; Rome becomes independent of, 122; Latin conquest of, 189, 190; won back by Michael Palaiologos, 190; be-

sieged by Amurath II., 226; by Mahomet, II., *ib.*; becomes capital of the Ottoman Empire, 227
Constantius, Emperor, father of Constantine the Great, 95
Constantius, Emperor, son of Constantine the Great, reunion of the Empire under, 96
Constanz, Peace of, granted by Frederick I., 178; Council of, 207
Constitution of England, 6, 166, 183, 184
Consuls, power of the Roman Kings transferred to, 55; Plebeians first chosen, 56
Copenhagen, Treaty of, 295; bombardment of, 327
Cordova, Ommiad dynasty founded at, 126; seat of the Western Caliphate, *ib.*
Corfu, Venetian possession of, 227, 248; attacked by the Turks, 294
Corinth, early foundation of, 26; joins the Confederacy against Sparta, 37; Alexander's synod at, 39; joins the Achaian League, 44; destroyed by Mummius, 65
Corsica, its ancient inhabitants, 49; subject to Carthage, 59; ceded to Rome, 69; its relations to the Eastern Empire, 114, 120; revolt of, against Genoa, 312; annexed to France, 312, 314.
Cortez, Hernando, his conquest of Mexico, 276
Corvinus, Matthias, King of Hungary, 231
Cornwallis, Marquess, his administration in India, 344
Cosmo de' Medici, *see* Medici
Council, nature of, among Aryan nations, 6, 163
Councils of the Church, *see* Church
Courtray, battle of, 219; why famous, *ib.*
Cracow, Commonwealth of, 343; suppression of, 360
Crassus, Marcus Licinius, defeated and killed by the Parthians, 75
Crecy, battle of, 215
Crete, Saracen conquest of in, 126; won back to the Eastern Empire, 143; Venetian possession of, 227, 248; conquered by the Turks, 293; their conquest of, *ib.*
Crimea, 267; Russian conquest of, 316; war in, 352, 359, 363
Crœsus, King of Lydia, conquers the Greeks on the coast of Asia, 32; conquered by Cyrus, *ib.*
Cromwell, Oliver, Protector, greatness of England under, 287
Crusade, First, preached by Peter the Hermit and Urban II., 157; taking of Jerusalem, *ib.*
Crusade, Second, preached by St. Bernard, 186
Crusade, Third, 187
Crusade, Fourth, character of, 188, 191; taking of Constantinople, 189
Crusades, beginning and causes of, 155; meaning of the name, 157; effects of, 158, 186; against the Albigenses, 191; against Sicily, 192; in the north of Europe, 193
Cuba, 365
Curland, Duchy of, 217
Culloden, battle of, 310
Cyprus, Phœnician settlements in, 23; Greek settlements in, 24, 26; separate Empire in, 189; subject to Venice, 227; conquered by the Turks, 248, 269
Cyrus, King of Persia, his conquests of Babylon and Lydia, 318; of the Greek settlements in Asia, *ib.*
Czar, origin of the name, 276
Czechs, 127
Czernagora, *see* Montenegro, 343

D.

Dacia, wars of, with Rome, 87; made a province of by Trajan, 88; given up by Aurelian, 91; Gothic kingdom in, 100; Romance language of, 107
Damascus, capital of the Ommiads, 125
Dandolo, Henry, Doge of Venice, his share in the fourth crusade, 189
Danes, their relations with Charles the Great, 127; their ravages and settlements of, 134; conquer Northern England, 135; their wars with Alfred, *ib.*; their settlements in Gaul, 136, 137; their final conquest of England, 144
Dante Alighieri, fixes the standard of the Italian language, 172; his attitude towards the Empire, 209; his birth and death, 212
Danube, Roman boundary crossed by the Goths, 81, 100
Darius, King of Persia, his expedition against Athens, 32
Dauphin, origin of the title, 218
David II., King of Scots, captive in England, 216
Davis, Jefferson, President of Confederate States, 366
Deccan, the, 9
Decius, Emperor, persecutions of Christians under, 92

Delaware Bay, Swedish Colony of, 300; Dutch conquest of, *ib.*
Dêmêtrios Poliorkêtês, King of Macedonia, 43
Democracy, meaning of the word, 28
Demosthenes, stirs up the Athenians against Macedonia, 39, 42
Denmark, greatness of, 163, 194; its decline in the 13th century, 229; reign of the House of Oldenburg in, *ib.*; its relations with Sleswick and Holstein, *ib.*; its separation from Sweden, 264; accepts the Reformation in, 265; wars of, with Lübeck, *ib.*; cedes Scania to Sweden, 295; becomes an absolute monarchy, *ib.*; Sleswick and Holstein united with, 32; her exchange of territory in 1814, 324; becomes a constitutional state, 363; loss of the Duchies, *ib.*
Dermot, Irish King, 185
De Ruyter, Dutch admiral, 287
De Witts, murdered, 295
Dictator, his office at Rome, extent of his power, 56
Diet, German, in Middle Ages, 167
Dijon, capital of the Duchy of Burgundy, 131
Diocletian, Emperor, his division of the Empire, 93; his abdication, *ib.*; persecution of the Christians under, 94
Dionysios, Tyrant of Syracuse, 59
Directory in France, 329
Ditmarschen conquered by Denmark, 265
Dominic, Saint, founder of the Dominicans, -70
Dominicans attacked by Wickliffe, 207
Domingo Saint, *see* Hayti
Domitian, Emperor, 86, 87
Dorians, their migration, 30
Drusus, campaigns of, in Germany, 83
Dunkirk, cession of, to England, 272; sold by Charles II. to France, 288
Dupleix, governor of Pondicherry, 320
Dutch, settlements of High and Low, 108
Dutch colonies in America, 278, 300; in India, 300

E.

Eadgyth, *see* Edith
Ear, a common Aryan word, 5
East, the, character of its history, 2, 81; prevalence of Mahometanism in, 117
East-Angles, kingdom of, 133
East-Saxons, kingdom of, 133
Eastern Caliphate, *see* Caliphate, Eastern
Eastern Church, *see* Church
Eastern Empire, separated from the Western, 123, 125; its greatness under the Basilian dynasty, 142, 143; Slavonic invasions, *ib.*; decline of its power, 155; cut short by the Seljuk Turks, 156; its revival under the Komnênian dynasty, *ib.*, 189; becomes practically Greek, 162; uncertainty of succession in, 168; its decline, 189; its restoration, 190; becomes more strictly hereditary, 190, 191; its advance and decline in 14th century, 224; end of, 227
Eastern Mark, *see* Austria
East India Company, its beginning and growth, 298, 299, 320; its powers transferred to the Crown, 321, 364
Ecgberht, King of the West Saxons, his supremacy, 135
Edgar, King of the English, reign of, 144
Edith, daughter of Edward the Elder, marries Otto the Great, 144
Edmund, Magnificent, King of the English, his wars with the Danes, 136
Edmund Ironside, King of the English, his wars with Cnut, 144
Edmund, son of Henry III. of England, crown of Sicily offered to, 192
Edward the Elder, King of the English, his wars with the Danes, 136; receives the homage of all Britain, *ib.*
Edward the Confessor, King of the English, son of Æthelred, 145; his alliance with the Emperor Henry II., 148; last of the West-Saxon dynasty, 150, 151
Edward I. of England, his crusade, 188; his conquest of Wales and Scotland, 214
Edward II. of England, 215
Edward III., his claim to the French crown, 215; his alliance with the Emperor Lewis, *ib.*; gives up and reasserts his claims, 216
Edward VI. of England, 262
Edward the Black Prince, his rule at Bordeaux, 216; restores Peter of Castile's crown, 228
Egbert, *see* Ecgberht
Eginhard, his life of Charles the Great, 137
Egypt, submits to Alexander the Great, 40; rule of the Ptolemies in, 41, 71; Roman conquest of 79; Saracen conquest of, 118; separate Caliphate in, 156, 186; recovered by Saladin, 187; campaign of Saint Lewis in, 188; annexed by Sultan Selim, 268; campaign of Buonaparte in, 330; its modern relation to Turkey, 358

Eirênê, deposes Constantine VI., 122
Elagabalus, Emperor, takes the names of Aurelius and Antoninus, 89
Elba, Buonaparte exiled to, 333; his return from, *ib.*
Eleanor of Aquitaine, wife of Henry II. of England, 153
Electors of the Empire, origin of, 167
Elizabeth, Empress of Russia, 316
Elizabeth, Queen of England, final settlement of the Reformation under, 262; conspiracies against, 263; her war with Philip, *ib.*
Elizabeth of Parma, wife of Philip V. of Spain, 306
Elizabeth, daughter of James I. of England, married to Frederick, Elector Palatine, 270
Elsass, French annexations of, 272, 275, 312, 328; given back to Germany, 353
Emmanuel Filibert, Duke of Savoy, 261
Emperor-elect, title of, 250
Empire, Roman, *see* Roman Empire
Empire, Eastern, *see* Eastern Empire
Empire, Western, *see* Western Empire
England, foundation of the kingdom of, 136; its connexion with the Western Empire, 144; Danish conquest of, *ib.*; restoration of West Saxon Dynasty, 145; Norman conquest of, 150, 152; relations with France, 150, 180; growth of Feudal ideas in, 165, 166; growth of its constitution, 183, 185; its connexion with Ireland, 185, 186; final union of Wales with, 214; relations with Scotland and France, 215, 217; loss of her possessions in Aquitaine, 216, 217; historians of, 231; religious and social movements in, 242; decline of villainage in, *ib.*; civil wars in, 261, 264; the Reformation in, 232; its later relation and union with Scotland, 263, 264; its colonies, 277, 278, 301, 363; wars of, with France, 285, 286; greatness of, under the Parliament and Protectorate, 287; her wars with the United Provinces, *ib.*, 288; degradation of, under Charles and James, *ib.*; effects of the Revolution in, *ib.*; legislative union of Scotland with, 289; growth of her power in India, 298, 299, 321, 344; growth of her maritime power, 300; her foreign wars, 309, 310; revolt of her American colonies, 310; her colonization in Australia, 323, 344; her wars with Napoleon Buonaparte, 329, 331, 340; with the United States, 341; with Russia, 363; her later wars, 364; her relations with Ireland, *ib.*
English, the early home of, 76, 109; their conquest of Britain, 109; its difference from other Teutonic settlements, 110; keep their own language and religion, *ib.*; their kingdoms in Britain, 132, 133; their conversion, 133; history of their language, 152, 232; later settlements of, 273
Epaminôndas, restores Messênê, 38; killed in the battle of Mantineia, *ib.*
Epeiros, relations of its people to the Greeks, 20, 25; kingship in, 27; its greatness under Pyrrhos, 43; reckoned as a Greek state, *ib.*; becomes a Federal commonwealth, 46; helps Macedonia against Rome, 64; Roman conquest of, 65; despots of, 190
Epidamnos, submits to Rome, 63
Estates, assemblies of, 184; established in France by Philip the Fair, 184, 185
Esthonia, 193
Etruria, doubtful origin of its people, 50; Confederation of, *ib.*; Gaulish invasion of, 56
Eugenius IV., Pope, 207; holds a council at Ferrara and Florence, 208
Eumenês, King of Pergamos, 67
Euripidês, 34
Europe, its geographical character, 10; its three great peninsulas, 11; settlement of the Aryans in, 12–15; its characteristics in modern times, 236; spread of Christianity in, 238
Evesham, battle of, 185

F.

Family Compact, 313
Farel, William, 260
Fatimites, their Caliphate in Egypt, 186; put down by Saladin, 187
Federation, nature of, 44
Ferdinand III. of Castile, finally unites Castile and Leon, 195; his conquests from the Mahometans, *ib.*
Ferdinand, King of Naples, 228
Ferdinand of Aragon, marries Isabella of Castile, 228; their conquest of Granada, 229; his conquest of Navarre, 242; his treaty with Lewis XII., 245; his conquest of Naples, *ib.*; joins in the League of Cambray, *ib.*; his death, 246
Ferdinand VII. of Spain, 338, 360; death of, *ib.*
Ferdinand I., Emperor, 251
Ferdinand II., Emperor, his successes in the Thirty Years' War, 269; his death, 270
Ferdinand III., Emperor, 270

Ferdinand V., of Hungary and Austria, 356, 357
Ferrara, Council of, 208
Feudal Tenure, origin of, 165; its difference from allodial tenure, *ib.*; effects of, 165, 166
Fiefs, *see* Feudal Tenure
Finland, Russian conquest of, 341
Fins, a remnant of the non-Aryan people of Europe, 8
Flamininus, Titus Quinctius, proclaims the freedom of Greece, 64
Flanders, Counts of, 131; a fief of the French crown, 210; united to the Duchy of Burgundy, 222; freed from homage to France, 247
Florence, Council of, 208; subjection of Pisa to, 211; constitution of 211, 212; power of the Medici in, 212; the birthplace of Dante, *ib.*; gets rid of the Medici, 245; obliged to take them back, 246; siege and subjugation of, 248; the Medici made Dukes of, *ib.*; Sienna added to, *ib.*; becomes the temporary capital of Italy, 356
Florida, Spanish colony. 312; ceded to England, *ib.*; given back to Spain, 323
Forest Cantons, the three, league formed by, 219
France, origin of name, 104; Duchy of, 131; beginning of the kingdom, 132; end of her connexion with the Empire, 141; relations of, with England, 152, 153; effects of the Norman conquest on, *ib.*; effects of the Feudal Tenures on, 167; the crown becomes hereditary, 168; relations of, with England under Henry II., 180; conquest of English possessions in, 181; growth of the royal power in, 182; advance of her dominion, 183; constitution of, 184, 185; suppression of Templars in, 206; allied with Scotland against England, 215; wars of, with England, 215–217; further extension of her dominion, 218; Duchy of Burgundy annexed to, 223, 242; peasant revolts in, 232; acquires Roussillon and Artois, 243; rivalry of, with Spain, 244, 246; advance of the power of, 253; her annexation of Britanny, *ib.*; her wars with England, 254; wins back Calais, *ib.*; her wars with the Empire, *ib.*; annexes the three Lotharingian bishoprics, *ib.*; her wars with Spain, 255; persecution and civil wars in, *ib.*; dealings of, with Savoy, 261; her part in the Thirty Years' War, 270; further annexations of, 272; her settlements in America, 277; greatness of, under Lewis XIV., 282; Grand Alliance formed against, 285; persecutions of Protestants in, 286; wars of, 305, 306, 310; position of, in 18th century, 311; her annexations of Lorraine and Corsica, 312; allied with Spain against Portugal, 313; her wars with England in India, 320, 321; her loss of Canada, 322; beginning of the Revolution, 328; divided into departments, *ib.*; annexes Venaissin and Avignon, *ib.*; becomes a Republic, 329; wars and conquests of the revolution, *ib.*; rule of Buonaparte, 330; extent of his Empire, 332; restoration of the Bourbons, 333; her North-American possessions bought by United States, 345; revolutions in, 350, 351; late wars of, 352; last republic of, *ib.*
Franche Comté, *see* Burgundy
Francia, meanings of the name, 104, 129; extent under Charles the Great, 127
Francis I. of France, his rivalry with Charles V., 246; his wars in Italy, *ib.*; his captivity and release, *ib.*; makes peace with Francis, 247; his conquest of Savoy, 254; character and death of, *ib.*
Francis II. of France, reign of, 255; persecution of the Huguenots under, *ib.*; marries Mary of Scotland, 263
Francis, Duke of Loraine, marries Maria Theresa, 306; succeeds to the Grand Duchy of Tuscany, *ib.*; *see* Francis I., Emperor.
Francis I., Emperor, 307
Francis II., Emperor, 308; resigns the Imperial crown, 334; his title of Emperor of Austria, *ib.*; President of the German Confederation, 336; reign of, 356
Francis Joseph of Austria, 357; crowned King of Hungary, *ib.*
Francis, Saint, founder of the Franciscan order, 170
Franciscan order, foundation of, 170
Franconia, origin of the name, 147
Franconian Emperors, 147; end of their dynasty, 148
Franken, *see* Franconia
Frankfurt (am Main), free city, 336 annexed to Prussia, 354
Franks, first heard of, 91; their settlements in Gaul, 103; their advance under Chlodwig, 103, 104; their dominion in Italy, 121; greatness of, under Charles the Great, 127; divisions of their kingdoms, 128; union of, under Charles the Fat, 129; East-

ern, use of the name, 157; Franks, East, choose Arnulf king, 130; their kingdom grows into Germany, *ib.*
Franks, West, choose Odo king, 130; their kingdom grows into France, 131
Frederick I., Emperor, surnamed Barbarossa, 177; his dealings with the Italian cities, *ib.*; with the Popes, 178; with the Kings of Sicily, *ib.*; with the Eastern Empire, *ib.*; dies on the Third Crusade, *ib.*, 187
Frederick II., Emperor, his two elections, 179; called the "Wonder of the World," *ib.*; flourishing state of Sicily, under, *ib.*; his dealings with Germany, Italy and the Popes, *ib.*; wins back Jerusalem, 187; favours Teutonic knights, 194
Frederick III., last Emperor crowned at Rome, 204
Frederick I., King of Denmark and Norway, 265
Frederick II., 265
Frederick III. of Denmark, the kingdom becomes an absolute monarchy under, 295
Frederick VII. of Denmark grants a free constitution, 362
Frederick, Elector of Saxony, protector of Luther, 251
Frederick, Elector Palatine, chosen King of Bohemia, 269; driven out, *ib.*
Frederick of Aragon, King of Sicily 214
Frederick of Austria, double election of, with Lewis of Bavaria, 203
Frederick of Swabia, brother of Conrad III., 177
Frederick William I., the Great Elector of Brandenburg, 266; joins the league against Lewis XIV., 284
Frederick I., first King of Prussia, 266, 290
Frederick William I., King of Prussia, 290
Frederick II. (the Great) of Prussia, his claims to and conquest of Silesia, 307; growth of Prussia under, 308; his share in the partition of Poland, 317
Frederick William III. of Prussia, his annexation of Hanover, 335
Frederickshall, Charles XII. killed at, 295
Freedmen obtain Roman citizenship, 72
French, Dukes of, 131
French, Romance speech of Northern Gaul, 107, 131; use of, in England, 152, 232; its mediæval literature, 172, 231, 279
Froissart, his history of the Hundred Years' War, 231

G.

Gades, Phœnician colony, 23
Galatia, settlement of, 42
Galba, Emperor, 86
Gallienus, Emperor, 90
Ganganelli, *see* Clement XIV.
Garibaldi, 356
Gascony, Duchy of, 131
Gaul, Cisalpine, 49; Roman conquest of, 67, 68; invaded by Cimbri and Teutones, 70
Gaul, Transalpine, Greek Colonies on the coast, 24, 69; Roman province in, *ib.*; Cæsar's conquest of, 76; reason of its importance, 77; settlement of Burgundians and Franks in, 103; Romance nations and languages in, 105, 107; Saracens in, 118; driven out of, 119; invasions and settlements of Northmen in, 136; *see* France
Gauls, their invasion of Greece and Macedonia, 42; their settlement in Galatia, *ib.*; defeat Romans at the Allia, 56; take Rome, *ib.*; help Samnites against Rome, 57
Gêlon, tyrant of Syracuse, 59
General Councils, *see* Church
Geneva, preaching of Farel in, 260; besieged by Dukes of Savoy, *ib.*; Calvin's influence in, 261; annexed to France, 339; freed, 340
Genoa, its position in 14th and 15th centuries, 211; bombardment of by Lewis XIV., 284; revolt of Corsica from, 312; revolutions in, 314; joined to Piedmont, 337
Geoffrey, Count of Anjou, husband of Empress Matilda, 153
Geography of Europe, 10
George I. of England, 289, 309
George II. of England, 309
George III. of England, 310
George of Denmark, King of Greece, 358
George, Czerni, revolt of Servia under, 325
Georgia, colony of, founded, 301
German Confederation, the, 336
German Emperors of the West, 125
German language, *see* Teutonic, Dutch, High and Low—Germany
Germanicus, origin of his name, 85; death of, *ib.*
Germans, early government of, 6; Roman wars with, 85, 88, 99; their invasion and settlements in the Empire, 99
Germany, campaigns of Cæsar in, 77; united under Charles the Great, 127; beginning of the kingdom, 129, 136;

wars with the Hungarians, *ib.*; Saxon Kings of, 139; union with the Roman Empire, 140; becomes the centre of the Empire, 162; effects of the Feudal Tenures in, 167; election of Kings in, *ib.*, 168; special greatness of Prelates in, 170; language of, 172; growth of towns in, 173; reign of Frederick II. in, 179; decline of the kingdom, 183, 198; effects of the Great Interregnum, 201; King of, use of the title, 206; its division into circles, 251; the Reformation in, 251, 253; results of Peace of Augsburg, 253; the Thirty Years' War in, 269, 271; state of, after the Peace of Westphalia, 271; state of literature in, 279; liberation of, from Buonaparte, 332; effects of the French Revolution in, 333, 335; end of the kingdom of, 333, 334; confederation of, 336; formation of the Zollverein in, 353; revolutions in, *ib.*; union and Empire of, 354
Ghibelin, origin and meaning of the name, 147
Gian Galeazzo Visconti, *see* Visconti
Gibraltar, taken by the English, 286, 289; defence of, 310
Glabro, Manius Acilius, defeats Antiochos at Thermopylai, 65
Gods, names of, common to Aryan nations, 6; Roman and Greek confounded, 52
Godfrey of Boulogne, King of Jerusalem, 157
Golden Bull, the, 204
Good Hope, Cape of, its discovery, 274
Gothic language, 91, 108
Goths, first heard of, 91; wars of, with Romans, *ib.*; defeated by Claudius, *ib.*, converted by Ulfilas, *ib.*; pass into the Empire, *ib.*; defeat Valens at Hadrianople, *ib.*; their settlement in Dacia, 100
Goths, East, their dominion in Italy, 104, 105; overthrow of their kingdom, 114
Goths, West, take Rome, 101; their kingdom in Gaul and Spain, 101, 103; lose and recover part of Spain, 114, 116
Gotland, Isle of, annexed to Sweden, 265
Gotthard Kettler, Grand Master of Livonia, his cessions to Poland, 266
Government, earliest form of, among Aryan nations, 6, 27; forms of, in Greece, 27; in ancient Rome, 52; effects of standing armies upon, 237;
Gracchus Tiberius and Caius, 72
Granada, Mahometan kingdom of, 230; conquered by Ferdinand and Isabella, 229
Grand Alliance, the, 285
Granikos, battle of, 40
Granson, battle of, 223
Gratian, Emperor, extinction of paganism under, 99, 100
Gravelines, battle of, 254
Great Britain, kingdom of 289 310; revolt of the American colonies from, 310, 322; position of, in 18th century, 311; Ireland united to, 340; possessions abroad, 344; extension and increased independence of her colonies, 363; less interference of, in continental affairs, 364; later wars of, *ib.*; firm union of, 300–364
Great Mogul, title of, 300, 364
Great Schism, 206
Great Interregnum, 200
Greece, Aryan settlement in, 12; its history earlier than that of Rome, 18; influence of its geographical character on, 11, 21; its earlier political advance, 21; early history of, how far trustworthy, 30, 31; first Persian invasion, 32; second, 33; supremacy of Philip, 39; Gaulish invasion, 42; character of its later history, 43; prevalence of Federal government in, 44, 45; the last days of its independence, 46; first dealings of, with Rome; freed from Macedonia, 64; practically dependent on Rome, *ib.*; final conquest, 65; influence of its culture in Asia, 67; lasting power of its civilization, 79; Slavonic settlements in, 143; Turkish conquest of, 227; War of Independence, 357; kingdom of, 358
Greek, an Aryan tongue, 4; use of, in the Eastern Empire, 112, 171; in Southern Italy, 123
Greek provinces of Rome, 81
Greeks, their kindred with Italians, 12, 20, 51; first Aryan nation mentioned in written history, 19; their relations to the neighbouring nations, 20; their relations with the Phœnicians, 23; extent of their colonies, 23, 24; distinction between them and the Barbarians, 25; their forms of government, 27, 28; their religion, 29; conquest of their cities in Asia Minor, by Crœsus, 32; by Cyrus, *ib.*; their disputes, with Persian Kings, *ib.*; submission of their colonies to Xerxes, 33; their Asiatic cities given up to Persia, 37; spread of their civilization in Asia, 40, 41; their colonies in Southern Italy, 50, 51; their colonies in Gaul, 69

Greenland, Scandinavian settlement in, 275
Gregory I. (the Great), Pope, sends Augustine to Britain, 133
Gregory II., Pope, withstands the Iconoclasts, 121
Gregory III., Pope, withstands the Iconoclasts, 121
Gregory VII. (Hildebrand), Pope, disputes of, with Henry IV., 148; driven out by Henry, *ib.*; his designs, 149
Gregory IX., Pope, opposes Frederick II., 187; preaches crusade against the Prussians, 194
Gregory X., Pope, his measures of pacification, 204, 205; his death, *ib.*
Gregory XI., Pope, brings back the Papal court to Rome, 206
Gregory XII., deposed by Council of Constanz, 207
Guelf, origin and meaning of the name, 177
Guise, family of, its relations with France, 255
Gunhild, daughter of Cnut, marries the Emperor Henry II., 148
Gunpowder, invention of, 209
Gustavus Vasa, King of Sweden, 264; growth of the kingdom under, *ib.*
Gustavus Adolphus, of Sweden, 265; his share in Thirty Years' War, 270; death of, *ib.*
Gustavus III. of Sweden, war of, with Russia, 341; murder of, *ib.*
Gustavus IV. of Sweden, reign and deposition of, 341
Gutenberg of Mainz, his invention of printing, 209
Guthrum, Danish King, Alfred's treaty with, 136

H.

Habsburg, House of, 202, 306
Hadrian, Emperor, 87; gives up the conquests of Trajan, 88
Hadrian IV., Pope, his disputes with Frederick I., 178; gives his Bull to Henry II. for the conquest of Ireland, 185
Hadrian VI., Pope, character of, 249
Hadrianople, battle of, 100; taken by the Ottomans, 225
Hamburg, commonwealth of, 174, *see* Hanseatic League
Hamilcar Barkas, growth of the Carthaginian power in Spain under, 62
Hannibal, general of the Carthaginians, takes Saguntum, 62; his campaigns in Italy, *ib.*; defeated by Scipio, 62; makes a league with Philip of Macedonia, 64
Hanover, Electorate of, joined to Prussia, 335; kingdom of, 336; annexed to Prussia, 354
Hanseatic League, formation of, 173; its wars with Scandinavia, 229; diminution of its power, 271; its cities annexed to France, 336; joins the German Confederation, *ib.*
Harold Blaatand, Danish King, wars of Otto II. with, 141; conversion of, *ib.*
Harold Hardrada, of Norway, invades England, 151
Harold, King of the English, defeated by William the Conqueror, 151
Hasdrubal, 62
Hastings, battle of, 151
Hastings, Warren, 321
Hayti, 275; revolutions in, 345
Hebrews, a Semitic nation, 7
Hedwig, Queen of Poland, marries Jagellon, Duke of Lithuania, 230
Heligoland, English possession of, 344
Hellas, meaning of the word, 20
Helvetic Republic, 339
Henry, Duke of Saxony, elected King of Germany, 138; his wars with the Magyars, *ib.*
Henry the Lion, Duke of Saxony and Bavaria, his wars with Frederick I., 178; marries Matilda, daughter of Henry II. of England, *ib.*; loss of dominions, *ib.*
Henry II., Emperor, 141
Henry III., Emperor, his dealings with the Papacy, 147; his alliance with England, 148
Henry IV., Emperor, revolt of the Saxons against, 148; disputes between him and Gregory VII., 148; his wars with his sons, *ib.*; drives Gregory from Rome, *ib.*; crowned Emperor by Clement III., *ib.*
Henry V., Emperor, his war with his father, 148; his disputes with the Popes, *ib.*; marries Matilda, daughter of Henry I. of England, *ib.*; ends the Franconian dynasty, *ib.*
Henry VI., Emperor, his conquest of Sicily, 178
Henry VII., Emperor, revival of the Empire under, 202; coronations of, at Milan and Rome, *ib.*; death of, *ib.*
Henry I. of England, marries Matilda, daughter of Malcolm of Scotland, 153
Henry II. of England, pedigree of, 153; marries Eleanor of Aquitaine, *ib.*; dominions of, 179; death of, 181; conquest of Ireland under, 185

Henry III. of England, reign of, 182; his wars with France, 183; civil wars of his reign, 184
Henry V. of England, his French victories, 217
Henry VI. of England, crowned at Paris, 217
Henry VIII. of England, takes Boulogne, 254; aspires to the Empire, 261; throws off the Papal power, 262
Henry I. of France, 153
Henry II. of France, his wars with the Empire, 254; annexes the three Bishopricks, *ib.*; persecution of Huguenots under, 225
Henry III. of France, 255, 256
Henry IV. of France and Navarre, leader of the Huguenots, 255; his possessions, 256; turns Catholic, *ib.*; his murder, *ib.*
Henry, Don, Infant of Portugal, maritime discoveries and conquests under, 228
Henry of Trastamara, civil war of, with Pedro of Castile, 227; kills Pedro, 228
Hêrakleia, long independence of, 42
Heraclius, Emperor, 115; his Persian campaigns, 116
Hermann of Salza, Grand Master of the Teutonic Order, 194
Hêrodotos, history of, 31
Heroes, children of the Gods, 29
Heroic Ages, 27
Hessen-Cassel, Electorate of, 334
High-Dutch tongue, influence of Luther on, 279
Hierôn, King of Syracuse, helps Carthage against Rome, 60; makes an alliance with Rome, 13
Hildebrand, favours the designs of William the Conqueror, 151, *see* also Gregory VII.
Hindostan, Aryan settlements in, 9
Hippias, Tyrant of Athens, 32
Hispaniola, *see* Hayti
History, different aspects of, 1; Eastern and Western, different characters of, 2; division of, into periods, 17; how soon trustworthy, 17, 18; writers of, at Constantinople, 171; English and French writers of, 231
Hohenstaufen, House of, 176
Holagou Khan, ends Caliphate of Bagdad, 197
Holland, Stadholdership of, 294; *see* Netherlands and United Provinces
Holstein, Duchy of, its relations with Denmark, 229, 318, 342, 362; a fief of the Empire, 229; joined to Prussia, 362
Holy League, the, 245
Homeric Poems, their value, 30
Honorius, Western Emperor, 101
Horace, 84
Hospitallers, foundation of, 171, 186; driven out of Rhodes, 268; their possession and defence of Malta, *ib.*
House of Commons, origin of, 185
House of Lords, origin of, 185
Hugh the Great, Duke of the French, 132; his wars with Lewis, *ib.*
Hugh Capet, Duke of the French, chosen King, 132
Huguenots, persecutions of, 255; massacre of, 256; colonize Carolina, 277
Hundred Years' War, 256; compared with Peloponnesian War, *ib.*; end of, 217
Hungarians, their settlement in Europe, 15, 138; their wars with Germany and conversion, 139, 168
Hungary, kingdom of, founded, 139, 163; ravages of the Moguls in, 197; its connection with the Empire, 203; its Angevin Kings, 230; threatened by the Turks, *ib.*; designs of Austria on, 231; Turkish conquests in, 268; crown passes to House of Austria, *ib.*; revolts against Ferdinand II., 269; reign of Leopold, 290; Turks driven out of, 291; crown made hereditary, *ib.*; civil wars in, *ib.*; dealings of Joseph II. with, 308; revolution and re-conquest, in, 356, 357; restoration of, 357
Huniades, John, exploits of, against the Turks, 231
Huns, driven out of China, 100; enter Europe, *ib.*; their dominion under Attila, 102; their defeat at Châlons, *ib.*
Huss, John, burning of, 207
Hussite War in Bohemia, 207

I.

Ibrahim lays waste Peloponnesos, 258
Iconoclasts controversy, 120, 141
Ignatius Loyola founds the Order of Jesuits, 250
Ikonion, capital of Seljuk Turks in Asia Minor, 158
Iliad, *see* Homeric Poems
Illyria, Greek settlements in, 24; war of, with Rome, 63; Roman Emperors from, 89, 91, 93
Imperator, title of, 78, 79
Imperial Chamber, 251
Infantry, use of, in war, 232
India, Aryan settlements in, 9; beginning of Mahometan conquests of, 156;

English and Dutch settlements in, 298; Mogul rule in, *ib.*, 299; beginning of the Company in, *ib.*; French and English struggles for supremacy in, 320; growth of English power in, 321, 344; mutiny of the native soldiers, 364; its government transferred to the British crown, *ib.*
Indies, West, discovery of, by Columbus, 275
Innocent II., Pope, 176
Innocent III., Pope, 179; his dealings with John of England, 182
Innocent IV., Pope, deposes Frederick II., 179, 182; protests against the taking of Zara, 189, 191; proclaims a crusade against the Albigenses, 191; offers crown of Sicily to Edmund of England, 192
Innocent VIII., Pope, 213
Interregnum, the Great, 201
Ionian Islands, Republic of, formed, under English protection, 341; incorporated with Greece, 258, 363
Ionians, their Asiatic colonies, 30
Iran, meaning of the name, 8
Ireland, Celtic inhabitants of, 108; English conquest of, 155, 185; Reformation in, 246; Cromwell's conquest of, 287; conquest of, by William III., 289; independence of, 310; rebellion in, 340; union of, with Great Britain, *ib.*; disaffection in, 357; disestablishment of Church in, *ib.*
Irish, a Celtic people, 108; *see* Scots
Irish tongue, 13
Isabella, wife of Edward II. of England, 215; Edward III.'s claim to the French crown through her, *ib.*
Isabella, Queen of Castile, marries Ferdinand of Aragon, 228; their joint rule, *ib.*; conquest of Granada under, 229; death of, 241
Isabella II., Queen of Spain, reign deposition of, 360
Issos, battle of, 40
Italian, a Romance tongue, 106; fixed by Dante's poems, 172
Italians, their kindred with the Greeks, 12, 51, 57; their relations to Rome, 58; rise against Rome, 73
Italy, one of the three great European peninsulas, 11; its Aryan and pre-Aryan inhabitants, 12, 13, 48, 50; geography of, 48; effect of its geography on its history, 50; language religion and government in, 52; Leagues in, *ib.*; Roman conquest, of 57, 59; invaded by Hannibal, 62; end of Emperors in, 102; passes into the hands of the Barbarians, 103; rule of Odoacer in, *ib.*; East-Gothic kingdom in, 104; flourishing state of, under Theodoric, 105; recovered to the Empire by Belisarius and Narsês, 114; Lombard conquest of, *ib.*, 120; decline of the Imperial power in, 121; dominion of the Franks in, 122; rule of Lothar in, 128; rival Kings, 130; kingdom united to Germany, 140; growth of the towns in, 174; decline of their power and freedom, *ib.*; dealings of Frederick I. with, 177, 178; Frederick II.'s wars in, 179; falls off from the Empire, 200; revival of learning in, 208, 209; use of printing and gunpowder in, 209; its Commonwealths in 14th and 15th centuries, 209 212; growth of Tyrants in, *ib.*; made the battlefield of Europe, 244, 292; rivalry of France and Spain in, 244, 246; wars of Charles VIII. and Lewis XII. in, 244–246; wars of Charles and Francis in, 246; dominion of Charles V. in, 247; Spanish rule in, *ib.*; no progress made by Reformation in, 249; state of, in the eighteenth century, 313; wars of the French Revolution in, 329, 337; Buonaparte's kingdom in, 331; restoration of the princes, 337; changes in, *ib.*; power of Austria in, 338; disturbances in, 354; revolutions and wars, deliverance of, 352–356; formation of the kingdom, 355, 356
Iturbide, Emperor of Mexico, 365
Ivan Vasilowitz, frees Russia from Moguls, 327
Ivan IV. of Russia, his wars, 266; takes the title of Czar, 267

J.

Jacob, Caliph of the Almohades, defeats Alfonso of Castile at Alarcos, 195; growth of the Mahometan power in Spain under, *ib.*
Jagellon, Duke of Lithuania, marries Hedwig, Queen of Poland, 230; his conversion, *ib.*
Jamaica, English conquest of, 287
James the Conqueror, King of Aragon, reign of, 195
James V. of Scotland, death of, 263
James I. of England (VI. of Scotland), union of England and Scotland under, 264; his foreign policy, *ib.*
James II. of England, reign and abdication of, 285, 288
James Francis Edward Stuart (Old Pretender), attempt of, abetted by

Lewis XIV., 309; by Spain and Sweden, *ib.*
Jamteland, annexed to Sweden, 265
Janissaries, origin of, 225; decay of, 297; end of, 358
Jassy, Treaty of, 319
Jehangir, Mogul Emperor, grants a Charter to the English, 298
Jena, battle of, 335
Jenghiz Khan, rise of the Moguls under, 196
Jerome Buonaparte, King of Westphalia, 335
Jerome of Prague, burning of, 207
Jerusalem, taken by Pompeius, 75; destroyed by Titus, 86; taken by the Crusaders, 157; kingdom of, *ib.*, 186; taken by Saladin, 187; won back by Frederick II., *ib.*; final capture of, by the Chorasmians, 188; end of the kingdom, *ib.*
Jesuits, order of, their foundation and growth, 250; power of, *ib.*; driven out of Spain and Portugal, 313; suppressed by Clement XIV., 315
Jews, a Semitic people, 7; religion of, *ib.*; subdued by Titus, 86; persecution of, in Spain, 244
Joachim Murat, King of Naples, 332
Joan of Arc, called the Maid of Orleans, 217
Joanna of Castile, 242; married to Philip of Austria, *ib.*
Joanna I., Queen of Naples, 213
Joanna II., Queen of Naples, 213
John, Chrysostom, Saint, Patriarch of Constantinople, 112
John XII., Pope, crowns Otto the Great, 140
John XXII., Pope, quarrels of, with Lewis of Bavaria, 203, 206
John XXIII., Pope, deposed, 207
John of Aragon, revolt of the Catalans against, 228
John of Austria, Don, 258
John, King of Bohemia, killed at Crecy, 202, 216
John of England succeeds Richard, 181; loses Normandy, *ib.*; quarrels with Innocent the Third, 182; signs the Great Charter, 184
John, King of France, taken prisoner at Poitiers, 216
John the Great, King of Portugal, 228
John VI., of Portugal, goes to Brazil, 338, 361
John of Salisbury, 198
John, Duke of Bedford, Regent of France, 217
John the Fearless, Duke of Burgundy, his murder, 222
John, Duke of Calabria, 228
John Tzimiskês, Eastern Emperor, murders Nikêphoros Phokas, 142; his wars and victories in the East, *ib.*; defeats the Russians, 143
John Komnênos, Eastern Emperor, revival of the Empire under, 189
John Vatatzês, Emperor at Nikaia, 190
Joseph I., Emperor, reign and death of, 291
Joseph II., Emperor, his reign and reforms, 308
Joseph Buonaparte, King of Spain, 332
Juarez, President of Mexico, 365; Maximilian killed by, *ib.*
Jugurtha, conquered by Marius, 73
Julian, Cæsar under Constantius, 96; campaigns in Gaul, *ib.*; his restoration, 96; reign and death, 97; paganism, 98
Julius II., Pope, his share in the League of Cambray, 245; his Holy League, *ib.*; his alliance with the Swiss, *ib.*; his policy, 249
Justinian, Emperor, reign of, 113; his buildings and code of laws, *ib.*; extent of the Empire under, 114
Jutes, a Low-Dutch tribe, 109; found the kingdom of Kent, 110
Juvenal, 84

K.

Kainardji, Peace of, 319
Kamel, Egyptian Sultan, gives up Jerusalem to Frederick II., 187
Kaminiec, won back to Poland by Augustus the Strong, 297
Karl, *see* Charles
Karlings, Frankish dynasty of, in Germany and Gaul, 121, 122; end of, in Germany, 130; end of, in Western-Frankish kingdom, 132
Karolingia, kingdom of, 129, 131, 140
Kasan, Mogul, 197; Russian conquest of, 266, 267
Kent, kingdom of, founded by the Jutes, 110, 132; the first Christian kingdom of the English, 133
Kephallênia, Roman conquest of, 65
Kettler, Gotthard, Grand Master of Livonia, his cessions to Poland, 266
Kiev, Lithuanian conquest of, 197
"King of France," title of English Kings, 216
Kings, ways of appointing, 167; increase of their power, 237
Kingship, common among Aryan nations, 27, 163; gradually abolished in Greece, 28; abolished in Rome, 54

Kleomenês, King of Sparta, greatness of Sparta under, 46; defeated by the Macedonians and Achaians, *ib.*
Kleopatra, Queen of Egypt, her influence over Antonius, 79; her death, *ib.*
Köln, its Archbishops and Electors, 170; French annexation of, 334
Komnênos, Byzantine dynasty, 156
Koran, the, 17
Korkyra, 24; submits to Rome, 63
Kossuth, 357
Kynoskephalê, battle of, 64
Kyrênê, 24

L.

Labourdonnais, French Governor of Mauritius, 320
Lamian war, the, 42
Languages, Aryan, their common origin, 3, 4; Romance, 106; Teutonic or Dutch, 108; use of, in the Middle Ages, 152, 231; growth of the study of, 182
Laon, capital of the Karlings, 131
Laps, remnant of non-Aryan people in Europe, 8, 168
La Rochelle, 256
Latin, use of the word in 13th century, 190
Latin language, classical writers in, 82; groundwork of the Romance tongues, 106; use of, dies out in Eastern Empire, 171; continued in the West, 172
Latin franchise, 58
Latin provinces of the Roman Empire, distinction of, from Greek and Oriental, 81, 82
Latins, 51; their league of Thirty cities, 52; their alliance and wars with Rome, 56, 57
Lauenburg, Duchy of, joined to Denmark, 342
Lausanne, Bisphoprick of, annexed by Bern, 260
Law of nations, 279
Leagues, nature of, 26; in later Greece, 44, 46; in ancient Italy, 52, 53
Learning in the East, 171; in the West, 172; revival of, in Italy, 208, 209; in 13th, 14th, and 15th centuries, 231; promoted by Leo X., 249; in 16th and 17th centuries, 278, 279; decline of, in Thirty Years' War, *ib.*; in 18th century, 302, 326; revival of, in Germany, 347
Leipzig, battle of, 332
Leo III., Pope, crowns Charles the Great, 123
Leo X., Pope, his alliance with Charles, 246; his policy and encouragement of learning, 249
Leo the Isaurian, Emperor, defeats the Saracens, 120; Inconoclast controversy under, *ib.*; decline of the Imperial power in Italy under, 121
Leon, its growth and union with Castile, 154, 162, 195
Leônidas, King of Sparta, killed at Thermopylai, 33
Leopold I., Emperor, alliance of, with the United Provinces, 284; reign of, 290; gives up Hungary to his son Joseph, 291
Leopold II., Emperor, 308; his previous rule as Grand Duke of Tuscany, 314
Leopold, Duke of Austria, defeated at Morgarten, 317
Leopold of Austria, defeated at Sempach, 221
Leopold, King of Belgium, 361
Lepanto, defeat of the Turks at, 243, 269
Lepidus, Marcus Æmilius, 79
Leuktra, defeat of the Spartans at, 37
Lewis I. (the Pious), Emperor, 128; divisions of the Empire under, *ib.*
Lewis, the German, extent of his kingdom, 129
Lewis II., Emperor, his reign in Italy, 129
Lewis the Child, last of the Karlings in Germany, 130
Lewis IV., Emperor, his disputed election, 203; his deposition, *ib.*; his alliance with Edward III. of England, 215
Lewis IV., King of the West-Franks, 132
Lewis V., last of the Western Karlings, 132
Lewis VI., of France, 181
Lewis VII., of France, 181; goes on the Second Crusade, 186
Lewis VIII., of France, the English crown offered to, by the Barons, 182
Lewis IX. (Saint), of France, 182; growth of the kingdom under, 183; his crusades and death, 188
Lewis XI. of France, his annexation of Provence, 218
Lewis XII., his Italian wars, 245; his death, 246; his marriage with Anne of Britanny, 253; his reign in France, 254
Lewis XIII., 246; his death, 270
Lewis XIV., accession of, 270, 283; his seizure of Orange, 272; his character and absolute dominion, 283,

311; his wars and annexations, 284, 285; his devastation of the Palatinate, *ib.*; his persecution of the Protestants, 286; revokes the Edict of Nantes, *ib.*; his intrigues with Charles II., 288; recognizes the claims of the Old Pretender, 309
Lewis XV. of France, his reign and wars, 306, 311
Lewis XVI. of France, his reign and execution, 327, 328
Lewis XVIII. of France, his restoration and reign, 333, 350
Lewis the Great, King of Hungary and Poland, 230
Lewis II. of Hungary, killed at Mohacs, 268
Lewis Buonaparte, King of Holland, 339
Lignitz, battle of, 196
Liguria, inhabitants of, 49; Roman conquest of, 68
Lincoln, Abraham, President of United States, 366; murder of, *ib.*
Lithuania, language of, 16, 193, 197; its conversion, growth, and union with Poland, 230
Literature, Roman, under the Empire, 83; early Teutonic, 172; Italian, beginning of, 198, 208
Liudprand, King of the Lombards, 121
Livonia, conquest of, by the Teutonic Knights, 171, 194; Swedish conquest of, 295; given up to Russia, 296
Livy, 84
Lodi, seeks help from Frederick Barbarossa against Milan, 177
Lollards, the followers of Wyckliffe, 232
Lombard League, 178; its wars with Frederick Barbarossa, 178
Lombards, their conquests in Italy, 114; take Ravenna, 121; victories of Pippin over, 122; conquered by Charles the Great, *ib.*
Lombardy and Venice, kingdom of, 337
London, Plague of, 288; Great Fire of, *ib.*
Lorraine, modern name of Lotharingia, 129; Duchy of, its relations to Charles the Bold, 222; with France, 255; settled on Stanislaus, 306; annexed to France, 312; part of given back to Germany, 353
Lorraine, House of, its relations with Austria, 306
Lothar I., Emperor, kingdom of, 128
Lothar II., Emperor, 176
Lotharingia, kingdom of, 129, 130
Lothringen, *see* Lorraine
Louis Philippe, King of the French, reign and deposition of, 350
Louisiana, French colonization in, 208, 304; divided between England and Spain, 225
Low-Dutch, *see* Dutch
Loyola, Ignatius, founder of the Jesuits, 250
Lübeck, Commonwealth of, 174; wars of, with Denmark, 265; annexed to France, 332, 336; joins the German Confederation, *ib.*
Lucca, Duchy of, 337
Lucius Sextius, first Plebeian Consul, 56
Lucretius, 84
Luneville, Peace of, 330, 334
Luther, Martin, preaching of, 251; condemned at Worms, 252; followers of, *ib.*; his death, *ib.*
Luxemburg, Duchy of, 361
Lydia, kingdom of, conquered by Cyrus, 32
Lykia, league of its cities, 41, 67
Lyons, Council of, 179; French annexation of, 218
Lysandros, Spartan admiral, defeats the Athenians at Aigos-potamos, 35

M.

Macedonia, its inhabitants, 20; Greek colonies in, 23; not at first counted as Greek, 25, 38; its relations with its Kings, 27; its rise under Philip, 38; invaded by the Gauls, 42, 43; reckoned as a Greek state, 43; its wars with Rome, 64, 65; its dismemberment and final conquest, 65; Slavonic settlements in, 143
MacMahon, Marshal, President of the French Republic, 353
Madras, English settlement at, 299; taken by the French, 320
Mæcenas, Caius Cilnius, 84
Magnêsia, defeat of Antiochos at, 66
Magyars, *see* Hungarians
Mahmoud I., Sultan, 319
Mahmoud II., Sultan, 344, 358
Mahomet, born at Mecca, 116; spread of his religion, 117
Mahomet II., Sultan, called the Conqueror, 226; his siege and conquest of Constantinople, *ib.*; his conquest of Greece and Trebizond, 227; death of, *ib.*; defeated by John Huniades, 231
Mahomet IV., Sultan, 297
Mahomet Almohade, his defeat at Tolosa, 195
Mahomet Ali, Pasha of Egypt, 358
Mahrattas, revolt of the, 299

Mainz, its Archbishops and Electors, 170; French annexation of, 334
Majorian, Emperor, 102
Malta, given to the Knights of Saint John, 268; Turkish siege of, *ib.*; English possession of, 341
Mamelukes, 344
Manfred, King of Sicily, crusades preached against, 192; defeated and slain by Charles of Anjou, 193
Mantineia, battle of, 38
Manuel Komnênos, Eastern Emperor, his relations with Italy, 177, 178; his defeat by the Turks, 189
Manzikert, battle of, 156
Marathôn, battle of, 32
Mardonios, Persian General, defeated at Plataia, 33
Margaret of Flanders, married to Philip, Duke of Burgundy, 222
Margaret, Queen of Norway, union of the Scandinavian kingdoms under, 229
Maria, Queen of Portugal and Brazil, 364, 365
Maria Theresa of Spain, marries Lewis XIV., 283
Maria Theresa, Empress and Queen of of Hungary, her marriage, 306; her disputed succession, 307; her part in the Seven Years' War, 308; in the partition of Poland, 317
Marignano, battle of, 246
Marius, Caius, his wars with Jugurtha and victories over the Teutones, 70, 73; his civil war with Sulla, 73, 74
Mark, 139
Markos of Keryneia, general of the Achaian League, 45
Marlborough, Duke of, 286
Marseille, *see* Massalia
Martin V., Pope, 207
Mary, Duchess of Burgundy, 223; marries Maximilian, 242, 250
Mary, daughter of Lewis of Hungary, marries Siegmund, 230
Mary, Queen of Scots, her marriage, reign, and beheading, 263
Mary I. of England marries Philip II. of Spain, 262; loss of Calais under, *ib.*; restoration of the Pope's power under, *ib.*
Mary II. of England, her marriage and election as Queen, 288
Maryland, 277; settlement of, 278
Massalia, Ionian colony, 24; alliance with Rome, 69
Massinissa, King of Numidia, ally of Rome against Carthage, 63
Matilda, daughter of Henry I. of England, marries Henry V., 148; marries Geoffrey, Count of Anjou, 153, 180
Matilda, daughter of Henry II., marries Henry of Saxony, 178
Matilda, daughter of Malcolm, marries Henry I., 153
Matthew Paris, 198, 231
Matthias I., Emperor, 251
Maurice, Emperor, his wars with the Avars, 115; murdered by Phocas, *ib.*
Maurice of Orange, leader of the war in the Netherlands, 258
Maximian, joint Emperor with Diocletian, 93; his enforced abdication, *ib.*; persecution of the Christians under, 94
Maximilian I., King of the Romans, marries Mary of Burgundy, 242, 250; his share in the League of Cambray, 245; his death, 246; his new titles, 250; his reforms, 251
Maximilian II., Emperor, 251
Maximilian, Emperor of Mexico, 365
Mayence, *see* Mainz
Mayors of the Palace, 121
Mazarin, Cardinal, 270
Mecca, birthplace of Mahomet, 116
Medici, their power in Florence, 212; their banishments and restorations, 245–248; established as Dukes, 248.
Medici, the elder Cosmo de', his power at Florence, 212
Midici, Lorenzo, de', his power at Florence, 212
Medici, Cosmo de', Duke of Florence and Grand Duke of Tuscany, 344
Mediterranean Sea, the centre of the three old continents, 10; Phœnician and Greek colonies on, 23, 24
Megalopolis, foundation of, 38; joins the Achaian League, 44
Merowingians, Frankish dynasty of, 121
Merwings, *see* Merowingians
Messênê, Spartan conquest of, 30; freed by Epaminôndas, 38
Metz, Bishoprick of, seized by Henry II. of France, 254; given back to Germany, 353
Mexico, Spanish conquest of, 276; revolution in, 365
Michael Palaiologos, Eastern Emperor, wins back Constantinople, 190
Michael Romanoff, Czar of Russia, 267
Middle Ages, application of the name, 174
Miguel, Don, of Portugal, 361
Milan, dwelling-place of the Western Emperors, 93; crowning place of the Emperors as Kings of Italy, 140; her oppression of smaller cities, 177; Duchy of, under the Visconti, 210; under the House of Sforza, *ib.*; submission of Genoa to, 211; conquest of, by Lewis XII. of France, 245; re-

stored to House of Sforza, 246; taken by Francis I., *ib.*; by Charles V., 242; granted to his son Philip, 247; part of its territory ceded to Savoy, 306; Napoleon Buonaparte crowned at, 331; annexed by Austria, 337; revolts against Austria, 355
Milêtos, flourishing period of, 27
Military Orders, 171, 186
Mill, a common Aryan word, 5
Milosh, Obrenowitch, revolt of Servia under, 343
Miltiadês, Athenian General, defeats the Persians at Marathôn, 32
Minnesingers, 198
Minorca, taken by the English, 289; restored to Spain, 310
Mithridatês, King of Pontos, his war with Rome, 74; defeated by Sulla in Greece, 75; his final defeat, *ib.*
Moguls, their invasions and conquests, 196; their religion, *ib.*; their dynasties at Kasan and in Persia, 197; overthrow the Caliphate and the Seljuk Turks, *ib.*
Mohacs, battle of, 268
Moldavia, union of, with Poland, 296; Russian influence in, 320; beginning of Greek war of independence in, 357; its union with Wallachia, 359
Monstrelet, his history of the Hundred Years' War, 231
Montenegro, its relations with Turkey, 344, 357
Morad, *see* Amurath
Morat, battle of, 223
Morgarten, battle of, 220
Moriscos, driven out of Spain, 244
Morosini, Francesco, conquers Peloponnêsos, 294; chosen Doge, *ib.*
Moscow, capital of Russia, 230
Mummius, Lucius, destroys Corinth, 65
Murat, Joachim, King of Naples, 332
Murten, *see* Morat
Mustapha III., Sultan, 319
Mykalê, Persians defeated at, 33
Mykênê, its early greatness, 26

N.

Nabis, Tyrant of Sparta, 64
Najara, *see* Navarete
Nancy, battle of, 223
Nantes, Edict of, its revocation, 286
Naples, kingdom of, its separation from Sicily, 193; disputes for its succession, 213; conquered by Ferdinand of Aragon, 242, 245; reign of Joachim Murat, 332
Narbonne, conquered by Saracens, 118
Narses, finally subdues the Goths, 114
Narva, battle of, 295
National Assembly of France, 328; dissolution of, 351
National Convention of France, 329
Navarete, battle of, 228
Navarino, battle of, 358
Navarre, kingdom of, conquered by Ferdinand of Aragon, 242
Nelson, Lord, 331
Nero, Emperor, deposition and death of, 85
Nerva, Emperor, 87
Netherlands, their connexion with Burgundy, 222, 223; with Spain, 242; their revolt, 243, 257; Spanish provinces transferred to Austria, revolts in, 319; annexed to France, 334, 339; kingdom of, 339; separation of Southern provinces from, 361
Neufchatêl, its connexion with Prussia, 290
New Amsterdam, capital of New Netherlands, 30; *see* New York
New England, colony of, founded, 277, 278.
New Jersey, colony of, founded, 301
New Netherland, Dutch colony of, 278; annexes Delaware Bay, 300; English conquest of, 301
New Orleans founded, 301
New Rome, *see* Constantinople
New York, origin of, 301
Nice, *see* Nikaia and Nizza
Nicholas, Emperor of Russia, 359
Nicolas V., Pope, 213
Nikaia, council of, 97; capital of the Seljuk Turks, 156; Empire of, 190.
Nikêphoros, Phokas, Eastern Emperor, wins back Crete, 142; murder of, *ib.*
Nikomêdeia, capital of Diocletian, 93
Nikopolis, battle of, 231
Nimwegen, Peace of, 284
Nizza, Turkish siege of, 269; annexed to France, 352
Norman Conquest, effects of, on England and France, 151
Normans, conquests in Italy and Sicily, 155
Normandy, foundation of the Duchy of, 136, 137; its growth, 150; French conquest of, 181.
Northmen, their settlements, 134, 136.
North-German Confederation, the, 354
Nova Scotia, origin of, 301
Novara, battle of, 355
Novgorod, becomes a republic, 193
Nushirvan, *see* Chosroes

O.

Octavius, *see* Augustus
Odyssey, *see* Homeric Poems
Odenathus, reign of, at Palmyra, 90
Odo, Count of Paris, King of the West Franks, 130; does homage to Arnulf, *ib.*; defends Paris against the Northmen, 136
Odoacer, reign of, in Italy, 103
Olaf, King of the Northmen, his war in England, and conversion, 144
Oliva, Treaty of, 295
Olynthos, conquered by Philip, 39
Omar, Caliph, 117
Ommiads, dynasty of, at Damascus, 125; at Cordova, 126
Orange, Principality of, 257; seized by Lewis XIV., 272
Orchomenos, victory of Sulla at, 75
Orleans, siege of, raised by Joan of Arc, 217
Orleans, Regent Duke of, 309
Oscans, 51
Ostend, siege of, 258
Othman, Caliph, 125
Othman gives his name to the Ottoman Turks, 224
Otho, Emperor, 86
Otho of Bavaria, King of Greece, driven out, 358
Otranto, taken by the Turks, 227
Otto the Great, defeats the Magyars, 139; subdues Berenger, King of Italy, 140; crowned Emperor, *ib.*; death of, 141; marries Edith, daughter of Edward the Elder, 144
Otto II., Emperor, his wars with the Danes, 141
Otto III., Emperor, called the Wonder of the World, 141
Otto IV., Emperor, 179
Ottocar IV., Emperor, King of Bohemia, 202
Ottoman Turks, beginning and growth of their dominion, 225, 243; their advance in Europe, 225; their levy of tribute-children, *ib.*; take Constantinople, 226; take Otranto, 237; their defeat at Lepanti, 243, 269; greatness of, under Suleiman the Law-giver, 268, 269; their wars with Persia, 268; with Hungary and the Empire, 290, 291; with Venice, 293, 294; with Poland, 296; their decline, 297, 319, 343; their wars with Russia, 342, 343, 344, 358, 359; revolts of subject nations against, 343, 357; wars with France, 344; with Egypt, 358
Ovid, 84
Oxford, rise of the University, 198

P.

Paganus, meaning of the word, 98
Palaiologos, dynasty of, 191
Palmyra, kingdom of, destroyed by Aurelian, 90
Palatine, first Roman settlement on, 53
Palatinate, ravaged by Lewis XIV., 285
Paoli, the, leaders of the Corsican revolt from Genoa, 312
Papists, origin of the name, 241
Paris, capital of the Duchy of France, 131; of the kingdom of France, 132; siege of, 136; rise of the University, 198; peace of, 310; taken by the Allies, 332; German siege of, 352
Parliament, English, 184, 185
Parliament of Paris, humiliation of, by Lewis XIV., 283
Parthenôn, 294
Parthia, kingdom of, founded by Arsakês, 64; wars with Rome, 75, 87, 90; revolt of the Persians from, 90
Passarowitz, Peace of, 291, 294
Patrician, title of, 122
Patricians at Rome, 55, 71, 72
Paul IV., Pope, war of Philip II. with, 243
Paul, Emperor of Russia, murdered, 342
Paullus, Lucius Æmilius, defeats the Macedonians at Pydna, 65
Pavia, battle of, 246
Pedro, King of Aragon, defeated by Simon of Montfort, 192
Pedro of Aragon, King of the Island of Sicily, 193
Pedro the Cruel, King of Castile, expulsion and restoration of, 227, 228
Pedro, Dom, Emperor of Brazil, 319; King and Regent of Portugal, 360
Pedro, II., of Brazil, 366
Peisistratos, Tyrant of Athens, 29
Pelopidas, greatness of Thebes under, 37
Peloponnesian War, 34
Peloponnêsos, Turkish conquest of, 227; Venetian conquest of, 294; reconquered by Turks, *ib.*
Pennsylvania, colony of, founded, 301
Penn, William, colonizes Pennsylvania, 301
Pergamos, kingdom of, 41, 66; its greatness under Eumenês, 67; becomes a Roman province, *ib.*
Periklês, his greatness at Athens, 34; effect of his influence on the government, *ib.*
Perseus, King of Macedonia, 65
Persia, growth of, under Cyrus, 31; wars and alliance with the Greeks,

32–35; revival of, under Artaxerxes, 90; wars with Rome, 90, 112, 184; greatness of, under the two Chosroes, 114, 115; victories of Heraclius over, 116; Saracen conquest of, 119; rise of Turkish dynasties in, 156; Mogul dynasty in, 197; beginning of the modern kingdom, 268; wars with the Ottomans, *ib.*; with Russia, 342
Persians, their Aryan origin, 9, 31
Peru, Spanish conquest of, 276
Peter, King of Aragon, Castile, and Portugal, *see* Pedro
Peter the Hermit, preaches the First Crusade, 157
Peter the Great, rise of Russia under, 315; his title and policy, 316
Peter III. of Russia, murder of, 316
Pharsalos, battle of, 78
Philip II. of Macedonia, rise of Macedonia under, 38; conquers Olynthos, 39; his supremacy in Greece, and death, *ib.*
Philip V. of Macedonia, his wars with Rome, and defeat at Kynoskephalê, 64
Philip Augustus of France, his crusade, 181, 187; annexes Normandy, 181; wins the battle of Bouvines, 182
Philip the Fair of France, founds the Estates of France, 184; his quarrel with Boniface VIII., 205; subservience of the Popes to, *ib.*; destroys the Templars, 205; seizes Aquitaine, 215; annexes Lyons, 218
Philip I. of Castile, his descent and marriage, 242
Philip II. of Spain, 241; his persecution of the Moors, 244; marries Mary of England, 262
Philip III. of Spain, decline of the Spanish power under, 243; expels the Moriscos, 244
Philip IV. of Spain, loses Portugal, 243; his wars with France, *ib.*
Philip V. of Spain, disputed succession of, 286, 305
Philip of Valois, Duke of Burgundy, marries Margaret of Flanders, 222
Philip the Good, Duke of Burgundy, growth of the Duchy under, 222
Philip of Swabia, disputes the crown with Otto of Saxony, 179
Philippi, battle of, 79
Philippine Islands, Spanish settlements in, 274
Philopoimên, General of the Achian League, 45, 64
Phocas, Emperor, usurpation and death of, 115
Phœnicians, their origin and colonies, 22; their relations to the Greeks, 23
Picts, in Britain invade the Roman province, 108
Piedmont, French annexation of, 329; recovered by King of Sardinia, 337; Genoa joined to, *ib.* despotic government in, 338
Pippin, King of the Franks, his wars with the Lombards, 122
Pisa, subject to Florence, 116; conquers Sardinia, 154; its Ghibellinism, 177; Council of, 207
Pitt, William, Earl of Chatham, 310
Pius II., his writings and attempted crusade, 213
Pius VII., Pope, 337
Pius IX., Pope, 355, 356
Pizarro, Francesco, his conquest of Peru, 276
Plassy, battle of, 321
Plataia sends help to the Athenians at Marathôn, 32
Plebeians at Rome, their origin, 55; their disputes with the Patricians, 56, 71
Podolia, given up to the Turks, 296
Poitiers, battle of, 215
Poland, rise of, 139; its conversion, 168, 193; Mogul invasion of, 196; its union with Lithuania, 230; its greatness under the Jagellons, 265; its wars with Sweden and Russia, 266, 267; its crown made purely elective, 266; its decline, 267, 296; partitions of, 317; new kingdom of, united to Russia, 343; revolts of, against Russia, 359, 360
Poles, Slavonic people, 15, 127
Polish Election, war of the, 306
Polybios, history of, 66
Pombal, Marquess of, 313
Pomerania, shifting of territory in, between Sweden, Denmark, and Prussia, 277, 296
Pompeius, Cnæus, his eastern wars, 75; his civil war with Cæsar, 77; his defeat at Pharsalos and death, 78
Pondicherry, 321
Pontos, kingdom of, 42
Popes, beginning of their power, 120; disputed elections of, 147, 178, 207; their disputes with the Emperors, 148, 150; theory of their power, 179, 203, 206; their claim to dispose of kingdoms, 185; seat of, removed to Avignon, 205; brought back to Rome, 206; their position in the 15th century, 208; increase of their temporal power, 212, 213, 248; discontent with, 238, 239, 250; their character in the 16th century, 249, 250; end of their

authority in England, 262; their character in the 18th century, 314; end of their temporal power, 356
Portugal, wars of her Kings with the Mahometans, 195, growth of her power, 228; annexed to Spain, 243; restoration of, *ib.*; her settlements in Africa and India, 274; her share in the war of the Spanish Succession, 292; attack of Spain and France on, 313, expulsion of the Jesuits from, *ib.*; liberation of, 338; revolutions and civil wars in, 361
Posen, Grand Duchy of, given back to Prussia, 343
Pragmatic Sanction, the, 305
Pressburg, Treaty of, 334
Pretender, the Old, *see* James Francis Edward Stuart
Pretender, the Young, *see* Charles Edward Stuart
Printing, invention of, 209
Protestant, origin of the name, 241, 252
Provence, origin of the name, 69; county of, a fief of the Empire, 192; held by Charles of Anjou, *ib.*; French annexation of, 218
Provinces, Roman, condition of, 61; Latin, Greek, and Oriental, distinction of, 81
Provincials, Roman, 61, 71
Prussia, Gregory IX. preaches a crusade against, 194; conquered by the Teutonic Knights, *ib.*; Western Prussia annexed to Poland, 230; Duchy and kingdom of, 266; growth of, 290; Silesia annexed to, 307; its share in the partitions of Poland, 317; dismembered by Buonaparte, 332; war with France, 352–354; forms the Zollverein, 353; revolutions in, *ib.*; war with Austria, 354; annexes Sleswick and Holstein, 362
Ptolemies, kingdom of the, in Egypt, 41
Pultowa, Charles XII. defeated at, 295
Punic, Latin form of Phœnician, 60
Pydna, battle of, 65
Pyrenees, Peace of the, 288
Pyrrhos, King of Epeiros, killed at Argos, 43; helps the Tarentines against Rome, 58; goes into Sicily, 59; defeated by the Romans at Beneventum, *ib.*

Q.

Quadruple Alliance, the, 305
Quebec taken by the English, 322

R.

Raleigh, Sir Walter, founds the colony of Virginia, 277
Radstadt, treaty of, 286
Ravenna, Exarchate of, 120; taken by the Lombards, 121; won back by Pippin, 122; battle of, 245
Raymond, Count of Toulouse, crusade preached against, 192
Reformation, the, chief causes of, 238, 239; different forms of in different countries, 240
Regulus, Marcus Atilius, 61
Reign of Terror, the, in France, 329
René, Duke of Lorraine, helped by the Swiss League, 223
Rene, King of Sicily, and Count of Provence, 228
Rhine, the, boundary of the Roman province of Gaul, 77; Confederation of the, 334
Rhodes, commonwealth of, 42; held by the Knights of St. John, 227; the Knights driven out of, 268
Richard I. of England, his crusade, 181, 187
Richard, Earl of Cornwall, elected King of the Romans, 201
Richelieu, Cardinal, growth of the royal power under, 256; his share in the Thirty Years' War, 270
Rienzi, Cola di, his Tribuneship, 212
Robert, Duke of the French, his grant to Rolf, 137
Robert, King of Naples, 213
Robert of Geneva, or Clement VII., anti-pope at Avignon, 206
Robert Wiscard, his conquests in Southern Italy, 154
Robespierre, 329
Roger II., King of Sicily, 155; league of East and West against, 177
Roger Bacon, 198
Rolf, first Duke of the Nornams, his settlement and baptism, 137
Roman Empire, greatest extent of the Empire, 17; beginning of, 79; extent of, 80, 83; distinction of its Latin, Greek, and Oriental provinces, 81; nature of its dominion, 82, 87; all its inhabitants become Romans, 82, 89; rule of, passes from the Cæsarian family, 86; Emperors chosen by the army, 88; the Tyrants, 89; wars with the Persians and Germans, 90, 91; threatened by the Goths, *ib.*; growth and persecutions of Christianity in, 92, 94; division of, under Diocletian, 93; united under Constantine, 94; capital fixed at Constan-

tinople, 96; changes under Constantine and his sons, *ib.*; establishment of Christianity in, 97, 99; various forms of Christianity in, 98; Teutonic settlements in, 99, 100; reunited under Zeno, 104; continued in the East, 111, 113; its extent under Justinian, 114; wars with Avars and Persians, 115; with the Saracens, 22; decline of its power in Italy, 120; its final division, 123, 124
Roman Law, *see* Civil Law
Roman Catholics, origin of the name, 241
Romance nations, origin of, 105; history of their languages, 106, 172
Romansch, language, 107
Rome, the centre of European history, 16–18; her probable origin, 53; character of her history, 53, 54, 55; her kings, 54; dynasty of the Tarquinii, *ib.*; the commonwealth, 55, 56; makes a treaty with Carthage, 56, taken by the Gauls, *ib.*; gradual conquest of Italy, 56, 59; war of, with Pyrrhos, 58; condition of the Italian States under, 59; first wars with Carthage, 60, 63; her provinces, 61; takes Sardinia and Corsica, 62; second war with Carthage, 63; her first possessions beyond the Hadriatic, *ib.*; first and second wars with Macedonia, 64; conquest of Ætolia, 65; final conquest of Macedonia, *ib.*; war with Antiochos, 66; her first province beyond the Ægean, 67; conquest of Cisalpine Gaul, 67, 68; of Liguria and Venetia, 68; of Spain, 68, 69; her first province in Transalpine Gaul, 69, 70; invasions of the Cimbri and Teutones, 70; relations with Egypt, 71; her great power the cause of her final fall, *ib.*; her constitution, *ib.*; internal disputes, 71, 72; revolt and submission of the allies, 73, 74; first civil war, 73; wars with Mithridates, 74, 75; conquest of the kingdom of Pontos, 75; conquest of Syria, *ib.*; first dealings with Parthia, *ib.*; internal disputes, 76; conquest of Transalpine Gaul, 76, 77; first dealings with Britain, 77; civil wars, 77, 79; conquest of Egypt, 79; beginning of the Empire, *ib.*; her position under the Emperors, 82; literature and art of, 83; ceases to be the seat of government, 93; taken by Alaric, 101; growth of the Papal power, 120, 148; decline of the Imperial power, 121; threatened by the Lombards, *ib.*; saved by Pippin, 122; separated from the Eastern Empire, 123; crowning place of the Western Emperors, 125; return of the Popes to, from Avignon, 206; revolution of Rienzi at, 212; sack of, 247; held by the French, 355; the capital of united Italy, 356
Rouen, settlement of Rolf at, 137; taken by Henry V. of England, 217
Rousillon, shiftings of, between France and Aragon, 228, 243, 272
Rousseau, 325
Rudolf of Swabia, his election and death, 148
Rudolf of Habsburg, elected King, 202; not crowned Emperor, *ib.*; his reign, *ib.*; grants the Duchy of Austria to his son Albert, *ib.*
Rudolf II., Emperor, 251
Rudolf, last King of Burgundy, 147
Russia, state of, in the 13th century, 193; subjection of, to the Moguls, 197; Lithuanian conquest of the Western provinces of, *ib.*; deliverance of, from the Moguls, 230; growth of, 266, 267; her conquest of Siberia, 274; greatness of, under Peter the Great, 315, 316; her conquest of Crim Tartary, 316; share of, in the partitions of Poland, 317; her annexations of Carelia, *ib.*; dealings with the nations subject to the Turks, 319, 320, 324; Buonaparte's invasion of, 332; wars with Sweden, Turkey, and Persia, 342, 350; French invasion of, 343; kingdom of Poland united with, *ib.*; her new European position, 358; revolts of the Poles against, 359, 360; abolition of serfage in, 360
Russians, a Slavonic people, invade the Eastern Empire, 143; defeated by John Tzimiskês, *ib.*; conversion of, to Christianity, 145
Ryswick, Peace of, 285

S.

Saguntum, taken by Hannibal, 62
Saint Domingo, *see* Hayti
Saint Helena, Buonaparte banished to, 333
Saint John, knights of, *see* Hospitallers
Saint Petersburg, foundation of, 315
Saint Quentin, battle of, 254
Saint Sophia, church of, built by Justinian, 113
Saladin puts down the power of the Fatimites, 187; takes Jerusalem, *ib.*

Salamis, battle of, 33
Saluzzo, joined to Savoy, 261
Samnites, their wars with Rome, 57; join the Marian party, 73; finally conquered by Sulla, 74
San Marino, Commonwealth of, 174, 248, 337
Saracens, rise of, 116; accept the doctrine of Mahomet, 117; their conquests from the Empire and the Goths, 118; driven out of Gaul, 119; division of their Empire, *ib.*; their conquest of Persia, *ib.*; repulsed from Constantinople, 120
Sardinia, its ancient inhabitants, 49; its relations to Carthage and Rome, 59, 62; recovered from the Saracens by Pisa, 154; reconquered by Spain, 305; Dukes of Savoy become Kings of, 305; rule of the Carignano dynasty in, 355; wars of, with Austria, *ib.*, 356
Sassanides, dynasty of, in Persia, 90
Savoy, Counts and Dukes of, 219, 259; their relations with Switzerland, 260; their loss and gain of territory, 261; growth of their power, 292, 306, 314; become Kings of Sicily, 293, comparison of Savoy and Sweden, 296; become Kings of Sardinia, 305; neutrality of the northern part guaranteed, 340, 352; annexed to France, 352
Saxons, their invasion and settlement in Britain, 109, 110; their settlements in Gaul, 109; the English so-called by the Celts, *ib.*
Saxons, Old, conquered and converted by Charles the Great, 127; revolt against Henry IV., 148
Saxony, Duchy of, broken up, 178; alliance of, with Prussia, 335; electorate and kingdom of, *ib.*
Scandinavia, conversion of, 145, 168; union of the kingdoms of, 229, wars of, with the Hanseatic League, *ib.*
Schaffhausen, canton of, formed, 260
Schwyz gives its name to the League, 220
Scipio, Lucius Cornelius, defeats Antiochos at Magnêsia, 66
Scipio, Publius Cornelius, defeats Hannibal at Zama, 62
Scipio, Publius Cornelius Æmilianus, takes Carthage, 63; takes Numantia, 69
Scotland, settlement of the Northmen in, 134; position of the Kingdom, 163; dealings of, with England and France in the 14th century, 214, 215; her independence acknowledged, 214; Reformation in, 240, 263; her Kings become Kings of England, 264; union of, with England, 287; effects of the Revolution in, 288; final union with England, 289
Scots in Ireland and Northern Britain, 108; invade the Roman Province 133; their early relations to the English, 135; serve in French armies, 215
Seleukids, extent and decline of their kingom, 41, 46
Selukos, his kingdom, 41
Selim the Inflexible, Sultan, conquests of, 268
Selim II., Sultan, 269; Selim III., Sultan, 343; murder of, 344
Seljuk Turks, rise, growth and decay of their power, 155, 156
Semitic nations, their history, 7; their influence on religion, *ib.*
Sempach, battle of, 221
Senlac *see*, Hastings.
Septimania, *see* Narbonne
Serfage, general abolition of, in 346; Russia, *ib.*, 359
Sertorius, revolt of, in Spain, 72
Servia, Turkish conquest of, 225; revolts and independence of, 343, 357
Seven Weeks' War, the, 354
Seven Years' War, the, 308
Severus, Alexander, Emperor, 89; his wars with Persia, 90
Severus, Septimius, Emperor, 88
Seville, won back from the Mohametans by Ferdinand III., 195
Sforza Francesco, Duke of Milan, 210
Shah Ismael, founder of the Sophis in Persia, 268
Shah Jehan, Mogul Emperor, 299
Siberia, Russian conquest of, 274
Sicily, its inhabitants, 20, 25; Phœnician and Greek settlements in, 23, 24; their wars, 24, 59; origin of its name, 51; Pyrrhos helps the Greeks against the Carthaginians, 59; battle-field of the Aryan and Semitic races, 60; becomes a Roman province, 61, 62; Saracen conquest of 126; Norman conquest of, 155; kingdom of, *ib.*; union with the Empire, 178; reign of Frederick II. in, 179; conquered by Charles of Anjou, 193; revolt and separation of the island, *ib.*; united to Aragon, 214, 228; to Savoy, 293; reunited, to Naples, 306, 314; delivered by Garibaldi, 356
Siculi, give their name to Sicily, 51
Siegmund, Emperor, his dominions, 203; his zeal for ecclesiastical reformation, 204, 207; marries Mary

of Hungary, 230; defeated by Bajazet at Nikopolis, 231
Siegmund, Duke of Austria, 223
Sienna, annexed to the Duchy of Florence, 248
Sigismund I., of Poland, abolishes the Teutonic order, 266
Silesia conquered by Frederick the Great, 307
Sikyôn, joins the Achaian League, *ib.*
Simon of Montfort the elder, his crusade against Toulouse, 192
Simon of Montfort, Earl of Leicester, his constitution of Parliament, 184, 185; killed at Evesham, 185
Sixtus IV., Pope, 213
Sixtus V., Pope, reign of, 250
Slave, meaning of the word, 15
Slaves, third Aryan swarm in Central Europe, 15; dealings of the German kings with, 38; their settlements in the Eastern Empire, 142, 143; their conversion to Christianity, 143; revolts of, against the Turks, 319, 324
Slavery, abolition of, in British colonies, 366; in United States, 366
Sleswick, Duchy of, its relations with Denmark, 229, 318, 366; annexed to Prussia, *ib.*
Smalcaldic League, the, 252
Sobieski, John, King of Poland, delivers Vienna from the Turks, 291; his election, 296; his Turkish victories, *ib.*; his death, 297
Solon, lawgiver of Athens, 30; his poems, 31
Sophis, dynasty of, in Persia, 268
Sophocles, 34
Spain, remains of non-Aryan people in, 8, 13, 68; its geographical character, 11; Celtic settlements in, 13, 68; Phœnician and Greek settlements in, 23, 24, 68; Carthaginian dominion in, 62; Roman conquest of, 62, 68, 69, 83; Gothic kingdom in, 101, 103, 105; settlement of the Vandals in, 104; growth of the Romance language in, 106; southern part won back to the Empire, 114; conquered by the Saracens, 118; growth and decline of their power, 154; end of the Western Caliphate in, *ib.*; advance of the Christian states, 162; growth of new Mahometan dynasties in, 195; end of the Mahommetan power, 241; under Ferdinand and Isabel, 242; under Charles the Fifth, *ib.*; decline under his successors, 243, 244; expulsion of the Moriscos, 244; rivalry with France, *ib.*; wars with Elizabeth of England, 263; with France, 272; her colonies, 274, 276; aggressions of Lewis XIV. on, 283; disputes as to her succession, 292; temporary revival of her power, 305, 313; alliance with France against England and Portugal, 313; expulsion of Jesuits from, *ib.*; dealings of Buonaparte with, 338; Peninsular war, *ib.*; later revolutions and civil wars in, 360
Spanish Succession, war of the, 285
Sparta, her conquest of Messênê, 30; joins with Athens against Xerxes, 33; helps to defeat Mardonios at Plataia, *ib.*; war of, with Athens, 34; gives help to Syracuse, 34; overcomes Athens, *ib.*; her supremacy in Greece, 36; makes war upon Persia, *ib.*; wars with Athens and Thebes, 37; destroys Olynthos, *ib.*; in alliance with Athens, 38; wars with the Achaian League, 46
Speyer, Diet of, 252
Spice Islands, Dutch settlements, 298; massacre of Englishmen in, *ib.*
Spinola, Marques, his siege of Ostend, 258
Stadholder, office of, 294; abolished, 294, 295
Stanislaus Leszczynski made King of Poland by Charles XII., 297; his second election, 306; Duchy of Lorrain settled on, *ib.*
States General of France becomes the National Assembly, 328
Stephen III., Pope, asks help of Pippin, 122
Stilicho, Roman general, checks the West-Goths, 101
Stralsund, siege of, 295
Strassburg seized by Lewis XIV., 284
Suleiman the Lawgiver, Sultan, besieges Vienna, 252; wars and conquests of, 268, 269
Suliots defend their independence against the Turks, 344
Sulla, Lucius Cornelius, his civil war with Marius, 73; his dictatorship, 74; his victories in Greece over Mithridatês, 75
Suraj-ad-dowla takes Calcutta, 321; defeated at Plassy, *ib.*
Surat, first English settlement at, 299
Sweden, separated from Denmark, 264; her wars with Poland, 266; her share in the Thirty Years' War, and relations to the Empire, 271; becomes an absolute monarchy, 295; greatest extent of her power, *ib.*; compared with Savoy, 296; her loss of power and territory, 317; union

of Norway with, 342; reforms in, 363
Swegen, son of Harold Blaatand, his apostasy, conquest of England, and death, 144
Sweyn, *see* Swegen
Swiss, serve in foreign armies, 223; their infantry, 232; their defeat at Marignana, 246
Swiss Confederation, the, 340
Swiss League, beginning of the, 219; its extension, 220; relation of, to the Empire, France, and Austria, *ib.*; war of, with Charles the Bold, 223; effects of the Burgundian war on, *ib.*; growth of its power, 259; *see* Switzerland
Switzerland, beginning and growth of the League, 219, 220; origin of the name, *ib.*; their relations to Austria and the Empire, *ib.*; the Burgundian war and its effects, 223; growth of the Confederation in, 259; annexations of, *ib.*; admission of the new Cantons, *ib.*; the Reformation in, 260; relations with the Dukes of Savoy, *ib.*; formal acknowledgement of her independence, 271; relations to the French Republic and Empire, 330; the Helvetic Republic and act of mediation, 339; the Swiss Confederation, 340; war of the Catholic and Protestant cantons in, 362; establishment and reform of the Federal constitution in, *ib.*
Swords, Knights of, joined with the Teutonic Knights, 194
Sybaris, flourishing period of, 27
Syracuse, flourishing period of, 27; Athenian siege of, 35; its Tyrants, 59; taken by the Romans, 62
Syria, Seleukid kingdom of, 67; Roman conquest of, 75; Saracen conquest of, 118; Ottoman conquest of, 268

T.

Tacitus, 84, 87
Tangier, English possession of, 289
Taras, *see* Tarentum
Tarquinii, dynasty of, at Rome, 54
Tartars, the, *see* Moguls
Tarentum, Greek city of, asks help of Pyrrhos, 58
Tasmania, English colonization in, 289
Templars, military order, foundation of, 171; chief strength of the kingdom of Jerusalem, 186; suppression of, 205, 206
Temujin, *see* Jenghiz Khan
Teutones, their invasion of Gaul and defeat by Marius, 70
Teutones, second Aryan swarm in Western Europe, 14; their settlements in the Empire, 99, 160
Teutonic Constitution, changes in, 164
Teutonic Knights, military order, their establishment in Prussia and Livonia, 171, 194; defeated by the Moguls at Lignitz, 196; their wars with Poland, 230, 265; abolished, 266
Texas, annexed to the United States, 79, 366
Thebes, chief city of Bœotia, 26; helps Xerxes, 33; in alliance with Sparta, 34; joins the confederacy against Sparta, 37; her greatness and wars with Sparta, 37, 38; joins Athens against Philip, 39; her revolt and destruction under Alexander, *ib.*
Themistoklês, commands Athenian fleet at Salamis, 33
Theodisc, meaning of the word, 15
Theodore Laskarês, Emperor at Nikaia, 190
Theodoric, King of the East-Goths, his reign in Italy, 104; extent of his dominions, 105
Theodoric, King of the West-Goths, killed at Châlons, 102
Theodosius the Great, extinction of paganism under, 99; his reign and penance, 101
Theognis of Megara, his poems, 31
Theophanô, sister of Basil II., marries Otto II., 143
Thermopylai, battle of, 33; defeat of Antiochos at, 65
Thessalonica, massacre of the inhabitants of, 101
Thessaly, its inhabitants, 20, 25
Thiers, M., President of the French Republic, 353
Thirty Years' War, the, 269, 271
Thucydidês, his history of the Peloponnesian War, 34
Tiberius, Emperor, reign of, 84, 85
Tigranês, King of Armenia, subdued by the Romans, 77
Tilly, his share in the Thirty Years' War, 240
Tilsit, Peace of, 335
Timour, rise of, 225; defeats Bajazet at Angora, 226; death of, *ib.*
Titus, Emperor, destroys Jerusalem, 86; succeeds Vespasian, *ib.*; his popular name, *ib.*
Togrel Beg, founds the Seljuk dynasty, helps the Caliph Al Kayem, 156
Toledo, won back by Alfonso VI., 154

Tolosa, battle of, 195
Toul, Bishoprick of, annexed to France, 254
Toulouse, capital of the West-Gothic kingdom, 103; crusades against, and annexed to France, 183, 191, 192
Tours, battle of, 119
Towns, growth of, 173
Trafalgar, battle of, 340
Trajan, Emperor, 87; his conquests, 87, 88
Trapezous, *see* Trebizond
Trebizond, Greek Empire of, 190; outlives the Empire of Constantinople, 191; conquered by Mahomet II., 227
Trent, Council of, 250
Trèves, *see* Trier
Trier, dwelling place of the Western Cæsar, 93; its Archbishops, and Electors of the Empire, 170; French annexation of, 334.
Triple Alliance, its object, 288
Troyes, Treaty of, 217
Tunis, taken by Charles V., 269
Turan, meaning of the word, 8
Turanian nations, their position in Europe and Asia, 8; their later settlements in Europe, 15
Turenne, his part in the Thirty Years' War, 271
Turkey, *see* Ottoman Empire
Turks, their settlement in Europe, 16; when first heard of, 115; *see* Ottoman and Seljuks
Tyrants, meaning of the word, 28, 78; in Greece, 29, 32; in Sicily, 29, 31, 59
Tyre, taken by Alexander the Great, 40
Tyrtaios, his poems on the wars of Sparta and Messênê, 30

U.

Ulfilas, Bishop, preaches Christianity to the Goths, 100; his translation of the Bible, *ib.*
Ulrica, Queen of Sweden, 295
Umbrians, 51
United Provinces, their union, 284; their independence formally acknowledged, 284, 271; their power, 259, 294; their wars with France, 258, 259, 295; with England, 287, 288; join the Triple Alliance against France, *ib.*; high position of, in Europe, 294; the Stadholdership made hereditary, 318; their decay, *ib.*; the Batavian Republic, 339; the Kingdom of the Netherlands, 352
United States, 310; their union and independence, 322; formation of new states, 345; purchase of Louisiana by, *ib.*; abolition of slavery in the Northern States, *ib.* annexation of Texas, 366; secession and re-conquest of the Southern States, *ib.*; final abolition of slavery, *ib.*
Universities, growth of 231; colleges founded in, *ib.*
Unterwalden, Canton of, 219
Urban II., Pope, holds the Council of Clermont, 157
Urban IV., Pope. offers the crown of Sicily to Charles of Anjou, 192
Urban VI., Pope, his disputed election, 206.
Uri, Canton of, 219
Utrecht, Treaty of, 286, 289, 290

V.

Valens, Emperor, his reign in the East, 100; killed at Hadrianople, 101
Valentinian, Emperor, his reign in the West, wars of, with the Germans, 99, 100
Valerian, Emperor, taken prisoner by the Persians, 89; persecutions of Christians under, 92
Valais, *see* Wallis
Vandals, their settlement in Spain and Africa, 104
Van Tromp, Dutch admiral, 287
Varna, Wladislaus of Poland, killed at, 231
Varus, Publius Quinctilius, defeated by Arminius, 83
Vasco da Gama, his discovery of the Cape of Good Hope, 274
Vaud, liberation of, 339
Veii, Roman conquest of, 56
Venaissin, French conquest of, 218; given up to the Popes, *ib.*; French annexation of, 328
Venetia, Roman conquest of, 68
Venice, rise of, 114; her relations to the Eastern Empire, 115; her share in the fourth crusade, 189; her Eastern dominion, 190; her constitution and power by land, 211 her wars with the Turks, 243, 248, 293; League of Cambray formed against, 245; annexed to Austria, 337; revolt and reconquest of, 355; united toItaly, 356
Vercellæ, defeat of the Cimbri at, 70
Verden, Bishoprick of, annexed to Sweden, 271; given up to Hanover, 296
Verdun, Bishoprick of, annexed to France, 254

Vespasian, Emperor, reign of, 86
Victor, anti-Pope, 178
Victor Amadeus II., Duke of Savoy, growth of his power, 292; becomes King of Sicily, 293
Victor Emmanuel II., of Sardinia, 355; chosen King of Italy, 356
Vienna, besieged by the Turks, 252, 268, 291; Congress of, 336
Vienne, sale of the Dauphiny of, 218
Villehardouin, writes an account of the taking of Constantinople, 198
Virgil, 84
Virginia, English colony of, 277
Visconti, Gian Galeazzo, first Duke of Milan, 220; Filippo-Maria, 220
Vitellius, Emperor, 86
Voltaire, 315

W.

Wagram, battle of, 336
Wales, its final union with England, 214
Wallachia, united with Poland, 296; Russian influence in, 320; Greek war of independence begins in, 357; united with Moldavia, 359
Wallenstein, his share in the Thirty Years' War, 269
Wallis, its conquests from Savoy, 260
Walpole, Sir Robert, 309
Warsaw, Grand Duchy of, 335, 343
Washington, George, President of the United States, 321
Waterloo, battle of, 333
Welf, heads the Saxon revolt against Conrad III., 177; *Guelfs* called from, *ib.*
Waibling, *Ghibelins* called from, 177
Wellesley, Marquess, Governor-General of India, 344
Wellington, Duke of, 332
Welsh, meaning of the name, 107, 110
Wenceslaus, King of the Romans, 203; founds the Duchy of Milan, 209
Wends, 127; conversion of, 162
Wessex, kingdom of, 132; supremacy of in Britain, 145; Danish invasion of, *ib.*
West, characters of its history, 2, 3
Western Empire, separation of, from the East under Charles the Great, 123; beginning of its German character, 124; its extent under Charles, 128; restored by Otto the Great, 140; its union with the German kingdom, 140, 162; connexion of, with England, 144; kingdom of Burgundy united to, 147; relations of, with the Papacy, 149, 160; becomes more and more German, 161, 162; relations of Bohemia to, 163; growth of towns in, 173, 178; decline of its power, 179, 200, 237, 271; the great Interregnum in, *ib.*; its connexion with Hungary, 203; with the House of Austria, 204; its relations with the Swiss League, 220; with the dukes of Burgundy, 222; becomes purely German, 251; abolition of, 333, 334
Westphalia, Kingdom of, 335
Westphalia, Peace of, 271
William of Malmesbury, 198
William the Silent, Prince of Orange, leads the revolt in the Netherlands, 257
William II. (IX. of Orange), Stadholder, 294
William of Orange, Stadholder, his defence of the United Provinces, 284; his marriage and election to the English crown, 285, 288
William IV. made hereditary Stadholder, 288
William V., 318
William the Conqueror, greatness of Normandy under, 150; his claim to the English crown, 151; defeats Harold at Senlac, *ib.*; crowned King, *ib.*
William the Bad, King of Sicily, 178
William the Good, King of Sicily, 178
Winfrith, *see* Boniface
Wismar annexed to Sweden, 271
Witt, John de, murder of, 295
Wladislaus, King of Hungary and Poland, killed at Varna, 231
Wolfe, General, 322
Worms, Diet of, 252
Wulfila, *see* Ulfilas
Wycliffe, John, his writings, 207; spread of his opinions in Bohemia, *ib.*

X.

Xenophôn, his history of the Peloponnesian War, 35
Xerxes, son of Darius, his invasion of Greece, 33

Y.

York, 93; Constantine the Great begins to reign at, 94

Z.

Zakynthos, Roman conquest of, 65
Zama, battle of, 62

Zara, taken by the Crusaders, 189
Zaragoza won by Aragon, 154
Zeno, Eastern Emperor, reunion of the two Empires under, 103
Zenobia, Queen of the East, 90
Zeus, chief Greek God, 29; confounded with the Latin Jupiter, 52
Zollverein, the, 353
Zug, joins the Swiss League, 220
Zürich, joins the Swiss League, 220; preaching of Zwingli in, 260
Zwingli, Ulrich, preaching and death, 260

www.ingramcontent.com/pod-product-compliance
Lightning Source LLC
LaVergne TN
LVHW021143110826
845150LV00005B/1111
* 9 7 8 1 4 2 5 5 4 7 5 0 9 *